The Limits of Alignment

The Limits of Alignment
Southeast Asia and the
Great Powers since 1975

John D. Ciorciari

To Rosemary with my gratitude! This book certainly wouldn't have been possible without all of the guidance and support you've provided over the years. I hope the finished product reflects at least some of the wisdom you've shared with me!

Very best wishes,

~ John

Georgetown University Press ✸ Washington, D.C.

Library of Congress Cataloging-in-Publication Data

Ciorciari, John D. (John David)
   The limits of alignment : Southeast Asia and the
great powers since 1975 / John D. Ciorciari.
        p.   cm.
   Includes bibliographical references and indexes.
   ISBN 978-1-58901-696-5 (pbk. : alk. paper)
 1. Southeast Asia—Foreign relations—20th century.
 2. Southeast Asia—Foreign relations—21st century.
 3. Great powers. 4. World politics—1945–1989.
 5. World politics—1989– 6. Alliances—Case studies.
 7. International relations—Case studies. 8. National
security—Southeast Asia—Case studies. I. Title.
   DS525.8.C56 2010
   327.59—dc22

                              2010001634

15 14 13 12 11 10   9 8 7 6 5 4 3 2
First printing
Printed in the United States of America

Contents

Illustrations

Acknowledgments

In writing this book I have benefited from the generous encouragement and guidance of many distinguished scholars. The book grew out of my doctoral thesis at the University of Oxford, where Yuen Foong Khong provided scholarly inspiration and wise counsel as my advisor. Between 2002 and 2004 I had the honor of being the Wai Seng Senior Research Scholar at the Asian Studies Centre at St. Antony's College, working closely with Rosemary Foot. Others who provided valued feedback and guidance on my thesis included James G. Sherr, Steve Tsang, Jonathan R. C. Wright, and Jürgen Haacke, who served as my external examiner. Generous grants from the Fulbright Commission, Clarendon Fund, American Friends of Christ Church, and Harvard Club of the United Kingdom also made my doctoral work possible.

I have enjoyed numerous opportunities to conduct field research and study Southeast Asian foreign policies. In 2003 and 2004 I was a Visiting Research Fellow at the Institute of Defence and Strategic Studies in Singapore, which has since become the S. Rajaratnam School of International Studies (RSIS) at Nanyang Technological University. I am grateful to Dean Barry Desker and many others at RSIS who helped me hone my research. I am also grateful to the Institute of Southeast Asian Studies in Singapore, which I visited on numerous occasions; to the University of Malaya in Kuala Lumpur, which welcomed me for a brief visit in early 2004; to the Institute of Strategic and International Studies at Chulalongkorn University in Bangkok, which I visited in October 2005; to the Institute for International Relations in Hanoi and Thai Ministry of Foreign Affairs, both of which I visited briefly in early 2008; and to the Documentation Center of Cambodia in Phnom Penh, where I have often conducted research over the past decade.

Between 2004 and 2007, as an official in the U.S. Treasury Department, I was able learn firsthand about the practice of international relations in Southeast Asia. Among many others, I am grateful to Tim Adams, Andy Baukol, Bob Dohner, Clay Lowery, Randy Quarles, and John Taylor for giving me opportunities to work on important issues in the Asia-Pacific and granting me occasional leave to further my academic research.

Many officials and scholars have helped me with this book project by discussing ideas or parts of earlier drafts in seminar settings or personal interviews. They include—but certainly are not limited to—Amitav Acharya, Muthiah Alagappa, Mushahid Ali, Jennifer Amyx, Ang Chen Guan, Mely Caballero-Anthony, Dennis Arroyo, Maitrii Aung-Thwin, Bob Axelrod, K. S. Balakrishnan, Suchit Bunbongkarn,

Sunait Chitintaranond, Youk Chhang, Chong Ja Ian, Derek Da Cunha, Ralf Emmers, Naranyan Ganesan, Evelyn Goh, Aruna Gopinath, Ruhanas Harun, Roger Haydon, Khairy Jamaluddin, Roslina Johari, Suzaina Kadir, Hiro Katsumata, Bilahari Kausikan, David Koh, Kwa Chong Guan, Kyaw Yin Hlaing, Lee Lai-to, Mel Levitsky, Vincent Lim, Joseph Chinyong Liow, Vorasakdi Mahatdhanobol, Mak Joon Nam, John Mearsheimer, K. S. Nathan, Carmelito Pangatungan, Bob Pape, Gene Park, Pham Cao Phong, Kumar Ramakrishna, Leonard Sebastian, Mala Selvaraju, Kusuma Snitwongse, Tan See Seng, Jatswan Sidhu, Dajlit Singh, Ranjit Singh, Ian Storey, Martin Stuart-Fox, Tin Maung Maung Than, Pranee Thiparat, Phillips Vermonte, Christian Von Luebke, Stephen Walt, Panitan Wattanayagorn, Bridget Welsh, Danny Wong, and Maung Zarni.

I owe further debts of gratitude to the people and institutions that helped me expand, reorganize, and refine my dissertation and turn it into a book. From 2007 to 2009 I was a postdoctoral fellow at Stanford University, first at the Walter H. Shorenstein Asia-Pacific Research Center and later as a National Fellow at the Hoover Institution. Don Emmerson served as an informal mentor at the Southeast Asian Forum and taught me a great deal about the region and about analyzing complex political problems. I am appreciative to Ambassador Michael Armacost, Bob Carroll, Gi-Wook Shin, and Dan Sneider, for offering comments on my arguments or parts of the manuscript and providing me with opportunities to share my work. Last but not least, I thank my colleagues at the University of Michigan's Gerald R. Ford School of Public Policy and Center for Southeast Asian Studies for giving me the support to bring the book to fruition.

Abbreviations and Acronyms

AFP	Armed Forces of the Philippines
AMS	Agreement on Maintaining Security (Indonesia and Australia)
ANZUK	Australia, New Zealand, and the United Kingdom
APEC	Asia-Pacific Economic Cooperation forum
ARF	ASEAN Regional Forum
ASEAN	Association of Southeast Asian Nations
ASEAN-6	The first six members of ASEAN (Singapore, Malaysia, Indonesia, Brunei, Thailand, and the Philippines)
ASEM	Asia-Europe Meetings
BCP	Burmese Communist Party
BITAC	U.S.-Malaysia Bilateral Training and Consultative Group
BSPP	Burmese Socialist Program Party
CARAT	Cooperation Afloat Readiness and Training
CGDK	Coalition Government of Democratic Kampuchea (including the Khmers Rouges, royalists, and other anti-Vietnamese groups during the 1980s)
CIA	U.S. Central Intelligence Agency
CIS	Commonwealth of Independent States
COMECON	Council for Mutual Economic Assistance (USSR and allies)
CPP	Cambodian People's Party (Kanakpak Pracheachon Kâmpuchéa)
CPT	Communist Party of Thailand
CSCAP	Conference on Security and Cooperation in the Asia-Pacific
DK	Democratic Kampuchea (Cambodia, 1975–1978)
EAS	East Asia Summit
FMS	Foreign Military Sales credit program (United States)
FPDA	Five-Power Defence Arrangements (Malaysia, Singapore, Australia, New Zealand, and United Kingdom, 1971)
Fretilin	Revolutionary Front for East Timorese Independence
IMET	International Military Education Training program (U.S.)
IMF	International Monetary Fund
JI	Jemaah Islamiah
LPDR	Lao People's Democratic Republic
LPRP	Lao People's Revolutionary Party
MILF	Moro Islamic Liberation Front (Philippines)
NAM	Non-Aligned Movement

NATO	North Atlantic Treaty Organization
NLD	National League for Democracy (Burma/Myanmar)
NPA	New People's Army (Philippines)
PAVN	People's Army of Vietnam
PKI	Communist Party of Indonesia (Partai Komunis Indonesia)
PRC	People's Republic of China
PRK	People's Republic of Kampuchea (Cambodia, 1979–1990)
SEATO	Southeast Asia Treaty Organization
SLORC	State Law and Order Restoration Council (Myanmar, 1988–1997)
SOFA	Status of Forces Agreement (U.S.-Philippines)
SRV	Socialist Republic of Vietnam
TAC	Treaty of Amity and Cooperation (1976)
UMNO	United Malay National Organization
UNTAC	U.N. Transitional Authority in Cambodia
VCP	Vietnamese Communist Party
VFA	Visiting Forces Agreement (U.S.-Philippines)
ZOPFAN	Zone of Peace, Freedom, and Neutrality

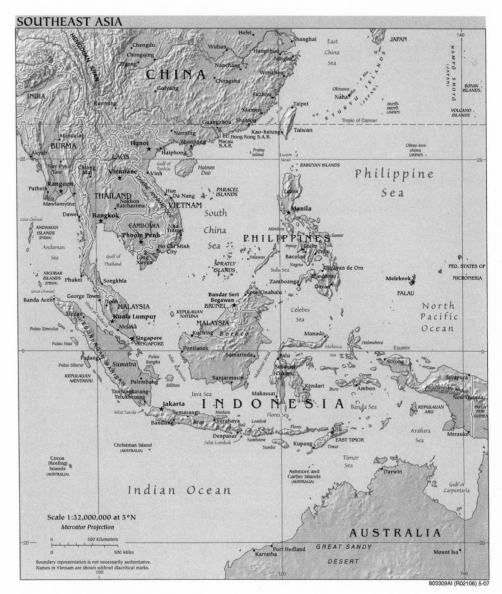

Map 0.1 Southeast Asia after 1975

Source: University of Texas Libraries

Introduction

This book is about alignment politics in the Global South. By alignments, I refer specifically to agreements between two or more states to undertake defense-related security cooperation.[1] In the pages that follow, I attempt to address a critical question for international relations theory and practice: how do the small states and middle powers of the Global South tend to align with the great powers in pursuit of their security interests?

The Global South—sometimes called the developing world or third world—is the home to most of the earth's population and many of the most pressing challenges to international security. As defined here, it includes the Middle East, Africa, Latin America and the Caribbean, and most of Asia and Oceania. Only Europe, North America, and the highly industrialized democracies of Japan, South Korea, Australia, and New Zealand are excluded. Within the developing world, only China has the military, nuclear, and economic muscle to be considered a bona fide great power alongside the United States, Russia, and arguably France and the United Kingdom. The rest of the Global South is populated by small states and middle powers. These states—which I label developing countries (DCs) despite the imperfections of that term—generally lack formidable independent power capabilities. Unlike the great powers, they usually cannot affect the international security landscape dramatically on their own. However, many occupy strategic positions, and collectively their choices have enormous consequence.

The alignment preferences and policies of developing countries are important for a number of reasons. They affect the overall global distribution of power by adding to the resources of some great powers and constraining others. They also shape the strategic character of particular regional environments. Sometimes DCs align in a manner that fosters peace and stability in their environs. At other times they align, either intentionally or accidentally, in a way that contributes to instability and conflict. That they do is important, because interstate conflict since 1945 has usually occurred in various parts of the developing world, not on the home turf of the great powers. Finally, in an era of globalization and asymmetrical conflict, the most dangerous exporters of insecurity are not necessarily the mightiest of nations. Cooperation from DCs can be the key to great-power efforts to meet the menaces of terrorism, nuclear proliferation, and other nontraditional security threats.

With so much at stake, international relations theory needs to address the alignment behavior of states in the Global South. To date when theorists have addressed this topic, they have focused primarily on explaining how states choose sides amid great-power competition. Consequently they have clung to a trichotomy that implies that states have only three basic options: *balance* against the great power that appears the most powerful or menacing, *bandwagon* with it, or remain as neutral as possible. In the real world, as any policy practitioner knows, DCs and other states have a wider range of alignment options. Theory needs to better account for that fact.

In this book I argue that DCs usually attempt to stake out positions between the stark alternatives of balancing, bandwagoning, and neutrality. In most cases, they do tilt toward one or more great powers and establish security cooperation to manage the principal perceived challenges to their interests. They usually try to limit their alignments, however, stopping shy of stalwart military pacts and hedging their bets in various ways. This behavior is nothing new. Great powers have long sought to drive strategy in meeting international security challenges, obtaining help from allies near and far. The governments of DCs play a different game, seeking maximum great-power commitment to their security interests while trying to minimize the price of obtaining that support. In a nutshell, they seek the greatest rewards at the smallest risk.

The past several years have certainly confirmed that dynamic. In late 2001 U.S. President George W. Bush cast the options of balancing and bandwagoning in moralistic tones, boldly declaring that states were "either with us or against us [in] the war on terror."[2] Most DCs have tilted toward America in the campaign against terrorism, but few have offered the unflinching support that U.S. officials demanded. Limited alignments have been the order of the day. In Afghanistan the United States has led an international force to oust the Taliban, but its allies have offered different levels of support. Some have been willing to fight, some to provide humanitarian relief, and some only to commit money. The military and intelligence services of America's most important regional ally—Pakistan—have provided support that helps keep the Taliban on their feet. U.S. efforts to track down terrorists have met with some close cooperation but also with elements of resistance and frequent Pakistani attempts to keep the relationship at arm's length. This behavior should not come as a great surprise; America's Cold War cooperation with Pakistan was similarly characterized by shades of gray.

The Iraq War is an even more striking example. In 2003 the United States drew up war plans only to find that two of its key friends in the Middle East—Turkey and Saudi Arabia—would deny use of their territories for an invasion. Assembling a coalition for the controversial war required expending an untold sum of U.S. political capital, and coalition membership plunged when the going got tough. For better or worse, the fact that so many DCs have withheld stalwart support for the Bush administration's multifaceted campaign has constrained America's ability to drive the international security agenda. Again, these patterns are hardly new. America's allies in the developing world split over Vietnam, European nuclear defense, Middle East policy, and a range of other issues during the Cold War. Then as now, a general reluctance among DCs to forge tight alliances has imposed significant limits on great-power prerogatives, blurring the lines between friends and foes and complicating the execution of grand strategies. Limited alignments have thus had profound international security consequences that leading theoretical approaches—which cling to the trichotomy of balancing, bandwagoning, and neutrality—are apt to miss.

Developing country alignments will continue to exert a heavy influence on the course of international security in the coming decades, and limited alignments are likely to be the continuing norm. Most DCs will seek some external security aid and protection, but without obvious, Cold War–variety strategic lines in the sand, most DCs will see little reason to forge rock-ribbed defense pacts. That pattern could eventually change as China, Russia, and India rise. As a more robustly multipolar world begins to take shape, DCs will have to choose whether and how to adjust their alignment positions. If strong threat-balancing tendencies prevail, a rising power like China may face a ring of containment by solid American allies. If DCs bandwagon in an effort to ride the wave of the future and secure future gains, China or other ascending giants could win friends that help propel it toward superpower status and usher in a more genuinely bipolar or multipolar era.

If limited alignments are the norm, the Global South will be a more complicated but somewhat less polarized place. DCs will forge flexible security relations with their great-power protectors, adjusting their positions subtly over time to reflect regional and domestic concerns and the changing global balance of power. The United States will find it increasingly costly to play the role of global sheriff and maintain clear strategic primacy if ambivalent security partners offer fewer basing privileges and if coalitions shrink. However, if DCs eschew tight alliances, other great powers will also find it more difficult to mount a serious challenge to the status quo. I argue that this pattern of alignments is the most likely. It is important for both theorists and policymakers to understand why.

MY ARGUMENTS

In this book I contend that DCs generally favor limited alignments, particularly in the post–Cold War order. I argue that DCs rarely remain strictly nonaligned; they usually tilt toward one or more great powers to obtain some measure of security support. However, they usually try to avoid tight alliance relationships when they have a meaningful choice in the matter. They normally prefer and pursue limited alignments, because they believe flexible security arrangements will provide the best ratio of risks to rewards under conditions of strategic uncertainty. Alignment with a great power brings rewards—such as defense support and various forms of aid—but also carries the risk of diminished autonomy and the related hazards of dependency, abandonment, or entrapment. Both the risks and rewards of a stalwart alliance often exceed those of a more limited, flexible security arrangement. I contend that unless a DC faces an unmanageable threat and identifies a credible and capable great-power ally, its leaders usually expect the marginal risks of a tight alliance to outweigh the marginal rewards. Thus they conclude that a middle position between neutrality and outright alliance maximizes their security utility, and they have an incentive to tilt only partway toward their preferred great-power protector.

I argue further that limited alignments are likely to be particularly preponderant in the current era of American strategic primacy. Allying tightly against the United States is dangerous, whereas close alliance with America presents heightened risks of entrapment or abandonment due to unrivaled U.S. might. Moreover, few DCs perceive the need to forge tight defense pacts with or against America in a period of relative peace among the great powers.

Balancing, Bandwagoning, and Neutrality

My arguments attack one of the key conceptual structures in international security studies—the trichotomy of balancing, bandwagoning, and neutrality.[3] Contemporary theories generally present alignment politics as a choice between those three basic options. The first option is to balance. The dominant claim in the literature is that countries align to pool their capabilities against common adversaries when they cannot stand safely on their own. Structural realists like Kenneth Waltz argue that the anarchic nature of the international system gives states of all sizes an incentive to align against the most powerful state in the system. Thus "secondary states, if they are free to choose, flock to the weaker side."[4] Implicit in his argument is the assumption that an unrivaled great power will at least sometimes use its might to dominate others. States either balance to avoid subjugation, or they may eventually disappear.

Most scholars agree that DCs do not align strictly on the basis of power distributions, and Stephen Walt improved on the balance-of-power thesis by arguing that states generally align to balance against the foreign state or coalition that poses the greatest threat. Steven David, Deborah Welch Larson, and others have rightly argued that internal politics, economics, and ideational factors also affect alignment policies. Those critiques offered a valuable contribution by drawing much-needed attention to the power of domestic imperatives in shaping security strategies, particularly in the Global South. However, like Walt, they focus on how states choose sides amid great-power competition, concluding that DCs and other secondary states normally align to balance against the sources of both internal and external security threats.[5]

The second option in the conventional alignment trichotomy is to bandwagon. Walt defines bandwagoning as aligning with the state that poses the principal external threat and argues that it is rare, usually occurring only when states are very weak, when allies are unavailable, or when the spoils of war are about to be divided.[6] Randall Schweller defines bandwagoning differently, as alignment with the most powerful or promising state in the international system. He asserts that states often "bandwagon for profit" to secure revisionist gains rather than protection.[7] Like most other alignment theorists, he focuses on how states choose sides and tells us little about the forms that security cooperation is apt to take.

Both outright balancing and bandwagoning strategies are ideal types that imply tight alliance. Walt concedes that "balancing and bandwagoning are ideal types," which tell us more about the motives for an observed alignment than the form it takes. He argues that "states that choose to bandwagon will not leave themselves completely vulnerable, and they may offer only modest support to the dominant power." Similarly, "states that choose to balance may also seek cordial relations with their opponents, while simultaneously obtaining protection against them."[8] Walt thus acknowledges the occurrence of limited alignments but downplays it theoretically. His objective is to explain as parsimoniously as possible how states choose sides, not to account for the extent of their resulting security cooperation.

In this book I do not attempt to distinguish between balancing and bandwagoning behavior or to resolve which definition for bandwagoning is better. That debate largely focuses on the motives for security cooperation: do states usually align defensively to meet threats or to advance more offensively minded interests? In practice, those assessments are difficult to make. A state that is better equipped to protect itself is often better able to expand its power as well, and governments doubtlessly align for a mix of motives in individual cases. My goal is not to disentangle the offensive and defensive interests that drive DCs to align. Instead I focus on determining how often DCs pursue limited alignments, and how often they embrace tight ones—whether for profit, protection, or both.

The third ideal-type option states have is to keep their heads down and try to remain neutral. Paul Schroeder has referred to this strategy as one of "hiding" from great-power competition.[9] Staying entirely neutral is difficult and often dangerous, however, and true nonalignment is comparatively rare. Most DCs perceive the need for outside support in defending their security interests, and unless larger states deem a country to be strategically and politically unimportant, external pressures to align are normally considerable. Robert Rothstein thus describes nonalignment as an "eternal myth," often desired but seldom viewed as feasible in practice.[10]

The alignment trichotomy has been theoretically attractive, partly because it is relatively elegant and easy to understand. The centrality of that conceptual structure in Cold War theoretical discourse also reflects the fact that Western scholars and statesmen had obvious policy interests in understanding how states choose sides in a divided world order. However, by trying to identify the foremost threat or opportunity that drives a country to choose sides, existing theories downplay the complexity of alignment politics. They also give short shrift to the importance of risk and uncertainty in alignment decisions. In the real world, governments clearly have a range of possibilities between neutrality and tight balancing or bandwagoning alignments. DCs usually do not declare strict allegiances or hide from the great powers; more often, they attempt to maneuver subtly and use great-power feuds as a source of leverage. Theory needs to come to grips with reality and explain nuances in alignment politics, not just idealized forms of behavior.

The Middle Path
International relations theorists have only begun to explore the range of options between strict neutrality and tight balancing or bandwagoning alliances. They have

done so largely by focusing on ways that states can either soften existing alliances or hedge their bets to reduce reliance on alliance structures.

Soft Balancing

Some scholars have focused on how policymakers attempt to reduce reliance on rigid alliance structures by using other means to constrain potentially menacing or overbearing states. Robert Pape and T. V. Paul have developed the notion of *soft balancing* as an alternative to the *hard balancing* concept that dominates the traditional literature. Whereas hard balancing implies the use of military buildups and strong countervailing alliances to keep a problematic great power in check, soft balancing implies an ad hoc strategy of using multilateral institutions and loose diplomatic ententes for the same purpose.[11]

Pape and Paul argue that major powers have engaged in soft balancing behavior in recent years, seeking to limit American influence by denying some U.S. requests for security support and mobilizing opposition to America in the United Nations, the North Atlantic Treaty Organization (NATO), and other diplomatic forums. Sometimes states engage in both soft balancing and a degree of hard balancing against a potential adversary. For example, as Pape and Paul note, China and Russia often opposed the United States diplomatically in the early post–Cold War period and also entered a very limited countervailing alignment through their 1996 "strategic partnership."

At other times, soft balancing implies more of an effort to restrain one's friends. For example, Pape and Paul use the concept to describe French and German behavior before the 2003 Iraq War. In such cases, the term *soft balancing* can be a bit confusing because America's NATO allies were not aligning against the United States in an overall strategic sense.[12] France and Germany remained U.S. treaty allies—engaging in extensive cooperation in counterterrorism, Afghan reconstruction, and many other areas—but sought to restrain their mighty ally, especially on the question of Iraq. Rather than forging a military alliance against America, they merely sought to put some limits on their tight security relationship with the United States.

Soft balancing resembles what Schroeder has referred to as "transcending"— attempting to constrain a great power through norms and institutions rather than alliances.[13] These related concepts certainly point to an important facet of international relations, but they are better considered a supplement (or alternative) to security alignments than a type of alignment strategy per se. Through diplomacy, norms, and institutions, states can reduce their dependence on alliance structures to some degree. This often makes it easier for DCs and other states to keep their alignments limited.

Hedging

In recent years numerous international relations theorists have used the term *hedging* to describe efforts by states to provide for their security while avoiding overly antagonistic alliance relationships. Evelyn Goh defines hedging as a set of contingency-planning strategies in "a situation in which states cannot decide upon more straightforward alternatives such as balancing, bandwagoning, or neutrality" and instead cultivate a foreign policy that avoids "choos[ing] one side at the obvious expense of another."[14] Although few other scholars have defined the term as clearly, most treat hedging as an overarching foreign policy strategy in which a state engages with a potential rival through economic and political means while taking countervailing protective measures in the security sphere.

Defined this broadly, hedging is ubiquitous in the contemporary order. Robert Art sees European states "hedging their security bets" to avoid too much dependency on the United States. Eric Heginbotham and Richard Samuels assert that Japan has engaged in a "dual hedge," preserving an alliance with the United States while opening to greater commerce with China, and Rosemary Foot describes China as hedging by expanding political and economic ties with Washington while setting up bilateral and multilateral security structures in case of a rainy day.[15]

Similar behavior is evident throughout the Global South. William Wohlforth argues that "hedging [has been] the dominant strategy among Russia's neighbors" since the mid-1990s as they seek to come out from under Moscow's shadow. Daniel Markey describes Pakistan's ambivalent relationship with the United States since September 2001 as an example of hedging. Benjamin Miller argues that U.S. allies in the Arab world are choosing to hedge their bets and limit their alignments with America to avoid falling too far into the U.S. orbit and antagonizing their own populations. Analysts have pointed to a particularly important and obvious pattern of hedging behavior in Saudi Arabia.[16] Several analysts of Southeast Asia have seen similar patterns of risk-averse foreign policy behavior as countries try to hedge their bets in the context of an uncertain Sino-American relationship and other shifting international currents.[17]

The literature on hedging in foreign policy is helpful, both because it depicts an important behavioral trend and because it rightly draws attention to the importance of risk aversion and uncertainty in the formulation of security strategies. Risk and uncertainty are particularly critical in driving the actions of vulnerable DCs, which often perceive themselves as small ships in a tempestuous ocean of international affairs. However, the literature is not specific enough about the relationship between broad hedging strategies and security alignments. Leading works on hedging imply that even stalwart alliances can be part of broad hedging strategies if accompanied by robust political and economic engagement. For example, some of America's most rock-ribbed allies engage routinely with some of its greatest potential strategic nemeses. Japan's behavior toward China is a case in point. If any type of alliance can be part of a hedging strategy, the concept is not terribly useful in helping illuminate the nuances in alignment politics.

This book focuses more narrowly on the security dimension of interstate relations. My argument that DCs tend to pursue limited alignments is not at all inconsistent with the empirical observation that they often hedge their bets in various ways. Indeed, I argue that one of the benefits of limited alignments is that they avoid drawing lines in the sand, thus leaving doors open to DCs to diversify their economic and diplomatic relations. I do not endeavor to provide a composite theory of foreign policy, however. My goal is to explain the precise types of alignments that DCs tend to pursue with great powers in the security sphere: tight alliances, limited alignments, or no significant security ties at all.

The Meaning of Limited Alignment

Empirically I distinguish between tight alliances, limited alignments, and nonalignment based on the different levels of security cooperation that each entails. Tight alliances are often established by formal treaties and generally involve deep, institutionalized defense relationships. They often carry mutual defense obligations as well. These formal alliances—such as NATO, the Warsaw Pact, or the U.S.-Japan alliance—often carry the greatest commitments, partly because they require a public signature or ratification process and legislative or judicial review. Tight alliances are not always based on formal treaties, however. Sometimes tight informal alignments form, cemented not by legal and bureaucratic features but by a sense of shared interests, private commitments, and established cooperation through basing facilities, intelligence sharing, and substantial joint military operations. Examples include the Sino-Vietnamese alliance during the Vietnam War or U.S. ties to Israel since 1967.

Limited alignments entail lower commitment and a less binding security relationship. They typically include arrangements for preferential arms sales, joint training exercises, and other forms of military aid. Such relationships are usually public, but they do not carry a general pledge of military support in the event of a crisis or a general commitment to engage in joint combat operations. Limited alignments seldom give a great power basing privileges. Instead, great-power partners may enjoy commercial access to military facilities and some degree of logistical or technical assistance. Examples include contemporary U.S. ties to Egypt, Jordan, and Saudi Arabia.

In this book a tight alliance refers to an arrangement involving at least two of the following features: a formal defense treaty or widely acknowledged informal pact, semipermanent or permanent basing rights, joint combat operations, or a significant alliance bureaucracy. When two states do not have at least two of those features, I consider them to be in a limited alignment. Even when a formal treaty is in place, if none of the other elements is apparent, I describe the relationship as a limited alignment. The substance of security cooperation is the determining factor for this analysis.

Finally, genuine nonalignment implies the lack of significant security cooperation with any great power. A nonaligned DC may exchange defense delegations from time to time, and it may share some information with a great power, but it does not engage in serious joint exercises or training, and it usually does not grant great powers access to defense facilities, even on a commercial basis. Figure 0.1 schematically summarizes the basic alignment options that DCs possess vis-à-vis a great power.

Genuine nonalignment	Limited alignment	Tight alliance
	Tilting for protection or gain	*Assertive Balancing or Bandwagoning*

Figure I.1 Range of Options

Source: Author's compilation

When a state pursues limited alignment, it steers a middle path between the stark ideal-types of outright, decisive alliance and genuine nonalignment.

Why DCs Favor Limited Alignments

The leaders of DCs try to limit their alignments for many of the same reasons people often resist firm commitments in everyday affairs. In international politics and in other domains, people seek to strike the best possible balance between the risks and rewards of cooperation and to keep their options open. On Wall Street, investors seldom put all of their money on one stock; at the racetrack, spectators rarely bet their life savings on a single horse. In affairs of the heart, partners seek love and fulfillment but often limit their commitments or see other people when they fear abandonment or a loss of freedom. In each of these cases, the actor in question tries to preserve options as a form of insurance, because it is unclear what the future holds. That DCs behave similarly should come as no surprise. After all, international politics is conducted by officials pursuing many of the same kinds of interests as ordinary people—interests including power, wealth, safety, and status.

When the leaders of DCs decide how to align, they carry out the same informal risk-and-reward calculus that informs people's choices in other areas of life. They try to maximize their expected utility, obtaining as many rewards as possible at a minimum level of risk. The rewards of great-power alignment include protection from internal and external threats, as well as economic and political assistance. If alignments bore no costs, DCs would have every incentive to form tight alliances with powerful protectors to secure military, economic, and political aid. However, stalwart security arrangements with powerful partners do entail real hazards for DCs. They can diminish the weaker partner's independence, alienate other states and domestic actors, and create significant risks of entrapment or abandonment.

The rewards of an alignment tend to rise as security cooperation tightens, but so do the risks. I argue that DCs usually perceive limited alignments as a utility-maximizing strategy and seek to enter into such relationships. Both the rewards and risks of alignment depend on variables at the international and domestic levels, which I examine in some detail in chapter 1. Existing theories often focus on factors at the international level, such as balances of power and external threat perceptions. However, domestic and ideational variables also provide powerful drivers for DCs' alignment choices and expose them to certain risks that are less acute for wealthy, democratic developed states. This makes DCs particularly likely to favor limited ties and helps explain why pacts like NATO are generally unappealing to states in the Global South.

Uncertainty adds another key reason for limiting security ties and keeping options open. In a fluid international environment, neither the rewards nor the risks of alignment are certain. Thus limited alignments are not only a way of seeking to optimize risks and rewards; they are also a convenient default strategy when policymakers cannot decide on the more risky alternatives of tight alliance or strict nonalignment. DCs usually prefer tight alliance only when the expected rewards are particularly great because they face clear threats and identify a capable and credible great-power protector. In most cases, the magnitude of various threats is unclear or internally disputed, and limited alignment is the safest course of action. Limited alignments reduce the risks of security cooperation but still provide some insurance against the possibility of a grave future threat. They also leave DCs enough autonomy and flexibility to shift course if conditions change.

This is not to suggest that entering a limited alignment is a fail-proof security strategy. In interpersonal affairs, resisting firm commitments often suggests a lack of trust or even a degree of duplicity. When a contract lawyer holds out for a better deal in negotiations, she may win plaudits from a grateful client. Conversely, when she responds to a marriage proposal by saying she would rather date, she may elicit a much less favorable reaction. International politics lies between these extremes. A certain degree of cold-blooded calculation may be accepted as par for the course, but human relationships and reputations also matter. The danger of pursuing flexible, limited ties is that a great power may not rescue or support a DC that it perceives as a lukewarm or fair-weather friend. Consequently, alignment strategies need to be carefully calibrated. In chapter 1, I develop these theoretical arguments in greater detail.

Why Limited Alignments Are So Common Now

Limited alignment strategies are particularly preponderant in the current era of American primacy for several reasons. First, as Wohlforth has argued, unrivaled U.S. power makes it dangerous for DCs to ally tightly against the United States.[18] The comparatively liberal nature of the U.S.-led international order also reduces the demand for assertive balancing strategies, as John Ikenberry, John Owen, and others have claimed.[19] The United States has tremendous military and economic largesse to share with friendly states, and DCs have strong incentives to tilt toward Washington except in rare cases when America presents a clear and present threat to their regimes (as in Iran, Venezuela, or Cuba). Ironically, U.S. power also makes it easier for DCs to pursue only limited security ties to America. U.S. might has reduced the likelihood of aggression by other large powers, giving DCs less need for tight American alliances to stare down potential adversaries.

Limited alignments are also strongly preponderant today because the risks of tight alliance with an unrivaled power are particularly great. Military and economic muscle gives the United States the capacity to bully smaller partners, which lack an obvious strategic counterweight to its influence. The risk of diminished autonomy is therefore acute, giving rise to concerns even when short-term American intentions appear friendly. DC officials also have added reason to fear abandonment now that an omnipresent Soviet threat no longer compels the United States to come to their defense. Moreover, the risk of entrapment is severe because America seldom needs permission from its allies to exercise its will unilaterally. U.S. leaders can easily override or ignore objections from most of their weaker allies, as long as a few countries provide platforms for the projection of U.S. power. Kenneth Waltz has argued that this fact makes a unipolar system inherently unstable.[20] The knowledge that they lack any kind of veto rights inclines DCs to limit their security ties with a leading power that could otherwise drag them into unwanted conflict or tie them to unpopular foreign policies. The war in Iraq is a striking case in point. I elaborate on these arguments in chapter 1.

TESTING MY CLAIMS

I test my claims against ten cases from modern Southeast Asia—the maritime states of Singapore, Malaysia, Brunei, Indonesia, and the Philippines and their mainland neighbors of Vietnam, Cambodia, Laos, Thailand, and Myanmar. I do not include East Timor, which only recently became independent. I examine each state's relations since 1975 with the three relevant great powers—the United States, China, and the Soviet Union. I code each state's alignment posture in each calendar year as a single observation, judging it to be in a limited alignment, tight alliance, or nonaligned position. That data enables me to test my two basic contentions—that DCs generally pursue limited alignments and that they do so with particular frequency in the contemporary era.

An important point is in order. In their effort to forge limited alignments, DCs do not always succeed. Consequently, a DC's preferences are not always reflected in alignment outcomes. In some regions of the world and at some time periods, there may be considerable differences between the security arrangements that DCs seek and what they obtain. I thus focus not only on what Southeast Asian states did, but also on what they sought to do, noting discrepancies between apparent preferences and outcomes. As I will show, outcomes provide a reasonably good indicator of preferences in a modern Southeast Asian context.

A finding that a large majority of Southeast Asian states sought limited alignments during a particular period would not prove that DCs do so in all times and places, but it would add meaningful support for my arguments. By contrast, evidence that Southeast Asian states generally sought strict neutrality or tight defense pacts would considerably weaken the force of my argument. If limited alignments have been less prevalent in Southeast Asia since the end of the Cold War, my second claim suffers a significant setback, if not a definitive death blow.

Why Southeast Asia?

I focus on Southeast Asia partly because of the area's obvious strategic importance. Southeast Asia is located on the front line of the two most significant generational developments in the international security order: the growth of Islamic extremism and the rise of China. It is a diverse region with a sizable share of the world's Muslim population, and it has been an important front in the global campaign against terrorism. The nature of the cooperation that Southeast Asian states undertake with America and other external powers will affect the severity and longevity of the terrorist challenge. These factors alone make the region an important subject of study for international security.

In addition, Southeast Asia is at the crossroads of Asia's economic explosion, which is shifting the overall balance of influence in world politics toward the Pacific. Based on its geographic location beside the awakening Chinese colossus, Southeast Asia is one of the first regions in which the People's Republic of China (PRC) can function as a bona fide great power. It thus provides a possible bellwether for how DCs may align as China becomes more influential in other parts of the world. Numerous analysts have prophesied that the world is embarking on a "Pacific Century." Southeast Asian alignments will play a key part in determining whether the rise of Asian economic and military powers has a stabilizing or destabilizing effect on international security, both within and outside of the region.

There are also good methodological reasons for choosing Southeast Asia. I select a bundle of ten Southeast Asian cases partly to balance the competing objectives of breadth and depth that often bedevil social science research. Modern Southeast Asia provides enough observable alignments to draw meaningful conclusions from the data, but a study of ten countries over three decades is not overly broad. I am still able to undertake a deep enough historical inquiry to ascertain government leaders' perceptions and link them to particular alignment decisions.[21]

Modern Southeast Asia provides an excellent set of case studies for other reasons as well. First, Southeast Asia matters to the great powers, both for strategic and economic reasons. The Soviet, Chinese, and American governments, among others, have all actively pursued influence in the region. Unlike Eastern Europe or parts of Latin America during the Cold War, Southeast Asia has also been relatively up for grabs in a strategic sense; no great power has enjoyed clear hegemony over the region. This gives Southeast Asian governments some leverage in determining their alignment postures and makes their decisions important for international security more broadly—by tilting one way or another, they can meaningfully affect the balance of great-power influence in their area.

Second, the states of Southeast Asia are diverse, varying widely in size, ethnic and religious composition, wealth, geography, and ideological orientation. They include wealthy and poor countries; large and small states; island and landlocked territories; Buddhist, Muslim, and Catholic populations; communist and capitalist regimes. To the extent that they exhibit similar alignment behavior, such behavior cannot easily be dismissed as an exclusively Buddhist, communist, poor-country, or island-nation phenomenon. By contrast, examining only the Arab Gulf states or Caribbean countries would raise the possibility that their alignment behavior results not from a general logic of foreign policy but instead from their status as Muslim-majority or small island nations. Any set of case studies can be faulted for validating or refuting a theory only in a limited geographic and temporal sphere, but the diversity of Southeast Asian countries diminishes the force of that critique.

Third, Southeast Asian states entered the post–Vietnam War period with very different alignment portfolios. Some were heavily aligned and others were relatively neutral. This diversity in starting points adds interest to a study of modern Southeast Asia, enabling one to examine the path-dependence of alignment strategies. Do states that are closely aligned tend to remain that way because of bureaucratic institutions and force of habit? Do states that are less aligned tend to remain that way?

Finally, a number of Southeast Asian countries present what Harry Eckstein famously described as crucial cases—cases that offer particularly easy or difficult tests for a hypothesis.[22] If a hypothesis passes a hard test, it scores a major victory. If it fails an easy one, it suffers a potential knockout blow. Southeast Asia presents both types. Indonesia, Malaysia, and Burma have been leaders of the Non-Aligned Movement (NAM) since its inception in 1955 and should present relatively easy cases for me. If they fail to conform to my expectation, my core argument suffers a significant setback. By contrast, Thailand and the Philippines were strong U.S. allies in the Vietnam War era, and Vietnam was a close Soviet security partner. Those three countries present tougher tests; if they exhibit a preference for limited alignments, my argument gains significant credibility.

Why Start in 1975?

There is no single correct time frame for analyzing Southeast Asian alignments, but I select 1975 as the starting point for several reasons. First, 1975 was a clear watershed in Southeast Asian history. In April of that year, communist Khmer Rouge forces streamed into Phnom Penh, winners of an ugly five-year civil war. Weeks later Vietnamese communist tanks crashed through the gates of the presidential palace in Saigon to punctuate their victory in the war against America. The triumph of communists in Laos soon followed. Communist gains and the U.S. withdrawal from Indochina did not create a tabula rasa in Southeast Asia, but those developments did signify the definitive end of an era in regional politics and forced governments to reassess their alignment policies. In addition, by 1975 almost all the states of modern Southeast Asia had emerged from colonial rule or chaotic civil war and become capable of formulating coherent, relatively independent foreign policies.

Starting in 1975 also enables me to evaluate Southeast Asian alignment behavior for roughly similar periods under both the Cold War and post–Cold War eras, and thus also the claim that limited alignments are likely to be particularly preponderant in the contemporary era. During the Cold War Southeast Asia was characterized by intense strategic and ideological rivalry between the superpowers, with China playing an increasingly important role and contributing to the emergence of a kind of skewed bipolarity—or lopsided tripolarity—in Asia. The demise of the Soviet Union ushered in an era of relative unipolarity as the United States raced ahead of its peers in economic and military terms. In recent years China's booming economy, modernizing military, and greater political assertiveness have led many to believe that the Asia-Pacific region is returning toward a more bipolar or multipolar system. U.S. embroilment in Iraq and Afghanistan has had a similar effect. The time frame I have chosen enables me to assess how different strategic conditions can affect DCs' alignment preferences.

Ascertaining Perceptions and Explaining Alignment Choices

Selecting an appropriate case study is not my only methodological challenge. Another difficulty is to ascertain the perceptions of the relevant policymakers. Most scholars agree that elite executive branch officials are the dominant decision makers in Southeast Asia, and I focus my attention accordingly. The most reliable method for ascertaining policymakers' perceptions is careful historical research. Elite interviews, public statements, the few official memoranda available to the public, and secondhand accounts in the scholarly literature can all contribute to an accurate understanding.

Public statements by Southeast Asian officials must be weighed with particular care to assess their sincerity, since they can be instrumentally motivated. Former Malaysian Prime Minister Dr. Mohamad Mahathir illustrated the point when he said, "Why should we fear China? If you identify a country as your future enemy, it becomes your present enemy."[23] I rely partly on public statements but primarily on a broad reading of secondary sources, drawing on the observations and judgments of leading country and regional experts.[24] I also base my empirical conclusions on newspaper articles, official documents, and interviews with current or former officials. Where possible, I compare evidence from multiple sources and triangulate to ascertain the most accurate historical picture of modern Southeast Asian alignment politics.

To explain alignment decisions as results of policymakers' perceptions and beliefs, I rely primarily on process tracing. I use historical sources to show that policymakers identified particular security interests and consciously pursued alignment policies designed to advance them. Statements by leaders, sound inferential reasoning, and conclusions in the secondary literature also provide support for the conclusions I draw. At times, counterfactual reasoning also helps me establish the factors that drove Southeast Asian alignment preferences and policies.

OUTLINE OF THE BOOK

Chapter 1 begins by developing my two core claims. First, I argue that DCs gener-
ally pursue limited alignments with their preferred great-power protectors. Second,
I contend that they are particularly apt to do so in the contemporary, post–Cold
War international system. Chapters 2 and 3 provide a narrative of Southeast Asian
alignment politics since 1975 to furnish data and test my two basic claims. Chapter
2 examines the era from the end of the Second Indochina War to the Paris Peace
Accords in 1991, and chapter 3 discusses the period between 1992 and the present.
In chapters 4 and 5 I explain why Southeast Asian states have so frequently favored
limited alignments, drilling down and analyzing each government's policies and
perceptions in some detail. In chapter 6 I examine how changes in the international
system have made Southeast Asian states even more likely to prefer and pursue
limited alignments during the post–Cold War period. I conclude by reviewing key
findings and drawing out some broader implications of this study for international
security.

The Appeal of Limited Alignments

I HAVE CLAIMED THAT DCs USUALLY PREFER to enter into limited alignments, tilting toward one or more great powers but stopping shy of tight, deeply embedded alliances. I have also argued that limited alignments are particularly likely today. This chapter attempts to explain why.

I begin with the premise that states generally prefer alignments they expect will deliver the greatest rewards at the least possible risk under conditions of strategic uncertainty. Security cooperation with a great power carries both dangers and benefits for a small state or middle power in the Global South. I review some of these risks and rewards and argue that limited alignment is usually the optimal strategy. Genuine nonalignment tends to leave DCs too vulnerable, whereas tight alliance often renders them too susceptible to great-power domination or dependency. Limited alignment is usually an appealing intermediate option, delivering adequate benefits at an acceptable price.

Of course DCs do not decide the forms of their alignments alone. Their great-power friends also have a meaningful say in the matter. Sometimes great powers simply impose security arrangements on unwilling weaker partners. The pressure to align is often considerable and makes it difficult for most DCs to pursue true nonalignment, even when they wish to do so. Even DCs willing to engage in limited security cooperation sometimes find themselves coerced into tight, rigid alliances by a mightier protector. In other instances DCs have the opposite problem: they seek security cooperation with a great power only to be rebuffed and left to fend for themselves. Great powers do not always seek to cultivate tight alliances, either because they do not wish to commit the necessary resources to a particular state or because forging a tight alliance with one DC would complicate the great power's relations with other states in the same region. When DCs do demand tight pacts they may not find a supply.

It is thus crucial to distinguish in this study between *preferences* and *outcomes*. My argument is one about preferences. I contend that DCs usually prefer limited alignments and usually pursue that outcome. This pursuit is observable in DCs' foreign policy behavior, even when they fail to achieve their desired outcomes. I argue that DCs seeking limited alignment do in fact obtain their preferred outcomes in many cases (and perhaps most).

The argument that DCs' alignment preferences depend on weighing perceived risks and rewards raises an obvious question: what factors determine those potential hazards and payoffs? The second part of this chapter addresses that question. There is no simple formula. Material and ideational factors at both the domestic and international levels influence DCs' assessments of risks and rewards. Nevertheless, I attempt to identify some of the variables that are likely to be the most important in the greatest number of cases. I conclude by discussing why changes in the structure and nature of the international system have made limited alignments even more common in the Global South since the end of the Cold War.

THE BASIC ARGUMENT

In their pursuit of national interests, the leaders of DCs undertake the same kinds of rough risk-reward assessments that ordinary people do every day. They consider security cooperation with great powers as a way to obtain a number of rewards. Sometimes they seek only state or regime survival in a dog-eat-dog security environment. Other times they seek above all to stay afloat economically, and the price for great-power aid is fealty in the security sphere. Motives can also be personal: elites are sometimes driven by greed or a lust for material power that only a great power's coffers or arsenal can satisfy. Similarly, a desire to ride the coattails of a powerful protector can provide psychic benefits to leaders in search of prestige or legitimacy. Most DCs align at least to some degree because the world is a dangerous place for small countries and middle powers, and few want to take their chances unprotected. Spurning all great-power allies can leave a DC highly exposed and vulnerable to conquest from outside or from within.

The rewards make some degree of security cooperation with a great power appealing most of the time. However, there is no free lunch in international security affairs. Great powers seldom hand out guns, butter, and security guarantees without demanding some obeisance from their weaker partners in return. Alignments thus come with substantial risks as well as rewards. The tighter an alignment, the higher these risks tend to be. DCs are always constrained to some degree by their international environments, but aligning too tightly with a powerful protector can make matters worse. It can turn a DC into a dependent satellite or stooge of an overbearing protector, or it can lead to entrapment in unwanted conflict. A DC also runs a risk if it brandishes the sword while standing confidently beside a mighty ally: it might later find itself abandoned in an hour of need.

Entering a tight alliance is like signing a big business contract or deciding to get married. The possible rewards are tremendous, but such commitments also narrow options, tie one party's fate to another, and carry a certain risk of betrayal. For small states and middle powers in the developing world, picking the wrong partner can have grave consequences in blood, freedom, and treasure. Thus it is hardly surprising that when they have a choice, DCs usually prefer limited alignments that keep their options open. When they have a meaningful choice, DCs usually prefer dating to marriage.

DCs can also try to pursue strict nonalignment, which carries a different kind of risk-and-reward profile. An investor who hides his money in a mattress is relatively unexposed to stock price fluctuations, and a Romeo who never asks Juliet to the dance faces little chance of refusal. However, such extreme risk-avoiders also forego the possible rewards of a booming portfolio or a fulfilling relationship. DCs can try to split the difference and they usually do. They can avoid the high risks of rigid defense commitments by cooperating in a more ad hoc, informal, and flexible way. At the same time, limited alignment gives them some security ties to a great power that can develop into closer cooperation if conditions warrant.

In short, the leaders of DCs usually consider limited alignments to be utility-maximizing in that they deliver the best possible ratio of risks to rewards. Clearly, keeping a powerful protector at arm's length is not always the best strategy. A DC that refuses to ally tightly may similarly find itself written off by a great-power friend, just as a vendor who, to preserve wiggle room, refuses to sign a long-term contract with a buyer may soon lose the deal. I argue that in the dangerous arena of international security, limited alignments are usually more attractive to DCs than the ideal-type options of balancing, bandwagoning, or strict neutrality, especially when the risks and rewards of alignment are difficult to gauge. The sections that follow examine the principal hazards of alignment, as well as the main benefits.

Risks

The principal risks of alignment to a DC are the dangers of diminished autonomy, abandonment, entrapment, and domestic backlash. These dangers vary from case to case, but they are usually greater in tight alliances than in limited alignments. This is the main reason DCs often prefer to stay at arm's length, even if that means passing up the arms, cash, and other benefits that flow from rock-ribbed security pacts.

Diminished Autonomy and Dependency

As just mentioned, one risk of alignments—and especially tight ones—is that they can turn DCs into satellites or stooges of a great power. Most DCs have been victims to military occupation, colonialism, or other forms of imperial rule during modern history. Unsurprisingly, most are loath to accept external masters if they believe they can run their own affairs independently. Many DCs won their independence from colonial or imperial powers only after the end of World War II or more recently. Their leaders' personal legacies and political regimes are often intimately identified with national independence movements. Most remain wary of a return to subordinate status. States that pried their independence away from colonial or imperial powers—often at no small cost in human lives—are rarely apt to seek alignments that dramatically undercut their hard-earned freedom.[1]

Policy flexibility. Autonomy implies foreign and domestic policy flexibility. George Kennan argued that, because of the fluid nature of international politics, "most wise and experienced statesmen usually shy away from commitments likely to constitute limitations on a government's behavior at unknown dates in the future in the face of unpredictable situations."[2]

Most DCs have seen economic, political, and military dependency as the way neo-imperial powers would wedge their way into the drivers' seats of national policymaking. This enables a great power to rule the roost and treat its ally with disdain. The more tightly a DC aligns—and the more dependent it becomes on a great power—the more constrained it will be in formulating independent policies. Even a friendly great power is likely to demand some fealty as the price of protection and security support. Reduced policy flexibility denies the DC the flexibility to change its position as strategic conditions evolve over time. In 1983 Colombian President Belisario Betancur clearly explained the rationale for avoiding tight alliances when possible: "It is a question of not being a satellite of any one power center and of maintaining our own power of decision."[3]

Concerns about independence tend to be particularly strong in the developing world. This point is crucial, because it largely explains why limited alignment strategies are likely to be of particular appeal to the states of the Global South (and why northern states more often exhibit a willingness to enter strong defense pacts). Many DCs are economically weak and only partially coherent as modern nation-states. Their governments often possess questionable legitimacy, their borders are often arbitrary, and some elements of their populations often have only a diffuse sense of belonging to the state. To the extent that leaders seek to build domestic legitimacy and viable nation-states, the appearance of relative autonomy can be critical. Some leaders—like Ngo Dinh Diem in Vietnam or Babrak Karmal in Afghanistan—have banked on heavy great-power support to consolidate their positions, but that strategy carries enormous risks of dependency and domestic dissatisfaction. The leaders of DCs are almost always sensitive to the risk that tight alliances can turn their countries into mere client states and themselves into puppets.

Dependency. Fears of diminished autonomy are inextricably linked to the dangers of dependency and loss of leverage. For some DC leaders, dependency is accepted as the price for survival or kleptocratic gains; the development of the nation-state is a secondary concern. However, for many other governments in the Global South, survival is not enough. Their leaders also seek to build viable states that can stand on their own. Leaning on a great power often provides a helpful aid in the process of economic and military development, but it can also retard growth in some cases by providing too great a crutch. Local authorities sometimes become too dependent on its aid or markets and avoid making the difficult decisions necessary for building strong independent security forces and a robust economy. Moreover, in a highly dependent relationship, a DC often has to devote some of its modest resources to fighting the great power's causes rather than its own. Subordination of its security policies to the goals of its larger partner can skew the development of the DC's own forces and leave it unprepared to meet its independent needs.

Modern history reveals many cases of limited alignments motivated largely by a desire to guard national autonomy and preserve some leverage and flexibility. For example, a long history of U.S. and other great-power intervention in the region has made most modern Latin American governments fearful of dominance by their mighty northern neighbor. Under considerable U.S. pressure, almost all Latin American governments signed the Rio Treaty of 1947, which committed them to repel any attack (presumably a Soviet one) on a member state.[4] Nevertheless, most governments sought to limit ties, and by the 1960s, most had joined the NAM as members or observers, and the Rio Treaty became largely moribund.[5] Latin American governments generally sought to confine military ties to the U.S. International Military Education and Training (IMET) program, joint training exercises, and some arms provision. Few contributed any troops or money to America's wars in Korea, Vietnam, and elsewhere. Even during the conflict-ridden years of the Second Cold War in the late 1970s and early 1980s, only a few states in the region became tight American allies by choice. As Lars Schoultz has argued, "To Latin Americans the long history of U.S. armed intervention in the region militates against inviting the camel to stick its nose under the tent once again."[6]

African relations with the Soviet Union provide numerous other examples. During the Khrushchev and Brezhnev eras, the USSR sought to build a network of alliances with African states, essentially by trying to swap arms for bases and political influence. It met with relatively little success. African governments that had recently shaken off the shackles of a century or more of European rule were hardly eager for Russian apparatchiks to set up a new imperial order. Only five sub-Saharan African states agreed to sign friendship treaties with Moscow, and only Somalia (briefly) and later Ethiopia agreed to grant the Soviets basing rights.[7]

Angola and Mozambique became reliant on Soviet arms to fight off domestic rivals and the South African army, but after suffering the brunt of Portuguese rule, they turned down Soviet requests for military facilities and willingly suffered some aid cutbacks as a price. The governments of Congo and Guinea-Bissau followed a similar path, turning down Soviet entreaties for tight alliances and basing rights that would have jeopardized their newfound independence. In a host of other African countries—such as Mali, Benin, Guinea, Zambia, Kenya, Uganda, and Madagascar—Soviet aid generally met with a similar refrain: thanks for the arms, but scant interest in Soviet bases or tight, deeply embedded alliances.[8] American administrations sought less energetically than the USSR to establish strong defense relationships in sub-Saharan Africa, but when they did, they usually received a lukewarm response for similar reasons.[9]

Post-Soviet states provide further cases of limited alignments driven largely by a desire to avoid continued dependency on Russia and subordination to the Kremlin. Russia and the surrounding Commonwealth of Independent States (CIS) signed a collective security agreement at Tashkent in 1992, which Russia's neighbors generally felt compelled to sign due to their deficient or nonexistent stand-alone military capabilities. However, almost all CIS governments feared Russian domination, and as soon as they were able to stand on their own two feet, almost all sought to wean themselves off of Russian security dependency by reducing bilateral defense links to Moscow and engaging with the West and the United States, largely through NATO's Partnership for Peace (PfP) training program. Some invited Russian forces to resolve episodic crises, such as the risk of a spreading Afghan civil war in the mid-1990s, but the overall trend was toward limited ties.

By 1998 Russian Defense Minister Igor Sergeev said that Russia only had three "close allies [with] fairly advanced military contacts"—Armenia, Belarus, and Kazakhstan. Two of those, Belarus and Kazakhstan, worked to limit their alignments with Moscow by espousing policies of neutrality and establishing military links to the West. In general, post-Soviet states have pursued "strategic partnerships" (or similar informal arrangements) with Russia and limited ties to NATO to achieve autonomy without making unnecessary enemies in Moscow.[10]

Leverage. As noted, maintaining one's distance from a great power is not only a form of self-protection. Maintaining flexibility can also deliver added leverage to a DC. When a great power has no reason to fear that a weaker ally will defy it or defect to a rival bloc or coalition, it may take that ally for granted. In the 1980s, when the United States essentially purchased a tight alliance with Honduras to conduct operations in neighboring countries, some U.S. diplomats disparagingly referred to it as Washington's "Central American whore."[11] Nobody aspires to that status, and the line between friend and stooge can be thin.

By contrast, if a DC keeps a good measure of autonomy, rival great powers are more apt to vie for its allegiance, and it can play them off against one another to its advantage. Robert Keohane has described the ability of weaker states to manipulate their great-power protectors as something of a "ridiculous paradox" in international affairs. Indeed, DCs can often punch above their weight in an asymmetrical relationship by preserving a measure of strategic ambiguity.[12] Limited alignment sometimes gives them that leverage; tight alliances usually do not. This is an important point, because limited alignments are not just a defensive strategy. They can also be part of relatively assertive, proactive DC strategies by helping relatively weak states pursue their interests more effectively.

During the Cold War DCs of all sizes frequently limited their allegiance and declared themselves nonaligned to obtain external aid yet keep both superpowers at bay.[13] This strategy appealed to many. Some used the strategy as they sought to move toward major-power status. India combined rhetorical nonalignment with a tilt toward Moscow to obtain aid without exposing itself to dependency on a new imperial power or becoming too embroiled in the superpower fray.[14] Limited alignment was also appealing to kleptocratic regimes driven largely by the goal of filling their family coffers. For example, Mobutu Sese Seko in Zaire found that a tight alliance was unnecessary to secure superpower aid; limited security ties kept both American and Soviet spigots open. A wide range of countries with other features and security goals followed a similar path. Nigeria, Ghana, and Yugoslavia, for example, steered a middle course during the Cold War to secure arms or aid, either for narrow regime interests or national development, without paying a large price in dependency or drawing lines in the sand.

Abandonment

A second major risk of alignment, related to dependency, is the possibility of abandonment. The risks of abandonment and entrapment (discussed shortly) are ever-present dangers that create what Glenn Snyder has called the basic security dilemma of alliance politics.[15] Both risks tend to rise with tighter alliance pacts. The more dependent a DC becomes and the more tightly it integrates its military operations with a great power, the more vulnerable it will be if its stronger ally leaves it in the lurch.[16] Small or weak DCs are particularly vulnerable to abandonment because they are usually less important to a great power and can be more easily sacrificed. If abandoned, they have few stand-alone means to protect themselves.

Although DCs sometimes enter tight alliances believing strong ties will reduce the probability of abandonment, history casts doubt on that logic. In one study of the reliability of formal alliances, Alan Sabrosky found that even treaty allies abandoned one another (either by staying neutral or switching sides during a war) in more than 70 percent of observed cases.[17] Tight alliances thus provide no guarantee of support but do make a DC vulnerable to a greater security shock if an ally fails to come to its defense.

Pakistan is an example of a critical state in the Global South that has accused the U.S. government of being unreliable and has thus tried (with mixed success) to limit its alignment with America. As Daniel Markey argues, "The past six decades of on-again, off-again bilateral cooperation have undermined Pakistani confidence in long-term U.S. partnership." Pakistan viewed U.S. opposition to the Pakistani nuclear weapons program during the 1990s as a betrayal, especially because India had already developed its own nuclear arms. The rapid reduction in America's interest in Afghanistan after the Soviet withdrawal was similarly seen as evidence of U.S. unreliability. Pakistani ties to the Taliban and other militant groups thus form part of a strategy by the army and the government to "hedge against abandonment by Washington."[18]

The risk of abandonment points to another important benefit of limited alignments—they sometimes enable a DC to develop meaningful security cooperation with more than one great-power partner. It is difficult and dangerous to pursue stalwart alliances with two or more rival great powers, because one or both behemoths will see close ties to the other as a form of betrayal. By contrast, establishing limited alignments with multiple great-power partners is sometimes possible. As noted, some African countries did so during the Cold War, and a number of post-Soviet states have done so since the mid-1990s. When DCs develop limited offsetting alignments with two rival powers, they hedge their security bets much like the financial trader sets up alternative options to manage financial risk. As David Lake argues, two or more independent alignments reduce a weaker state's dependency on any protector and increase its leverage by establishing an outside option.[19]

Entrapment

As noted, a further risk that flows from diminished autonomy is the danger of entrapment. When a DC becomes dependent on or subservient to a great power, it runs the risk of being dragged against its will into the great power's conflicts. DCs often do not have enough leverage to dissuade great-power allies from controversial foreign policy initiatives—including decisions to go to war—but can endure serious consequences when a great power steers it into harm's way. Even if treaty obligations do not compel allegiance, dependency makes it politically costly and difficult to rebuff an ally's entreaties. A great power can also embroil a weaker ally in conflict by launching attacks from the DC's soil. Before it can raise objections, a DC can quickly become implicated in conflict, pushing it into a further state of dependency.

An important point follows from this logic. James Morrow and Glenn Snyder have argued that alignment choices basically involve a security-autonomy trade-off; tighter alignment usually means more security and less autonomy, and looser alignment means the opposite.[20] In fact, as both scholars acknowledge, a DC that becomes too dependent on its great-power protector can lose both security and autonomy. Excessive dependency on a great power can doubly backfire, stunting a country's independent security development and entangling it in conflicts it would rather avoid. All DCs are vulnerable to entrapment, but small or weak countries are particularly at risk. They usually do not have extensive influence on a great power's policies but can suffer devastating consequences when their great-power protectors drag them into battle. A fear of being dragged into conflict also helps explain why Costa Rica resisted tight alliance and basing agreements with the United States during the 1980s even though its leaders saw the Sandinistas in neighboring Nicaragua as a serious threat.[21]

Even if they do not become caught directly in the cross-hairs of conflict, DCs risk antagonizing other governments or domestic groups when they become identified as the stooges of a great power, especially a great power with unpopular foreign policies. Alignment with a great power can clearly pollute a DC's relations with that power's rivals and adversaries. If foreign policy elites often subscribe to the view that my enemy's enemy is my friend, it is equally true that my enemy's friend is my enemy. Third parties may impose a variety of penalties for alignment with a great power. Military attacks or blockades are among the most extreme options. Efforts to strangle a country economically, isolate it politically, or foment domestic resistance against its government are more common.

Entrapment concerns have often encouraged DCs or rising powers to avoid tight defense pacts. When America was still a developing country of sorts, its leaders sought to avoid tight alliances for fear of losing autonomy and suffering entrapment. George Washington wrote in his farewell address that the United States should avoid permanent alliances because it would be unwise "to implicate ourselves, by artificial ties, in the ordinary vicissitudes of [European] politics, or the ordinary combinations and collisions of her friendships or enmities. Our detached and distant situation invites and enables us to pursue a different course . . . we may safely trust to temporary alliances for extraordinary emergencies."[22] James Madison would later issue a similar admonition against "entangling alliances." The United States was not the only country to follow that path; small European states often attempted to duck out of the way of big-power rivalries during the nineteenth century.[23]

Fears of retaliation also help explain why during the Cold War most Latin American governments that opposed the United States—such as Chile under Salvador Allende in the early 1970s and Nicaragua under the Sandinistas after 1979—avoided tight military alliances with the Soviet Union and offered no basing facilities to the USSR.[24] The Bay of Pigs episode, Cuban Missile Crisis, and U.S. military interventions in the Dominican Republic and Grenada made it clear that inviting America's wrath could have dire consequences.[25] Sometimes great powers penalize their rivals' close allies as part of a deliberate wedge strategy to make the alignment more costly and encourage the weaker party to pull away. At other times, they do so to weaken their rivals by bleeding their allies.

Alienating Domestic Groups

Of course, alignments can offend domestic groups as well. Here again, internal political factors can play major roles in determining alignment preferences and outcomes. In most cases, the governments of DCs face significant internal challenges to both their control and their legitimacy. This situation was apparent during the Cold War, when opposition groups punished their governments for aligning with an ideologically disfavored superpower. For example, in the late 1980s Ecuadorian President Léon Febres Cordero sought to strengthen security ties with the United States by inviting rotating units of 600 U.S. soldiers to assist in post-earthquake reconstruction. Leftist groups in the country immediately accused Febres of compromising the country's sovereignty and facilitating a neo-imperial American effort to secure bases in Ecuador. The Ecuadorian congress passed a resolution calling for the troops' withdrawal, and within months, U.S. forces departed.[26] Conservative groups similarly challenged Soviet-allied regimes. As Mohammed Ayoob and others have emphasized, these internal challenges to state formation and development are often at the heart of security concerns in the developing world.[27] DCs thus disfavor external security relations that jeopardize domestic stability.

This phenomenon has been apparent in recent years, especially in the Middle East. Even when elite policymakers are able to put their own suspicions of U.S. intentions aside, public perceptions that America is targeting Islam raise the domestic and regional costs of alignment for governments with large Muslim populations. Numerous U.S. allies have faced the fury of domestic Islamist groups, who accuse their governments of aiding and abetting the American crusade. Proponents of radical reform in the Arab world have attacked regimes allied to the United States for decades, launching both physical and political campaigns to discredit what they describe as puppet governments.

The most famous case is Saudi Arabia, where Osama bin Laden and others used the U.S.-Saudi alignment as evidence of apostasy and fomented unrest.[28] Jordan, with a majority population of ethnic Palestinians, and several other U.S. friends from Morocco to the Gulf have similarly conducted a delicate balancing act to secure the benefits of American security cooperation without exposing themselves to domestic or regional attack.[29] In Pakistan President Musharraf survived multiple assassination attempts by radical groups, despite wavering in his cooperation with Washington. Cozying up to Uncle Sam entails serious risks in many states.

In DCs where the government enjoys firm domestic control and legitimacy, or where the government can credibly present an alignment as a prerequisite for survival in a hostile neighborhood, those costs can be manageable. In most cases, however, policymakers in DCs have a great incentive to consider the possibility of domestic political backlash.

Rewards

The previous section hardly offered a ringing endorsement for seeking great-power security support. With all of the risks that such bonds entail, why do DCs align at all? Sometimes a great power points enough guns or withholds enough butter to leave them little choice. Great-power pressure often makes it particularly difficult to maintain a position of strict neutrality, especially during times of ongoing or imminent conflict and in regions that are hotly contested due to their strategic location or prized resources. Resisting the pressure to align is likely to be easy only in times of relative great-power peace for out-of-the-way states.

In addition to being a difficult position to maintain, strict nonalignment is usually not the preferred course of action for most DCs. In most cases, DCs choose to align voluntarily—at least up to a point—because they need help in advancing or defending their security interests and related objectives. Whether those goals include defense of the status quo, revision of the existing order, or simply personal enrichment, alignment with a great power can often carry considerable rewards. Strict nonalignment usually leaves them too vulnerable to security threats or too weak to pursue more offensively minded interests.[30] Under some circumstances the expected rewards are high enough that a DC prefers to enter a tight alliance, but I argue that the expected payoff is usually enough only to justify limited security cooperation.

Security Support

Alignment with a great power offers a number of potential rewards. The most obvious reward from security cooperation is help in meeting perceived military threats. A great power can help a DC deter or fight off potential attackers, build up its own armed forces through training and technology transfer, and meet a variety of nontraditional security challenges. Great powers are often the only realistic providers of the types of defense hardware, advanced training, and deterrent capability that a DC desires. By helping meet external defense burdens, a great-power ally can also help its weaker partner devote time and money to national development and social spending.

In many cases, however, the security rewards of alignment are modest. Great powers do not always have the defense goods and services that a DC seeks. For example, Vietnam moved away from Chinese military aid and toward Soviet assistance during the 1960s, because only Moscow had the high-tech tools to fight American air power. Egypt moved away from the Soviet embrace after the October War of 1973 partly because Anwar Sadat believed that only America had the power to deliver security vis-à-vis Israel. Similarly, some post-Soviet states, such as Georgia and Ukraine, moved away from tight alliance with Russia in the 1990s in part because Russia lacked the capacity to help them build state-of-the-art security systems.

Great powers have particular limitations when faced with local separatist or dissident movements. Adversaries can often negate their size and technological edge by blending into the population and using asymmetrical tactics. Great-power military bureaucracies are lumbering giants that can be slow to adapt to a counterinsurgency campaign, and the political will of great powers to fight insurgencies is notoriously short lived.[31] Recent research suggests that the mechanization of advanced industrial armies makes them even less effective in waging counterinsurgency than great powers of the past.[32] Depending on them to fight local adversaries is a dangerous business.

Spillover Benefits

Spillover benefits also exist. Economic aid and trade are perhaps the most concrete nonmilitary payoffs of alignment. For many DCs, the fear of economic failure often constitutes a more existential threat than any armed external or internal menace. Economic weakness contributes to insecurity and prevents DC governments from advancing their policy goals, such as wealth, power, or public welfare. Thus, as Deborah Welch Larson argues, the governments of DCs sometimes align with great powers largely to secure economic resources and solidify their positions in power.[33] Whether they seek financial support to develop their countries or line their own pockets, DC leaders seldom enter into security arrangements without considering the possible economic payoffs.

Aid and trade give even wealthy DCs incentives to align. For example, Saudi Arabia and other Gulf States have aligned with the United States for decades partly to secure a vast market for their prodigious oil reserves.[34] Joanne Gowa and Edward Mansfield have found evidence that security alignments usually do lead to considerable increases in trade between allies.[35]

Alignments can also offer certain political rewards. The clearest political benefits involve great-power protection in diplomatic forums. For example, Israel is frequently the target of hostile resolutions in the United Nations. American vetoes (or threats of vetoes) in the Security Council and lobbying in the General Assembly have been crucial in helping Israel weather the diplomatic storm. The Soviet Union similarly shielded its allies during the Cold War. China and Russia frequently protect states like North Korea and Iran from American efforts to build multilateral sanctions regimes today.

In theory, alignments can give a DC some influence over a great power's policies as well by establishing the weaker partner as a confidante.[36] The United Kingdom has long tried to punch above its weight diplomatically by functioning as a pivot between the United States and Europe. Australia has sought a similar role in Asia. American leaders do not always listen to their counterparts in London and Canberra, but those special relationships do give British and Australian officials added status in diplomatic affairs. Cuba became influential during the Cold War partly because it served as eyes and ears for the USSR in Latin America. Most DCs cannot expect to achieve meaningful influence on a great power's foreign policy, but those with considerable power resources or diplomatic sophistication can expect modest benefits. Finally, alignment can sometimes add to a government's status by making it a member of a prestigious group—contemporary eastern European interest in NATO is perhaps the best example.

Striking the Optimal Balance

When deciding how to align, DC policymakers informally assess how the rewards of tight alliance would likely compare with those that would flow from limited (or nonexistent) security cooperation. Would the great power provide more arms and training? Would its guarantees be more reliable? Would the spillover economic and political benefits be more substantial? The marginal risks are also important. How much lost autonomy would a tight alliance pact entail? How much more vulnerable would the weaker partner be to abandonment or entrapment? Tight alliances are unnecessary if a great power can be counted upon to support a DC anyway; they make sense only when they deliver marginal rewards that outpace the risks that a tighter pact entails. A number of alignment theorists have recognized this logic. For example, Hans Morgenthau wrote that states will avoid alliances "if the burden of the commitments resulting from the alliance is likely to outweigh the advantages to be expected," and Glenn Snyder suggests that "the principle of marginal utility applies" as states choose the extent of their cooperation.[37]

Optimizing risks and rewards is difficult in an ever-changing international environment, and policymakers are never able to do so in a perfectly scientific or rational manner. To the extent that they are able to pursue policies rationally, DCs are likely to tilt toward a great-power protector only until the marginal risks of alignment (i.e., the added risks flowing from closer alignment) come to outweigh the marginal rewards. At that point they maximize their expected utility from security cooperation. High perceived risks and low expected rewards give DC policymakers incentives to enter limited alignments or avoid security cooperation altogether. Conversely, the lower the risks and higher the expected rewards, the more attractive tight alliance becomes. Figure 1.1 illustrates these incentives schematically.

The key to explaining a DC's alignment preferences is to determine the magnitude of risks and rewards that its leaders expect to flow from various alignment strategies.

DC Preferences and Outcomes

The high risks and variable rewards of alignment are likely to lead DCs to prefer limited alignments most of the time. They do not always achieve their preferred outcomes,

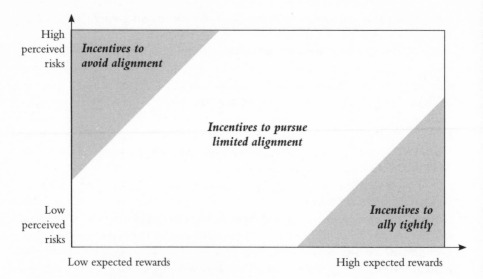

Figure 1.1 Alignment Strategies

Source: Author's compilation

however. As noted, great powers can sometimes impose alliances by using force, threats of force, or overwhelming economic and political pressure. When the stakes are high enough, a great power can bring considerable pressure to bear on even a large, relatively strong DC. Do the preferences of developing countries really matter?

I argue that they do. Because great powers are usually in the market for security partners, they are seldom apt to reject a DC's requests for limited security cooperation. Thus few DCs are likely to be genuinely nonaligned simply because no great-power partner accepts them. Great powers are also unlikely to compel close allegiance by large numbers of DCs. It is extremely costly in financial, military, and political terms for a great power to impose tight alliances on unwilling partners.

This is especially true in the modern era. In the colonial period, European states with teeming populations and tremendous power advantages were able to send boatloads of soldiers and civil servants around the world to administer unequal relationships with weaker peoples. That is much more difficult to do today. DC populations are larger, and nationalism and the norms of sovereignty and self-determination are strong. Great powers are apt to face significant resistance to compulsory alliances from the population of the weaker state. Imposing a tight alliance often means applying a credible threat of force and other forms of pressure. These are often in short supply because wealthy states have fewer willing troops and ever-increasing pressures to spend financial resources domestically. Great powers may also face significant domestic political criticism, either because the alliance requires an unpopular military occupation or because citizens oppose the coercive relationship on normative grounds.

For all of these reasons, great powers are likely to be satisfied with less costly security relationships involving the weaker party's consent. DCs therefore usually have significant influence on the form that an alignment takes, and their preferences are often likely to be reflected both in their observable efforts to achieve a particular security arrangement and in the final outcome.

CALCULATING RISKS AND REWARDS

I have argued that DCs align to strike the optimal balance of risks and rewards. But how do DCs calculate the dangers and payoffs of various alignment options? The answer is not simple. Both the risks and rewards of alignment depend on a number of material and ideational factors at the domestic and international levels. These factors tend to be highly interrelated, and the weight that policymakers give to each varies from case to case. This militates against a neat and parsimonious account of the independent variables that determine specific DC alignment preferences. Only a relatively nuanced historical analysis can explain most individual cases in enough detail. The theoretical challenge, then, is to identify some of the most important variables that tend to influence DCs' alignment decisions. This section examines a number of factors that are apt to influence a DC's alignment calculus and offers arguments about which tend to be more or less important.

Power Considerations

Hard power capabilities—that is, raw military and economic resources—are clearly factors that influence DCs' assessments of the risks and rewards of alignment. The distribution of power in the international system matters, as do the relative capabilities of the DC and its prospective great-power ally. However, the following discussion makes it clear that power alone does not determine the hazards and benefits of alignment.

The Systemic Distribution of Power

The systemic distribution of power is one factor apt to influence DC alignment calculations. Whether the international system is relatively multipolar, bipolar, or unipolar has implications for the likely risks and rewards of alignment in the Global South, though the effects of power distributions depend on the nature of great-power relations as well as the balance of capabilities between them.

Risks and rewards in a multipolar order. In a multipolar order, no single great power has the ability to dominate others. If the relationship among the great powers is basically peaceful, DCs are likely to perceive only modest need for external security support and to shun tight alliances, which are only worth bearing when they deliver substantial payoffs. However, a rich body of literature suggests that multipolarity often gives rise to tensions among the great powers, which form shifting ententes as they jockey for influence and security in the absence of an unrivaled leader that can impose a measure of discipline. The Concert of Europe is often touted as an exception, but it burst at the seams when German power grew in the late nineteenth century, leading to a competitive multipolar system and two world wars in the first half of the twentieth century.

To the extent that multipolarity spawns insecurity by encouraging rival powers to vie for the top spot, it likely leads DCs to see higher rewards in security cooperation. Small states and middle powers can be easily trampled when giants do battle. From the age of European mercantilism to the mid-twentieth century, rival great powers sailed and marched around the globe, seizing territory, establishing empires, and fighting frequently against one another. The hapless small states and middle powers that stood in their way were often conquered and subdued by force. Some saw little alternative to forging tight alliances.

The risks of tight alliances are likely to be relatively high in a multipolar order, however. Entrapment is a particularly serious concern in an unstable multipolar order, as major-power war can easily drag smaller allies into the fray. To make matters worse, allies in a multipolar world, where lines are not drawn clearly in the sand, may often perceive very different threats. A DC may find itself required to fight a country that it thought was its friend. Fears of entrapment gave a number of small European states an incentive to pursue relative neutrality in the era of the two world wars. Domestic political costs of alignment also exist, as do the risks of dependency and abandonment. The only consolation may be that a DC can keep an otherwise domineering great power from dominating or abandoning it by threatening to defect to a rival alliance bloc.

Because of those risks, limited alignment is still likely to be common, and probably preponderant. This is especially true for DCs that are primarily concerned about internal security threats and have less fear of external attack based on their geographic location or lack of desired resources; the rewards of tight alliances may be modest despite the dangerous systemic environment.

DC alignments in a bipolar system. In a bipolar order, where two roughly matched giants stand at the top of the international security hierarchy, the system can again be characterized by relative peace or intense strategic competition. After World War II the old great-power game began to change. A head-on collision between the superpowers became less palatable for a number of reasons, including the advent of nuclear weapons, greater public resistance to military mobilization, and the decreasing economic importance of physical territory in the post-industrial age. Kenneth Waltz has famously argued that a bipolar system is inherently more stable than a multipolar one.

Even if Waltz's argument is correct—and many have challenged it—a stable balance at the systemic level does not necessarily mean peace and quiet in the Global South. During the Cold War, proxy wars flared throughout the developing world as the superpowers vied for advantage outside of the core geographic area of NATO and the Warsaw Pact. From the Korean Peninsula to South Asia, the Horn of Africa, and the Near East, interstate war among DCs was relatively common, especially in hotly contested areas outside of clear U.S. and Soviet spheres of influence. Superpower rivalry also contributed to intense, muscular armed antigovernment insurgencies in many parts of the world. Occasionally, in places like Afghanistan and Central America, the superpowers even intervened directly to prosecute their interests. The nature and intensity of conflict during the Cold War made tight alliances attractive to DCs that saw little alternative if they sought to survive.

In a competitive bipolar system, DCs in hotly contested areas may have particularly strong incentives to extend their hands for close great-power support as an opposing superpower and its well-armed friends seek to dominate the neighborhood. Intense bipolar rivalry can also moderate some of the risks of alignment. The risk of abandonment tends to recede, because a superpower protector is likely to fear losing allies to its rival. Entrapment and alienation of domestic constituencies remain real concerns, but at least DC leaders are more likely to share a broadly similar threat perception with their great-power allies. When threat perceptions converge, a DC is more likely to accept or support conflicts instigated by the great power.

Despite the higher likelihood of tight alliances in competitive bipolar systems, limited alignments are still likely to be the preferred norm. Even DCs located in a region torn by conflict often try to keep their heads down and dodge security challenges. For example, in the tempestuous Middle East and North Africa, limited alignment has been a common (if not dominant) strategy, especially among minor states. Syria, Lebanon, and South Yemen all allied tightly with one of the superpowers for brief periods during the Cold War era, but for most of the past half century they have sought to avoid such clear allegiance. Libya and the Maghreb countries have all limited their alignments with great powers and sought to avoid embroilment in the region's interstate conflicts.

Unless they are directly in harm's way, DCs frequently pass the buck and rely on others to deal with international security threats. As John Mearsheimer argues, "Threatened states are reluctant to form balancing coalitions against potential hegemons because the costs of containment are likely to be great; if it is possible to get another state to bear those costs, a threatened state will make every effort to do so."[38] William Wohlforth adds that "if buck-passing temptations appeal to great powers, they are likely to be nearly irresistible to weak regional states whose potential contribution to a balancing coalition is marginal."[39] There is no reason to bear the risks of allying tightly when a DC can seek out a middle position and stay out of the scrum.

Aligning in a relatively unipolar context. In a relatively unipolar system, certain of the dangers of aligning either with or against the leading power rise due to that state's unrivaled might. Balancing assertively against the leading power is dangerous, especially for the first few countries to attempt it, because it runs the risk of making a very influential (and perhaps even unstoppable) enemy. Wohlforth argues that when the leading state reaches a certain threshold level of relative might, counterbalancing becomes prohibitively costly, even for major powers.[40] Small or mid-sized DCs are likely to be even more fearful of poking the hornets' nest.

Tilting toward an unrivaled power is an attractive and sensible strategy for most DCs, particularly if the leading power is viewed as basically benign. They can gain security and spillover benefits, and they avoid antagonizing the behemoth. However, when any state possesses unmatched capabilities, close security cooperation with it carries particularly acute risks, because a DC has little leverage to prevent its mighty ally from becoming domineering, reckless, or unreliable.

First, the leading power has the capacity to use brute force or other means to bully DCs, which lack an obvious strategic counterweight to its influence.[41] A DC faces a heightened risk of domination, because it cannot credibly threaten to defect to a rival security bloc. Shortly after the end of the Cold War, Iraqi Deputy Prime Minister Tariq Aziz put the case bluntly by writing that "when the Soviet Union existed and was internationally active, my country and many other countries, especially in Asia and Africa, enjoyed a greater degree of independence," because the superpowers "had to be careful about their policies toward, and relations with, the majority of nations . . . to avoid a shift in the balance of power." Aziz noted that even the threat of defecting or moving toward a rival would earn a state greater attention and respect.[42] In a unipolar order, the leading power knows that there is no easy option for DCs to defect, and it has less incentive to strike a favorable bargain with its weaker allies in terms of autonomy and aid.

Second, the risk of abandonment is particularly high in a unipolar system. Because the leading power is much mightier than all potential competitors, it can sacrifice an ally more easily than a great power functioning in a competitive bipolar or multipolar system. Abandonment is particularly likely when the threat perceptions of a DC and its great-power ally diverge. DCs—and especially small or weak countries—usually see the primary threats to their interests emanating from their immediate neighborhoods. A great power sometimes views the same threats as systemically inconsequential, because the local actors feared by its friends in the Global South lack the apparent willingness and capacity to damage their core security interests. Consequently the great power has an incentive to abandon its allies in peripheral areas and conserve its power resources for protecting core strategic assets.

Peruvian President Alberto Fujimori thus lamented that in the post–Cold War order, "only one superpower acts as the arbitrator in international matters. And it becomes involved only when its own vital interests and priorities are on the line. When that is not the case, it makes a graceful exit, arguing that [it] cannot solve everything."[43] In a bipolar or multipolar setting, a great power has more incentive to stay engaged in peripheral regions simply to deny influence to an adversary. Losing an ally in such an environment is more costly. In a unipolar system, the leading power has more discretion to pick and choose.

Third, the absence of clear competitive poles in the international system makes it more likely that the leading power and its allies will develop widely divergent threat perceptions.[44] During the Cold War U.S. and Soviet policymakers were apt to perceive ideological and strategic adversaries lurking behind every tree. (Even when they were incorrect, DCs in search of aid could often use the specter of a rival to secure a superpower's assistance.) In a more unipolar order, some of the local or regional threats that preoccupy many DCs are of less concern to the leading power, because they are not viewed as opportunities for the expansion of a serious strategic rival. The converse is also true; DCs are not apt to share the leading power's threat perception unless those threats are clearly related to security challenges at home.

The increased likelihood of divergent threat perceptions raises the risk that DCs will be entrapped in an unwanted conflict instigated by the leading power. If the leading power is powerful enough to exercise its will unilaterally or with partial international support, it can override objections from many or most of its allies in the developing world. Thus DCs are often unable to exert great policy influence on the United States, which can take unilateral foreign policy decisions—including decisions to go to war—without worrying about its allies defecting to a rival bloc.

The benefits of tight alliances with or against the leading power in a relatively unipolar system depend largely on the character of the leading power. If an unrivaled power were to embark on a campaign of global military conquest—as Hitler hoped to do after defeating rivals in Europe—some DCs might see substantial rewards in forming tight counterbalancing alliances. However, when DCs view the leading power as benign, or when they perceive it primarily as a defender of the status quo, most are apt to expect only modest benefits from assertive counterbalancing strategies. I argue that this has generally been the case in the post–Cold War era.

The rewards of alignment with the leading power can be substantial. In addition to advanced military systems and economic might, the leading power typically heads international institutions and can assist friendly states in a variety of indirect ways. However, the leading power's preponderance often diminishes its allies' need for security support. To the extent that the leading power is able to enforce peace and hold other potentially aggressive states in check, DCs have less to fear and are less likely to accept the risks of tight alliances.[45]

Relative Capabilities

The relative capabilities of the DC and its potential great-power protector contribute somewhat less predictably to the alignment calculus. Developing countries, as I have defined them, include rich countries and poor ones, behemoths and shrimps. A large middle power like Mexico, Turkey, or South Africa bears little resemblance to the world's smallest and weakest states, such as the island states of the South Pacific. Given their differences it is not unreasonable to expect that such states will pursue very different alignment policies. Nevertheless, I argue that the preference for limited alignments is likely to cut across all types of DCs without great variation according to DCs' independent material capabilities.

All else being equal, weaker DCs are likely to perceive greater rewards from allying tightly with a great power. They are, by definition, the countries with the least capacity to advance or defend their own interests independently and typically have the greatest need for economic and military aid. One might thus imagine that weak DCs are least able to survive or prosper without hitching themselves tightly to great-power patrons. However, the same vulnerabilities make it likely that weak DCs will see higher risks in alignment, because they are easier to exploit and more easily trampled or torn asunder if their larger ally entraps or abandons them. These considerable dangers are likely to offset high expectations of rewards.

Stronger DCs may have less pressing need for great-power support, and thus may be more capable of pursuing their interests without entering tight defense pacts. Yet depending on their location and other features, they may still face plenty of security threats that they cannot meet alone. They may also be slightly less concerned about great-power domination and dependency, which in some cases could make them less hesitant to form alliances than weaker DCs.

The need of a DC for external support depends less on its independent capabilities than the character of its neighborhood and internal environment. For example, sizable DCs, such as Pakistan and North Korea, have massive security forces precisely because they face dire perceived threats or find it difficult to control large territories. Despite their might, they may see the need for robust external support. Others, such as Brazil, may not perceive significant need for great-power security backing. Small, relatively weak states, such as Lebanon or Kuwait, have a very different need for support than some tiny island states of the Caribbean. What matters is the extent to which a government believes its own means are not enough to advance its security interests and the degree to which it thinks a great power offers the tools it needs.

Here the difference between preferences and outcomes is again worth stressing. Great powers sometimes pressure their DC partners to form tight alliances. In such cases, a small, weak DC may have a tougher time resisting such pressure than a large, strong one. The argument here is that DCs of all shapes and sizes are likely to prefer and pursue limited alignments most of the time.

Conclusions on Power

The effects of system-level changes on DCs' alignment behavior are clearly relevant to contemporary international security. The global strategic environment is never truly unipolar, but it became more so than at any point in recent centuries after the collapse of the Soviet Union. The United States survived as the world's dominant military power as well as the clear leader in political and economic affairs. The global order can still be described as relatively unipolar today, at least in the security sphere. The United States spends more on defense than the next nine countries combined and has no serious rival in terms of aggregate defense capabilities. Over time the United States may maintain a decisive advantage or lose its lead. It is thus important to consider how shifts in the distribution of power are apt to affect the alignment preferences and behavior of states throughout the Global South.

The preceding discussion suggests that the power distribution does matter. All else being equal, multipolar and bipolar orders are likely to generate more tight alliances than a relatively unipolar system. Yet this depends heavily on the character of relations among the major states, not just their relative capabilities. Moreover, the effects of changes in the systemic power distribution are indirect. They influence DCs' alignment behavior by affecting other variables—such as perceptions of local or regional threats and allies' credibility—that serve as the more proximate causes for alignment preference in the Global South.

Threat Perceptions

The threats that a DC's leaders face are usually much more crucial to their risk-reward assessments than power alone. The magnitude of threats is important, because it partly determines a DC's need for external support. The nature of the menace as is important as the severity of the security challenge. As discussed in the following section, the primacy of internal and nontraditional threats in many DCs diminishes the anticipated benefits of alignment and drives up the dangers.

External Menaces

The magnitude of external security threats is one of the key variables affecting the rewards of alignment. Most alignment theorists agree that the more dire an external menace a state faces, the greater benefits it will expect from great-power protection. Sometimes a DC has no balancing option and is forced to appease its menace, but when a potent ally is ready and willing, the incentives to align tend to peak on the eve of conflict or in the heat of war, when a great power can deter adversaries or help its weaker partner wage a common struggle.[46]

Geography often contributes as much as power or perceived intentions to the intensity of threat perceptions. As Thomas Christensen and Jack Snyder have argued, states on the front lines of conflict have particularly strong incentives to form robust countervailing alignments to avoid a knockout blow, especially when they believe their adversaries possess formidable offensive capabilities.[47] It is no coincidence that regions like western Europe, the Korean peninsula, and the Near East showed the most frequent numbers of tight alliances during the Cold War. European countries living under a Soviet shadow, Korean rivals staring across the 38th parallel, and Middle Eastern states embroiled in successive regional wars often judged the rewards of tight alliance to be worth the risks. Greater external threats also tend to reduce the domestic political risks of alignment, because they make it easier for DC leaders to justify alliance with a great-power protector.

By contrast, a DC that is basically content with its security situation—either because it bears no revisionist intentions or enjoys an unthreatening neighborhood—will expect lesser rewards from alignment. As Patricia Weitsman argues, governments in such circumstances "have incentives to *hedge* their bets by forging low-commitment-level agreements."[48] The same is true when threats recede. Alastair Buchan has rightly asserted that tight alliance becomes less appealing "once the period of clear and present danger is past," because they risk "restricting the freedom of both without giving either a decisive influence upon the policy of the other."[49] Why endure the risk of diminished autonomy when one has little need for the rewards of tight security cooperation? South America provides examples. Interstate war has been rare in modern history, and only a few states (especially Colombia) have faced serious and prolonged armed insurgencies. Given fears of dependency, most South American governments have seen no reason to invite the U.S. army to a neighborhood that has little need for a sheriff.

For similar reasons, numerous scholars have argued that despite their high degree of institutionalization, NATO and other Cold War–era alliances are weakening (or will soon weaken perceptibly) unless resurgent threats from Russia, Iran, China, or other sources replace the Soviet menace that sustained those alliances during the Cold War.[50] NATO's survival provides a reminder that though threats do provide the most common and reliable incentive for security cooperation, they are not the only factors that hold allies together. Similarly, levels of threat are not the only determinants of the tightness of a DC's preferred alignment.

Internal or Nontraditional Threats

The types of security challenges facing a DC are as critical as the magnitude of threats in determining the risks and rewards of a prospective alignment. Many states in the Global South see their primary security challenges as domestic, partly because they lack the democratic features, rule of law, or economic performance to earn robust public legitimacy. The lack of established peaceful mechanisms for political succession magnifies leaders' fear of internal threats, because losing power can result in a prison term or execution. Postcolonial geography also contributes because arbitrary borders often cut across national, ethnic, or religious lines and increase the likelihood of ethnoreligious rivalry and sectarian strife. In most parts of the world, coups are far more likely to bring about the demise of a government than occupation by foreign powers. The prevalence of internal security challenges is one of the factors that most clearly differentiate DCs from the wealthier, more consistently democratic states of the developed world. It is also one of the principal reasons why limited alignment is more common in the Global South.

First, the primacy of internal security challenges often lowers the expected rewards of great-power support. As noted, great powers are often unable to provide the right kinds of resources to deal with internal threats. DCs usually have better local information and more familiarity with the local territory and population than a great power. They are also in a better position to deal with the political fallout from collateral damage.[51] If a great power cannot advance internal security—or if its involvement is counterproductive—the rewards of alignment are often severely diminished.[52]

Second, when a DC faces strong internal security challenges, the risks of tight alliances tend to rise. Cold War conflict in Central America, sub-Saharan Africa, and elsewhere showed that the price of identification as a lackey is high, exposing a government to subversion or even attack.[53] Foreign troops are an asset when they are sitting in tanks or cockpits and confronting a conventional military foe, but they are usually less helpful in mopping up insurgencies or building local legitimacy. White American faces in uniform did little to build the postcolonial credentials of South Vietnamese leaders, and Soviet apparatchiks won few friends for the Soviet-allied regime in Afghanistan after 1979. Foreign troops can galvanize local resistance to the regime, escalate conflict, alienate key domestic constituencies, or draw neighbors and opposing great powers into the melee. DCs with compromised legitimacy or popularity are particularly susceptible to the risks of alignment, because they can easily be painted as apostates or stooges of a great power.

Similar logic applies to nontraditional security threats. Some DCs focus increasing attention on human security and nonmilitary contingencies—such as transnational crime, migration, or natural disasters. To the extent that such concerns predominate over military-oriented threats, the need for robust alliances decreases. Meeting such contingencies requires the ability to cooperate with numerous partners, through either flexible bilateral ties or institutions. Traditional defense pacts usually offer limited support and may exacerbate problems by antagonizing third parties whose cooperation is needed to resolve a given crisis.

Conclusions on Threat Perceptions
Threat perceptions are not as easily measurable as capabilities, because they involve factors like geographic proximity and perceived intentions, but they offer more powerful explanations for alignment preferences. They can be considered first-order variables in DCs' calculations of risks and rewards. Again, both the magnitude and nature of threats are important—something conventional alignment theories tend to overlook. Higher levels of external threat usually raise the rewards of alignment and lessen the risks at the margins. Thus they make tight alliances more probable. Severe internal security challenges have different effects, often raising the domestic political hazards of alignment at least as much as the expected benefits and encouraging a DC to limit its great-power security ties. DCs facing low levels of domestic and foreign menaces are most likely of all to favor limited ties.

Perceived Great-Power Intentions
Power and threat perceptions—the focus of most realist theories—are certainly not the only factors affecting the risks and rewards of an alignment. A great power's perceived intentions affect DCs' calculations as well. DC policymakers are likely to focus on two things: whether a great power appears broadly committed to its interests and whether that great power's pledges of support are credible. The perceived friendliness of a great power is an obvious consideration. If a great power shares similar interests and values, it is more likely to behave in a way that benefits its DC partner and less likely to impose undesired policies.

Credibility is a critical part of the glue that holds alignments together and profoundly affects the expected risks and rewards of security cooperation. Policymakers frequently cite the importance of credibility in alliance politics. For example, in 1983 President Ronald Reagan justified taking a hard line against the Sandinista regime in Nicaragua and allied leftist movements by saying, "If Central America were to fall, what would the consequences be for our position in Asia and Europe and for alliances such as NATO? . . . Which ally, which friend [would] trust us then? . . . Our credibility would collapse, our alliances would crumble."[54]

The more a DC can rely on a great power's promises, the more those pledges of support are worth. However, the inverse is also true. Where a great power lacks credibility, the risk of abandonment rises, and the likelihood of timely assistance recedes. Israeli Foreign Minister Abba Eban expressed a similar logic by comparing an alliance without credibility to "an umbrella which is taken away as soon as it begins to rain."[55]

A great power's friendliness and credibility can be tested in minor ways every day, but they are ultimately tough to gauge. Even joint exercises and public pronouncements of support cannot erase uncertainties. The risks of alignment thus depend heavily on DCs' assessments of the ultimate character of the great-power partner. The great power's military doctrine and broader foreign policy, its history of honoring commitments, and its public and private assurances all carry weight, as do intangible factors such as ideological and cultural affinity.

Great-Power Policies

A great power's announced or implicit policies clearly affect its appeal to DCs as an alignment partner. The content of a great power's policies is one relevant factor. If the great power appears domineering or belligerent, concerns about domination or entrapment are bound to rise. If its policies are widely disfavored domestically or viewed as illegitimate internationally, the political risks of alignment increase, and limited alignment becomes more likely. For example, the Turkish government has long been wary of allowing the United States to use its facilities for Middle Eastern operations, fearing a popular backlash in the neighborhood and within its own borders. Those concerns rose sharply after 9/11, when the U.S. government embarked on a muscular and controversial "war on terror." The Turkish government has thus denied U.S. aircraft use of Incirlik Air Base for Middle Eastern missions in recent years.[56]

The consistency of great-power policies also matters. When a great power's foreign policy shifts dramatically over time, DCs are more likely to perceive high levels of risk. A great power that is friendly today may become menacing or simply abandon its partners tomorrow. Policy inconsistency has been a particular challenge for the United States, where new administrations arrive every four to eight years, often redefining foreign policy priorities.

In numerous Latin American, Middle Eastern, and African states, the relative oscillation of U.S. policy between strategic ally and human rights critic also tended to heighten fears of abandonment and promote limited alignments. Iran and Peru opened doors to the USSR in the late 1960s, partly on the basis of concerns about the intentions of their U.S. allies; Chile, Argentina, and other military-led Latin

American regimes also reduced ties in the late 1970s as the Carter administration focused attention on their woeful human rights records and cast doubt on the extent of U.S. commitment to their regimes.[57] The case of wavering U.S. ties to Pakistan is also an excellent example. That is not to suggest that American pressure for democracy or human rights was ill founded; the point here is that the high degree of variation in U.S. policy over subsequent administrations made many DCs cautious about aligning too closely with America lest their great-power ally turn on them in a time of need.

Ideological Affinity

Many alignment studies downplay the role of ideology—defined here as a coherent system of beliefs about how governance systems ought to be organized[58]—arguing that security policies result from more rational evaluations of countries' security interests. Charles Kegley and Gregory Raymond assert that "necessity, not ideological affinity, is . . . the cement of most alliance bonds."[59] John Mearsheimer similarly argues that when confronting a serious threat, states "pay little attention to ideology as they search for alliance partners,"[60] and Stephen Walt argues that ideology was not a very important determinant of alignment behavior in the Middle East between 1955 and 1979.[61] Indeed, states often shift ideological considerations toward the back burner when confronted with serious threats. Ideological lines are easily redrawn in such cases, as governments seek common ground to strengthen or justify strategically motivated ententes. For example, the U.S. government often painted conservative military regimes as ideological allies against communism during the Cold War, despite their illiberal, undemocratic nature.

Ideology cannot be dismissed entirely as a factor in DCs' alignment calculus, however. It affects DCs' risk-reward calculations by shaping perceptions of great powers' trustworthiness and credibility and by raising or reducing the domestic political costs of security cooperation. Ideological affinity can create the perception that a foreign government belongs to one's in-group, helping establish trust and a sense of shared purpose that encourages strong alignment.[62] It is certainly no coincidence that during the Cold War, most liberal democratic states aligned with the United States, and most communist countries sided with the Soviet Union, with or without compulsion.[63]

As James Morrow suggests, ideology affects the utility function that governments use in weighing the pros and cons of alignments.[64] Victor Cha has similarly argued that "identity consonance"—encompassing a sense of shared political traditions and values—provides a significant part of the glue for tight alliances.[65] Paul Dibb argues, referring to the strong U.S.-Australian pact, that "alliances are not merely the product of rational calculations of national interest. They involve shared values and belief systems and a shared history of doing things together."[66] Of course, ideology can also drive a wedge between security partners. The divisive effects of ideology are apt to be most important for DCs that base their legitimacy heavily on ideological credentials, because a government that professes stridently to govern according to communist, democratic, or Islamist principles will have a harder time explaining a decision to throw in its lot with a great power of different ideological leaning.[67]

Ideology is seldom the most important determinant of alignment behavior, and its effects vary widely from case to case. It is best considered a secondary factor in the risk/reward calculus, one that seldom determines outcomes but can tip the balance in close cases. All else being equal, two states with similar ideological outlooks can be expected to ally tightly more often (and for a longer period) than states with sharply differing ideologies.

Cultural Bonds

Most theorists also discount the role of cultural identities. Jack Snyder has argued that cultural explanations for international behavior should be a last resort because they "tend to be vague in their logic, with causes that are quite distant in time and sequence from their purported consequences."[68] Clearly, cultural identities are not the sole determinants of DCs' alignment decisions. Samuel Huntington overstated the importance of cultural factors in alignment politics when he argued that "countries tend to bandwagon with countries of similar culture and to balance against countries with which they lack cultural commonality. . . . Power attracts those who are culturally similar and repels those who are culturally different."[69] American alliances with Japan and South Korea or former Soviet alliances with Egypt, Syria, Cuba, or Nicaragua are among many examples of tight alliances that cut across civilizational lines. In addition, the effects of cultural factors are notoriously difficult to test, because identity is vague and intersubjective, particularly in religiously, ethnically, and linguistically diverse regions.[70]

Although the problems with relying on cultural explanations are clear, they do not justify rejecting the role of culture in alignment politics altogether. Like ideology, cultural values can affect a DC's perception of a great power's friendliness and credibility.[71] It is difficult, for example, to argue that the tight, long-standing bonds between the United States and the United Kingdom or Australia owe nothing to cultural affinity. In at least some cases, cultural similarities can contribute to a sense of shared identity and purpose.

Conversely, cultural differences can raise suspicions of a great power, domestically or in a surrounding regional neighborhood. U.S. alignments with Arab or Muslim-majority countries provide the most obvious contemporary example. Many policymakers in states such as Egypt, Turkey, and Pakistan have doubts about the American commitment to their long-term regime stability. Others believe that the U.S. government is hostile to Islam. Public outrage at U.S. policies—and thus pressure on governments to hedge—is rooted partly in a popular sense that Muslims are under threat from imperious western powers. Although cultural factors are rarely the primary drivers of alignment behavior, a DC is marginally more likely to limit its ties to a great power from a clearly distinct linguistic and civilizational group. Like ideology, culture is best considered a secondary explanatory variable.

Past Relations

Lurking behind contemporary statements of policy and ideological and cultural ties, DCs' past dealings with great powers also affect their perceptions of the risks of alignment. For many DCs, colonial or other imperial legacies contribute to abiding suspicion of great powers and fears of domination and dependency. Most cases of limited DC alignment in regions including Latin America, Africa, and the former USSR can be attributed partly to memories of colonial or imperial subordination.

Past relations do not always induce suspicion or resentment, however. Where DCs broke from colonial or imperial rule on relatively amicable terms, historical domination does not always militate against a strong alignment relationship. Perhaps more importantly, a long history of working together as independent nations can increase trust between alignment partners, reducing the risks of alignment and raising the expected rewards. This is especially true when the great power embeds itself in formal bilateral or multilateral institutions that give its weaker partners a meaningful voice in key security decisions.

Robert Keohane and others have argued that formal alliances sometimes spawn "cybernetic" bureaucracies that take on a life of their own, but governments ultimately do have the power to pull out, and Scott Bennett has shown empirically that they often do.[72] The survival of some alliance institutions can be attributed to the confidence they provide to member states, not just the self-preservation instincts of alliance bureaucracies. For example, Eastern European states were eager to escape the rigid Warsaw Pact, whereas interest in NATO membership has remained relatively strong. In part, that difference stems from NATO's more democratic institutional structure, which makes the alliance more rewarding and less risky for its smaller members.

Conclusions

Individually, great-power policies, ideational and cultural affinity, and past relations are usually not the dominant variables driving DC alignment choices. Taken together, however, these factors quite often do exert a meaningful impact by influencing a DC's perceptions of a prospective great power partner. These factors frequently point in the same direction, because states with common ideological and cultural features often share historical links and experience of cooperation. Such states also tend to approach policy issues in a broadly similar manner. Realist alignment theories downplay messy ideational and historical factors, but by doing so, they lose the ability to explain important differences in alignment preferences. Ideational factors are likely to be particularly relevant in explaining borderline cases in which power relations or threat perceptions alone cannot offer clear guidance on whether a DC will favor tight or limited security ties.

Economic Aid and Trade

Economic aid and trade are likely to be more modest contributors to DCs' assessments of the risks and rewards of alignment than perceptions of threats and a prospective great-power ally's intentions. Many realists give economics little weight when explaining military alignments. For example, Robert Ross discounts the independent effect of the great powers' relative economic might on DC alignment decisions.[73] Walt argues that "although the desire to obtain economic and military aid has been a common motive for establishing close relations with a wealthy and powerful ally, the choice of which potential patron to prefer is determined by other factors."[74]

Those arguments are somewhat overdrawn; economics cannot be dismissed entirely. Many DC leaders enter into alignments largely because they seek either funds for national development or spoils to stash away in Swiss bank accounts. Economic lifelines are often precisely what DC leaders believe they need to meet security challenges as well, enabling them to mobilize armies, co-opt rivals, and pacify restless segments of the population. Economic aid and trade are thus important spillover benefits of alignment. The flow of money and goods can also strengthen alignments by demonstrating the great power's commitment to a DC.[75]

Nevertheless, aid and trade alone are not usually enough to make a DC prefer a tight alliance when other factors (namely, perceived security challenges and great-power intentions) point toward the desirability of a limited alignment. These economic benefits have to be weighed against some considerable risks. Historically, dependency on a single great-power market has often meant exploitation for DCs. Great powers strip them of resources while reaping the profits of higher-value-added products.

Many DC officials believe that too much reliance on a great power skews the development of local economies toward functions at the low end of the economic food chain and locks them in a cycle of debt and dependency. In fact, an entire school of research called dependency theory grew out of Latin America during the Cold War to highlight the perils of unequal economic relationships. Most of the governments of African countries, South Asian states, and Soviet satellites similarly concluded that great-power aid could sometimes be a poisoned chalice. Some developing economies—such as South Korea and Taiwan—pursued tight alliances with the United States and managed to develop strong independent economies, but the fear of economic dependency encouraged other DCs to limit their ties to Uncle Sam and diversify.

Tight alliances also raise the risk that a third party will retaliate by slapping on sanctions or sealing off its markets to trade.[76] Sanctions can have a crushing effect, especially when backed by the UN Security Council, International Monetary Fund (IMF), World Bank, or a coalition of major trading partners. They can compound a DC's domestic security threats, undermine the government's ability to provide law and order, and diminish its performance legitimacy.[77] Consequently DCs have a strong incentive to shy away from security strategies that will draw lines in the sand and add to the likelihood of hostile economic responses. No government wants to follow in the financial footsteps of Cuba, Libya (until recently), or North Korea. Even steps far short of sanctions can severely curtail a country's economic development and drive it further into dependency on its great-power ally.

Except in the poorest DCs private trade and investment flows usually dwarf international aid flows; globally economic aid has historically hovered at around 1 percent of the value of global trade.[78] Consequently a great-power ally normally needs to provide quite a large aid package to outweigh the risk of reduced access to third-party markets. Tight alliance can indeed provide rewards, but the risks quite often exceed them, especially in an economic system characterized by high levels of trade and relatively few barriers. The argument advanced here is that an interest in securing aid and trade usually adds modestly to a DC's incentives to pursue limited alignment. Aid and trade are rarely likely to drive the formation of a tight alliance absent grave security concerns; DCs usually do not sell their autonomy cheaply.

Alternatives or Complements to Great-Power Protection
A final set of factors affecting the risks and rewards of great-power alignment relate to the availability of other security options to a DC. Alignments take place within a broader strategic framework. When a DC lacks the muscle to advance its security interests independently, it does not necessarily need to ally tightly with a great power. Self-help remedies, discussed earlier in the section on power capabilities, offer one obvious alternative. A DC can also rely on pacts or informal arrangements with other secondary states (i.e., small states or middle powers). Last, they can participate in multilateral forums and promote international norms that promote security and limit the scope for external predation. Like a DC's independent power capabilities, these alternative security structures can affect alignment politics in the Global South both by influencing DCs' preferences and, in some cases, by helping them resist great-power pressure to achieve desired outcomes. Like economic factors, these are apt to be lesser factors in the alignment calculus, but they are not insignificant.

Secondary-State Security Cooperation
Great powers are not the only possible security partners. DCs can forge ties with other secondary states and thus reduce dependence on great-power patrons. Egypt's periodic alignments with Arab nationalist regimes in the 1950s and Iran's contemporary ties to Syria are possible examples. At other times these arrangements serve as alignments by proxy to great powers, mitigating some of the risks of direct security ties. Cuban alignment with revolutionary states in Africa and Latin America during the Cold War is a case in point. African security ties to U.S. allies like Britain or France are also good examples. When a DC faces only modest security threats, these secondary-state arrangements are sometimes enough. However, secondary states are usually less able than great powers to provide major military, economic, and political assistance in a crisis. Thus secondary-state partners are usually seen more as complements than alternatives to great-power protectors. Such arrangements reduce the need for robust great-power support and thus the expected rewards of a tight alliance.

Multilateral Institutions and Norms

A further option for DCs is to rely on norms and multilateral forms to add to their security and advance their interests. Norms and institutions are usually far from the most important variables in the risk–reward calculus, but on the margins, they can reduce some expected rewards of tight alliance and increasing certain political risks.

Realist models downplay the effect of norms and institutions, describing alignment politics as ruthlessly amoral and based solely on considerations of national interest in a dog-eat-dog, self-help anarchical environment.[79] In the security arena, they argue, the risk of armed attack often makes states prioritize relative gains and adopt muscular defense postures when they perceive threats.[80] Indeed, most scholars agree that international cooperation through shared norms and institutions has been somewhat easier to achieve in economic affairs than security relations.[81]

Liberal theorists nonetheless argue that institutions can lessen the need for antagonistic arms races or confrontational defense pacts by serving as forums where states can develop shared norms of behavior, engage in confidence-building, and work to resolve or defer disputes peacefully. In addition to the United Nations and other global organizations, many regional groups seek to reduce neighborly and extramural threats to their members. The Association of Southeast Asian Nations (ASEAN) is a regional organization of particular relevance to this study. Another is the Gulf Cooperation Council (GCC), formed by Saudi Arabia and neighboring Arab Gulf states in 1981 to manage a perceived threat from revolutionary Iran, to cooperate in internal security affairs, and to build economic links in the region. Other multilateral forums include the Arab League, Andean Pact, Mercosur, African Union, European Union, Organization of American States, Organization of the Islamic Conference, and GUAM (Georgia, Ukraine, Azerbaijan, and Moldova).

The project of building multilateral forums and institutions relates closely to the effort to blunt the edges of naked power politics by establishing strong international norms. DCs routinely invoke the norms of state sovereignty and noninterference to shield themselves from neighborly or great-power predation. In some instances these norms help fend off external or internal political attacks. (Whether and when these norms are desirable are separate questions.) In western Europe, a strong norm of peaceful dispute resolution has emerged since the end of World War II, significantly obviating the need for ready defenses against neighbors, if not from more distant potential foes. To the extent that DC leaders believe norms and institutions have taken hold, they are apt to perceive lower levels of insecurity. This reduces the perceived need for great-power protection and thus the expected rewards of tight alliance.

Some norms and institutions are specifically designed to reduce DCs' need to pursue tight alliances or endure involuntary pacts. The prime example is the NAM, established in the 1950s and including most of the states of the Global South. The NAM's founding states—India, Algeria, Ghana, Yugoslavia, and Egypt—sought to reduce DCs' dependency on and vulnerability to the superpowers by stressing third world solidarity. Solidarity has been tough to achieve (or even feign) in a forum that includes both India and Pakistan, both Iraq and Iran, and many other pairs or groups of historical enemies. The NAM has also not prevented tight alliances; numerous members have drifted into tight alliances when facing serious security challenges. Soviet allies such as Cuba and North Korea and American friends such as Saudi Arabia and the United Arab Emirates are examples. Even some of the NAM's founding leaders, such as Egypt and India, allied tightly with the Soviet Union at certain points.

Some DCs have also advanced regional variants of the norm of nonalignment. For example, during the 1950s Argentine President Juan Perón championed a "third position" between the superpowers, emphasizing relative neutralism, independence, and a rejection of rigid military alliances. In the same era Egyptian President Gamal Abdel Nasser championed the pan-Arabist movement, stressing fraternal solidarity among Arab states and limits on superpower dependency. Iran under the Ayatollah Khomeini later espoused a foreign policy of "neither East nor West."

In most cases norms emphasizing nonalignment reflect DCs' desire to avoid tight alliance for other reasons. They are more symptoms than causes. However, governments that consistently espouse policies of nonalignment do become somewhat bound to those policies over time, because domestic constituencies and foreign friends see deviations from nonalignment as betrayals of principle. In a security crisis governments have ample reason to bear those accusations, but in peacetime, past commitment to the norm of nonalignment adds a reason to avoid tight alliance. India is perhaps the best case in point; despite facing considerable threats from terrorist organizations and fearing the rise of China, leaders in New Delhi would face a significant political price for allying tightly with America, and this is partly attributable to the government's long-standing emphasis on the norm of nonalignment.[82]

Norms and institutions rarely eliminate the perceived need for great-power protection. In most parts of the Global South, conflict is a frequent fact of life. When push comes to shove, DCs are seldom willing to pass up great-power support in the hope that norms or institutions will shield them from attack. Like secondary-state arrangements, institutions are usually complements—they reduce the expected rewards of tight alliance by moderating threats emanating from neighbors or extraregional powers. However, Southeast Asia provides a good test for this proposition, because the ASEAN states have developed a more robust normative framework—centered around noninterference and peaceful dispute management—than almost any area of the Global South.

The Role of Uncertainty

In practice, policymakers can seldom if ever draw up a neat list of risks and rewards as they formulate alignment policy. Alignment studies often downplay that fact, assuming for simplicity that governments have relatively clear and unified views of the intentions of friends and foes. Occasionally that assumption is appropriate.

Kim Jong-Il, Mahmoud Ahmadinejad, and Than Shwe can have little doubt about American hostility, and Israel has almost daily reminders of the hostility of many of its neighbors. However, other actors' intentions are not always so obvious. Are foreign foes spouting vitriol for the benefit of domestic constituencies, or might they actually attack? Are domestic dissidents merely rabble-rousers, or do they reflect serious regime vulnerabilities? Even the most obvious gathering menaces are sometimes misread, as in Europe during Adolf Hitler's digestion of Austria and Czechoslovakia.

When policymakers cannot arrive at a reasonably clear view of other actors' intentions, judging the risks and rewards of alignment is difficult. Limited alignments are a sensible default strategy because they are easier to unwind that tight ones. They do not involve high degrees of institutionalization or entrenched military and bureaucratic interests. As both Evan Medeiros and T. V. Paul have argued, limited alignments thus tend to leave economic and diplomatic doors open for engagement with a potential adversary while setting up an alignment structure that can be strengthened if tensions rise.[83] In other words, limited alignment is often the safest default strategy, because it enables DCs to adjust their posture as conditions change or if their initial perceptions of other actors' intentions prove to be wrong. Ultimately, maintaining multiple actions in an hour of need can be better protection than an alliance.[84]

Uncertainty would arise even if an ideal-type rational actor made a state's alignment decisions, and it is even more challenging in the real world. The formulation of alignment policy results from negotiation among agencies, political parties, interest groups, and branches of government that often have different views on the relative risks and rewards of a particular alignment strategy. Randall Schweller has rightly argued that a lack of consensus among senior policymakers often makes it difficult for governments to adopt high-risk alignment policies.[85] When a government cannot arrive at a clear collective view of the best security strategy, it is apt to seek out middle ground, buying time to wait and see as conditions change and the risks and rewards of alignment become clearer.

Summary of Major Variables

As the preceding analysis suggests, a number of variables go into the calculation of risks and rewards. This fact militates against a neat, parsimonious theoretical model. Although I began by arguing that the systemic distribution does tend to exert an impact on alignment patterns, systemic factors do not offer the most convincing explanations of individual states' alignment choices. The effects of systemic change are mediated through other variables that serve as the more proximate causes for DC alignment preferences.

The relative importance of various factors in DC alignment calculi vary from case to case. It is nevertheless possible to present a rough hierarchy of factors that inform DCs' assessments of the dangers and benefits of alignment (see figure 1.2). At the top of the hierarchy are external and internal threat perceptions. Mainstream

Favoring Weaker Alignments		**Favoring Tight Alliances**
Background Variable: Systemic Distribution of Power		
Relative unipolarity	$\longleftrightarrow$	Bipolarity or multipolarity
First-Order Variables: Perceptions of Threat and Great-Power Intentions		
Weak or unclear external threats	$\longleftrightarrow$	Clear, pressing external threats
Preponderant internal security challenges	$\longleftrightarrow$	Preponderant external military challenges
Weak great-power capability	$\longleftrightarrow$	Strong great-power credibility
Second-Order Contributing Variables		
Weak reliance on great-power aid and trade	$\longleftrightarrow$	Strong reliance on great-power aid and trade
No past institutionalized alliance	$\longleftrightarrow$	Past institutionalized alliance
Controverial or inconsistent great-power policy	$\longleftrightarrow$	Uncontroversial and consistent great-power policy
Ideological difference	$\longleftrightarrow$	Ideological affinity
Cultural difference	$\longleftrightarrow$	Cultural affinity
Option to align with other secondary states	$\longleftrightarrow$	No option to align with other secondary states
Strong DC confidence in norms and institutions	$\longleftrightarrow$	Weak DC confidence in norms and institutions

Figure 1.2 Key Variables

Source: Author's compilation

theories of alignment tend to give priority to external threats, but I argue that domestic security concerns are comparably important in the risk-reward calculus of most DCs and largely explain why they favor limited alignments more often than wealthy developed states. The perceived risks are usually higher, and the rewards less appealing, to a DC government focused above all on domestic challenges.

I have also argued that alignment preferences often cannot be explained without reference to the DC's perceptions of a prospective great-power partner. I identified a cluster of second-order variables related to the perceived intentions and credibility of a prospective great-power partner: namely the nature of its policies, its ideological and cultural features, and its experience with the DC in question. These variables are seldom decisive individually, but they are often correlated. When they are, they can often tip the balance, explaining why two DCs facing similar threat environments prefer to adopt different alignment postures.

I then presented additional second-order factors including economic ties and the availability of other security options to the DC, such as secondary-state arrangements and norms and institutions. I place these lowest on the hierarchy not because they are always unimportant but because their effects are likely to be visible only on the margins.

No single variable can reliably account for DCs' decisions to pursue tighter or more limited alignments, and their relative contributions vary from case to case. In any given instance, some factors raise the risks, and some reduce them; some heighten the rewards, and others diminish them. The more factors that point toward high risks and low rewards, the more apt a DC is to favor limited alignment, and vice versa. When the ultimate calculus is unclear, DCs are also likely to steer a middle path in the hope of preserving flexibility in an uncertain environment.

Heuristic Examples of the Alignment Calculus

The way these various factors influence calculations of risks and rewards can perhaps best be illustrated through a series of brief heuristic examples. These examples illustrate reasons why a DC might prefer limited alignment or tight alliance under different circumstances.

Contemporary Brazil-U.S. relations are the first example. Modest security ties benefit Brazil by contributing to healthy overall relations in the political and economic spheres and by furnishing some desired technical assistance and hardware. Tight alliance would provide little added value, however; officials in Brasília simply see no need for stalwart security guarantees or American bombers and bases without a serious enemy breathing down their necks. The risks of limited alignment with America are modest, because the two governments share broadly compatible ideational outlooks, but perceived risks would rise sharply in a tight alliance, as historical experience and misgivings about U.S. foreign policy would likely give rise to concerns about diminished autonomy, public backlash, and association with risky U.S. military ventures. Figure 1.3 illustrates this logic schematically, showing that in this case, Brazil maximizes its utility through a limited alignment.

Algeria would likely arrive at a very different calculation of risks and rewards when considering security ties to the United States. The Algerian government faces no imminent external predators but must contend with serious domestic resistance from violent Islamist groups. Although some U.S. training, materiel, and money are useful, a stalwart alliance carries few added rewards; troops and tanks simply cannot defuse the threat. Moreover, the marginal risks of a tight alliance are likely to be grave. The Algerian and U.S. governments have major policy differences, a checkered history, and divergent ideational features. A lack of trust would likely contribute to real fears of diminished autonomy or abandonment. Finally, the Algerian government could also be painted as a U.S. lackey, helping drive recruits into the arms of the insurgency. Figure 1.4 presents such a situation. Again, limited alignment is the utility-maximizing strategy.

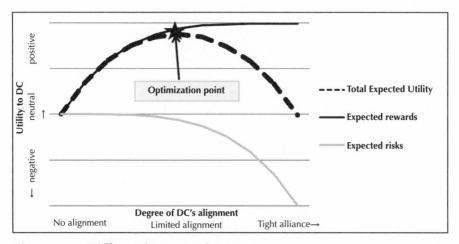

Figure 1.3 Diffuse Threat Environment

Source: Author's compilation

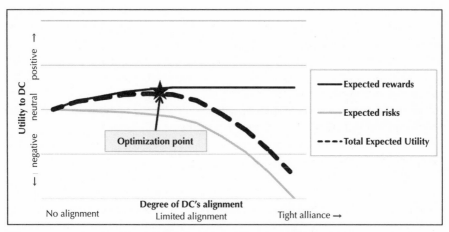

Figure 1.4 Lack of a Suitable Great-Power Ally

Source: Author's compilation

Of course, DCs do not always pursue limited alignments. An example of a state that likely preferred tight alliance with the United States is Georgia after the Rose Revolution of 2003. The Georgian government faced a clear external security threat from Russia, perceived the United States as having political and military power that could help diffuse it, and saw the Bush administration as committed to the defense of allies and democracy. The apparent friendliness of the U.S. government diminished some of the risks of tight alliance. The added benefits of tight alliance appeared substantial, and the marginal hazards manageable (figure 1.5).

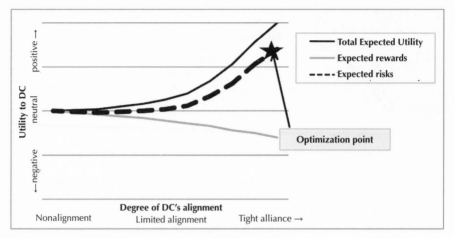

Figure 1.5   Conditions for a Tight Alliance

Source: Author's compilation

Georgia thus pursued NATO membership and closer bilateral security links to Washington. Ultimately, NATO's failure to prevent the Russian invasion of South Ossetia in 2008 was a reminder that DCs cannot always choose their alignments alone.

I contend that the first two scenarios are more common than the third. Thus DCs usually conclude that tight alliances are too risky, and genuine nonalignment leaves them too unprotected. Staking out middle ground between these extremes normally leaves them in the best possible position.

WHY LIMITED ALIGNMENTS ARE SO LIKELY TODAY

One proposition that flows from the theoretical model developed in this chapter is that DCs are particularly prone to favor limited alignments today. A cursory review of post–Cold War evidence supports that claim. In most regions of the world—including Latin America, the Middle East, Africa, and Central Asia—tight alliances have become considerably less numerous since the end of the Cold War. Only the rush of several Eastern European states to join NATO stands out as an obvious exception.

I argue that for many DCs, several key variables in the risk-reward calculus have changed since the collapse of the USSR. Changes in both the power structure and nature of the international order have added to the prevalence of limited alignments. First, the power distribution has shifted from bipolarity to relative unipolarity. Second, the nature of the international order has evolved to reflect the particular characteristics of American leadership. The United States has not always pursued economic openness and democratic norms and institutions since 1991, but in comparative historical terms its leadership has been quite liberal. This is critical, because it helps explain the nonexistence of tight anti-American pacts, which traditional balance-of-power theory would predict.

The preponderance of U.S. power and the liberal nature of the U.S.-led order have diminished the likelihood of major-power war and made many DCs less fearful of external attack by challengers to the existing order. These changes in the external threat environment have driven down the appeal of tight alliances for most DCs, which now face security threats that are primarily either internal or nontraditional. At the same time, concerns about U.S. policies have magnified some of the domestic political dangers of tight alliances with Uncle Sam, making limited ties more appealing.

Other factors have also contributed modestly. Economic globalization provides added incentive to favor limited alignments by raising the risks of antagonistic pacts. Norms and institutions have evolved, most notably by drawing the likes of China and Russia further into the fold and raising opportunities to pursue political engagement that smoothes some of the rough edges of international politics. Both economic interdependence and political engagement help to moderate threat perceptions and ease DC demand for tight alliances. These developments are closely related, but I separate them here to add some theoretical clarity.

Finally, it is worth noting that in addition to preferring limited alignments, DCs that tilt toward America are more likely to achieve their desired outcomes in the contemporary context. Without the Soviet Union staring across a Cold War divide, the U.S. government is likely to be more tolerant than it would otherwise be of DCs that prefer dating to marriage.

Power Considerations

One reason for the added prevalence of limited alignments in the contemporary era is structural. Relative unipolarity has added to certain risks of forging tight alliances with or against the United States. America is certainly not without critics and adversaries in the Global South, but they have good reason to avoid tight defense pacts that the United States might construe as hostile balancing coalitions. If America's enemies had any doubts about U.S. willingness to exercise its military superiority, the campaigns in Bosnia, Kosovo, Afghanistan, and Iraq showed the concrete danger of defying Washington. Governments in Venezuela, Syria, Cuba, North Korea, and Iran have all sought to build ties with other major powers like China and Russia, but none has proposed organizing a robust alliance against America. Even if they were to do so, China and Russia would likely have little interest.

Most DCs are apt to align with the United States to varying degrees in the post–Cold War context to stay on America's good side and reap certain benefits.[86] Nevertheless, DCs have incentives not to align too tightly with America. In the post–Cold War context, the United States does not depend heavily on weaker security partners to face down a serious strategic challenger. For DCs aligned with the world's sole superpower, acute power asymmetry raises fears of domination and concerns about abandonment.[87] The knowledge that they lack any kind of veto rights gives DC policymakers an added reason to limit their allegiance. If they ally tightly, treaty obligations or other dependency could make it hard to escape embroilment in unwanted conflict. Pressure on U.S. allies to send troops to participate in the controversial Iraq War in 2003 provides one obvious case.

Threat Environment

In the theoretical model developed in this chapter, threat perceptions are even more critical than power configurations in determining the expected risks and rewards of alignment. The threat environment in a relatively unipolar order depends not just on the power distribution but also on the character of the leading power and its relations with other major states. In the post–Cold War period, the extent and nature of U.S. primacy has contributed to a kind of hegemonic peace among the big powers.

Most DCs see lower rewards from tight alliances in the post–Cold War period, because they simply do not face the same types of existential external military threats that menaced them in previous periods of history. Civil wars and ethnic conflicts proliferated during the 1990s, but serious bids for military expansion or conquest by other large states or middle powers are unlikely as long as the United States defends the status quo with overwhelming might. John Mueller has even argued that interstate war among the great powers has become virtually obsolete.[88] Without the fear of traditional military attack, DCs have less reason to seek the rewards of tight alliance with America and less reason to bear the risks. For example, states such as Italy and Turkey no longer need large U.S. military bases to keep the Soviets in check.[89]

To the extent that rival powers do challenge the existing order, they are most likely to do so through asymmetrical or nonmilitary means, such as Iranian or Syrian support for Hezbollah and Hamas or Venezuelan loans to leftist movements in Latin America. The vast majority of conflicts that have erupted after the end of the Cold War have been domestic or local. The most common form of conflict has involved rival domestic groups competing, often along ethnic or religious lines, for ascendancy over contested or inchoate nation-states. As discussed earlier, meeting asymmetrical security challenges is usually not the strong suit of great powers. DCs that face these types of revisionist threats—such as Lebanon or Colombia—often find that close great-power backing does not strengthen their hand as much as the kind of quiet, low-key technical and economic support that flows from limited alignments.

Perceptions of U.S. Intentions and Policies

Perceptions of American intentions and policies are also critical to explaining why DCs are particularly apt to prefer limited alignments today. These factors are, of course, closely related to the character of the contemporary threat environment.

Although the U.S. government is not universally trusted or beloved, most DCs do not view America as a significant direct threat to their security. As John Ikenberry has argued, American governments exercised strategic restraint over the past several decades—and especially after World War II—and led the establishment of multilateral institutions that now limit U.S. capacity to abuse its unrivaled power.[90] John Owen adds that the penetration of liberal democratic norms in many governments has made them less fearful of the United States than they would otherwise be of a country possessing America's vast power resources.[91] Many officials in the Global South also believe that American behavior can be modified meaningfully by engaging with the United States at public and official levels. America's democratic system of government, open economy, free press, and leadership of a plethora of multilateral institutions provide numerous avenues for peaceful dissent. Tight anti-American alliances are unnecessary when diplomatic and other levers will do.

For DCs that do not see America as menacing, tight counterbalancing alliances would offer little obvious benefit. In fact, a reasonable number of DCs quietly support the U.S. role as a kind of global policeman—not because they adore America, but because they have existed under much more onerous forms of hegemony. Eastern European countries are perhaps the best examples. They see little reason to balance against a liberal superpower by allying tightly with a historically overbearing neighbor.

Although most DCs do not see America as a direct threat to be balanced, many do have considerable bones to pick with U.S. foreign policies. As noted earlier, when a great power pursues widely disfavored policies, it drives up the political risks for its allies. As the leading power in the international system, and as the principal sponsor of a host of controversial policies, the United States is the object of widespread resentment by disaffected governments and populations. Close identification with its policies can be costly for a DC's leaders. The U.S. campaign against terrorism is the most obvious example, but arms sales and other support to Israel, American sanctions regimes, and other policies are also widely chastised. When DCs have a choice, they are likely to keep a distance.

Economic Globalization

A modest additional incentive to favor limited alignment in the post–Cold War era is economic. The contemporary international economic system is relatively open by historical standards. Part of this process of globalization is due to technological strides, but the policies of the leading economic powers—such as the United States, European Union, Japan, Russia, India, and China—have also enabled former Cold War foes to integrate rapidly into the broader world economy. Economic openness relates to alignment politics, because when a DC has diverse trade relationships, the risk of aligning against any of those partners goes up.[92]

For example, during the Cold War, many small Caribbean and Latin American countries were tied closely to the U.S. economy, depending heavily on American export markets and finance. Very few entered the period with economic ties to the USSR. Consequently, those countries ran tremendous economic costs when they aligned with Moscow against America but suffered only modest trade and investment losses when aligning with the United States against the Soviet Union. Since the end of bipolar competition, Russia and China have significantly expanded the scope of their economic relations with former Cold War friends and foes alike, making it more risky for many DCs to ally tightly against them.

Institutional Evolution

A final (and comparatively modest) reason for the added prevalence of limited alignments since the end of the Cold War is the evolution of international institutions. Of particular importance to alignment politics has been the increased role played by Russia and China. Although officials from Moscow and Beijing were members of the United Nations and other international groups, their multilateral engagement was highly constrained before the early 1990s. Since then they have been able to plug into many more institutional forums. The 1993 founding of the ASEAN Regional Forum, 2001 establishment of the Shanghai Cooperation Organization, and 2003 creation of the G-20 are just a few examples. Russia has joined the G-8 and built more institutional ties to Europe, and China has become a key member of Asian forums like ASEAN Plus Three and the East Asia Summit. These institutions do not provide members with credible guarantees against attack, but engagement through them has helped foster robust political engagement and moderate threat perceptions.

Like developments in the international economy, the evolution of international institutions is clearly related to changes in the structure of the global system: namely, the nature of American leadership and the relations among the great powers. All of these related variables point broadly in a similar direction, diminishing the appeal of tight alliances to many DCs.

CONCLUSIONS

I have argued that the best way to understand states' alignment preferences in the Global South is to consider them products of rough calculations of risks and rewards. Using that model, I have made two key, empirically testable claims. First, DCs generally prefer limited alignments when they have a meaningful choice in the matter. Second, they are particularly likely to do so in the contemporary era of U.S. primacy.

These claims challenge conventional theories of alliance politics, most of which focus on how states choose sides and ignore the forms of alignment. Theory needs to better account for options in between the ideal-types of balancing, bandwagoning, and neutrality. The examples used throughout this chapter show that countries in regions around the Global South—including the Middle East, Asia, Africa, and Latin America—often favor limited alignments. I do not attempt to prove systematically that my hypotheses are valid in all times and places but have tried to establish a prima facie case for my two core claims, which appear to find support in a number of regions and time periods.

Explaining the forms of alignment is a complicated matter, which largely explains why theorists have steered away from the subject. As Stephen Walt has argued, "The specific commitments that allies accept will reflect a host of idiosyncratic features that are unlikely to be easily generalized."[93] That certainly does not make the subject unimportant or undeserving of study, but it does mean that a theoretical explanation for the forms of alignment needs to be nuanced. To provide adequately deep explanations of individual states' alignment choices, I focus on a limited set of Southeast Asian cases. If my arguments are valid, I should be able to show that those countries preferred and pursued limited alignments considerably more often than tight alliances or genuine nonalignment, especially in the post–Cold War period. I attempt to do so in the chapters that follow.

Chapter 2

Latter Stages of the Cold War

DURING THE LATTER STAGES OF THE COLD WAR, Southeast Asia experienced considerable tension and turmoil. The end of the Vietnam War brought only a fragile peace as superpower rivalry continued in the region, fanning the flames of ideologically laced local conflict. By 1979 an ugly new war erupted, pitting Vietnam and its Soviet sponsors against Cambodian rebels backed by China, the United States, Thailand, and other anticommunist Southeast Asian states. The Third Indochina War became the central fault line in regional security until the late 1980s, when a negotiated withdrawal of Vietnamese troops from Cambodia paved the way for a peace settlement. Throughout the late 1970s and the era of the Third Indochina War, Southeast Asian leaders adjusted their alignments to address changing security threats and deal with uncertainty about Chinese, Soviet, and American intentions.

This chapter reviews the alignment politics of the region during that period and shows that Southeast Asian states frequently favored limited alignments and attempted to build flexible security arrangements, even amid ideological cleavage and conflict.

THE INTERWAR PERIOD, 1975–1978

Momentous change came to Southeast Asia in 1975. Vietnamese communist tanks rolled into Saigon, sounding a definitive death knell to U.S.-backed forces in Indochina. Communist revolutionaries had already taken power in neighboring Cambodia, and North Vietnamese officials quickly began unifying Vietnam. In Laos communist forces also marched toward an increasingly certain victory. Believers in the domino theory anticipated that communist victories in Indochina would have a knock-on effect throughout the region, but they underestimated the depth of tensions within the socialist camp after the Sino-Soviet split. U.S. withdrawal from Saigon removed the cork from a bottle of simmering intracommunist rivalry in the region. Without a unifying American adversary, suspicions grew between the once-fraternal communist parties of Cambodia and Vietnam, which began to polarize into two rival groups around China and the Soviet Union.

The dramatic reduction of American power in mainland Southeast Asia also prompted U.S. allies, especially Thailand and the Philippines, to revisit their alliance policies and put a bit more distance between themselves and Washington. As America retreated from Vietnam and sought to limit its military expenditures, Brezhnev's Soviet Union continued a massive arms buildup. By the late 1970s Soviet force capabilities in the Pacific approached America's for the first time. China also entered the region more prominently as an alternative patron for local communist parties and as a possible ally to complement American security guarantees. The relatively bipolar superpower struggle of the early Cold War years thus gave way to a more triangular great-power dynamic in the region, and Southeast Asian governments adjusted their alignments to cope with new strategic realities.

Intracommunist Rumblings in Indochina

During the early years of the Cold War, communist groups had appeared relatively cohesive in the Indochina theatre. Khmer Rouge, Pathet Lao, Viet Minh, Viet Cong forces had united to a considerable degree against France and later America and their "reactionary" local allies. During the 1960s, however, the acrimonious Sino-Soviet split showed serious chinks in the armor of socialist solidarity. Border clashes along the Ussuri River in 1969, China's rapprochement with the United States in 1971–1972, and mutual recriminations during peace talks in Vietnam exacerbated Sino-Soviet tensions.

Strains between Vietnamese and Cambodian communists had also increased over time. During the Vietnam War Viet Cong forces increasingly spread onto Cambodian soil and became the targets of American air attack. The Khmers Rouges helped their Vietnamese communist siblings in many respects, helping move troops and arms along the Ho Chih Minh Trail. However, the presence of Vietnamese soldiers on Cambodian soil touched some raw nerves in a country where phobia of Vietnam was historically strong. Pol Pot, Khieu Samphan, and other Khmer Rouge leaders harbored a long-standing sense of mistrust toward their Vietnamese mentors, believing the latter sought to recolonize Cambodia and turn it into a "Vietnamese puppet" within an Indochinese federation.[1]

Democratic Kampuchea Reluctantly Aligns Itself

The first of the three conservative Indochinese regimes to fall in 1975 was the U.S.-backed military government of Lon Nol in Cambodia. In April, as American backing for Lon Nol's forces ground toward a halt, waves of ill-clad Khmer Rouge revolutionaries emerged from the countryside and streamed into Phnom Penh. Hardened by years of brutal civil war in the jungle, and practicing a radical agrarian ideology, the Khmer Rouge forces almost immediately began to line up and shoot members of the ancien regime. Within days they evacuated the teeming city of Phnom Penh to break apart and reeducate the feared bourgeois population, embarking on a brutal campaign to cleanse the country of unwanted foreign and capitalist influence. Their foreign and domestic policies revealed intense paranoia and xenophobia; after years of fighting, the Khmer Rouge leadership perceived threats lurking behind every tree.

Internally the Pol Pot clique became obsessed with rooting out alleged spies, traitors, and other "no-good elements" that might undermine the creation of a radically independent, agrarian socialist state. Externally the Khmers Rouges also perceived omnipresent threats to their nascent regime, which they renamed Democratic Kampuchea (DK). To the west DK forces clashed with right wing rebels bankrolled by the Thai military and U.S. Central Intelligence Agency (CIA). To the east Viet-Cambodian solidarity barely survived the Khmer Rouge victory celebration. The two countries clashed over disputed islands in the Gulf of Thailand just days after the American retreat from Saigon.[2]

Although Pol Pot and his colleagues saw threats on all sides, they did not initially seek tight great-power alignment. They were intensely focused on preserving independence from foreign powers, especially the dreaded United States, which had sent scores of B-52 bombers over Cambodia and supported Lon Nol's military machine during the country's civil war. The Khmers Rouges also shut off all diplomatic ties with the USSR, which had betrayed them by recognizing the Lon Nol government and negotiating with the United States over Vietnam in the early 1970s. To the radical Pol Potists, Soviet talks with the Nixon and Ford administrations over détente were reminders of the 1954 Geneva settlement, when the USSR had agreed to divide Indochina with the hated imperialists. Close Soviet-Vietnamese ties only added to DK distaste for the Soviet "hegemonists."[3]

The PRC was the only great power that DK leaders perceived as friendly. Ideological affinity, a history of cooperation in guerilla conflict, and common suspicion of Vietnam made China the most attractive external patron for Democratic Kampuchea. Although the Khmers Rouges espoused a policy of nonalignment, tremendous economic hardship and insecurity soon forced them to turn to China for help. In May 1975 Khmer Rouge forces captured the U.S. ship *Mayaguez* in the Gulf of Thailand. The American military responded decisively, rescuing the ship and inflicting significant casualties, and no foreign power came meaningfully to Democratic Kampuchea's defense. The incident likely demonstrated to the Khmers Rouges the danger of strict nonalignment. To manage dire economic conditions and numerous security challenges, Phnom Penh thus aligned in a limited fashion with Beijing. Chinese ships moved into the port of Sihanoukville shortly after the *Mayaguez* affair, and Pol Pot and other senior DK officials made a series of trips to Beijing that spring and summer.[4] China pledged economic support, military training, and technical assistance in exchange for Phnom Penh's political support in advancing Chinese foreign policy objectives, particularly in the context of the PRC's mounting dispute with Moscow.[5] The first bilateral accord signed by the new DK regime was an August 1975 agreement in which Beijing promised to send military and economic aid with few strings attached.[6]

Vietnam Moves toward Moscow

Vietnam's alignment policy also shifted after the war. Following the U.S. withdrawal from Saigon, the leaders of the Vietnamese Communist Party (VCP) tried to steer a more neutral course, refusing to ally tightly with the USSR for fear of losing independence, alienating China, and foreclosing a possible mending of fences with the United States.[7] VCP leaders saw both China and the United States as potential trading partners and sources of much-needed aid as they turned inward to focus on unifying and reconstructing their war-ravaged country. They also saw the PRC and America as dangerous adversaries if their intentions toward Vietnam were hostile. Consequently, Vietnam initially tried to avoid a tight alliance. It refused to join the Soviet-led Council of Mutual Economic Assistance (COMECON) in 1976 at the Soviet Union's urging and denied Soviet requests to use the bases at Cam Ranh Bay. Soviet aid declined to its lowest level in over a decade.

Despite Vietnam's initial pursuit of a limited alignment, relations with China and the United States did not improve. The U.S. government remained hostile and tensions with the PRC grew steadily worse.[8] The Sino-Vietnamese drift had begun during the Vietnam War. Large numbers of Chinese troops in North Vietnam stoked age-old concerns about Chinese hegemony. Relations grew frostier in the late 1960s, when fears of dependency on China and a need for high-tech weapons to shoot down U.S. warplanes led the VCP to tilt more toward Moscow. Vietnamese leaders attacked the 1972 Sino-American rapprochement as a Chinese "stab in the back," and relations further deteriorated after China's seizure of the disputed Paracel Islands in January 1974.[9] Vietnam's persecution of ethnic Chinese traders in the south, whom the VCP feared would undermine the new communist order, also fueled Chinese ire, and Sino-Kampuchean ties engendered fears of encirclement in Hanoi.[10]

To rebuild their conflict-torn state and guard against China, VCP leaders saw little option but to turn to the Soviet Union. In October 1975 Le Duan traveled to Moscow and secured a large aid package of about $500 million spread across dozens of infrastructure and development projects.[11] Even that level of aid did not meet the tremendous costs of unifying the country, rebuilding Vietnam's war-torn infrastructure, and extending its centrally planned economy to the South. VCP leaders demanded more than $4 billion in aid from the United States as a form of reparations and tried to establish much-needed trade relations, but the U.S. government rebuffed them on all fronts. Vietnamese intransigence was partly to blame, but Sino-American hostility pushed Vietnam further into the arms of the USSR; as Democratic Kampuchea formed a limited alignment with China, Vietnam gradually drifted further from Beijing and closer to the Soviet Union.[12]

Laos Follows Vietnam

In late 1975, only six months after the fall of Saigon, the Pathet Lao—more formally known as the Lao People's Liberation Army—seized power in Vientiane, defeating the U.S.-backed royalist army and allied ethnic minority forces. The Pathet Lao leadership had worked closely with the VCP for decades, as both military allies and ideological understudies during the war of independence against the French, the Lao civil war, and the struggle in Vietnam. Since the 1960s some Lao communist officials had looked to the PRC to offset Vietnamese influence in Laos, but by 1975 the pro-Vietnamese faction in Vientiane was ascendant. When they finally sealed victory, the Pathet Lao promptly aligned with Vietnam, signing a twenty-five-year treaty of friendship and cooperation.[13] As Sino-Vietnamese tensions increased, and as Democratic Kampuchea veered toward Beijing, the revolutionary victory in Laos thus shifted the correlation of forces in Indochina back toward Moscow and Hanoi.

The United States lost almost all of its influence in the country, as the new Lao People's Democratic Republic (LPDR) swiftly implemented wholesale changes in domestic and foreign policy, expelling the U.S. Agency for International Development and terminating its agreement with the International Monetary Fund. Relations with America further deteriorated as ethnic Hmong rebels in northern Laos—former members of the CIA's Secret Army—led an anticommunist resistance movement that the Pathet Lao did not bring to heel until 1978. Lao leader Kaysone Phomvihane also identified threats from rebel groups along the border and accused Thailand of continuing to "follow evil imperialist schemes" by "fostering and supporting exiled Lao reactionaries and counter-revolutionary elements."[14]

For Kaysone and other Lao leaders, the key challenges were to subdue domestic rebels and build a functioning new state after a long and calamitous series of conflicts.[15] In addition to embracing Vietnam, Laos developed closer ties to the USSR, which provided significant economic aid, a few hundred technical advisors, and military hardware in addition to most of Lao's external economic aid. However, Laos did not offer the Soviets a formal alliance treaty or basing facilities, which would have alienated China and compromised Lao autonomy by making the alignment more permanent and pervasive.[16] Most Soviet aid to Laos came through Vietnam, which helped Laos limit the scope of its direct security ties to Moscow.

SEATO's Demise and ASEAN's Rise

As the end of the Vietnam War unmasked fissiparous forces among communist countries, it also generated concerns about the strength and credibility of U.S. alliances in Southeast Asia.[17] Thailand and the Philippines had been allies of America since the early years of the Cold War through bilateral ties and the U.S.-led Southeast Asian Treaty Organization (SEATO). The Vietnam War had further bolstered cooperation because officials in Manila and Bangkok feared a surge of communist resistance and the U.S. government provided extensive military and economic aid in exchange for the use of huge basing facilities. Nevertheless, after the U.S. evacuation of Saigon, SEATO fell apart, and conservative Southeast Asian governments invested more energy in ASEAN and the development of regional mechanisms to enhance their security and reduce dependence on external patrons. U.S. policies and shifting great-power relations provided much of the impetus for these changes. Evolving domestic conditions and the emergence of more confident governments in some Southeast Asian states also contributed significantly to the shifts.

SEATO Unravels

Since 1955 SEATO had underscored the American commitment to the defense of Southeast Asia against potential communist expansion. Thailand and the Philippines were the only regional members, but the United States, France, Britain, Australia, New Zealand, and Pakistan gave the alliance a broad membership. Dominated by the United States, SEATO was less genuinely multilateral than NATO and was arguably redundant given the strong Thai-U.S. and Philippine U.S. alliances. Nevertheless, it had important political and symbolic value as a statement of the West's intention to defend the noncommunist regimes of Southeast Asia. The 1969 Nixon Doctrine, which implied a great role for regional states in providing for their own defense, was an early sign that such support could not be counted upon indefinitely. The British pullout East of Suez in 1971 and the departure of American troops from Vietnam in 1975 added to a perception that SEATO was no longer a credible expression of Western intentions.[18]

Moreover, to most Southeast Asian governments, the main security threats came from within. All leaders in the region had to deal to varying degrees with communist rebels and ethnic insurgents of various stripes. Amitav Acharya has argued that SEATO simply "represented a flawed approach to regional security." The alliance was most useful in deterring "a threat of outright aggression, an unlikely scenario as far as many non-communist Southeast Asian states were concerned." It was less helpful in dealing with revolutionary social problems.[19] Consequently, in July 1975 Thai Prime Minister Kukrit Pramoj and Philippine President Ferdinand Marcos agreed to phase out the alliance, believing that SEATO would complicate relations with Vietnamese communists without adding to the reliability of the U.S. defense commitment. In September SEATO members announced that the organization would dissolve by mid-1977.

ASEAN and the ZOPFAN Principle

Even before the enunciation of the Nixon Doctrine and the British pullout, conservative Southeast Asian governments had moved to develop security structures that would increase their stand-alone security capacity and reduce the need for reliance on great-power protectors. The most important of these was ASEAN, created at a meeting in Bangkok in August 1967 by Indonesia, Malaysia, the Philippines, Singapore, and Thailand.

Although the new association had support from the United States and other Western powers, it was not a defense pact like SEATO. It was instead a forum that prioritized ASEAN and promoted a respect for sovereignty, encouraged peaceful dispute management through consultation and consensus, and frowned on antagonistic military pacts. The organization sought above all to develop regional solutions to regional problems that would help member states enjoy security without having to depend on external powers, which all feared would jeopardize their hard-fought independence and possibly entrap them in great-power feuds.[20]

The need to buttress great-power alignments had become more apparent to ASEAN leaders after the British government announced its withdrawal from areas east of Suez in 1968 and the United States enunciated the Nixon Doctrine in 1969. U.S. efforts to "Vietnamize" the Vietnam War—by encouraging the regime in Saigon to assume added responsibilities—also reduced ASEAN confidence in America's commitment to Southeast Asia.[21] Led by Malaysia and Indonesia, ASEAN members signed a declaration in 1971 promoting a Zone of Peace, Freedom, and Neutrality (ZOPFAN). The ZOPFAN principle expressed the desire to reduce regional countries' dependence on great-power allies and avoid embroilment in superpower conflict by keeping the region free of external interference.

The ZOPFAN principle was in some respects a regional analog to the norm of nonalignment promoted by the NAM, which claimed all five ASEAN states as members. It was motivated in large part by perceptions of strategic necessity given the shifting tectonic plates of great-power rivalry. Without credible Western guarantees, alliances were not worth as much. However, ZOPFAN also reflected a growing sense of regional confidence as postcolonial ASEAN states became increasingly able to stand on their own.

By 1975 concerns about the U.S. withdrawal from Vietnam prompted ASEAN members to redouble their efforts to build norms and institutions that would improve their security and lessen reliance on America. ASEAN heads of state met for the first time in 1976 in Bali, prompted primarily by the events in Indochina the previous year. At the summit they hammered out a landmark document, the Treaty of Amity and Cooperation. It set out the main principles guiding ASEAN diplomacy, including the norms of sovereignty and noninterference and a particular style of diplomacy known as *musjawarah-mufakat* (consultation and consensus). The so-called ASEAN Way of diplomacy related more to process and emphasizes accommodation, confidence-building measures, and an incrementalist approach to conflict management. Combined with a strong norm against the use of force in dispute settlement, this process emerged as ASEAN governments sought to reduce regional infighting, withstand pressure from external powers, and build stable postcolonial states.

ASEAN members also prioritized national sovereignty through the norm of noninterference, which implied refraining from criticism of other members' domestic policies, denying sanctuaries to foreign rebel groups, and cooperating against subversion. The norm of noninterference was primarily a device to help ASEAN states meet common domestic challenges, including economic disruptions and threats from local communist groups and ethnic insurgents. These norms are often held up as reasons why ASEAN states have avoided intramural wars for the entire duration of the institution's existence.[22]

The ZOPFAN principle, introduced by Indonesia and Malaysia, thus gained a measure of acceptance by other ASEAN members, as evident in a key passage of the Treaty of Amity and Cooperation: "The High Contracting Parties shall endeavour to strengthen their respective national resilience in their political, economic, socio-cultural as well as security fields in conformity with their respective ideals and aspirations, free from external interference as well as internal subversive activities in order to preserve their respective national identities."[23]

The 1971 ZOPFAN Declaration had asserted ASEAN's collective objection to excessive great-power intrusion, stating somewhat idealistically that Southeast Asia should be "free from any form or manner of interference by outside Powers."[24] Indonesian Foreign Minister Adam Malik said when introducing the concept, "The nations of Southeast Asia should consciously work toward the day when security in their own region will be the primary responsibility of the Southeast Asian nations themselves. Not through big power alignments, not through the building of contending military pacts or military arsenals but through strengthening the state of respective endurance, through effective regional cooperation with other states sharing this basic view of our world affairs."[25]

Not all ASEAN leaders interpreted the ZOPFAN concept similarly. Indonesia and Malaysia, which were the principal sponsors of principle, favored a steep overall reduction in great-power presence in the region, whereas Thailand, the Philippines, and Singapore were more focused on limiting the scope for interference by hostile external states. In fact, ASEAN strategies represented varying degrees of pro-Western tilts rather than genuine nonalignment. At the 1976 nonaligned summit in Colombo, the NAM refused to endorse the ZOPFAN principle, because some left-leaning members accused the ASEAN states of supporting neocolonialism through military and economic cooperation with the West.[26]

Pro-American security tilts did not mean that ASEAN members were irrevocably committed to the U.S. agenda. ASEAN governments sought to limit external interference by hostile foreign powers, which could sponsor subversion, but also by stronger allies, which could clamp down on Southeast Asian governments and compromise their autonomy. The following year ASEAN held a symposium on the topic of national resilience and defined the term as follows: "National resilience is the dynamic condition of a nation, including tenacity and sturdiness, which enables it to develop national strength to cope with all challenges, threats, obstructions and disturbances coming from outside—as well as from within the country—directly endangering the national existence and the struggle for national goals."[27]

This concept of resilience, modeled on the idea of *ketahanan nasional* (national resilience) enshrined in the Indonesian constitution, emphasizes the extent to which Southeast Asian states sought independent strength to meet security challenges, with or without the help of great powers.

The notion of resilience also drew attention to the importance of nonmilitary aspects of national security; *ketahanan* (resilience) was quite distinct from *pertahanan* (defense). Most Southeast Asian states saw their principal security challenges emanating from within, in the form of either communist or ethnic separatist movements. Most policymakers believed that economic development and social welfare were the long-term solutions to such challenges, not military buildup through great-power alignments. Indonesian and Malaysian elites in particular subscribed to the view that tight alliance would tend to skew resources toward military machines that served the strategic and economic interests of the great powers, in some cases undermining national development and social reconciliation. Even government officials in U.S. treaty allies, such as Thailand and the Philippines, occasionally criticized the extent to which American pressure influenced the development of their own armed forces and their application of budgetary resources.

U.S. allies in the region were loath to sign away their policy prerogative to Washington. American policy during the Cold War focused largely on the containment of communism, the opening of markets, and (at least sometimes) the promotion of democracy and human rights. Although officials in the ASEAN states generally shared the desire to fight communism, they often differed on tactics and found the American approach too polarizing. They feared being used as pawns on a global chessboard to serve American interests rather than their own. Many were also suspicious of U.S. efforts to open their markets, fearing the thin edge of a wedge of U.S. corporate exploitation. Finally, the American democracy and human rights agenda was a significant threat to the comparatively illiberal governments in the ASEAN region. The result of these concerns was a convergence toward limited alignment postures among the ASEAN states in the late 1970s.

Wavering in the Western Alliance Structure: Thailand and the Philippines

The phase-out of SEATO accompanied significant changes in the bilateral Thai and Philippine alliances with Washington. In March 1975 Kukrit Pramoj announced his intention to seek the complete withdrawal of American forces within a year and declared, "this government will follow an independent foreign policy."[28] Many in the Thai military resisted the removal of U.S. forces, and Commander-in-Chief Boonchai Bamrungphong summarized their concerns: "We are asking our friends to leave while on the other side of the border they have powerful friends supporting them.... the U.S. forces should remain here." Singaporean Prime Minister Lee Kuan Yew said the same.[29]

In addition to problems with Vietnam, the Pathet Lao takeover also prompted an increase in Thai threat perceptions from Laos, because Thai officials viewed the Lao communists as sponsors of insurgency and as a major cause for increasing refugee flight into Thai territory. However, Thai leaders saw the presence of American troops in their country as more likely to provoke animosity and conflict with neighboring communist states than to prevent it.[30] To many in Bangkok, the *Mayaguez* affair was a particularly striking case in point: the United States had launched a military attack on Democratic Kampuchea from bases in Thailand without seeking any form of approval. The danger of entrapment was real.

Given the Vietnam syndrome in Washington, Thai officials also questioned whether U.S. forces would stand to defend Thailand in the event of neighborly conflict. By 1975 Thai officials were attempting to adjust to the reality of a lesser U.S. commitment to mainland Southeast Asia. Pramoj thus pursued a more limited alignment, distancing Thailand from Washington to a degree, establishing relations with Vietnam, and attempting to reorient Thai foreign policy to reflect the changing balance of power in the region. He also sought to mend fences with the PRC. In late June 1975 Pramoj traveled to Beijing and established diplomatic relations with China for the first time since the communist victory of 1949. Thailand established low-level security ties with the PRC, mainly because Thai leaders feared Vietnamese expansion but could not count on a continued U.S. commitment to mainland Southeast Asia.[31]

Pramoj's policy changes and rising activity by the Communist Party of Thailand (CPT) precipitated a backlash from the powerful armed forces, which executed a coup in 1976 and brought General Kriangsak Chomanan to power. Nevertheless the limited Sino-Thai alignment survived through periodic weapons supplies and military exchanges. Officials in Bangkok and Beijing found common interest in establishing security in northeastern Thailand, where large ethnic Lao and Vietnamese populations created the conditions for domestic subversion.

Officials in Manila shared their Thai counterparts' concerns about the reliability of the U.S. defense commitment and the possibility of antagonizing a powerful, unified Vietnam and the Soviet Union. In late 1976 Thai Prime Minister Tanin Kraivixien and Philippine President Ferdinand Marcos jointly expressed their intention to achieve "a just balance among the great powers" in Southeast Asia.[32] The 1951 U.S.-Philippine Mutual Defense Treaty remained, but Marcos began to demand revisions to the 1947 military bases and assistance agreements, insisting on greater Philippine sovereignty and demanding that continued use of the bases be tied to security assistance. Many Filipinos argued that the bases left the country with compromised sovereignty. In addition, they argued that the bases were not geared toward the security of the Philippines. Instead they were designed to serve U.S. strategic interests and could result in a Soviet conventional or nuclear attack on the country that would not occur without the American military presence. By 1979 revisions to the base agreements were made that gave back approximately 90 percent of the territory around Clark Air Field and Subic Bay to the Philippines as sovereign territory.

The end of SEATO and the weakening of the U.S. alliances with Thailand and the Philippines in the late 1970s were premised partly on the belief that external threats to the ASEAN states had significantly subsided. Military attacks by China against an ASEAN state was considered extremely remote, especially in the context of the Sino-Soviet split and Sino-American rapprochement. Vietnam, in the throes of unification and economic reconstruction, was also considered very unlikely to attack and would require massive aid from the USSR to do so. In the midst of détente, great-power support for Vietnamese aggression appeared quite unlikely. In July 1977 Thai Foreign Minister Upadit Pachariyangkun described the prospect of an external menace to an ASEAN state as "obsolete." He said, "We are more preoccupied with the possibility of increased subversive activities which get aid from outside. . . . I am sure that there will be no external aggression, not even from North Vietnam."[33]

Continued concerns about U.S. credibility also played a role. The Carter administration's priority on human rights—which manifested itself in reduced aid to

Thailand and many other countries accused of human rights violations—further strained defense ties and led officials in Bangkok to fear that American support was becoming less reliable.[34]

Pro-American Tilts in Indonesia, Malaysia, and Singapore

Indonesia, Malaysia, and Singapore also looked with concern at the withdrawal of U.S. power from Indochina. All were anticommunist and feared that Soviet or Chinese power would soon pour into the vacuum created by the American retreat, but none sought to forge tight alliance with the United States. Instead, they continued a policy that had emerged in the 1960s of pursuing limited security cooperation with the West while building stronger national and regional resilience to deal with local and regional security threats. The establishment of ASEAN, declaration of the ZOPFAN principle, and creation of the FPDA all helped soften the blow of America's withdrawal from Vietnam. By 1975 Indonesia, Malaysia, and Singapore were all engaged in modest defense cooperation with America, and the communist victories in Indochina that year did not fundamentally change their alignment strategies.

Indonesia: Crisis in East Timor and Modest Pro-American Alignment

Indonesia had long espoused a policy of nonalignment, serving as the host for the 1955 Afro-Asian summit, which led directly to the creation of the NAM. In fact, its policy could better be described as a limited tilt. During the 1950s and early 1960s, Sukarno had steered toward China and the USSR out of a fear of Western imperialism. After an alleged communist coup attempt in 1965, the conservative General Suharto took power, reversing course and siding loosely with the West. Nevertheless, he remained loyal to the notion that avoiding tight alliance was a way for Indonesia to steer between the shoals of Western imperialism and communist subversion.

To Indonesian officials the saga in Indochina in 1975 was an important but secondary concern in managing its relations with the great powers; domestic security was paramount for the huge, ethnically diverse archipelagic nation. It had been pressure from domestic communists, not the Soviet navy, that had propelled Suharto to power, and it was primarily economic weakness and domestic threats that had encouraged the New Order regime to ally loosely with America from the mid-1960s onward.

Local threats continued to drive Indonesia's alignment policy after 1975. The first major crisis unfolded in the tiny Portuguese-held territory of East Timor, where a largely Catholic and Portuguese-speaking population coexisted beside the Indonesian colossus. In 1974, after a left-leaning government toppled the conservative Salazar regime in Lisbon and granted independence to East Timor, clashes broke out among rival Timorese political groups. The leftist *Fretilin* (Revolutionary Front for East Timorese Independence) gained the upper hand and declared independence, but officials in Jakarta warned that *Fretilin* forces could use East Timor as a base for communist subversion in Indonesia. In December 1975 Indonesia sponsored a decisive and bloody campaign by military "volunteers," annexed East Timor, declared it an integral part of Indonesia, and harshly repressed local resistance groups.

The East Timor crisis of 1975 solidified Indonesia's limited alignment with the United States by reinforcing the perception that America was the great power most committed to the interests of the Suharto regime. Before the conflict Secretary of State Henry Kissinger assured Suharto that the United States would not recognize *Fretilin*'s proclamation of independence. By contrast, the Chinese government condemned the Indonesian occupation, describing the move as an oppression of the East Timorese "people's struggle against colonialism, imperialism, and hegemonism."[35] In 1978 Deng Xiaoping made PRC intentions toward Indonesia clear by refusing to end support for Southeast Asian communist movements, whereas Indonesian Defense and Security Minister General Maraden Panggabean publicly accused China of sending exiled Communist Party of Indonesia (PKI) leaders back to Indonesia to foment unrest.[36] Indonesian officials also considered the USSR an unattractive ally, perceiving the Soviets as geographically remote, economically weak, ideologically distant, and not fully committed to influence in the region.[37] Indonesia therefore turned more toward Washington for economic and military support, and shortly after the invasion of East Timor, the U.S. Congress approved a $4.8 billion aid package.

Defense and political cooperation did not result in a U.S.-Indonesian alliance, however. The Indonesian government opposed establishing any permanent or long-term U.S. basing facilities, fearing a loss of independence, popular resistance, and diminished regional prestige. Security ties remained limited and, despite its unofficial tilt toward the United States and need for Western economic aid, Indonesia remained rhetorically nonaligned and frowned on the idea of hosting foreign bases. As the largest country in Southeast Asia, relatively unthreatened from the outside, Indonesia stood much to lose and relatively little to gain from a tight alliance. The regime's nationalist credentials and the country's potential for regional leadership were better served by pursuing only limited alignment with the United States and stressing independence, resilience, and self-sufficiency.[38]

Pro-Western Orientations in Malaysia and Singapore
Malaysia and Singapore saw similar perils in forging a close alliance with Washington, but both continued to see the need for Western security support to manage regional uncertainties. Malaysian elites remembered Sukarno's "Crush Malaysia" campaign and policy of *Konfrontasi* (Confrontation) in the mid-1960s and were wary of being too exposed to their larger neighbor. Singaporean leaders also recalled their country's painful birth, when the tiny, mostly ethnic Chinese city-state was expelled from the Federation of Malaya in 1965 and left to fend for itself amid larger ethnic Malay populations. Communism posed a continuing threat to both governments. Malaysian elites in particular recalled their struggle with British authorities against the ethnic Chinese communist insurgency during the 1948–1960 Malayan Emergency.

In addition to participating in ASEAN and taking other regional measures to improve their security, Malaysia and Singapore continued to participate in the Five-Power Defence Arrangements (FPDA) that had been established in 1971. The FPDA was a limited multilateral security system created by Malaysia, Singapore, Australia, New Zealand, and the United Kingdom involving mutual training, basing access, and consultations in the event of a crisis. Although it did not provide a security guarantee, it was a way to assuage Malaysian and Singaporean fears of abandonment as the United Kingdom withdrew.[39] Neither Singapore nor Malaysia considered the FPDA ideal, but it was a partial compensation for the loss of more robust British support and an indirect way to plug into the Western alliance system.

Malaysia did not closely embrace the United States during the 1970s despite engaging in regular low-level security cooperation through the IMET program, Foreign Military Sales (FMS) program, and other channels. The recent experience of colonial domination and the politics surrounding America's role in the Arab-Israeli dispute help explain why Malaysia favored a limited alignment, cooperating only at a low level with the United States. Concerns about American credibility after the announcement of the Nixon Doctrine also encouraged Malaysian leaders to pursue a rhetorical policy of relative "equidistance" between the superpowers.[40] As a primary sponsor of the ZOPFAN concept in 1971, Malaysia generally sought to limit great-power involvement in the region and led efforts within ASEAN to promote regional "neutralization" among the great powers.[41] Leaders in Kuala Lumpur were primarily focused on local intra-ethnic relations and internal communist threats sponsored by China since the Malayan Emergency.[42] Residual distrust remained after the normalization of Sino-Malaysian relations in 1974, but Malaysian officials did not perceive a strong U.S. alignment as an appropriate tool to deal with remaining issues of internal instability.

Singapore disfavored the neutralization concept and was more inclined than Malaysia to pursue security cooperation with the United States as a supplement to the FPDA. Singaporean leaders feared that Malaysian calls for increased regional neutrality would precipitate a further American retreat from the region and leave the city-state vulnerable to domination by larger neighbors.[43] In addition to providing political support for the continued U.S. military presence in the region in ASEAN and other forums, modest defense cooperation extended through the 1970s and allowed U.S. forces to use Singaporean ports and recreational facilities, which generated income for Singapore and promoted friendly defense ties.

Burma Pursues Relative Neutralism

Whereas Malaysia and Indonesia used the ZOPFAN principle to keep the great powers at arm's length, Burma pursued a more genuine policy of nonalignment and was in many respects the most isolated Southeast Asian country. Neutralism was nothing new for Burma. After World War II nationalist opposition to the Japanese had shifted almost seamlessly to Aung San's Thakin movement to fight against reimposition of British rule. Neutralism was above all a means for Burma to carve out space for independence. The country's colonial history made authorities wary of Western domination, and Chinese and modest Soviet support for the rebel Burmese Communist Party (BCP) foreclosed close alignment with China or the USSR. Burma thus became a key founding member of the NAM. Although General Ne Win overthrew the civilian government in a 1962 military coup, he stuck to a similar foreign policy. Rangoon pursued an espoused policy of "positive neutrality" and developed only a *paukphaw* (fraternal) relationship with China to moderate the PRC and secure aid on its ersatz "Burmese path to socialism."[44]

By the mid-1970s the *paukphaw* relationship was under some strain because the Ne Win regime perceived the BCP as a primary threat to its interests.[45] However, relations with China improved late in the decade. Sino-Soviet and Sino-Vietnamese acrimony led the PRC to seek out friends in Southeast Asia. The turning point was the rise of the more pragmatic Deng Xiaoping. From 1975 to 1978 Ne Win exchanged multiple visits with Deng, and though Burma did not commit to significant security cooperation, it tacitly agreed not to align against China by siding with the Soviet Union and Vietnam. The PRC in return indicated that it would reduce support for the BCP.[46] A reduction of Chinese aid to communist groups helped the Burmese government address a number of other simmering and long-standing ethnic insurgent movements, particularly along the Thai border.

Despite friendly ties with China, Ne Win's Burmese Socialist Program Party (BSPP) continued to follow a policy of relative neutrality. The BSPP's primary security challenges were internal, and officials saw great-power alignments as inappropriate instruments to pacify diverse insurgent groups, solidify its domestic legitimacy, and secure its national territory. Ironically, it was Burma's commitment to nonalignment that caused it to withdraw from the NAM at the Havana summit of 1979. By the late 1970s many NAM members veered toward a militant anti-Western stance, but others aligned closely with the West. Decrying the attitude of Cuba, Vietnam, and other radical members of the NAM, Burmese Foreign Minister U Myint Maung said, "The principles of the movement are not recognizable anymore."[47] Frustrated by the wide range of alignment behavior in the NAM ranks, Burma retreated toward isolation.

Alignment Polarization

As the United States, Japan, and the ASEAN countries refined their security policies, intracommunist tensions in Indochina escalated. Opposing alignments began to crystallize around rising border clashes between Democratic Kampuchea and Vietnam, paving the way toward war. The DK regime became ever more preoccupied with internal threats to the regime and alleged spies set by Vietnam, Thailand, or their great-power allies. In 1976 and 1977 brutal purges of DK officials in the country's eastern zone began, and Khmer Rouge military units began to mount increasingly lethal attacks against Vietnamese border towns. When some Cambodian officers defected to Vietnam and began to build a resistance group, conflict spread and Phnom Penh turned to China for further support.[48]

The PRC did not send armed forces, but by 1977 thousands of military, technical, and economic advisors poured into the country. Beijing also sent larger weapons and food shipments to its cash-strapped and militarily weak ally. The relationship certainly was not without strains. Chinese leaders feared that a trigger-happy Pol Pot regime could lead them into conflict, and the Khmers Rouges resented Chinese influence and control. The xenophobic Khmer Rouge regime was never comfortable relying heavily on an external patron and was an ornery ally to the PRC. Nevertheless, as military conflict continued to escalate in 1978 Democratic Kampuchea moved toward tight alliance with China.[49] In November 1978 Pol Pot even asked for the deployment of Chinese troops to help defend Democratic Kampuchea against Vietnam, but the PRC rejected his request.[50]

Soviet-Vietnamese Alignment Hardens

In 1976 and 1977 Vietnam attempted to pursue a more moderate alignment policy, reducing dependence on the USSR and moving toward a more independent position, but rapprochement with the United States or China proved virtually impossible. In the United States a strong desire to put the Vietnam War era in the past and focus on healing the country's internal wounds prevailed. Enmity toward the Viet Minh and disgust at human rights abuses during the unification period also kept Washington at a great diplomatic distance, and the countries did not resume relations. In the absence of American economic assistance, VCP leaders felt compelled to suffer added dependency on the USSR.

Domestic upheaval in China surrounding the deaths of Mao and Chou Enlai, the ideological struggles surrounding the radical Gang of Four, and the rise of the relatively inexperienced Hua Guofeng initially kept China from pursuing major diplomatic initiatives. However, as Hua's government gained its footing, Vietnamese persecution of ethnic Chinese in Ho Chih Minh City added another significant irritant to Sino-Vietnamese relations. The VCP saw the ethnic Chinese merchant community as a critical obstacle to domestic stability and regime consolidation. They also may have seen an opportunity to rally the country's ethnic Vietnamese around a minority scapegoat. In March 1978 the VCP nationalized foreign trade, a measure that severely affected the ethnic Chinese, who had long been a principal motor of the south's capitalist economy. This and other forms of persecution led to a mass exodus of ethnic Chinese boat people and further aggravated Vietnam's relations with ASEAN and the PRC.[51]

In the absence of other economic and military support, and in the face of mounting Chinese and Khmer Rouge hostility, Vietnam accepted an increasingly tight alliance with the USSR in 1978. In June Vietnam became a member of COMECON and in November signed a twenty-five-year treaty of friendship and cooperation with the USSR. The text of the treaty left little doubt that it was designed to encircle the PRC, stating that "the Soviet-Vietnamese treaty has forged one more link in the system of treaties of alliance between the fraternal socialist countries." Two months later a secret protocol gave the Soviets exclusive rights to bases at Cam

Ranh Bay for twenty-five years.[52] As Khmer Rouge border provocations continued, and Pol Pot publicly commanded his troops to commit genocide in Vietnam,
the People's Army of Vietnam (PAVN) built up its forces with Soviet support and
prepared for war. With a treaty to underscore expanded basing rights and military
exchange, Vietnam thus entered a tight formal alliance with the USSR.[53]

Indirect Lao-Soviet Alignment via Vietnam

As tensions mounted between Vietnam and Democratic Kampuchea, Lao leaders
took sides with their mentors in Hanoi. Prime Minister Kaysone Phomvihane accused China of "big-power chauvinism" and pledged to support Vietnam against
"threats, pressures, trouble-making, provocation, violation, slander and sabotage,
committed by the imperialists and international reactionaries," which were widely
understood to be China and the Khmer Rouge regime.[54] After the Pathet Lao
takeover, 50,000 Vietnamese troops remained in Laos, and Vietnam became the
dominant force in shaping Lao domestic and foreign policy. Concerns existed in
Vientiane about the possibility that Laos would simply be absorbed into an Indochina Federation dominated by Vietnam, but in the context of ongoing Cold War
competition and Sino-American cooperation against the Soviet Union, the LPDR
regime depended heavily on Vietnam for survival. The Soviet Union also continued to play a more limited role in Lao security, providing training for Lao forces in
their use of MiG-21 aircraft and other advanced military systems. The presence of
tens of thousands of PAVN troops and technical advisors in Laos also provided an
indirect link to Moscow. Nevertheless, Laos continued to limit its direct military
ties to the USSR, largely to avoid alienating China.[55]

Regional Alignment Overview, 1975–1978

From 1975 to 1978 Southeast Asian alignment politics were characterized by three
major features. First, Indochina polarized into two increasingly antagonistic camps.
China and Democratic Kampuchea formed one axis as the Pol Pot regime drifted
into a tight informal alignment with Beijing. Thailand also built limited security
ties to China, preparing for the possibility of a more menacing Vietnam. On the
other side of the fence, Vietnam moved steadily toward a tight military alliance
with the Soviet Union as its relations with China and Cambodia deteriorated. Laos
clung to Vietnam, thus forging a limited and indirect alignment with the Soviet
Union as well. Border clashes between DK and PAVN forces intensified and both
sides prepared for war.

The Indochinese states did not enter the period seeking to tighten alliance
structures; all had experienced the brunt of great-power domination and entrapment before and were aware of the risks. Nevertheless, their preferences shifted as
increasingly intense ideological and strategic rivalry between the Soviet Union,
China, and their regional friends drove up the expected rewards of tight defense
pacts. These changes were related to a shift in the overall correlation of forces
between the Soviet Union and United States, but they are more convincingly

explained as a product of increased external threats only partly attributable to new power configurations.

The second feature of regional alignment politics during the period was the effort by Thailand and the Philippines to loosen ties to America after the U.S. departure from mainland Southeast Asia. Here the change in Southeast Asian preferences could be best explained primarily as a result of U.S. policy. The withdrawal diminished confidence in U.S. security guarantees, which lessened the expected rewards of alignment and raised fears of abandonment. The U.S. departure also altered the balance of power on the mainland peninsula, even if U.S. capabilities in the broader Asia-Pacific region remained formidable. What had once been the most robust alliances in the region came under heavy scrutiny in the late 1970s, and their futures were less certain.

Finally, four important countries—Indonesia, Malaysia, Singapore, and Burma—had only modest ties to a great power as each sought to advance its sovereign interests largely through other security devices. Without greater need for external security support, these states preferred to avoid the risks of tight alliances (see table 2.1).

EARLY YEARS OF THE THIRD INDOCHINA WAR, 1979–1985

In December 1978 Vietnamese forces and allied Cambodian resistance fighters swept across the border into Democratic Kampuchea, justifying its attack as a response to Khmer Rouge provocation and a mounting threat from China. If the end of the Second Indochina War had contributed to a more triangular pattern of alignments in Southeast Asia, the invasion of Cambodia pushed the region back toward a more bipolar alignment framework pitting Vietnam, Laos, occupied Cambodia, and the Soviet Union against a loose anti-Hanoi coalition including Khmer rebels, the ASEAN states, China, and the United States.

Table 2.1 Alignment Postures, 1975–1978

Country	Great Power	Alignment Status
Brunei		(UK protectorate)
Burma		No alignment
Cambodia	PRC	Limited alignment (1975)
		Limited alignment → tight alliance (1978)
Indonesia	USA	Limited alignment
Laos	USSR	Limited alignment
Malaysia	USA	Limited alignment
Philippines	USA	Tight alliance
Singapore	USA	Limited alignment
Thailand	PRC	No alignment → limited alignment (1976)
	USA	Tight alliance → limited alignment (1976)
Vietnam	USSR	Limited alignment → tight alliance (1978)

Source: Author's compilation

Alignments Intensify in Indochina

The decision to topple the Khmer Rouge regime had pushed Hanoi further into alliance with the Soviet Union, as the invasion and subsequent occupation would have been impossible without massive Soviet military and economic support.[56] The Soviet Union provided much of the weaponry and almost entirely funded the operation. The USSR also delivered two frigates to the Vietnamese navy before the attacks and deployed its own naval forces in the South China Sea in support of the invasion—the first major show of Soviet naval force in Southeast Asia. By early January 1979 the vastly superior PAVN forces took Phnom Penh, and surviving Khmer Rouge cadres and officials fled with Chinese assistance to the mountainous jungle areas in the western reaches of the country.

Only two months later China launched a punitive attack to "teach Vietnam a lesson," but the attack was costly and failed to achieve a Vietnamese withdrawal from Cambodia. Instead, the brief Sino-Vietnamese war solidified Hanoi's perception of China as the source of its primary threat and drove Vietnam further into the arms of the Soviet Union. Moscow supplied the PAVN war effort through airlifts during the conflict, and by late March, Soviet vessels were docked at Cam Ranh Bay. In April Soviet spy planes arrived from Vladivostok to take up positions at the former U.S. facility at Da Nang, and for the first time the Soviet Union had established a major military presence in the region that connected its Indian Ocean and Pacific naval fleets. Cam Ranh Bay soon became the largest Soviet military and naval base outside of the Warsaw Pact. The alliance was in many ways a simple quid pro quo: the USSR underwrote the Vietnamese invasion of Cambodia in exchange for access to bases that would help expand Soviet power in Asia.[57]

The USSR increased economic and military aid to Vietnam to help its ally fight an increasingly costly guerilla war against Khmer rebels along the Thai-Cambodian border. Broader strategic factors also pushed Vietnam and the Soviet Union closer together. In January 1979 China and the United States normalized relations, signaling their tacit alignment against the USSR and its allies. Vietnam increasingly threw in its lot with the Soviet Union, attempting to stress its continued independence and minimize international fallout by emphasizing that it would permit no permanent Soviet bases.[58]

Although Cambodia remained nominally independent, the Heng Samrin regime possessed limited independence in foreign policy matters and survived on a diet of Soviet and Vietnamese support. Traditional Khmer resentment of Vietnamese domination became quickly apparent, but Heng Samrin asserted that the country would require heavy Vietnamese aid as long as China, the Khmer Rouge, and allied "imperialist forces" menaced the People's Republic of Kampuchea (PRK).[59] Soviet planes delivered supplies to the frontline cities of Siem Reap and Battambang, and technicians from the USSR built a military communications facility near the Thai border and an improved port at Kampong Sam. By 1984 Foreign Minister Hun Sen, who had begun his career as a Khmer Rouge military officer, described China as an "expansionist, hegemonist power" and declared that the PRK would follow "solidarity and cooperation with the Soviet Union [and] militant alliance and special relations among the three countries of Indochina."[60]

Laos continued to follow Vietnam's lead and develop closer ties to Moscow. At the Third Congress of the Lao People's Revolutionary Party in 1982, Secretary-General Kaysone Phomvihane declared that "the Beijing hegemonists are an immediate, dangerous enemy of the Lao people" and accused China of financing and arming rebel groups to destabilize the LPDR.[61] Lao leaders particularly feared Sino-Thai cooperation and support for domestic tribal insurgents. The China threat drove Laos closer to both the Soviet Union and Vietnam, which together provided the vast majority of economic and military support to the weak Lao state. As the war continued, the USSR stepped up direct aid to LPDR; by 1983 Laos received roughly $85 million in military aid from the USSR, and nearly 3,000 Soviet technical advisors worked in the country. The Lao-Soviet alignment thus became a tight one.[62]

Tight alliance with the USSR was certainly not without serious costs. Soviet allies were pressed to adopt a moribund economic model based on an industrial form of Marxism-Leninism that bore little relevance to their largely agrarian economies. Tight alliance with the USSR also meant espousing an international communist line. Since there could be only one dictatorship of the international proletariat, following the Soviet line meant accepting a kind of derivative status.[63] That was hard for elites in Vietnam and Laos to swallow after millions of their people had suffered or died to win independent nation-states. Following Soviet doctrine also meant heading on a collision course with China, Japan, the United States, and the ASEAN countries. Allies of the USSR watched their markets become skewed toward trade with the Soviet bloc, which in most industries offered substandard goods and services and obsolete training and industrial technology.[64] Only dire perceived security needs associated with the occupation of Cambodia encouraged Vietnam, and to a lesser degree Laos, to endure these costs for a time.

ASEAN Alignment Responses to the Vietnamese Invasion

The Vietnamese invasion of Cambodia was the single most determinative event in the alignment politics of Southeast Asia between 1975 and the end of the Cold War. Only Laos and occupied Cambodia rallied behind Hanoi, whereas the five ASEAN members of Thailand, Malaysia, Singapore, Indonesia, and the Philippines all aligned to varying degrees with the United States against Vietnam and the Soviet Union. For Thailand the specter of Vietnamese hegemony in Indochina was a direct military threat. For the other ASEAN states and Brunei, local security concerns and the overall balance of influence among the great powers were more important than any direct threat. Increasing Vietnamese and Soviet power raised the possibility of new subversive threats in the ASEAN region, as well as the possible disruption of the maritime stability vital to the region's economic growth. At the same time some ASEAN officials feared that the Third Indochina War gave China an opportunity to develop undue influence in the region. These uncertainties drove the ASEAN members to increase bilateral military ties, as did periodic upsurges of communist insurgency at home.

By 1979 the PAVN and allied Cambodian forces had secured control over most of Cambodia's territory. To deny Vietnam a fait accompli, China, the United States, Thailand, and other ASEAN countries furnished support to the rebel Coalition Government of Democratic Kampuchea (CGDK), which included the Khmers Rouges, Prince Sihanouk, and right-wing republican factions. Despite large-scale Soviet support, 180,000 PAVN troops were unable to defeat the rebel forces, whose numbers were roughly 60,000. A series of annual dry-season offensives failed to dislodge the rebels, who increasingly relied on international support from the Thai side of the border. At the same time ASEAN states applied political pressure on Moscow and Hanoi through the United Nations and 1981 International Conference on Kampuchea, denying international recognition to the Vietnamese-backed PRK. This and a multilateral regime of economic sanctions against Vietnam drove up the material and political costs of continued occupation.

Thailand Increases Cooperation with China and the United States
The military stalemate in Cambodia evoked different responses across ASEAN capitals. As the frontline ASEAN state, Thailand was the most directly threatened by Vietnamese forces. Although the Thai government initially declared itself neutral, it soon began assisting Khmer Rouge guerillas in the border area. The PAVN took reprisal with a limited incursion into Thailand in March 1979. In addition to concerns about Vietnamese military aggression, officials in Bangkok were concerned that the declining threat from the Beijing-backed CPT would be replaced by a pro-Hanoi insurgency in the northwest of the country, where large ethnic Lao and Vietnamese populations were viewed as vulnerable to enemy infiltration. Thai officials also saw the increase of Soviet power in the region as menacing, both because it raised Vietnam's military confidence and capacity and could disrupt commerce in the region's heavily trafficked sea-lanes.[65]

Most Thai officials came to view the Vietnamese occupation of Cambodia as an intolerable menace to the country's security. It removed the traditional geographic barrier between the two powers and signified an advance of Soviet power in the region. Some Thai policymakers believed that Vietnam sought to incorporate parts of northeastern Thailand—where ethnic Lao peoples were in the majority—into a greater Indochina.[66] As Khmer rebels increasingly retreated onto Thai soil and the PAVN launched raids over the border, Bangkok's threat perceptions solidified and propelled Thailand to seek Chinese and U.S. support.

China responded clearly and decisively. In January 1979 Chinese and Thai officials entered into a stronger informal alignment. Although no documents were signed, the PRC gave assurances to the Thai government that it would intervene if the PAVN attacked.[67] The Chinese invasion of Vietnam two months later added credibility to China's informal security guarantee to Thailand. In addition to serving as a strategic deterrent, China increased its provision of (mostly light) arms to the Thai army. The Thai alignment with China was a relatively unambiguous bargain; Thailand agreed to help in supplying Chinese arms to the Khmers Rouges in their guerilla struggle against the PAVN, and China pledged that it would stop supporting the CPT, which had long menaced the anticommunist Thai regime.[68]

After General Prem Tinsulanon replaced Kriangsak as prime minister in April 1980, Thailand became more openly hostile to Vietnam, and continuing PAVN and Lao forays across the border hardened Thai policy.[69] The Thai alignment with China became relatively tight, characterized by a relatively clear pledge of support against an external adversary (Vietnam), significant operational cooperation on the ground, and large levels of military aid. China provided light arms for the Thai military, and the United States also reaffirmed the U.S.-Thai alliance. In February 1979 President Jimmy Carter promised Kriangsak that the United States would honor its commitments under the Manila Pact. The United States promptly delivered additional aid and weaponry, increasing Thailand's military sales credits tenfold in 1980.[70] The United States did not commit to direct military involvement, largely due to the residual effects of the American exit from Vietnam, but it did provide much-needed deterrence and support against a possible Vietnamese attack, airlifting supplies to the Thai army after the June 1980 PAVN incursion and sending warships to the Gulf of Thailand on a regular basis.[71]

Thai perceptions of U.S. credibility also improved because the Vietnamese invasion of Cambodia put American interests more directly at risk, and because the new Reagan administration demonstrated a muscular anti-Soviet policy in Asia. The Thai-U.S. alliance thus rebounded from its low point between 1976 and 1978 to become a tight alliance again by 1980, characterized by large infusions of American military aid, a clear commitment of American support for Thailand against a common foe, and continued U.S. access to Thai air and naval installations to facilitate American air and naval presence in the region.

Chinese and U.S. support served complementary roles; Beijing engaged most directly with Cambodian rebels and provided small arms and guerilla training, seeking to "bleed Vietnam white" in the costly conflict. The United States provided economic aid and high-tech equipment for the Royal Thai Armed Forces as they prepared for a possible PAVN attack. In 1984 and 1985 the Royal Thai Army stepped up cooperation with the PRC through training and supply shipments, though China did not commit significant ground forces or enjoy use of Thai ports or military airspace.[72] Still, China's imperial history and modern legacy of supporting antigovernment rebels throughout the region induced caution in Thai officials, who approached the alignment cautiously as they tilted toward Beijing during the Third Indochina War.[73]

Singapore Encourages U.S. Resolve

Like Thailand, Singapore viewed the occupation of Cambodia with grave concern. As a small trading state vulnerable to external attack and economically dependent on regional security, Singapore sought to draw U.S. attention and resources back into the region. The unabashedly anticommunist Singaporean leadership continued to pursue only a limited alignment with the United States but stridently pushed for a hard-line policy against Vietnam. In 1982 Singaporean Foreign Minister S. Rajaratnam publicly warned that Vietnam sought to become a "hegemonic" power in Indochina with "regional imperialist ambitions."[74] More than any of its neighbors, Singapore viewed regional security through the lens of global developments, including the Soviet invasion of Afghanistan and the events of Central America and southern Africa. Foreign Minister S. Dhanabalan, Rajaratnam's successor, stated Singapore's view plainly: "We see the emergence of the Soviet Union as a dominant superpower as the biggest threat to peace in the region. The Russians have made it very clear that they want to dominate the world, and part of the plan covers the use of client states like Vietnam. . . . The Soviet Union has in the past few years proved that it intends to carry out its plans."[75]

Lee Kuan Yew asserted that Moscow's aims in Southeast Asia were "first to make friends, then to be the Big Brother and finally to be the arbiter."[76] Ambassador-at-Large Tommy Koh later acknowledged that Singapore had lobbied aggressively—and successfully—in Washington for the United States to provide overt aid to the Khmer resistance.[77] Singapore stopped short of aligning with China or encouraging Thailand to bolster cooperation with Beijing, however. Singapore's ethnic Chinese leaders feared that its larger neighbors would see the Lion City as a Chinese Trojan horse in the region.[78] To avoid stoking animosity in Kuala Lumpur or Jakarta, Singapore remained relatively quiet on the issue of ASEAN alignment with China, content to await an Indonesian move before normalizing relations with Beijing.

Indonesia and Malaysia Align Loosely with the United States

The New Order regime in Indonesia and the governing United Malay National Organization (UMNO) in Malaysia were both anticommunist, and both were concerned that the Soviet-sponsored invasion of Cambodia made a mockery of ZOPFAN, inviting more unwanted great-power conflict and intervention in Southeast Asia. However, they did not share the Thai or Singaporean threat perception. Neither Malaysia nor Indonesia rated the danger of Soviet dominance of Southeast Asia highly. Both believed that the Soviet threat was directed more at the United States and China than themselves and had no desire to be used as pawns in America's crusade against the Soviet Union and Vietnam. They also sought to avoid a protracted conflict that would give the great powers added pretext for deploying their forces more aggressively in the region.[79]

Kuala Lumpur and Jakarta were more concerned with domestic menaces—communist subversion, radical Islamic groups, and ethnic separatists—than external threats.[80] Although the Vietnamese takeover of Cambodia heightened concerns about the overall correlation of forces in Southeast Asia, the communist groups of greatest concern to Malaysia and Indonesia were trained by China and loyal to Beijing, giving the PRC subversive capacity in both countries. Their leaders saw Maoism, with its agrarian roots, as a much more formidable ideological challenge than the more urban variety of Marxism-Leninism espoused by the Soviet Union. Moreover, the 1979 Sino-Vietnamese War had suggested to some observers that the PRC would be willing to use force in certain instances to defend ethnic Chinese populations in Southeast Asia. Officials in Jakarta and Kuala Lumpur thus saw China as the principal great-power menace to their regimes' security.[81]

In 1980 Suharto and Prime Minister Hussein Onn of Malaysia therefore declared the Kuantan principle, asserting that both China and the USSR should cease intervention in Indochina to preserve peace in the region. Indonesian and Malaysian policymakers viewed a moderate Vietnam as the best option, secure enough to decline greater Soviet intervention and strong enough to serve as a bulwark against PRC expansion into Southeast Asia.[82]

Indonesian and Malaysian officials also feared that a protracted conflict and strong Sino-Thai alliance would lead to an unacceptable rise in China's regional influence and justify greater Soviet engagement in the region. The West's assistance with China's Four Modernizations thus contributed to the perception of China as a threat. Officials in Kuala Lumpur and Jakarta perceived China mostly as a long-term menace in the 1980s because the PRC was still unable to project serious military or economic power into the region. They feared, however, that Western support for China's economic, technological, and military growth would help China become a strong imperial power. The Soviet-Vietnamese menace would eventually pass, leaving ASEAN states to face a hostile and muscular PRC by themselves. Lee Kuan Yew said that ASEAN policymakers recognized "America's need to balance Soviet influence in East Asia" but had "apprehensions that a well-armed China may become a greater problem for Southeast Asia."[83] In the nearer term, Malaysian and Indonesian officials feared that American military support for China against the Soviet Union would result in arms finding their way southward to insurgents in the ASEAN states.[84]

Malaysian leaders were concerned that their desire for low-profile relations with Washington was translating into a low-priority American approach to Malaysia. Malaysian Deputy Prime Minister Datuk Musa Hitam said in 1983, "[We] like to think that you think Malaysia is important to you. But we don't get that impression."[85] Nevertheless, in 1984 Malaysia also began secret military cooperation with the United States through the Bilateral Training and Consultative Group (BITAC). The BITAC arrangements involved low-key joint training exercises, naval and air visits to Malaysia, and repairs of American ships in Malaysian docking facilities. Alongside the BITAC arrangements, Malaysia continued to purchase fighter planes and other advanced weapons systems from the United States. Malaysia continued to favor limited alignment, but its decision to bolster its modest security arrangements with America reflected concerns about communist expansion in Southeast Asia, diminished fears about a U.S. desire to dominate the region, and a perception that Washington was best equipped to help modernize the Malaysian armed forces.

Indonesia continued to tilt toward Washington as well, engaging in low-level cooperation with the United States but taking a slightly more equidistant position between the superpowers. In 1983 the Golkar government announced an "intensification of Indonesia's independent and active foreign policy," and Foreign Minister Mochtar Kusumaatmadja likened alignment choices between Washington and Moscow as navigating between two coral reefs. The Indonesian government continued to tolerate the U.S. bases in the Philippines but expressed the view that they should be only temporary.[86] Indonesian officials feared that U.S. officials attached too little importance to their country and took its alignment for granted.[87] Indonesia's expressed intent to pursue a more independent foreign policy was both a demand for increased U.S. attention and an effort to reinforce Jakarta's regional leadership and standing among rhetorically nonaligned nations.

When the United States continued to support China, Indonesia and Malaysia took occasional steps to signal greater neutrality and suggested to Washington that their pro-Western alignments could not be taken for granted. In 1984 Indonesian officials made a number of high-level visits to the USSR to improve ties and demonstrate that Jakarta had other options if the United States neglected ASEAN concerns about Sino-American ties. In a 1984 move widely interpreted as a demand for attention from Washington, Malaysia announced that it was interested in purchasing military equipment from the Soviet Union, and state-owned papers described the move as a "warning to the West."[88]

Independent Brunei Sides with the West

In the midst of the Cambodian conflict, a sixth member joined ASEAN when Brunei Darussalam became independent in 1984. The former British protectorate's alignment was decidedly pro-Western, primarily through the continuation of links to London that had obtained since 1888. British Gurkhas remained to provide security for the sultanate in exchange for political support and access to Brunei's extensive petroleum reserves. Tiny Brunei's sense of vulnerability to its immediate neighbors, more than any concern about Soviet attack or communist subversion, also encouraged Bandar Seri Begawan to join ASEAN.[89] Malaysia had supported the Bruneian government-in-exile and rival *Parti Rakyat* until the 1970s, whereas Indonesia had supported the 1962 Brunei revolt, in which rebels seized the valuable Seria oil installations and held a number of senior executives of the Royal Brunei Shell Company hostage. Even with the Cambodian conflict raging, the *istana* (palace)—in which a narrow group of the sultan's family and senior *menteri* (advisors) conduct foreign policy—remained most focused on the protection of the country's oil installations from possible Malaysian or Indonesian-backed advances. Economic and regime security interests thus bound Bandar Seri Begawan to London and encouraged a limited alignment with Washington that involved low-level naval cooperation and U.S. port calls at Bruneian facilities.[90]

Promoting a Balance of Influence in the Maritime ASEAN Area

As Muthiah Alagappa has argued, ASEAN governments generally sought to promote a healthy "balance of presence" among major external actors in Southeast Asia.[91] For Malaysia and Indonesia, the best long-term solution to regional security was to diminish the footprint of all of the great powers. One manifestation of that view was an effort in both Jakarta and Kuala Lumpur to reinvigorate a proposal to establish a Southeast Asia Nuclear-Weapons Free Zone (SEANWFZ). America opposed the proposal, which would have excluded some U.S. nuclear vessels from the area. Malaysia and Indonesia did not abandon the initiative, which eventually bore fruit in a 1995 treaty, but neither government wanted the balance of great-power influence to shift precipitously. Leading Indonesian foreign policy advisors asserted that an "increase of U.S. Seventh Fleet presence in the Asia-Pacific region [was] needed as a counterbalance" to increased Soviet might at Cam Ranh Bay.[92] The ambivalence of Indonesian and Malaysian officials about the U.S. role in Southeast Asia helps explain why both adopted limited alignment strategies.

The governments of Singapore and Brunei were somewhat more comfortable with a strong Western footprint in the region. Still, they agreed that keeping any one power from dominating Southeast Asia would improve their leverage as DCs. In the Cold War context, ASEAN governments could exploit superpower rivalry to their advantage by occupying middle ground. That made limited alignment strategies attractive to the governments of those four maritime ASEAN states, which believed they could meet their basic security needs without massive U.S. assistance. They avoided tight alliances in part to position ASEAN as a kind of fulcrum between the external powers. Singaporean Deputy Prime Minister Lee Hsien Loong stated the principle clearly in a 1984 address: "This policy depends on the competing interests of several big powers in the region, rather than on linking the nation's fortunes to one overbearing partner. The big powers can keep one another in check and will prevent any one of them from dominating the entire region, and so allow small states to survive in the interstices between them . . . a small state [cannot] manipulate the big powers with impunity. The most it can do is to influence their policies in its favour."[93] By establishing better relations with each of the great powers than the great powers had with one another, ASEAN states sought both security and influence out of proportion to their size.[94]

Internal Challenges Underscore the U.S.-Philippine Alliance

The Philippines shared the view that Chinese-sponsored communist groups and other local insurgents constituted greater menaces than the PAVN or the Soviet Pacific Fleet. However, the scale of the internal threat that Manila faced in the early 1980s was much greater, and the government's relative inability to defeat the movement brought President Marcos back to a closer ties with Washington. The country's most serious threat came from the communist New People's Army (NPA)—the military wing of the Philippine Communist Party—which grew rapidly after 1977 as the power of the corrupt and authoritarian Marcos regime waned. In fact, by the late 1970s some analysts concluded that the Philippine communist movement was the only one in the ASEAN region with a reasonable chance of seizing power from the established government.[95]

The NPA grew to roughly 23,000 members after the high-profile assassination of political opposition leader Benigno Aquino in 1983. Between 1980 and 1984 clashes with government forces rose from eighty-three to 3,500 per year, and communist rebels killed nearly 5,000 Philippine soldiers. The NPA also broke out of its traditional heartland in central Luzon to spark a nationwide insurgency across fifty-nine fronts throughout the rural Philippines, operating in about 20 percent of the *barrios* (local administrative units) in the country. In 1983 Defense Minister Juan Ponce Enrile said that the communist NPA was the only present security threat to the Philippines.[96] However, the long-standing ethnic rebellion among the Muslim Moro population in the southern Philippines also continued to simmer in Mindanao.

The Rise in Intramural Security Cooperation

During the Third Indochina War, the six ASEAN states also began to form intramural alignments and undertake confidence-building measures to enhance defense cooperation and build a stronger regional security community under the rubric of One Southeast Asia. ASEAN governments gradually expanded their cooperation against local threats, which included sharing information about the movements of guerilla groups across borders, establishment of mutual extradition treaties, and joint border patrols and counterinsurgency operations. Singapore was particularly active in developing joint air and naval exercises with its neighbors. By the mid-1980s this subregional network of alignments also developed a greater outward-looking dimension as ASEAN states' militaries began conducting joint ground and naval exercises and training to help protect against the possibility of Vietnamese expansion in the region.[97]

Burma Remains Isolated in Neutralism

Among the countries of Southeast Asia, only Burma could be described as nonaligned during the years following the Vietnamese invasion of Cambodia. Burmese leaders criticized the Vietnamese invasion of Cambodia but refused to participate on either side of the Indochina conflict. Burma also refused to take clear sides in the ongoing Sino-Indian rivalry and eschewed large aid packages from all of the great powers. In 1981 Ne Win declared that the Burmese Socialist Programme Party would follow in the spirit of U Nu's concept of "positive neutrality" by adhering to an "independent and active foreign policy." Rangoon asserted that it was "everybody's friend but nobody's ally."[98]

The BCP remained the most serious security challenge to the Burmese regime, but this diminished as relations with China improved when Deng Xiaoping's more pragmatic government came to power. China began to withdraw support from the BCP, diminishing communist insurgents as a threat. Beijing resumed economic aid to Burma and showed good intentions by expelling the BCP headquarters from the city of Manshi in southern China. This forced the BCP to relocate in northern Burma, where authorities in Rangoon could suppress communist activities more effectively. By the mid-1980s Chinese support for the BCP had all but evaporated.[99]

To manage threats from ethnic minorities and communist insurgents, Burma preserved an arm's-length *paukphaw* relationship with China. Rangoon subscribed to the one-China policy and refused to join the U.S.-led containment structure, and in exchange Beijing moderated its support of rebel groups along the long and porous Sino-Burmese border. Chinese economic aid to Burma increased but did not result in significant defense cooperation.

Regional Alignment Overview, 1979–1985

The Cambodian conflict became the most defining fault line in regional security during the latter stages of the Cold War and affected Southeast Asian alignment preferences and policies in a number of ways. First, the early 1980s were an era in which several Southeast Asian states deviated from their usual preference for limited alignments due to high expected payoffs from tight alliances. Threats emanating from the war drove Vietnam, Laos, and the new PRK to pursue tighter alliance with Moscow and encouraged enhanced ASEAN cooperation with the United States. The conflict also drew the attention and resources of governments in Washington and Moscow, both of which appeared to have the will to provide major military support to their allies as the so-called Second Cold War ignited. Again, it was great-power policies more than capabilities that contributed to shifts in Southeast Asian preferences.

Second, the conflict led Thailand and the United States to cooperate more closely with China, which ceased to support the Thai Communist Party and began to make its first significant inroads into the ASEAN alignment network. Third, the struggle in Cambodia and concerns about communist advances galvanized ASEAN members to enhance their own bilateral ties, which began to assume some of the regional security vacuum that British and American force reductions had created in the 1970s.

Table 2.2 Alignment Postures, 1979–1985

Country	Great Power	Alignment Status
Brunei	USA	Limited alignment (1984)
Burma		No alignment
Cambodia		Under occupation
Indonesia	USA	Limited alignment
Laos	USSR	Limited alignment → tight alliance (1983)
Malaysia	USA	Limited alignment
Philippines	USA	Tight alliance
Singapore	USA	Limited alignment
Thailand	PRC	Limited alignment → tight alliance (1980)
	USA	Limited alignment → tight alliance (1980)
Vietnam	USSR	Tight alliance

Source: Author's compilation

TAIL END OF THE COLD WAR, 1986–1991

The Third Indochina War continued unabated into the late 1980s, but regional security affairs entered a transitional phase after 1985. Mikhail Gorbachev introduced his policy of New Thinking, Soviet support for Indochina declined, and the Cold War standoff in Southeast Asia began to thaw. Gradual Sino-Soviet rapprochement eased tensions between Beijing and Hanoi, which were central to the struggle in Indochina. The Cambodian conflict remained the principal fault line in Southeast Asian security, but after two Jakarta Informal Meetings and bilateral Sino-Soviet and Sino-Vietnamese talks, the conflict moved toward resolution. In early 1989 Hanoi agreed to begin withdrawing troops from Cambodia unconditionally later that year. In September 1989 Vietnam withdrew many of its troops from Cambodia. Moscow began to pull back from the region, and the heavyweight struggle that had defined the Cold War security landscape in the region drew toward a close. By August 1990 the five permanent members of the Security Council agreed on a framework for resolving the international dimension of the conflict, which later became the basis for the Paris Peace Accords of 1991 and the consequent deployment of the UN Transitional Authority in Cambodia. In this changing strategic environment, Southeast Asian states again reviewed and updated their alignment policies.

Decline of Soviet Support to Indochina

The most pronounced changes in regional alignments again occurred in Indochina. The Soviet Union, eager to embark on much-needed economic and political reforms and beleaguered by costly guerilla wars in Cambodia, Afghanistan, and elsewhere began to withdraw its military support for Hanoi. The VCP reacted quickly and with great concern, establishing its own reform policy of *doi moi* (change and newness) in 1986 and considering ways to move toward a less dependent position. That process was difficult. For several years Vietnam's alliance with the USSR had effectively precluded relations with other major world powers and left Hanoi utterly dependent on Moscow for political support and military hardware.[100] China remained a real perceived threat, accentuated in 1988 when PLA and PAVN forces clashed again over the disputed Spratly Islands. The United States appeared no closer to normalizing relations, and a U.S.-led sanctions regime was crippling the country, frustrating the government's development plans, and undermining the regime's performance legitimacy in an era when communist governments were under siege throughout Eastern Europe.

The VCP Politburo began to reorient its security strategy, entering into negotiations on withdrawal from Cambodia and seeking other possible alignment partners. In May 1988 Hanoi introduced the landmark principle of "multidirectional foreign policy," which represented a profound shift away from Hanoi's unidirectional foreign relations with the Soviet bloc.[101] The withdrawal of troops from Cambodia began in 1989, weakening the mutual defense treaty between Hanoi and Phnom Penh but helping avert a Vietnamese economic collapse. In 1990 Vietnam tried to shore up the all-important alliance with Moscow, but Soviet officials announced that aid for the next Vietnamese Five-Year Plan would be reduced and that Soviet force levels in the country would also diminish steeply.[102] Vietnam thus worked quickly to reorient its security relations to reduce reliance on Moscow.

Laos faced similar problems as external support from Moscow via Hanoi receded in the late 1980s. During the mid-1980s direct Lao ties to the USSR had increased, partly on the basis of Soviet concerns about the effectiveness of aid channeled to Laos through Hanoi. That trend continued in the late 1980s as the USSR sought to expand its influence in Southeast Asia and lessen dependence on an increasingly uncooperative and faltering Vietnam. Soviet technicians and military advisors became more numerous in Laos, and training and military exchanges increased.[103] Lao-Soviet cooperation thus became more direct and substantial, and by 1986 could be described as a tight informal alignment. Economic aid from the USSR also continued to support the Lao economy, but soon the prospect of a precipitous drop in Soviet aid forced the Lao People's Revolutionary Party (LPRP) to reorient its foreign policy considerably.[104] Laos normalized ties with China in 1989 and, like Vietnam, significantly reoriented its security policy away from the USSR.

For the PRK government in Cambodia, the reduction of Vietnamese forces in 1989 began an era of heavy UN and great-power engagement that continued to limit the country's independent foreign policymaking capacity. An estimated 5,000 members of the PAVN remained in Cambodia, serving primarily as technical advisors or command-and-control advisors to the newly renamed State of Cambodia forces.[105] The five permanent members of the UN Security Council and major regional actors eventually came to agreement on how to establish a peaceful transition in the battle-weary nation in the 1990 Paris Peace Accords. Those accords paved the way for the UN Transitional Authority in Cambodia (UNTAC), prohibiting all foreign military aid to Phnom Penh and effectively neutralizing the country after years of bloody conflict.

ASEAN Uncertainty

By September 1989, as Vietnam began its withdrawal from Cambodia, a new age was beginning in ASEAN security relations as well. The resolution of the international dimension of the Cambodian conflict meant that the Moscow-Hanoi entente receded as an external threat to ASEAN governments. The gradual implosion of the USSR also lessened fears that Moscow would be able or willing to support local Communist groups in Southeast Asia. Once-menacing Vietnam pursued a new foreign policy of "friends everywhere" and moved toward ASEAN membership. Nevertheless, ASEAN officials saw risks in the new security environment, including regional tensions, internal ethnic fighting, and insurgency. Many feared that the end of superpower struggle would mean an end to the U.S. commitment to Southeast Asia and a possible rise of Japanese, Chinese, or possibly Indian militarism.[106] Some ASEAN leaders saw the 1988 Spratly Island clashes as evidence that China would endeavor to step into any strategic vacuum created by the diminished Soviet presence and possible U.S. withdrawal. Chinese and Japanese plans to participate in the UN peacekeeping mission in Cambodia also stirred regional anxieties.

Malaysian, Singaporean, and Bruneian Outreach

Malaysia and Singapore were among the first states to update their alignments in anticipation of the post–Cold War security environment. Malaysian officials were particularly concerned about Chinese behavior in the South China Sea, viewing PRC naval encroachment as Malaysia's principal external security threat. Malaysia did not move visibly closer to the United States, but it signed an MOU with Britain in 1989 to upgrade its defense forces, which was widely interpreted as part of an effort to manage a perceived maritime menace from China.[107] The Malaysian government also harbored ongoing concerns about intramural Southeast Asian security, as it continued to endure territorial disputes with all five of its ASEAN neighbors. In addition to fearing territorial losses, Malaysia was concerned that regional conflict could precipitate renewed clashes between Malays and the country's economically dominant ethnic Chinese minority. To enhance its security and promote regional stability, particularly in the economically and strategically vital South China Sea, Malaysia reaffirmed its existing security ties and pursued stronger regional defense cooperation, concluding a 1989 training agreement with Singapore, continuing joint training exercises with Indonesia, and promoting enlarged FPDA exercises.[108]

Indonesia also continued to tilt toward the West but emphasized its policy independence during the late 1980s, in part because the Indonesian government sought to play a leadership role in resolving the Cambodian crisis.[109] Indonesian leaders believed that their past struggle against imperialism helped them better understand Vietnam's predicament. They also believed that resolution of the conflict would marginalize the great powers and assert Southeast Asia's capacity to manage problems intramurally. Through the Jakarta Informal Meetings, which drew the competing parties in Cambodia to the table, the Indonesian government did play a significant part in breaking the stalemate in Indochina and reducing the region's dependence on the great powers.

Singapore remained more strongly opposed to Vietnam and the USSR, but its leaders were also concerned about Chinese encroachment and ever-present threats from its larger neighbors. To manage its relations with Jakarta and Kuala Lumpur and to build collective regional capacity, Singapore increased defense ties to Indonesia in 1989. At the same time, Singapore also pursued a stronger alignment with the United States, as fearful as any ASEAN government about an American pullback from Southeast Asia. Singapore offered to host more substantial deployments of U.S. naval and air forces, and Prime Minister Goh Chok Tong signed a 1990 MOU that gave the U.S. military access to the Sembawang Dockyard, allowed training at Paya Lebar Airport, and permitted some U.S. service personnel to be stationed in Singapore.[110]

Assuring its neighbors that it was not becoming a permanent base for American forces, Singapore also increased training cooperation and strategic consultation with the United States, clearly taking the alignment from a limited form to a more substantial one. Malaysian Defense Minister Ahmad Badawi saw the stronger Singapore-U.S. alignment as an effort to strengthen Singaporean defenses against Malaysia, asserting that Singapore continued to view Malaysia "as a threat to [its] existence" and that the alignment was "a deterrence directed against us."[111] Indeed, Lee Kuan Yew was often blunt in expressing his perception of the United States as a "benign superpower" that could help protect Singapore from potentially aggressive neighbors.[112]

Brunei also tilted further toward Washington. The sultan of Brunei reportedly funneled some $10 million to help U.S.-backed Contras in Nicaragua in 1986.[113] To manage the uncertainty of the changing balance of power in the South China Sea, Brunei also joined Singapore in offering U.S. forces greater access to its ports and other facilities in July 1990. Brunei's tilt toward America was further reflected in the sultanate's support for the U.S. liberation of Kuwait in 1990.

Durable Thai Cooperation with the United States and the PRC

As the Cambodian conflict dragged on, Thailand's alignments with both the United States and the PRC remained strong. Thai perceptions of vulnerability increased somewhat in 1988, when Laos and Thailand fought a three-month bloody border war that failed to dislodge Lao troops from a disputed area along the countries' frontier. American aid helped Bangkok protect against domestic challenges and the continued external menace from the PAVN. Thailand and the United States signed an MOU on logistics support in October 1985 and an agreement on the creation of a war reserves stockpile in January 1987. Nevertheless, the U.S. alliance had its limits, in that American forces did not participate in combat operations and U.S. supplies were mostly high end. Bangkok also continued to cooperate with China, which provided less expensive small arms and applied considerable political pressure on Vietnam.

Thailand began to wean itself off Chinese and American support only toward the end of the 1980s, when Prime Minister Chatichai Choonhavan and other Thai officials began to see the fruits of great-power negotiations over Indochina and Vietnamese withdrawal became imminent. Chatichai said that politics would take a back seat to economics and famously declared that Thailand would "turn a battlefield into a marketplace," establishing a *Suvannaphum* (golden land) in mainland Southeast Asia. Tight alliance and polarization had delayed market integration, and Bangkok perceived some economic incentives to pursue more great-power limited alignments when threats receded.[114] As the PAVN prepared to withdraw, Thai military cooperation with China and the United States declined toward the more moderate levels of the late 1970s. The tight Thai alignments of the mid-1980s thus gave way to a more limited pair of alignments with Beijing and Washington that involved lower levels of military aid and a less clear great-power commitment to Thai defense.

Continuation of the U.S.-Philippine Alliance

During the late 1980s the Philippine–U.S. alliance also proved durable despite the absence of a direct external threat from Vietnam. From the Philippine standpoint the alliance was mainly a tool to manage threats from the NPA and seperatist groups that represented disenchanted Muslim populations in the south of the country. Domestic rebellions were intimately tied to the failures and excesses of the Marcos regime, which plunged the Philippines into debt and closed off legitimate avenues for peaceful political dissent. In 1986 public frustration with Marcos led to the People's Power revolution and the ascent of Corazon Aquino to the presidency. Interestingly, although the United States had allied itself closely with the widely resented Marcos regime, the People's Power revolution did not result in a rejection of the alliance. Aquino's threat perceptions were partly responsible for the continuing friendship. She immediately faced serious economic problems, and without major economic, political, and military reforms, the NPA menace would soon present an existential threat to the Philippine government.[115] However, many in Manila (and in Washington) believed that the Philippine–U.S. relationship was broad and deep enough to transcend changes in governments and even political regimes.

Rise of SLORC and Burma's Alignment with China

For years Burma had been a backwater in regional alignment politics as Ne Win steered clear of regionalism in favor of neutrality, with a slight political tilt toward Beijing. That posture changed dramatically after the 1988 military coup and the State Law and Order Restoration Council (SLORC) regime was established. The SLORC leadership faced serious threats from the opposition National League for Democracy (NLD) and ethnic rebel groups in the north of the country, and China stopped providing significant support to the BCP. China was also one of the few countries that defied the Western boycott on the new Union of Myanmar and did not shun its military-backed regime. Myanmar turned to Beijing for security support and, within a month of the September 1988 crackdown, General Than Shwe led a high-level military delegation to Beijing and secured Chinese defense supplies.[116]

Facing Western sanctions and widespread international condemnation for its treatment of the NLD, Yangon's dire economic problems greatly exacerbated the regime's sense of insecurity. By 1989 Myanmar was bankrupt, in desperate need of foreign exchange with which to pay its international debts and fund military and civil operations in the country, including major infrastructure projects. The SLORC regime again turned to China for support, opening the border to direct trade, which increased considerably. Chinese merchants and financiers flocked into Myanmar, soon dominating the country's external trade relations.

The 1988–1990 period thus represented a significant turning point in Sino-Myanmar relations as Yangon began to veer away from relative neutrality toward clear alignment with the PRC. The limited Sino-Myanmar alignment of the late 1980s became a relatively tight informal alignment after the 1990 elections and

Chinese provision of a $1 billion package of military aid including aircraft, tanks, guns, and other military equipment. The PRC also began to train Myanmar forces and expressed an interest in Indian Ocean listening posts and possible access to naval facilities in the future.[117]

Regional Alignment Overview, 1986–1991

The late 1980s saw the reversal of some of the trends of the preceding years (see table 2.3). Changes in Soviet policies reduced the confidence of its allies and contributed a change in preferences in Hanoi and Vientiane, where officials feared abandonment (or inadequate support) and sought to move toward a more limited tilt. In Thailand the reduction of external threat accompanying the Vietnamese withdrawal from Cambodia had a similar effect. Maritime Southeast Asian alignment policies and preferences remained relatively stable. Burmese preference changed sharply in the late 1980s mainly as a result of domestic developments, as an unpopular SLORC government struggled to survive by leaning on China.

CONCLUSION

The latter years of the Cold War present a relatively stiff test for the hypothesis that DCs usually favor limited alignments. Southeast Asia was deeply caught up in great-power rivalries and polarized along strategic and ideological lines. The intensity of conflict presented most governments in the region with significant security challenges. Governments in the region sometimes entered willingly into strong, antagonistic alliances when they faced dire threats and when their great-power partners evinced a willingness to provide reliable support. Nevertheless, limited alignments were the most common observed behavior. The Cold War data show the power of the argument advanced in this book, because they suggest that limited

Table 2.3 Alignment Postures, 1986–1991

Country	Great Power	Alignment Status
Brunei	USA	Limited alignment
Burma	PRC	Limited alignment → tight alliance (1990)
		No alignment → limited alignment (1988)
Cambodia	USSR	(Semi-autonomous alignment via Vietnam)
Indonesia	USA	Limited alignment
Laos	USSR	Tight alliance → limited alignment (1989)
Malaysia	USA	Limited alignment
Philippines	USA	Tight alliance
Singapore	USA	Limited alignment (1990)
Thailand	PRC	Tight alliance → limited alignment (1989)
	USA	Tight alliance → limited alignment (1989)
Vietnam	USSR	Tight alliance → limited alignment (1989)

Source: Author's compilation

alignments are likely to be common or preponderant even in regions wracked by conflict and polarization.

Figure 2.1 summarizes the data from the period. Black boxes signify tight alliance, white boxes refer to nonalignment, and grey boxes denote limited alignment. Thailand, the only country in the region with two simultaneous great-power alignments, is coded according to the stronger of the two alignments at any given time. This avoids stacking the deck in favor of my hypothesis; I count any DC engaged in a tight alliance with any great power as tightly allied overall. In fact, the Thai-U.S. alliance and Sino-Thai alignment strengthened and weakened more or less simultaneously.

Southeast Asian governments that allied tightly during the period generally did so reluctantly, even if they were not compelled to do so by their powerful partners. All the countries in Southeast Asia—with the possible exception of the Philippines—started off the period attempting to avoid highly confrontational balancing or bandwagoning strategies. Even the Philippines tried to loosen its ties with America somewhat and mend fences with old adversaries to improve its leverage and stress its independence. Vietnam and Thailand steered back toward tight alliances only as tensions on the peninsula erupted into renewed regional warfare, when Thai and VCP leaders believed their security needs as frontline states were too great to be met without extensive great-power succor. Laos initially tried to limit its direct ties to the USSR, succumbing to tight alliance slightly later. Occupied Cambodia became nominally identified with the Soviet bloc as well, but with 180,000 Vietnamese troops and countless advisors in the country, it lacked the capacity to formulate an independent alignment policy.

Black = tight alliance
Gray = limited alignment
White = no alignment

Country/Year	75	76	77	78	79	80	81	82	83	84	85	86	87	88	89	90	91
Brunei	(British protectorate)																
Malaysia																	
Indonesia																	
Singapore																	
Thailand★																	
Philippines																	
Vietnam																	
Laos																	
Cambodia					(under occupation; later UN administration)												
Burma																	

Figure 2.1 Summary Data, 1975–1991

Source: Author's compilation

Note: ★ significant defense cooperation with both China and the United States (entire period)

Other Southeast Asian governments pursued limited alignment strategies throughout the latter stages of the Cold War. To preserve flexibility and avoid embroilment in great-power feuds, Burma and the five maritime states did not pursue strong alliances with Beijing and Washington even when the Third Indochina War reached its peak. When the great powers offered support, they approached security cooperation with caution and declined any explicit or implicit invitations to forge more substantial defense pacts. To support their limited alignment strategies, the maritime ASEAN states all began to develop stronger intramural defense ties and reemphasized normative and institutional complements to great-power (and particularly U.S.) security support.

A variety of factors informed the alignment calculi of Southeast Asian states during the period. Those factors will be examined further in chapters 4 and 5, but a few brief conclusions from this chapter are in order. First, Southeast Asian experience between 1975 and 1991 shows that the systemic distribution of capabilities does have some ripple effects and contributes to broad patterns of alignment behavior. As Soviet power waxed relative to U.S. might in the late 1970s, superpower competition intensified in the region, and alliances tended to harden. As it waned in the late 1980s, the same alliances tended to weaken, especially in the Indochina countries.

Second, the evidence supports the claim that the magnitude and nature of threats offers a much more convincing explanation than power alone for alignment preferences. Even when the Soviet-American balance shifted, it affected Southeast Asian states differentially—primarily based on geography. It is no coincidence that most of the states welcoming tight alliances (namely, Thailand and the Indochina states) did so at times when they faced pressing overland challenges from external military foes. States with internal threats foremost in mind generally steered toward limited security cooperation.

Third, the period shows that threats cannot explain alignment preferences alone. Perceptions of the intentions of great-power friends are also crucial. Perceived U.S., Soviet, and Chinese intentions had obvious effects on the preferences of their Southeast Asian friends on numerous occasions. Policy changes were particularly important, both because they affected credibility and because they altered the balance of power in the regional environment (i.e., Indochina). U.S. policy shifts in 1975–1976 and 1980–1981, the Soviet reorientation after 1985, and China's move toward moderation after 1979 were the most critical.

Ideological factors sometimes contributed to changing alignment preferences, most notably in cases of regime change in Cambodia and Burma. Experience appears to have mattered somewhat; all the tight alliances that existed during the period grew out of existing security relationships. Path-dependence was perhaps particularly relevant in the Philippines, where tight alliance structures probably would not have existed in the 1980s if not for the long-standing existence of a relatively embedded and institutionalized defense pact. Cultural factors appear to have played only minor roles in most parts of the region but stand out as a possible contributor to the longevity of the U.S.-Philippine alliance.

Fourth, the experience of 1975–1991 suggests only a modest role for economic aid and trade in shifting Southeast Asian alignment preferences. When states in the region moved from limited alignment to tight alliance postures, they did so much more clearly in response to military necessity than economic need. Larger aid packages did tend to follow tight alliances, especially for the Indochina states, but those handouts were offset by harsh economic sanctions imposed by the capitalist states, providing a reminder that tight alliances are often a bad way for a DC to promote its economic interests.

Fifth, the evidence offers modest support for the argument that norms, institutions, and other security alternatives can reduce the demand for tight alliances. The three countries that Donald Emmerson has called the "core" ASEAN states— Malaysia, Singapore, and Indonesia—invested heavily in regional security solutions and were indeed more prone to limited alignment than others in the region. Part of the explanation lies in the fact that those states were able to manage their own relations more peacefully, using ASEAN as an important vehicle for cooperation. However, the lower intensity of external military threats and different domestic political conditions better explain the core ASEAN states' more consistent preference for limited alignment. After all, Thailand and the Philippines were also ASEAN members and deviated from the limited alignment norm.

Chapter 3

The Post–Cold War Era

ALTHOUGH LIMITED ALIGNMENTS were common during the Cold War era, they have become much more dominant in Southeast Asia since the end of the Third Indochina War. As discussed in chapter 1, a number of related variables explain that change. Structurally, the United States has enjoyed clear primacy in power capabilities, particularly in the military area. America's superior might has driven up certain of the risks of tight alliance with or against the United States. The nature of the contemporary environment has also contributed. The past two decades have seen relative peace among the great powers, which diminishes major interstate threats in many corners of the Global South and thus DCs' perceived need for tight alliances. The relatively liberal character of the post–Cold War order has also facilitated economic and diplomatic engagement, often through multilateral forms. A sense of greater interdependence and expanded opportunities for dialogue has led many DCs to perceive diminished threats from erstwhile big-power foes, thus reducing the demand for tight security pacts.

The narrative in this chapter supports the claim that DCs generally favor limited alignments, particularly in the contemporary, relatively unipolar international system.

EARLY POST–COLD WAR PERIOD, 1992–1996

As the Cold War drew to a close, the most pervasive questions in regional alignment politics surrounded the changing levels of great-power interest and involvement in Southeast Asia. The United States appeared less willing to project its power in the region, and the Soviet Union declined precipitously as a military and political factor in the region. Japan was economically influential, but in the security sphere it remained a sleeping giant that many Southeast Asian officials did not wish to awaken. Only China appeared eager to assume a greater role as the diminished Soviet and U.S. roles created something of a military power vacuum in the region.

By 1992 American forces were pulling out of the Philippines, Thai-U.S. military cooperation was suspended, and both alliances appeared in some jeopardy.

Despite improved Singapore–U.S. ties, the continuing American role in the region was not beyond doubt. The three countries of Indochina, which had depended on Soviet sponsorship for more than a decade, also entered the post–Cold War period groping for policies that would ensure economic stability and security. Russia was retreating from its stronghold in Cam Ranh Bay, military aid to Indochina slowed to a trickle, and communist regimes in Eastern Europe were ironically falling like dominos.

Closure of Subic Bay

The most serious challenge to the U.S. alignment system came in the Philippines, where a series of contentious negotiations surrounded the future of the U.S bases at Subic Bay and Clark Air Field. The base negotiations became heavily politicized as many politicians in Manila attempted to project a more nationalistic line in the post-Marcos era. The Philippine government ultimately demanded much higher rent for the bases, and when the U.S. government balked, the Philippine Senate voted by a 12 to 11 margin in September 1991 to close the bases. The presence of U.S. troops had long been a sensitive issue in the Philippines, and opponents of the U.S. presence argued that the American bases represented neocolonialism and an intrusion into Filipino sovereignty.

From a military standpoint some Philippine officials came to see the alliance as unnecessary. Shielded by its geographic position, the Philippines had little to fear from its regional neighbors, whose power-projection capabilities were limited. Although Manila was suspicious of Chinese intentions in the South China Sea, the prospect of a resurgent China or a remilitarized Japan was initially considered quite distant. The country's primary security threats were internal. The communist NPA was losing influence, but the rising Moro Islamic Liberation Front (MILF) posed a major concern in the southern parts of the country.[1] It was unclear how a large U.S. military presence would counter the threat posed by such guerrilla and terrorist insurgent groups.

Moreover, some Philippine officials tended to take U.S. security support for granted. Defense Secretary Renato de Villa said in 1992, "We still have a defense treaty with the United States. If we are attacked from the outside—which is not likely to happen in the first place . . . the United States will have to come to our aid in defending us."[2]

Philippine perceptions that the bases were a strategic imperative for the United States help to explain why officials in Manila played hardball with their U.S. counterparts in the negotiations, which ultimately fell through. Most Filipino citizens and the defense establishment supported the bases, which they perceived as major reasons for U.S. material aid and the ongoing security guarantee.[3] The decision nevertheless stood, and U.S. forces began to pull out from their long-standing hub in Southeast Asia. What had been the most stable tight alliance in the region became a limited alignment.

The alliance did continue to function at a low level, and U.S. forces continued to use military installations in the Philippines. The Philippine-U.S. Mutual Defense

Board, set up in 1958, continued to devise plans for defending the Philippines and stockpiling materiel in case of an attack on the Spratly Islands. Military exercises, exchanges of information, training, and logistical cooperation also continued, most notably through the annual Balikatan (shoulder-to-shoulder) joint military exercises. However, U.S. military aid to the Philippines virtually disappeared after the closure of Subic Bay, and the alliance reached its weakest point in decades.[4]

Wavering Thai-U.S. Alliance

The end of the Cambodian conflict initially had only a modest effect on the Thai–U.S. alliance, despite the fact that Thailand had been a frontline state and was changing gears to promote economic development and friendly relations with its neighbors. Annual Cobra Gold joint military exercises continued, the largest involving American forces in Asia. Thai elites and soldiers also continued to train in the United States under a large military aid program. Even more tellingly, U.S. forces used Thai air bases as staging points during the 1990–1991 Gulf War.

However, the alliance came under stress after an unexpected Thai military coup in February 1991 and crackdown on pro-democracy demonstrators in May 1992. The George H. W. Bush administration suspended defense cooperation as a penalty for the authoritarian behavior of the new Thai regime. That decision showed that times had changed; without a looming Soviet threat on the horizon, America would be more willing to cut off allies whose domestic practices it disfavored. The Bush administration's move added to fears in Bangkok and other ASEAN capitals that Washington was less credibly committed to Southeast Asian defense. Without the USSR pressing on American interests, Southeast Asian allies could more easily be abandoned.

Relations improved when Chuan Leekpai's new civilian government came to power in Bangkok. Large Cobra Gold exercises and many smaller exercises returned in 1993, and Thailand again permitted U.S. forces to use its airports and seaports for refueling and maintenance. Thailand welcomed this limited restoration of the alliance due to concerns over growing Sino-Myanmar ties and a possible two-pincer Chinese military advance into Southeast Asia through the Eastern Indian Ocean and the South China Sea.[5] An interest in preserving access to world-class American hardware, training, and cooperation against drug trafficking and other nontraditional security challenges also made limited alignment attractive to Thai officials.

The limits of the resurrected alliance soon became apparent, however. In September 1994 President Bill Clinton proposed anchoring a floating naval facility in the Gulf of Thailand to accommodate six vessels and serve as a permanent pre-positioning naval base like the eight-ship flotillas in Diego Garcia and Guam. Chuan was initially receptive to the proposal, but the plan soon came under heavy domestic attack as an infringement on Thai sovereignty and a provocation to neighbors. Many Thai officials resisted the notion of a return to an embedded alignment involving permanent bases akin to the Cold War alliance.[6] In October Thailand formally rejected the plan, arguing that the move would frustrate relations with China and its peninsular neighbors. Malaysia and Indonesia also voiced their disapproval of the plan, arguing that it would "violate the policy of nonalignment" and "contribute to regional hostility."[7] Military cooperation remained, but U.S.-Thai defense relations were considerably more limited than they had been in the past. Thailand would no longer play host to U.S. bases, and the perceived value and credibility of the U.S. security commitment to Thailand declined without a common threat from Vietnam and the USSR.

Indochina and Myanmar

Like their ASEAN neighbors, Myanmar and the three states of Indochina encountered a new set of security challenges in the post–Cold War era. For Myanmar the principal difficulty flowed from domestic ethnic insurgencies, which flourished amidst the country's economic weakness and growing international ostracism. The SLORC further backed itself into a corner by refusing to honor national election results in 1990 and imprisoning opposition leader Aung San Suu Kyi. A new round of Western sanctions added to the SLORC's already precarious political and strategic situation. To stay afloat, Myanmar pursued a stronger alignment with China. The PRC, undeterred by Myanmar's domestic malfeasance, underwrote the SLORC's naval modernization program and supplied naval attack vehicles in exchange for permission to set up some naval intelligence facilities in the Andaman Islands. Large arms shipments also continued, helping the *tatmadaw* (armed forces) wage war against ethnic rebels. The Sino-Myanmar alignment became what one scholar called a "de facto military alliance" during the early 1990s.[8]

Vietnam, Laos, and Cambodia also entered the post–Cold War period with few friends in the neighborhood. Their anemic centrally planned economies required rebuilding, and their governments had to compensate for a drastic reduction in Soviet aid, which had bankrolled them throughout the 1980s. The collapse of the USSR and Eastern Bloc meant that Hanoi had to seriously reorganize its dealings with Moscow and develop other sources of aid and trade.[9] Although Russia continued to send arms and munitions, it was clearly turning inward. With its great-power status eroded, Moscow was no longer able to provide a worthwhile security guarantee. With its Soviet patron gone, Vietnam rushed to develop an alternative foreign security policy based on neutralism and cultivating friends everywhere. Improving relations with China and the United States became major goals in Hanoi. Fortunately for Vietnam, Chinese officials were like minded, and the two erstwhile foes normalized relations in 1991.[10] Hanoi also inched toward reestablishing relations with Washington. At the same time Vietnam mended fences with its Southeast Asian neighbors and pursued ASEAN membership. Vietnam's extension of olive branches to America and ASEAN was part of an effort to build economic and political ties in the region that would improve its resilience vis-à-vis the great powers, particularly China. In a few short years Vietnam thus moved from a very tightly aligned state to an essentially nonaligned one.

Laos found itself in a similar bind. As Soviet and Vietnamese support waned, the Lao military weakened considerably and an already feeble economy verged toward collapse. In addition, by 1989 Vietnam had withdrawn many of its battle-ready troops from Laos, including two infantry divisions it had stationed there during the 1979 border war with China. That military presence had long underscored the special friendship between Hanoi and Vientiane. The alliance remained, because the LPRP remembered who had brought them to power, but economic changes weakened the Lao-Vietnamese alignment after the late 1980s. Vietnam lacked the wealth needed to fill the void of lost Soviet support, and without its troops on Lao soil it offered little protection in case Thailand decided to settle old scores. The tight Viet-Lao alignment thus began to weaken.[11]

To compensate for the Soviet pullback, Laos began to pursue a more rounded foreign security policy akin to Vietnam's friends everywhere approach. In 1989, after a decade of hurling invective toward Beijing, Laos quietly restored party-to-party ties with China and asked for military assistance, though Beijing agreed only to sell arms on a commercial basis. After the withdrawal of PAVN forces from Laos and the subsequent reduction in Vietnamese aid in 1991, Lao relations with the PRC began to strengthen at the expense of Viet-Lao bonds, as Vietnam was hard pressed to provide support without Soviet patronage. Laos began to cooperate with China at a low level in security affairs, receiving modest amounts of arms and military aid.[12]

Cambodia also dealigned after the Berlin Wall came down and Cold War rivalries began to thaw. During the period when the PAVN phased out its military presence, the Khmer Rouge remained a credible threat with 30,000 to 40,000 men under arms. Subversive Khmer Rouge activity also took place throughout northwestern Cambodia. Nevertheless, the lessening of the Khmer-Vietnamese alignment was not entirely unwelcome in Phnom Penh. The 1982 Treaty of Friendship and heavy Vietnamese presence in Cambodia sustained the PRK regime, but the longer 180,000 Vietnamese troops and scores of civilian advisors remained, the more onerous the relationship became for Khmers, and the more resentment it produced. For much of modern history, Vietnamese domination has been the overriding long-term security concern of Cambodian leaders. King Norodom Sihanouk described Vietnam as a state that "used to take the kings of Cambodia and put them in cages and throw them into the ocean."[13] Thus, when the pro-Hanoi alignment became less useful as a weapon against the reviled Khmer Rouge, Cambodian leaders were eager to achieve a greater degree of independence.

To help fight the Khmer Rouge, the USSR had contributed massive material aid to the PRK regime, but the vast majority had flowed through Vietnamese hands. For Cambodian officials, continuing ties to the USSR (and later Russia) were nearly synonymous with their country's subordinated relationship to Vietnam. By the time Soviet and Vietnamese aid began to ebb in 1990, Cambodian leaders, including Chea Sim and Hun Sen, had begun stake out a more independent foreign policy position. Diminishing threats made that shift more practicable. The withdrawal of Vietnamese troops had eased Cambodia's relations with Thailand and the PRC, and by 1990 China announced that it was cutting off material support for the Khmer Rouge.[14] The Thai military also reduced its support for Pol Pot's rebel forces. These developments reduced Phnom Penh's need for external military support and allowed Cambodia to wean itself off of Vietnamese dependency. UN intervention imposed further changes in Cambodian foreign policy. In early 1992 UNTAC deployed and took over considerable responsibility for Cambodian security. In fact and by law, Cambodia was an internationally administered and nonaligned state for the eighteen months of UNTAC's mission.

The China Threat and America's Role

During the early 1990s fears remained in the maritime ASEAN states about a U.S. withdrawal from the region. The closure of Subic Bay, troubles in Thai-U.S. relations, and apparent disinterest in the Pentagon all made it appear that Uncle Sam was heading for the door. ASEAN leaders had little fear of their old nemeses in Moscow or Hanoi, because Vietnamese and Russian power had declined drastically in the region. India also was not a serious force. Japan's July 1991 entry into the U.N. peacekeeping mission in Cambodia stoked some Southeast Asian concerns, and Lee Kuan Yew famously exclaimed that UN acceptance of Japanese peacekeepers in Cambodia was "like giving chocolate liquors to an alcoholic."[15] However, Japanese domestic politics showed little movement toward increased militarization, and the 1992 reaffirmation of the U.S.-Japan alliance by President George H. W. Bush and Prime Minister Kiichi Miyazawa eased fears of a Japanese resurgence. Domestic communist insurgency also declined as a threat in most ASEAN countries, the only significant exception being the Philippines.

By contrast, China was becoming much more assertive. In February 1992 the PRC enacted a law unilaterally claiming the Paracel, Senkaku, and Spratly Islands as Chinese territory and authorizing China's armed forces to protect them. The Spratly disputes were of great concern throughout the region. The islands are believed to have oil reserves and occupy a considerable area in the South China Sea astride some of the region's busiest and most important sea-lanes. No fewer than six regional powers have laid overlapping claims: China, Vietnam, the Philippines, Taiwan, Malaysia, and Brunei. By 1992 every claimant except Brunei had stationed troops on the features they occupy, including three islands occupied by Malaysia, twenty-one by Vietnam, eight by the Philippines, one by Taiwan, and approximately eight by China. In the summer of 1992 China sent additional troops to six of its occupied islands, including Da Lac Reef, also claimed by Vietnam. Most Southeast Asian officials interpreted China's move as an effort to forcefully extend its territory deep into the heart of the region.[16] In response ASEAN foreign ministers drafted an official declaration on the South China Sea, the organization's first bona fide promulgation on regional security. The declaration insisted that competing claimants to the Spratly Islands settle the issue peacefully and issued an unprecedented public request for the U.S. military to maintain a presence in Southeast Asia.

China's military power remained suspect, but Beijing's assertive behavior in the South China Sea suggested that it would put some of its mounting economic might behind the development of a stronger navy.[17] Perceptions that China was becoming

both more potent and more domineering made the country a more immediate perceived threat to rival claimants. As Indonesian General Feisal Tanjung said in 1995, leaders in Jakarta feared that Chinese growth and assertiveness posed "a hegemonistic threat
to the region," if not to Indonesia directly. Indonesia sought to build its own defense
capacity to lessen dependence on friendly foreign powers, namely, the United States.[18]
The head of Malaysia's army also cited China's military growth as evidence of a plan to
dominate Southeast Asia: "The country to watch today would be the People's Republic
of China. Lately China has engaged in a large defence build-up . . . [If proposed pro-
curements occur,] China's military capabilities, especially in its power projection will be
significantly higher. Despite recent friendly utterances . . . it seems likely that [China's]
long-term aim is dominance, though not necessarily aggression. That surely must be
the meaning of the proposed large fleet and this factor immediately focuses attention
on the most sensitive territory in Southeast Asia—the group of Spratly Islands."[19]

In early 1995 China stationed armed naval vessels and building military structures on Mischief Reef, only 150 miles from the Filipino coast. The Mischief Reef
incident was a watershed in Southeast Asian security—China had flexed its military
muscle against a rival claimant other than Vietnam for the first time. Most ASEAN
officials saw the move as a blatant Chinese attempt to intimidate Southeast Asian
states and deter them from aligning with the United States against China in the
Spratly disputes.[20]

ASEAN threat perceptions ratcheted up another notch during the Taiwan Straits
crisis of March 1996, when the PRC conducted large exercises in the straits, including missile launches and seizure of a beachhead. Although tensions eased after
the elections, ASEAN officials generally saw a continuing pattern: China was increasingly willing to flex its military muscle to bully its neighbors. ASEAN leaders
did not rush to enter tight countervailing alliances with America, but they did inch
closer to Washington, forming limited alignments directed partly at the PRC.

Singapore Steps into the Breach
As Philippine-U.S. ties came into question, Singapore led efforts to supplement
the more limited American alliances of the post–Cold War era. In 1992 Singaporean officials approved the transfer of the U.S. logistics command for the western
Pacific from the Philippines to Singapore.[21] By 1992 Singapore was also allowing a
relatively constant rolling deployment of U.S. naval and air personnel, which represented a significant increase in security cooperation with America. Singaporean
leaders saw this arrangement as a way to preserve sovereignty while facilitating the
forward deployment of U.S. forces, which Singapore saw as a benign contributor
to the regional balance of power.[22] Interestingly, although Singapore's 1990 MOU
had initially provoked criticism from Malaysia, Indonesia, Laos, and Vietnam, those
countries did not loudly protest the transfer of the U.S. logistics command. Instead,
they quietly welcomed a slight restoration of the U.S. presence in the region to
manage the perceived China threat and quell regional tensions. Indonesia even announced that it fully agreed with the Singaporean move.[23]

Malaysia, Indonesia, and Brunei Tilt toward the United States

In addition to taking a softer position toward the U.S.-Singapore alignment, Malaysia marginally expanded its military ties to Washington, which included port calls, ship repair, air and naval exercises, and American use of Malaysian jungle combat facilities. Defence Minister Najib Razak said that Malaysia "would like to see a fair degree of American military presence in the region," which would have a "salutary countervailing effect," presumably with respect to China.[24] This was a noteworthy development for a state that had so stridently championed the ZOPFAN principle. In 1992 Malaysia and the United States signed an agreement allowing U.S. warships to be serviced at Malaysia's Lumut shipyard. Malaysia also offered to service U.S. warplanes at Subang airport and to host expanded joint exercises. That year the Malaysian government also publicly acknowledged the secret 1984 agreement between Malaysia and the United States to pursue defense cooperation through a bilateral training and consultative group. Further, U.S. and Malaysian officials acknowledged secret joint training exercises conducted since the 1970s.[25] Malaysia's quiet, limited alignment with America was essentially out of the closet.

Malaysia's more open alignment with the United States showed that despite frequent anti-American rhetoric, Prime Minister Mahathir Mohamad and his advisors saw a limited U.S. presence in the region as a key ingredient in regional security. While the Philippine bases were open, Malaysian leaders could benefit from the U.S. security presence even as they espoused strict nonalignment, but the closure of Subic Bay and Chinese pretensions in the Spratly Islands forced Malaysia to adjust. Malaysian Defense Minister Najib Razak declared that he was "happy [with] an expanding military relationship with Washington."[26]

As the closure of Subic Bay approached, Indonesia also helped to compensate by granting U.S. forces commercial access to naval ports and repair facilities on Surabaya in 1992. This occurred despite continuing congressional suspension over Indonesian IMET participation after the 1991 massacre in Dili. Indonesian officials were alarmed by PRC aggressiveness in the South China Sea, which posed a clear threat to Indonesia's interests. Politically, China also constituted a challenge to Indonesia's self-image as the natural leader of the region.[27] The PRC also claimed areas near Indonesia's Natuna Islands, which hold some of the largest proven reserves of natural gas reserves in the world. Chinese claims threatened Jakarta's ownership of those richly endowed islands and risked disrupting the heavy stream of maritime commerce vital to Indonesia's lucrative oil trade and economic well-being. Finally, the long-standing doctrine of *Wawasan Nusantara* (Archipelagic Outlook) demanded that the Indonesian armed forces defend every portion of its huge island chain to reduce the risk of maritime instability and a possible break-up of parts of the country's vast island archipelago.[28]

In 1996 the Indonesian navy conducted military exercises near the Natuna Islands. General Wiranto, leader of the forces, declared that they were intended as a signal to China and to deal with the possibility of a PRC threat in the South China Sea.[29] With China foremost in mind, Jakarta had begun open military exercises with the United States in 1990. The 1992 grant of access to shipyards in Surabaya added to that pro–U.S. alignment, although American criticisms of the Indonesian military's role in the 1991 Dili massacre in East Timor put a chill over defense relations for a time and the U.S. Congress suspended Indonesia's access to the IMET program.[30]

Although Indonesia and Malaysia did not ally tightly with America, they clearly became more open about their pro-American tilting behavior. At the 1992 NAM summit in Jakarta, Malaysian Prime Minister Mahathir Mohamad noted that the leverage of playing one superpower against the other was gone. "Where before we had the option to defect to the other side, now we have none."[31] Both Indonesian and Malaysian leaders—the strongest rhetorical adherents to nonalignment in Southeast Asia—concluded that the post–Cold War era demanded a slightly different strategy. Indonesian Foreign Minister Ali Alatas asserted that ASEAN states "can't keep [the United States, China, Japan, and Russia] out of the region" and acknowledged that the best alternative would be to achieve "equilibrium among them and between them and South-East Asia."[32] Donald Emmerson has referred to their new approach as "externalizing ZOPFAN" by seeking to engage the great powers in the region to promote the most favorable balance of outside influence in the region.[33] In practice, officials in both Jakarta and Kuala Lumpur agreed that the best balance would be struck through limited alignment with the United States.

Brunei also viewed Chinese claims to the Spratly Islands with grave concern and tilted toward Washington. Brunei has the smallest geographic claims in the South China Sea, but maritime stability in those waters is critical to the tiny, oil-trading state. To help protect its sovereign interests, Bruneian officials proposed an MOU roughly modeled on the 1990 U.S.-Singaporean agreement. In November 1994 the MOU took shape. It permitted U.S. naval visits to Bruneian facilities and committed the two states to enhanced defense cooperation via joint exercises, training, and other forms of military support. In addition, the sultan reinforced his alignment with Great Britain, concluding an agreement that ensured the Gurkha Rifles would remain in Brunei after 1998. The sultanate's stronger pro-Western ties, complemented by a stable alignment with Singapore, were intended to manage threats that it was ill equipped to deter with its own limited military means.[34]

Philippine-U.S. Ties Ebb and Flow

The Philippines was perhaps the most concerned about increased Chinese assertiveness in the South China Sea.[35] The 1995 Mischief Reef incident in particular raised Philippine interest in restoring its alliance with America and encouraged U.S. authorities to take a renewed interest in security cooperation. That year, American and Philippine forces conducted joint maneuvers near Mischief Reef and their largest Balikatan exercises since the closure of Subic Bay. In spring 1996, after another incident between Chinese ships and Filipino patrol boats, the Philippines held large joint exercises with U.S. forces near Manila Bay, and President Fidel Ramos declared that "the Philippines cannot be completely at ease in relations with China until the situation in [Mischief Reef]. . . is completely normalized." Philippine officials warned of China's "creeping invasion."[36]

The alliance was not without problems, however. Like Thailand, the Philippines did not want to serve as an American base, and Manila rejected a proposed U.S. acquisition and cross-servicing agreement in 1994 that would have given U.S. planes and ships increased access to the Philippines for a moderate fee.[37] In 1996 a larger setback occurred when the Philippine Department of Justice declared that the old Status of Forces Agreement (SOFA), which gave the United States jurisdiction over its troops stationed in the Philippines, was no longer legal. Without that provision, the Pentagon insisted that no further war games or joint exercises could occur. Although Ramos and others strongly supported continuing defense ties, neither the Philippine Department of Justice nor the Pentagon compromised, and despite Chinese naval pretensions, defense cooperation was suspended.[38]

Intramural Security Cooperation and Institutional Expansion

During the mid-1990s, the first six ASEAN members (the ASEAN-6 states) did much more than pursue limited alignments with the United States to promote their security interests. They also sought to solidify and expand their alignments with one another, creating what some have called a spiderweb of security cooperation. Although ASEAN members had made clear from the organization's founding that it was not a defense pact, bilateral defense cooperation among its members continued to increase gradually. Singapore was the most active in this regard, enhancing its bilateral military-to-military cooperation with Indonesia, Brunei, Thailand, the Philippines, Thailand, and Australia. Thailand reinforced defense ties with Indonesia through joint exercises and cooperated with Malaysia in a variety of ways to deal with the long-standing problem of insurgents near the Thai-Malaysian border. In September 1994 the Philippines and Malaysia achieved a breakthrough in their long-troubled relationship by concluding a defense cooperation pact that provided for joint military exercises, exchange of information, and possible limited use of one another's defense facilities. The Philippines also established low-level defense cooperation with Singapore through Anoa-Singa joint exercises begun in 1993, began talks with Brunei, and continued intermittent naval exercises with Indonesia.[39] These intramural links helped to unify ASEAN-6 members against external threats, smooth over regional tensions, and reduce dependence on Washington.

ASEAN-6 states also engaged Britain and Australia in regional security. Singapore and Malaysia participated in the revitalized FPDA. Britain retained strong ties to Brunei, where a battalion of Gurkha Rifles remained in Bandar Seri Begawan and continued to train and supply most of the Royal Brunei Armed Forces. Brunei also conducted military exercises with Australia. In 1996 the Philippines signed an MOU with the United Kingdom to pursue information exchanges, joint military exercises in the Pacific, and UK advisory assistance for Philippine defense. Most notably, Indonesia signed a 1995 agreement on maintaining security (AMS) with Australia. Although Foreign Minister Ali Alatas downplayed the alliance, General Hasnan Habib characterized the AMS as a military pact and asserted that the agreement "creates the impression that Indonesia has become part of the FPDA."[40] Cooperation with the

Anglo-Saxon powers added an extra layer to the spiderweb and functioned as part of a limited alignment strategy because they served as connections by proxy to the United States. Such arrangements helped increase the likelihood of U.S. support in the event of conflict without adding much risk of dependency or entrapment.

Partly to diversify their security options and reduce reliance on great-power alignments, a number of ASEAN governments (particularly the five original members of the group) also played a leading role in the explosion of multilateral organizations in the Asia-Pacific. ASEAN officials were key proponents of the Asia-Pacific Economic Cooperation forum (APEC) established in 1989 and the ASEAN Regional Forum (ARF) created in 1993.[41] ASEAN governments also helped create the Conference on Security and Cooperation in the Asia-Pacific (CSCAP) and the Asia-Europe Meeting (ASEM) in the early post–Cold War period. CSCAP is an informal track-two dialogue involving government officials, academics, and other experts in the region, who seek to build relationships and develop policy concepts for formal consideration by policy officials.

Alongside intramural alignments, confidence-building measures, and institutions, ASEAN members continued to advance norms geared to the promotion of interstate peace. Within the region, the norm of noninterference remained a cornerstone of ASEAN's approach, though that principle frequently came under legitimate attack for helping to shield repressive domestic practices from criticism. With regard to external powers, Southeast Asian states made their commitment to ZOPFAN principle more concrete by signing the Treaty on Southeast Asia Nuclear Weapon-Free Zone in 1995. Signatories were unable to convince great powers to accede to the treaty, but they did establish a new constraint on regional security affairs by agreeing not to develop, acquire, host, or otherwise facilitate the existence of nuclear weapons in the region.

Sheldon Simon has described ASEAN's efforts to establish norms and institutions alongside a protective alignment structure as the prongs of a "dual-track" strategy for regional security.[42] Alignments and national military development provide a traditional kind of protection against security challenges, and institutions and dialogue help to smooth the edges of power politics and reduce the need for regional arms races or antagonistic alignment politics. Lee Kuan Yew encapsulated the dual-track strategy in a 1996 speech at the Nixon Center in Washington: "President Nixon was a pragmatic strategist. He would engage, not contain, China, but he would also quietly, if I know him, set pieces into place for a fall back position should China not play in accordance with the rules as a good global citizen. . . . In such circumstances, where countries are forced to take sides, [Nixon] would arrange to win over to America's side of the chessboard, Japan, Korea, ASEAN, Australia, New Zealand, and the Russian Federation."[43]

In general, ASEAN-6 governments have established a fallback position by preserving limited alignments with the United States. Those arrangements ensure a soft form of American primacy in the region and provide insurance against the possibility of a threat from China or other external powers.

ASEAN-6 leaders generally viewed the dual-track strategies as compatible and mutually reinforcing. As Michael Leifer argued, the ARF was partly a way to complement alignment structures by keeping the United States engaged in the region, maximizing ASEAN's relevance, and limiting the scope for Chinese or Japanese domination. The Cold War rationale for a strong U.S. presence was gone, and Singapore's Foreign Minister Wong Kan Seng said, "I see multilateral security dialogues as another means of helping the U.S. stay engaged in this dynamic and economically important region. It creates a new rationale for a U.S. presence in the post–Cold War Asia-Pacific."[44]

To many ASEAN officials, a strong multilateral security community would reduce the necessity of living under great-power protection, and small states could wield greater influence in a system prioritizing consultative diplomacy.[45] Although the DCs of Southeast Asia could not challenge China or the United States in military terms, diplomacy could level the playing field somewhat and reduce ASEAN dependency on great-power protection.

China as an Emerging Mainland Ally

Although increasing Chinese power and assertiveness tended to provoke pro-Western alignments and a flurry of institutional initiatives in the maritime subregion, Beijing achieved closer military ties with several mainland Southeast Asian states between 1992 and 1996. All five accommodated Beijing to varying degrees, and all but Vietnam aligned with China in a limited way to manage more immediate local and neighborly security threats.

Thai-PRC Cooperation Continues

To complement the weakened Thai-U.S. alliance, the Thai government preserved informal security ties to China. The relatively passive American response to the closure of Subic Bay and Washington's suspension of ties with Thailand in 1991 had reinforced concerns that the United States would not use its military muscle to protect Thailand against regional encroachments. Like most of their ASEAN colleagues, many Thai officials feared PRC encroachment on the independence of Southeast Asian states and potential Chinese domination of the sea-lanes that are vital to Thai economic welfare. They also saw the possibility that Chinese influence would undermine Bangkok's prospective leadership of the peninsula and strengthen Thailand's traditional subregional adversaries.

However, most officials saw China as an uncertain long-term threat; Thailand's most immediate problems arose from insecure borders with its much poorer neighbors. As in the 1980s, Thai leaders saw arms purchases from China as a means to brace itself against security challenges emanating from Indochina and Myanmar.[46] Moreover, most in the Thai government saw little choice but to accommodate Chinese influence on the mainland. Cobra Gold exercises and access agreements helped keep U.S. forces engaged, but Thai officials doubted that America would be willing to confront the PRC on the Southeast Asian peninsula. Consequently,

Thailand followed its traditional policy of "bending with the wind." To manage uncertainty while securing support against short-term security challenges, it maintained limited alignments with both China and the United States.

Myanmar Builds Closer Links to Beijing

Next door to Thailand, Myanmar relied much more heavily on a strong, supportive relationship with Beijing. In 1990 opposition leader Daw Aung San Suu Kyi of the NLD swept national elections, but the junta defied the electoral results and placed her under house arrest. International opprobrium mounted steeply, and the SLORC regime became a bone fide international outcast. Myanmar turned to China, which unlike the West issued no serious criticism of the regime's behavior. For the PRC, Myanmar's misfortunes were a strategic opportunity to expand influence in Southeast Asia. The SLORC leadership was able to capitalize on Chinese interest, securing military supplies and logistical support that helped the *tatmadaw* combat or quell a number of ethnic insurgency movements through arms for peace arrangements. Among the aspects of deeper defense cooperation were substantial arms deals in 1990 and 1994, together totaling more than $1.5 billion. China helped Myanmar build conventional and counterinsurgency capabilities and provided artillery, missiles, patrol boats, fighter aircraft, and signals intelligence equipment.[47] The Sino–Myanmar security relationship thus evolved from a limited alignment to a relatively tight one.

By 1993 the back door to China appeared wide open, and Chinese influence and presence in Myanmar rose steeply. Myanmar allowed China to build up naval intelligence facilities along the Andaman Sea and contemplated granting the PRC extensive basing privileges as well. In November 1994 the two countries updated their agreements for weapons and other aid, cementing their ties and prompting the SLORC leadership to call China its "most trusted friend."[48] An agreement on sharing intelligence followed. However, fears of too much Chinese involvement in both economic and politico-military affairs began to raise concerns that the PRC would go from big brother to enemy.[49] Close alignment with Beijing also damaged Myanmar's relations with India and a number of ASEAN governments, which resented the prospect of PRC encroachment near the northwestern approaches to the Straits of Malacca. By the mid-1990s Myanmar officials thus began to put the brakes on their tightening alignment with China.

Laos and Cambodia Face New Uncertainty

Laos and Cambodia also turned toward China for security support during the early 1990s, but to a lesser extent. In Laos the long-lasting ethnic Hmong insurgency remained a challenge to the LPDR regime. The Hmong insurgents, descended from the forces supported by the U.S. and Thailand during the CIA's "Secret War" in Laos from 1961 to 1975, contributed to Lao officials' suspicion of Thai and American efforts to destabilize their regime.[50] Border clashes with Thai forces in the late 1980s had raised similar concerns about the need for foreign military support. As the Vietnamese role in Laos declined, the LPDR entered the first period in its modern history without a dominant external patron. Military and economic weakness meant that Laos had strong incentives to pursue positive relations with all of its neighbors. However, Vietnam had become much more insular, and distrust of Thailand and America put limits on the LPDR's willingness to embrace the West and its ASEAN allies. China instead began to emerge as Laos's most important security partner, surpassing Vietnam in some respects. The PRC did not give massive support like the USSR had provided during the 1980s, but it did supply modest amounts of arms and economic aid to Laos.[51]

Laos's limited alignment with China was directed to meet foreign threats as well as domestic ones. By 1994 increasing Thai influence, mainly through economic channels, concerned members of the ruling party. That year several Chinese military delegations visited Laos to discuss border security and other issues, and the two sides signed a military cooperation agreement.[52] Laos's relations with China were not without costs. The alignment was one reason why Laos was not admitted to ASEAN in 1995; some ASEAN officials saw Lao ties to the PRC as potentially destabilizing. Nevertheless, Lao and Chinese officials engaged in more frequent "ideological meetings," which Lao leaders saw as one way to avoid Thai domination or excessive dependence on a more inward-looking Vietnam.[53]

To the south, Cambodia emerged from years of occupation, civil war, and the UNTAC administration as a very weak state with insecure borders at land and sea. The Khmer Rouge remained a strong and pressing threat in the country's northwest during the annual dry season offensives in 1994 and 1995, prompting Cambodia to seek international help in fighting them. The government's appeal was not very successful. Thailand was concerned about supplying military muscle to Cambodia, because it feared spillover from increased border-area fighting. Western countries also offered scant military aid, though the United States and others offered technical and economic support.[54] Cambodia remained vulnerable and in search of allies.

Only in 1995 did Phnom Penh begin to make progress in achieving domestic security and external support through low-level cooperation with China. Ties to the PRC helped unlock the Khmer Rouge problem. The following year senior Khmer Rouge official Ieng Sary defected and signed an amnesty agreement with Phnom Penh, taking 3,000 troops with him and leaving Pol Pot's Khmer Rouge forces with only about 4,000 poorly organized guerillas. At nearly the same time, Phnom Penh realized a breakthrough in relations with China. The PRC agreed to a $1 million military aid package for the training and equipment of Cambodia's army. Shortly afterward Hun Sen visited Beijing and signed further agreements with Jiang Zemin on trade, investment, and an accord of cooperation between the Cambodian People's Party (CPP) and Chinese Communist Party. This modest alignment was a striking change from the years of Sino-Khmer acrimony during the era of Vietnamese occupation. By that point China had become a special friend of the CPP-led regime in Phnom Penh and the strategic backbone of Cambodia's security, helping keep Thailand and Vietnam at bay. By 1999 Cambodia was the top recipient of Chinese aid, receiving more than $200 million. China also expressed a growing interest in defense cooperation, and some analysts believed that Beijing sought naval access to the port of Kampong Sam.[55]

Vietnam Seeks Great-Power Support

Vietnam was the only mainland state that did not embrace a measure of security ties with China after the resolution of the Third Indochina War. Like its maritime neighbors, Vietnam reacted critically to China's 1992 claims in the South China Sea. Policymakers in Hanoi feared that it would gradually seize key islands and atolls, control lucrative oil and gas reserves, preside over vital sea-lanes and fishing areas, and otherwise exert dominance after the U.S. departure from Subic Bay. In addition to the Spratly Island dispute, the demarcation of Vietnam's land border and maritime border with China in the Gulf of Tonkin remained unresolved. VCP leaders believed that Vietnam could not stand up to China alone in a military conflict and sought external support.[56] Vietnam also continued to face severe economic problems that threatened to undermine the VCP's domestic position. Its mainland neighbors could provide little succor. Laos remained weak, Cambodia was in the midst of political upheaval, and Vietnam and Thailand built a new friendship that was fragile at best.

VCP leaders attempted to manage security threats not through an overt anti-Chinese alignment but by cautious accommodation and continuing efforts to join ASEAN and normalize relations with the United States. In November 1991 Vietnamese and Chinese officials met for the first time since normalization to end twelve years of estrangement. Vietnam pressed China to provide security guarantees that would have established a limited alignment of sorts. China refused, saying that the sides could be "comrades, but not allies."[57] At the same time, as Russian forces departed, Vietnam reportedly introduced the possibility of U.S. access to the large naval facilities at Cam Ranh Bay.[58] This drew a rebuke from China, which insisted that no foreign power establish a military presence in Vietnam. Although the United States and Vietnam normalized relations in 1994, and VCP officials sought some modest level of cooperation, no alignment materialized. This caused one Vietnamese official to conclude that "if the United States does not show some signs of support for the smaller states on the [Spratlys] issue, Vietnam will have no choice but to accommodate China."[59]

Vietnam continued to move toward ASEAN membership and pursued a new policy of "friends everywhere" to reduce its exposure to the PRC and shore up its domestic financial and political positions. It did not become enmeshed in the ASEAN-6 spiderweb of alignments—trust was still scarce between old adversaries—but it did renew its alignment with Russia through a new 1994 friendship treaty and an agreement for bilateral military cooperation. The unpublished agreement reportedly provided for bilateral consultations in the event of a crisis, but it offered little material aid. In fact, the Russian government announced that material support would fall once again.[60] Thus, Vietnam remained in search of credible external security support to offset the perceived threat from the north.

Table 3.1 Alignment Postures, 1992–1996

Country	Ally	Alignment Status
Brunei	USA	Limited alignment
Cambodia	PRC	No alignment → limited alignment (1995)
Indonesia	USA	Limited alignment
Laos	PRC	No alignment → Limited alignment (1992)
Malaysia	USA	Limited alignment
Myanmar	PRC	Tight alliance → limited alignment (1995)
Philippines	USA	Tight alliance → limited alignment (1992)
Singapore	USA	Limited alignment
Thailand	PRC	Limited alignment
	USA	Limited alignment
Vietnam		No alignment

Source: Author's compilation

Regional Alignment Overview, 1992–1996

The early post–Cold War period thus saw a gradual polarization of sorts in Southeast Asian alignments. The Thai and Philippine alliances to the United States were weakened, but other ASEAN states stepped forward to ensure that Washington remained the dominant great-power alignment partner for states in the maritime subregion. The 1995–1996 period was also the high-water mark for intra-ASEAN defense cooperation and ASEAN-6 ties to the ANZUK states of Australia, New Zealand, and the United Kingdom.

During the same period, however, China established itself in an increasingly central position in the alignment framework of mainland Southeast Asia. Some analysts even began to forecast a return to China's status as a suzerain power with ties to surrounding tributary states.[61] That analogy exaggerated China's influence in the subregion, but Beijing did make considerable inroads into mainland Southeast Asia during the early post–Cold War period. In many respects the PRC emerged as the preeminent external power engaged in peninsular security affairs, with four of five states entering limited alignments with the PRC (table 3.1).

FINANCIAL CRISIS AND ITS AFTERMATH, 1997–2001

The Asian financial crisis of 1997, turbulence in Indonesia, and the East Timor crisis of 1999 shook the confidence of ASEAN states. Coming on the heels of the haze crisis, during which toxic Indonesian smog engulfed some of its ASEAN neighbors, these crises damaged a number of bilateral ties and diminished ASEAN's perceived capacity to manage regional security threats. The introduction of Laos, Myanmar, and Cambodia into ASEAN between 1997 and 1999 also challenged the organization's solidarity on security matters and led to intra-organizational disputes about human rights and the norm of noninterference. Bilateral flare-ups and ethnic tensions became more frequent, and despite regional criticisms of an inadequate external response to the financial crisis, this tended to weaken the ASEAN "spider-web" of bilateral security cooperation and led Singapore in particular to put added priority on its alignment with the United States.

During the late 1990s China also continued to make economic and political in-roads into the region. Officials in Beijing began to take a more conciliatory diplo-matic approach to the South China Sea disputes, participated more fully in regional institutions like the ARF, and launched something of a diplomatic charm offensive garnished with economic aid. China's help for Southeast Asian capitals during the 1997–1998 financial crisis helped diminish short-term fears of the PRC. Neverthe-less, the steep ascent of China's economy and its growing military arsenal kept the PRC on the radar of many Southeast Asian leaders as a potential medium–term threat to regional independence and stability. That threat helped drive the resuscita-tion of the U.S.-Philippine alliance.

The Financial Crisis and ASEAN-6 Alignments

Between 1997 and 1999 the ASEAN states underwent a series of challenges that strained many relationships and led to changes in some governments' alignment policies. The most profound regional challenge was the Asian financial meltdown that reversed an unprecedented period of rapid ASEAN economic growth, spurred by massive foreign capital inflows. A number of factors arguably caused the crisis, including weak domestic financial systems, capital and current account imbalances, and excessive Western currency speculation. The result of these forces was a pre-cipitous collapse of the Thai baht and Bangkok stock exchange in July 1997. In the more interdependent post–Cold War economic system, panic soon spread to mar-kets throughout Southeast Asia and beyond, creating what some dubbed the "Asian contagion." From 1997 to 1999 per capita GDP in the ASEAN region declined by roughly 33 percent, seriously challenging the performance legitimacy of several Southeast Asian regimes.

After the crash, the Thai government was forced to secure an IMF bailout, and the Fund provided a loan of $17 billion. Indonesia had to seek even more exten-sive bailout led by the IMF, World Bank, and Asian Development Bank and total-ing some $40 billion. However, the IMF response hurt America's relationship with ASEAN capitals more than it helped; recipients complained that disbursement was too slow and that the harsh conditionality attached to IMF programs was inappro-priate for their specific country conditions. Some in the region even accused the United States of orchestrating the crisis to dampen Asian growth that challenged American economic supremacy.[62]

ASEAN Tumult and Ire

The Asian financial crisis injured most states in the region but wreaked greatest dev-astation on Indonesia, where GDP fell by a staggering 13 percent in 1998 alone.[63] The collapse of the rupiah and economic recession strained Indonesia's ability to pay its foreign debt and unmasked public frustration with the Suharto regime and latent resentment of the country's economically dominant ethnic Chinese minority. Government repression of rioters targeting Chinese-owned businesses added to the wave of popular dissent, magnified charges of corruption, and brought the collapse of the Suharto regime in 1998.

The crisis also hurt America's standing in Malaysia and Thailand, where officials perceived the United States as quick to criticize but slow to help regional economies in need. Prime Minister Mahathir Mohamed was the most vocal leader in the region espousing the view that Western currency speculators and other predatory financial actors had caused the crisis. Thai authorities held the U.S. government largely responsible for the perceived flaws of the IMF bailout package. In particular, they resented the pace of financial disbursement and requirements to liberalize the Thai economy, which resulted in foreign ownership of many local financial institutions. The U.S. failure to provide backup loans added to Bangkok's frustration.

Japan provided much of the financing for the bailout, but China was also a major beneficiary of ASEAN anger toward the West. The PRC did not offer as much money to the affected economies but came to the aid of Southeast Asian neighbors more quickly and with fewer strings attached. In particular, China provided Thailand with $1 billion of backup loans to supplement the IMF package. The PRC also refused to devalue the renminbi, which would have helped Chinese exporters but could have sparked another round of competitive devaluations in the ASEAN region. China's behavior won it considerable plaudits and helped the PRC develop greater soft power in the region. Nevertheless, alignment postures remained intact. U.S.-Malaysian cooperation continued beneath the strident critiques of Mahathir. Thai-U.S. defense cooperation increased modestly in the late 1990s in response to the pressing threat of drug-related conflict near the Myanmar border. In the absence of a clear external threat to Thai sovereign interests, this and other nontraditional security concerns became an increasingly important rationale for the alliance.

Singapore and the Changi Naval Base

If the financial crisis drove a wedge between the United States and some of its regional security partners, it had the opposite effect in Singapore. The Lion City did not perceive the Western response to the crisis as ideal by any means, but its frustration with Washington paled beside its fear of rising regional tensions. Shortly after B. J. Habibie took office in Jakarta in May 1998, Habibie referred to Singapore as nothing more than a "red dot" on the map, chiding its smaller neighbor for alleged discrimination against Malays and for being "a fair-weather friend" during the financial crisis.[64] A few months later worsening relations with Singapore led Malaysia to cancel its participation in the annual FPDA exercises.

As China gained regional influence and larger neighbors menaced the wealthy city-state, Singapore increased its defense ties with Washington. In early 1998 Singapore announced the construction of an expanded Changi naval base to facilitate and solidify an American naval presence in the region. The most important feature of the expanded Changi base is its ability to accommodate aircraft carriers—Port

Klang in Malaysia is the only other site in the region with that capacity. Singaporean officials acknowledged that the facility was specifically constructed to host U.S. forces. Lee Kuan Yew noted that no Asian power "will be able to balance China . . . the role of America as balancer is crucial if we are to have elbow room."[65] Defense Minister Tony Tan announced that U.S. aircraft carriers and warships would be welcome in the base as an alternative to off-shore anchorage and added, "it's no secret that Singapore believes that the presence of the U.S. military in this part of the world contributes to the peace and security of the region."[66] In November 1998 Singapore and Washington signed an addendum to their 1990 MOU, and in April 2000 the parties concluded an implementing arrangement to govern American use of the new facilities.

Philippine-U.S. Alliance Reinvigorated

The Asian financial crisis also had little negative effect on the Philippine-U.S. alliance, despite the considerable losses the Philippine economy suffered. Instead, mounting tensions with Beijing in the Spratly Islands tended to strengthen Philippine-U.S. security cooperation. Incidents around Mischief Reef, Scarborough Shoal, and Philippine-held Kota Island kept the China threat at the fore of Philippine defense concerns. One top Philippine official exclaimed, "[The PRC] would like to convert the South China Sea into their own lake. China is looking at these reefs as potential [aircraft] carriers."[67] Philippine officials also worried about intra-ASEAN tensions in the Spratlys. In July 1999 Malaysia and the Philippines sparred over a new Malaysian construction on Investigator Shoal in a Philippine-claimed area.[68] Philippine armed forces, described by one general in Manila as "an air force that can't fly and a navy that can't put to sea," were inadequate for the task.[69]

By 1999 perceptions of Chinese aggressiveness, ASEAN disunity, and a new form of Philippine nationalism prompted a reinvigoration of the U.S. alliance and a resolution of the SOFA issue that had paralyzed cooperation for more than two years. In May of 1999 the Philippine Senate overwhelmingly ratified a new visiting forces agreement (VFA) that allowed U.S. forces to come back to the Philippines without facing Philippine jurisdiction, and joint military exercises resumed. Philippine President Joseph Estrada publicly described the VFA as a check on "creeping assertiveness" by the PRC in the South China Sea, especially around Mischief Reef.[70] Senator Blas Ople added that "the one factor that restrains China's hawks is the realization that the Philippines is bound to the United States through the Mutual Defense Treaty.[71]

New ASEAN States Seek to Diversify

Between 1997 and 2001, as ASEAN-6 states adjusted their relations with the United States, the four newer members of ASEAN—Vietnam, Laos, Cambodia, and Myanmar—generally sought diversification of their alignments and reduced reliance on China. Perhaps the most obvious manifestation of that effort was that all four joined ASEAN as part of an effort to develop enhanced security relations with their Southeast Asian neighbors and to provide an institutional complement to traditional alignment structures. After Vietnam's 1995 accession, Laos and Myanmar followed in 1997, and Cambodia became the tenth member in 1999. These new members did not become part of the ASEAN-6 web of intramural security alignments, but with the exception of Cambodia, the new ASEAN states also took visible measures to form new alignments with extraregional partners.

Myanmar Comes Out of Its Shell

Myanmar had become the most dependent on China during the mid-1990s, but with its entry into ASEAN, it restored a modicum of international engagement. However, by allying tightly during the early 1990s, Myanmar officials found themselves drifting to an uncomfortable degree into China's strategic orbit, risking satellite status. The need for great-power security support remained high in Yangon. Insurgencies returned in force, and relations with Thailand deteriorated. Tensions revolved around renewed cross-border activities of the United Wa State Army, Shan United Revolutionary Army, and other insurgent groups that often flooded Thailand with illegal drugs to fund conflict. Thailand retaliated in part by cracking down on huge numbers of illegal Burmese immigrant workers. In 2001 Thai and Myanmar forces engaged in border clashes, one of the few incidents of intra-ASEAN armed hostility since the organization's founding in 1967. The SLORC regime continued to rely primarily on China for military support, but fears continued to rise about too much Chinese influence and mounting numbers of illegal Chinese immigrants. By the mid-1990s Myanmar thus began to pull away and limit its alignment with the PRC.[72]

After the mid-1990s Yangon and New Delhi improved their security relations, especially when the new Bharatiya Janata Party came to power in India in 1998. The two sides cemented bilateral security cooperation along the border and agreed on a range of other cooperative measures in 2000.[73] For Myanmar, rapprochement with New Delhi was partly a bid to reduce excessive exposure to Beijing.

Vietnam Seeks Friends Everywhere

By 1998 Vietnam shared the Indian concern about Chinese influence in Myanmar as well as PRC pretensions in the South China Sea. The VCP had been successful in eliminating significant armed insurgency in the country, and after normalizing relations, the perceived U.S. threat continued to diminish.[74] Relations with China generally improved after the December 1999 agreement on the land demarcation, but Spratly Island concerns remained. Immediately after his election as VCP secretary-general in 2001, Nong Duc Manh pledged an improvement in Sino-Vietnamese relations as part of the country's policy of diversifying its international ties to protect its sovereignty and independence. The CPV Central Committee expressed its intention to improve relations with "socialist countries and neighboring countries and with traditionally friendly countries."[75]

As part of its effort to diversify its security relations and moderate the Chinese threat, Hanoi cautiously and quietly approached the United States for limited contacts on defense issues. Military dialogue between the two countries expanded through increasingly high-level military delegations, culminating in a 2000 visit to Vietnam by U.S. Defense Secretary William Cohen. Vietnam was reluctant to press for a fuller military agreement with the U.S.—wary of offending China and still suspicious of the United States. The U.S. engagement in Kosovo frightened many Vietnamese officials, who saw the application of high-tech American weaponry through the lens of past experience and believed U.S. force could again be directed at Vietnam.[76] Instead of aligning with America, Vietnam pursued ties with other middle powers, signing separate bilateral agreements to engage in defense training and technical cooperation with Russia in 1999 and India in 2000.[77]

Vietnam continued to perceive domestic challenges from ethnic rebel groups, particularly in the central highlands. In early 2001 unpopular resettlement programs related to economic development projects sparked an uprising among indigenous minority groups that lasted for nearly two months before the army was able to quell the unrest. Hanoi announced that U.S.-backed Christian minorities had planned the uprising to establish an autonomous state called Dega in the central highlands. Vietnamese officials pointed to the Montagnard Foundation, based in South Carolina, as a primary sponsor of the rebel Christian forces.[78] The following month Cambodian officials arrested a number of alleged members of the United Front for the Liberation of Oppressed Races (FULRO), a group of ethnic rebels organized by the CIA during the Second Indochina War and still active in the jungles of Cambodian Mondulkiri and the Vietnamese central highlands. The American demand that they be granted asylum in the United States reinforced Vietnamese perceptions that certain domestic threats continue to relate closely to American efforts to undermine the regime.[79]

Laos Steers Back toward Vietnam

After the Asian financial crisis, Laos faced particularly severe difficulties meeting its military and economic requirements. The LPRP had relinquished its strict adherence to socialist principles in preceding years, and its dominant alignment concern had become an effort to preserve power and regime security. In general, the LPRP viewed Thailand as its greatest menace. More people of Lao ethnicity live in Thailand (roughly 20 million) than in all of Laos (approximately 5 million), giving the Thai government tremendous cultural levers, as well as military, political, and economic means, to disrupt the Lao regime. The primary debate within Lao foreign policy circles centered on which of two neighboring powers—China or Vietnam—was the more appropriate ally to help offset the perceived threat emanating from Thailand. Lao leaders of the older generation tended to continue to favor alignment with Vietnam, seeing the two countries as historically and ideologically "as close as lips and teeth." Younger officials generally favored rapprochement with China.[80]

The PRC remained Laos's chief external security patron at the outset; in 1998 Laos continued regular exchanges of military, party, and state delegations with China, and in 1999 the Lao minister of defense visited Beijing to discuss reviving a

1994 military cooperation agreement.[81] However, Viet-Lao security ties reemerged in the late 1990s, largely in response to renewed activity by Hmong rebels, whom the Lao People's Army was unable to defeat.[82] Internal strife—including a series of high-profile bombings in Vientiane—added to the country's economic woes and sense of regime insecurity. By 2000 Laos had requested and received Vietnamese troops to help fight off the escalation of a Hmong rebellion in the northeastern province of Xiang Khouang. This military cooperation was accompanied by more open and obvious increases in ideological and economic support. China also increased its economic ties to Laos, but by 2001 Chinese military involvement in Laos was less extensive than it had been in the mid-1990s.[83] Overall, Laos settled into a position characterized by limited ties to both Beijing and Hanoi.

Managing Chinese Leadership on the Mainland

Among the four new ASEAN states, only Cambodia showed little apparent interest in complementing its modest alignment with Beijing. China remained Cambodia's chief external partner, supplying limited military and substantial civilian aid.[84] That assistance was critical after an alleged coup by Hun Sen and the CPP in July 1997, in which the CPP marginalized the rival royalist party under Norodom Ranariddh. The alleged coup led to a cessation of American aid flows and an international cold shoulder to Cambodia. The limited Sino-Cambodian alignment thus resembles Myanmar's 1989 experience—officials in Phnom Penh had few places to go for much-needed aid, but China extended a welcoming hand. China was the first to recognize the reconstituted government and the first to provide military aid after the CPP solidified its grip on power. By 2003 Hun Sen hailed China as Cambodia's "most trustworthy friend."[85] That relationship signals a return to the ties that those states frequently displayed before 1979, an attraction based largely on a common wariness of Vietnam but also on the Cambodian government's need for economic support.

ASEAN's Expansion and Regional Institutional Changes

As Southeast Asian governments modified their alignments to cope with the stresses brought on by the Asian financial crisis, efforts to build stronger regional security institutions continued. The institutionalization of Southeast Asian security had considerable momentum during the mid-1990s—promising a strong complement to great-power alignments—but the Asian financial meltdown sapped that momentum considerably. ASEAN, APEC and the ARF all lost prestige after the financial crisis, the Indonesian haze crisis, and the East Timor crisis. The inability of those institutions to take meaningful independent action in such events suggested to most observers that they could not be counted on to serve central, decisive roles in a security crisis. In addition, ASEAN's expansion put strains on the relative normative cohesion of the organization, most evident in relations with Cambodia during the alleged coup of 1997 and with Myanmar after its admission in the same year.[86]

The stress on regional security became even greater with the 1999 East Timor crisis, in which government forces were heavily implicated in the violent suppression of the Timorese bid for independence. Indonesia's economic dependence on the IMF and multilateral development banks empowered the U.S. and Australian governments to criticize Indonesian human rights abuses and facilitate the creation of an independent East Timor. The East Timor crisis was a blow to intra-ASEAN unity, showing the fragility of the organization's largest member. It also gravely injured Indonesia's relations with the West. Immediately after Australia led international peacekeeping forces into East Timor, Jakarta abrogated its 1995 bilateral security treaty. In the meantime, the U.S. Congress imposed a suspension of military cooperation with Indonesia due to the alleged human rights abuses committed in East Timor.

For many Southeast Asian skeptics, the late 1990s showed that such institutions were of limited value in meeting real security challenges. Instead, they were best considered discussion forums to complement the region's complex web of bilateral relationships, keep the great powers engaged in dialogue, and smooth the rough edges of conflictual power politics.[87] Nevertheless, as APEC and the ARF lost prestige, ASEAN's institutional push continued through the formal creation in 1999 of the ASEAN+3 forum, which also included China, Japan, and South Korea.

One of the key objectives of the ASEAN normative-institutional agenda has been to socialize China and manage its rise without incurring undue PRC hostility. As Lee Kuan Yew emphasized, "The question is: Can the world develop a system in which a country the size of China becomes part of the management of international peace and stability? . . . we have to find a place for China when it becomes a major economic and military power."[88]

Regional institutions do appear to have provided a way for Southeast Asian officials to become more familiar with their Chinese counterparts (and vice versa) since the end of the Cold War. During the same period ASEAN leaders' threat perceptions of China generally appear to have diminished. The effect of norms and institutions is difficult to measure; economic ties and other factors have doubtlessly also contributed to changing perceptions of China as well. However, the sheer volume of meetings among ASEAN officials—now more than 600 per year—has created an epistemic community of officials that serves as a modest buttress against regional conflict by establishing expectations of peaceful dispute management. In a few cases, ASEAN has also helped Southeast Asian states stand up to China without requiring major U.S. support. In the early 1990s ASEAN was influential in deterring China from aggressive behavior in the South China Sea even after the U.S. government left Subic Bay and cast doubt on its intention to protect the Spratlys, and in the mid-1990s, Vietnam used ASEAN membership as one way to reduce their exposure to China. Institutions appear to have contributed to limited alignments by lowering the perceived need for tight balancing alliances.

Regional Alignment Overview, 1997–2001

From 1997 to 2001, alignment shifts in Southeast Asia were relatively subtle and complex (see table 3.2). The Asian financial crisis created strains among ASEAN members, particularly in the maritime subregion, and exposed the organization's

Table 3.2 Alignment Postures, 1997–2001

Country	Ally	Alignment Status
Brunei	USA	Limited alignment
Cambodia	PRC	Limited alignment
Indonesia	USA	Limited alignment
Laos	PRC	Limited alignment
Malaysia	USA	Limited alignment
Myanmar	PRC	Limited alignment
Philippines	USA	Limited alignment
Singapore	USA	Limited alignment
Thailand	PRC	Limited alignment
	USA	Limited alignment
Vietnam		No alignment

Source: Author's compilation

vulnerability. By weakening regional solidarity, the crisis tended to make great-power cooperation marginally more important to the ASEAN states.

Singapore aligned somewhat more clearly with the United States, and the Philippines resumed cooperation as its confidence grew in ASEAN's capacity to moderate Chinese advances in the South China Sea, though both alignments fell short of what this book would describe as tight alliances. Thailand modestly deepened its links with the United States as well, partly to manage some of the domestic insecurity that followed the country's economic plunge. Malaysia was highly critical of the U.S. role in the crisis response and endured vocal disputes with Washington on human rights issues, but in the absence of more attractive alternative security arrangements, bilateral defense ties remained intact. Only Indonesia moved away from the Western alliance structure, severing ties with Australia over East Timor and incurring congressionally imposed suspension of U.S. military aid.

The four new ASEAN members pursued somewhat divergent paths. Cambodia embraced closer ties to China, principally in the economic sphere but also involving a modest level of defense cooperation. The remaining mainland states showed decreasing enthusiasm for China as a dominant military ally. Added Indian involvement through modest defense cooperation with Vietnam and Myanmar was one sign; Laos's ties to Vietnam were also noteworthy. The alignment structure on peninsular Southeast Asia thus became marginally more complex, reflecting the lack of a shared security outlook among governments in the subregion. China remained in a central and highly influential position, but Vietnam, Laos, Myanmar, and Thailand all preserved, created, or reinstated alignments with other partners that buttress their security.

THE CONTEMPORARY PERIOD, 2002–2010

The attacks of September 11 marked another watershed in regional security and had several consequences for regional alignment preferences. Southeast Asia became identified as a second front in the campaign against terrorism, and the increased menace from regional al-Qaeda affiliates such as Jemaah Islamiyah added a new wrinkle to regional security, especially in the ASEAN-6 states. It drove up the need for external security support in the region but also reinforced some of the domestic perils of alignment with America. The effect of 9/11 and the ensuing U.S. war on terror differed across the region, primarily because of domestic political factors rather than systemic effects. Muslim-majority states have continued to cooperate quietly and to keep America at arm's length out of suspicion of U.S. motives and for fear of domestic backlash. States with non-Muslim majorities, particularly the Philippines, have veered somewhat closer to America, perceiving the U.S. government as broadly committed to their security and less fearful of internal political repercussions.

A related trend in regional security has been the increasing attention given by Southeast Asian defense planners to nontraditional security issues. These involve focusing military resources on threats such as terrorism, piracy, and transnational crime but also contingencies stemming from natural disasters, disease outbreaks, and the like. Addressing these complex international issues has required Southeast Asian states to work with multiple bilateral partners, international organizations, and civil society organizations. This has added incentives to keep ties flexible and avoid divisive, exclusive defense pacts.

The continued growth in Chinese power and influence in the region has been a third major external variable affecting alignment politics in Southeast Asia since 2001. China has expanded on a charm offensive, leaving ideological lectures behind and becoming a much more active, confident, and pragmatic player in regional diplomacy. At the same time its trade and investment ties have boomed. Engagement appears to have moderated perceptions of the China threat in many Southeast Asian capitals, and has certainly provided ASEAN governments with concrete disincentives to ally tightly against the PRC and risk its wrath. Thus China's rise has not prompted a major rethink of ASEAN alignment preferences or produced calls for either robust balancing or bandwagoning arrangements.

Reinforcement of Traditional U.S. Alignments

For Southeast Asian governments facing threats from local terrorist groups, the new American priority after 9/11 translated into additional resources for allies and additional credibility.[89] Some Southeast Asian terrorist groups also bear apparent connections to al-Qaeda, and the Bush administration has aggressively reached out to ASEAN states to cooperate in fighting local extremist groups. The war on terror has added a new wrinkle to the alignment politics of the region, because Washington now views some domestic insurgents in ASEAN states as threats to American security. In a sense, that development is reminiscent of the Cold War era, when U.S. and certain ASEAN officials shared a common fear of local communist movements in Southeast Asia.

The well-chronicled reemergence of Islamic extremism and terrorism in Southeast Asia has clearly affected regional threat perceptions. A number of known terrorist organizations have been active in the region, including the radical Islamic group Jemaah Islamiyah. Terrorist cells have been active across the region and have become major internal threats to a number of states in the region, by both challenging the governing regimes and jeopardizing economies through their adverse impact on finance and tourism. Senior Singaporean diplomat Bilahari Kausikan called it the number one threat in the region.[90] The October 2002 Bali blast and numerous smaller attacks—such as the 2003 bombs in the Davao City and attacks against military installments in southern Thailand—highlighted the growing problem. All five of the original ASEAN members have emerged as frontline states in the conflict against terrorism.

In Thailand, the Philippines, and to a lesser extent Singapore, simmering ethnic conflicts involving Muslim minorities have tended to magnify the ethno-religious dimension of governments' internal threat perceptions and create a sense of common cause with the United States. Although officials in Bangkok and Manila have tried not to characterize their conflicts with rebel groups in cultural terms, the struggles of the Malay peoples around Pattani and the Moros in Mindanao have always had an obvious ethnic dimension. Those conflicts also possess a religious aspect that has become more obvious since the 9/11 attacks and the subsequent Bali bombings in 2002 and Jakarta hotel bombings in 2003 and 2009. At times, struggles against ethnic Malay separatists have caused tension between Thailand and the Philippines and their Muslim-majority neighbors, Malaysia and Indonesia. Arab and South Asian links to local insurgent or terrorist groups have also drawn Thailand and the Philippines into the broader campaign against terrorism that many officials perceive—rightly or wrongly—as rooted in civilizational differences.

Philippine-U.S. Alliance

The war on terror has raised the degree of military and intelligence cooperation between Washington and several ASEAN states, especially the Philippines. Unlike Malaysia or Indonesia, the Philippines quickly and resolutely announced its support for the U.S. war on terror. During a November 2001 visit to Washington, President Gloria Macapagal Arroyo said, "The American and Filipino people stand together in the global campaign against terrorism."[91] Arroyo acknowledged the political costs of closer alignment but announced that the Philippines would be willing to pay a price for cooperation with the U.S.-led antiterrorist campaign. She offered American forces access to Clark Air Field and Subic Bay Naval Base for transit to Afghanistan, and some troops. Domestically, Arroyo defended her decision as a means to secure American aid in the country's battle against terrorism in the southwest Philippines, though some opposition voices accused her of using Abu Sayyaf as an excuse to rekindle a broader strategic alliance along the Cold War model.[92]

In January 2002 the Philippine government approved a U.S. proposal whereby hundreds of U.S. troops deployed to Mindanao to train Filipino soldiers in counterterrorism tactics and engage in joint exercises. American forces quickly established a number of logistical facilities and an operating base on the Abu Sayyaf stronghold of Basilan Island, and the Philippines became the only Southeast Asian country permitting the ground deployment of U.S. forces on its territory since 9/11. According to the terms of reference governing the cooperation, temporary U.S. bases were established, and the primarily American role was for training. However, American troops were permitted to fight in self-defense, opening both the possibility of wider American involvement and old debates about Philippine dependency on the United States.[93] By mid-2002 more than 1,000 American troops were active in the country, mostly on the southern Island of Mindanao. In August Philippine Defense Secretary Angelo Reyes and U.S. Defense Secretary Donald Rumsfeld signed an agreement that expanded bilateral ties through the creation of a political committee to supervise military-to-military programs.

The United States and the Philippines also signed a mutual logistics support agreement in 2002, and in 2003 the U.S. government designated the Philippines a major non-NATO ally. President Bush stood before the Philippine Congress and said that the two countries are "bound by the strongest ties that two nations can share."[94] Status as a non-NATO ally gave the Arroyo administration access to considerably greater military support. American military aid to the Philippines shot up from less than $2 million in 2001 to more than $125 million in 2004, making the Philippines the largest recipient of U.S. military assistance in East Asia. U.S. and Philippine forces held eighteen joint military exercises in 2004 alone, reflecting the rising security cooperation. The Philippines sent troops to Iraq briefly, though it elected to pull them back in the face of popular opposition at home. Increased cooperation with Washington has also provided economic benefits to the Philippines, because Arroyo secured a commitment for $4.6 billion in American military and economic aid. The relationship did not become as robust as it had been during the Cold War but became closer and can once again be described fairly as a tight alliance.[95]

The extended presence of U.S. troops on Philippine soil has reopened some old wounds, sparking occasional protests by domestic opponents of the alliance. The debate has focused largely on issues of sovereignty and national independence. After a high-profile rape case involving a U.S. soldier and allegations that American forces were engaging in combat operations, a group of nationalist political leaders challenged the constitutionality of the 1999 VFA, pursuant to which U.S. troops are allowed to operate in the country. The Philippine Supreme Court ruled that the VFA was constitutional and affirmed that decision in March 2010, but the dispute has reinforced the intensity of domestic opposition to a tight alliance relationship.[96]

A Stronger Singapore-U.S. Alignment

The September 11 attacks were deeply concerning for Singapore, which more publicly than ever identified itself as a friend of the United States. The small size of the city-state, its location, and its large Muslim minority population all made Singapore vulnerable to attack by radical Islamic groups. The importance of the local financial industry also meant that a single attack could be economically devastating by reducing confidence in local capital markets. Prime Minister Goh Chok Tong asserted that his country was a friend but not a client state or an ally of the United States. However, Singapore aligned itself strategically with the United States, and Goh acknowledged that its "interests coincide [with America's] in the short term, medium term and in a strategic sense."[97]

As the war on terror intensified, new Prime Minister Lee Hsien Loong made it clear that his government would seek protection through a solid U.S. alignment. Singapore was one of the few countries in Asia—along with Thailand and the Philippines—to join the American coalition of the willing in Iraq and send personnel to aid American forces. Its support for controversial American foreign policy endeavors arguably made Singapore the most important U.S. ally in the region. As Lee said, "Singapore and the U.S. have always shared a common vision of promoting stability, security and prosperity in Asia. Singapore has consistently supported a strong US presence in the region. While we are not treaty allies, we cooperate on many security matters. Singapore strongly supports U.S. efforts in the global war on terrorism and in countering the proliferation of weapons of mass destruction. We also support the war in Iraq."[98]

In July 2005 Lee and President George W. Bush signed a strategic framework agreement that defined Singapore as a major security cooperation partner of the United States.[99] The Changi naval base helped Singapore facilitate a more active role for the U.S. Navy in Southeast Asian waterways, as did the rotational deployment of American F-16 fighter aircraft. Roughly 100 U.S. naval vessels now visit Singapore each year, and Singapore has become a U.S. partner in the development of a new joint strike fighter aircraft. Primarily through Singaporean and Philippine alignments, American forces thus continue to play the role of a major offshore balancer in Southeast Asia, and through Singaporean and Philippine ties, the U.S. defense presence in the region was stronger by 2005 than any time since the closure of Subic Bay.[100] The American presence has remained relatively steady to this day.

Thai-U.S. Cooperation Rebounds

To a slightly lesser degree, Thailand has also responded to U.S. overtures for closer defense and security ties since 9/11. In 2003 Thailand became the first Southeast Asian country to obtain advanced Amraam missiles for its F-16 fighter aircraft. That year, head of the U.S. Pacific command Admiral Thomas Fargo praised Thailand for its "outstanding military-to-military relationship with the U.S.," and during a visit to the Royal Thai Army headquarters, President Bush designated Thailand a major non-NATO U.S. ally.[101] Non-NATO ally designation gives Thailand greater access to American military and economic aid, including credit guarantees for costly weapons purchases. Thailand contributed hundreds of troops to the U.S.-led wars in Afghanistan and Iraq, although Prime Minister Thaksin Shinawatra withdrew forces from Iraq in late 2004 under strong domestic pressure. Thai airfields and ports nevertheless remained critical in supporting U.S. transport of personnel and equipment to both Afghanistan and Iraq. Thailand also served as the primary hub for American relief efforts after the 2004 Indian Ocean tsunami that devastated a number of littoral areas in South and Southeast Asia.

In addition to reinvigorating military ties, Thailand and the United States cooperated more closely in law enforcement and counterterrorism measures after 9/11. The two countries established a Counter Terrorism Intelligence Center in 2001, providing a venue for close collaboration between Thai authorities and the CIA. In 2003 a joint Thai–U.S. operation led to the highly publicized arrest of the radical Islamic leader Hambali on Thai soil. The resumption of violence in Thailand's majority-Muslim southern provinces in early 2004 only underscored a common fear of terrorism between the Thaksin and Bush administrations.

Nevertheless, Thailand has not veered as far as the Philippines in the direction of a tight U.S. alliance. Its recent behavior still reflects a preference for limited alignment. Thai officials remain concerned about the domestic costs of identification with the United States and unsure of the usefulness of American assistance against mostly domestic threats.[102] The 2006 military-led coup against controversial Prime Minister Thaksin Shinawatra also raised an obstacle to defense ties, as U.S. law required a temporary suspension of military aid. Cobra Gold exercises and other forms of cooperation continued, but the episode highlighted the risk of depending too heavily on American defense support.

Malaysia and the United States—Public Criticism, Private Cooperation

Malaysian leaders have been publicly critical of the American war on terror, particularly after the invasions of Afghanistan and Iraq. In a speech to the Non-Aligned Summit in February 2003, Mahathir said that the attacks of September 11 have "removed all the restraint in the countries of the north. They now no longer respect borders international laws or even simple moral values. And they are now talking of wars, of the use of military conquests to change Governments. . . . It is no longer just a war against terrorism. It is in fact a war to dominate the world."[103]

Despite Mahathir's strident rhetoric, then Defense Minister Najib Razak noted in an address to the Heritage Foundation in Washington that bilateral defense cooperation had increased significantly after the 9/11 attacks, including more than 1,000 U.S. military flights through Malaysian air space per year and dozens of military port visits, including aircraft carrier stops at Port Klang. Malaysian and American naval forces participate in bilateral naval and ground training exercises, and Malaysia provides U.S. troops with jungle combat training facilities. Referring to the September 11 attacks, Najib later said that the "horrific events of that day galvanized our relationship as never before."[104] Quiet cooperation in counterterrorist and traditional military matters have continued alongside expanding economic relations, including the completion of a trade and investment framework agreement and initiation of free trade agreement negotiations.

Quiet U.S.-Indonesian and U.S.-Bruneian Security Cooperation

Since the fall of Suharto, Indonesian officials have been particularly circumspect about the intentions of foreign powers, particularly the United States. Indonesian suspicion of U.S. motives has led Jakarta to keep the relationship at arm's length. Shortly after the East Timor crisis, infuriated with perceived Western betrayal, President Abdurrahman Wahid proposed a new Asian coalition of China, India, and Indonesia to correct the "imbalance" in international affairs and "limit the scope for external forces to undermine Indonesia's sovereignty."[105] The Indonesian government also pledged that ASEAN would remain the cornerstone of its foreign policy and that the *bebas-aktif* (independent and active) tradition would continue.

After a brief hiatus imposed by the Pentagon during the East Timor crisis, Indonesian defense cooperation with the United States resumed in May 2001 despite the criticism of some human rights groups. That year joint humanitarian exercises resumed between the U.S. and Indonesian navies, and Indonesian military officers were invited to observe the annual Cobra Gold joint exercises including U.S., Thai, and Singaporean forces. President Megawati Sukarnoputri was the first leader of a Muslim-majority state to visit Washington after the September 11 attacks. Although she offered condolences and voiced her opposition to terror, she did not signal support for retaliatory invasion of Afghanistan or a significant turn in bilateral security ties. Indonesia has since cooperated with American authorities in antiterrorist activities quietly to avoid public recrimination.[106]

Terror attacks in Bali in October 2002 and Jakarta in the summer of 2003 increased the Indonesian government's concerns about radical Islamic groups. These episodes did not erase the perception gap between Washington and Jakarta but helped restore low-level cooperation. Human rights continue to be an irritant. The U.S. government has pressed for Indonesian military commanders to be tried for alleged crimes in East Timor, and Indonesia has been critical of the U.S. detention facilities at Guantanamo Bay. In 2003 the U.S. Congress also suspended a small amount of military aid to Indonesia over an alleged killing of American citizens by Indonesian armed forces in Papua.[107]

American sales of nonlethal military goods and services began again. A swift and effective humanitarian response by the U.S. military after the December 2004 tsunami improved bilateral ties. In 2005 the Bush administration issued a national security waiver to restore foreign military financing to Indonesia, mostly for maritime security. Secretary of State Condoleezza Rice also attested to Indonesian cooperation in the Timika killings, enabling Indonesians to participate again in the IMET program. Indonesia has since become more actively engaged in bilateral Cooperation Afloat Readiness and Training (CARAT) exercises and has stepped up military equipment purchases from the United States.[108] Thus military relations between the two countries normalized.

Continued acceptance of limited alignment with America has not meant Indonesian abandonment of the ZOPFAN principle. As Dewi Fortuna Anwar wrote in 2001, "Indonesia continues to hope that closer regional cooperation will eventually remove the underlying suspicions among ASEAN members, thus enabling the organization to develop a truly autonomous regional order in which members will no longer look to outside powers to guarantee their security."[109]

The country's traditional emphasis on national regional resilience, together with domestic political pressure, has encouraged Indonesian leaders—including Megawati and current President Susilo Bambang Yudhoyono—to impose considerable limits on its alignment with the United States. Since 9/11 and the October 2002 Bali bombings, Jakarta has had to engage in a delicate balancing act, engaging in quiet cooperation at the working level while vocally criticizing certain American policies and actions related to Iraq and the war on terror. Excessive identification with the United States could be politically fatal for an elected Indonesian government.

The arrival of the Obama administration was widely welcomed in Indonesia, because of both the new president's espoused policies and his childhood ties to Jakarta, but that change has not fundamentally altered the alignment equation. Terrorism remains a shared concern—as evident in the July 2009 bomb attacks against Western business groups in Jakarta—but Indonesia retains a strong preference for only limited security ties given policy difference, concerns about U.S. intentions, domestic political considerations, and the lack of a serious military threat.

Brunei's cooperation with the United States since 9/11 has followed a similar pattern. The sultanate has distanced itself politically from U.S. policies in the broader Middle East, but has continued to conduct military exercises with U.S., British, and Australian forces and to host port visits by American vessels. Quiet security cooperation—especially in naval and counterterrorist affairs—has helped the sultanate preserve strong political and economic ties with the West as it protects itself from ongoing perceived dangers in the South China Sea and from neighboring states.[110]

Vietnam and America Reengage

The most novel aspect of American security relations in Southeast Asia has been its increasing engagement with Vietnam. In 2005 Prime Minister Pham Van Dong agreed with President Bush to establish training for Vietnamese military officers in the United States under the IMET program. The two countries also set up channels for sharing intelligence on terrorism and transnational crime, and in 2006 they began to discuss possible sales of spare military parts. Vietnamese and American officials have also engaged in periodic discussions about American naval visits to Cam Ranh Bay, but VCP leaders remain hesitant, wary of American motives and eager to avoid confrontation with China.[111] Vietnam has continued to perform a delicate balancing act, seeking support from other middle powers where possible to limit its exposure to China or the United States. In recent years it has been the most genuinely nonaligned state in the region, at least if measured along a Sino-American axis.

Chinese Bridges to Southeast Asia

As the United States has expanded its security ties to many of the ASEAN states in the past five years, China has also been increasing its defense engagement gradually alongside its much more robust political and economic engagement. This has led some analysts to suggest that several Southeast Asian states have been bandwagoning with China or at least accommodating its rise.[112] Some of the progress has been multilateral. In 2003 China and the ASEAN states signed the Joint Declaration on ASEAN-China Strategic Partnership for Peace and Prosperity, which set out broad principles for enhanced cooperation. The next year ASEAN and China inked a five-year plan of action that promoted military exchange and training and contemplated possible joint military exercise and cooperation in peacekeeping.[113] These documents did not create any new alignments, but they did show that all states in the region were willing to engage with China at some level in military affairs—a far cry from the Cold War era.

Bilateral agreements also proliferated. China concluded a five-year joint action plan with Thailand for strategic cooperation in 2007. That deal followed the 2006 coup and temporary U.S. suspension of military aid and appeared to be a way of hedging Thailand's bets. Pursuant to the joint action plan, the two sides established additional training exercises—including China's first special forces training with a foreign country—concluded new deals for missile technology, and ramped up dialogue and exchange.[114] The Sino-Thai relationship is still not a tight alliance, but it has gotten progressively stronger. Much less sensational than the large U.S. Cobra Gold exercises and cutting-edge weapons programs, Sino-Thai exercises and arms deals have nonetheless grown quietly. The United States remains Thailand's primary external defense provider in material terms, but China is closing the gap and has established a special relationship that some analysts see as approaching the Thai-U.S. arrangement in importance.[115]

The PRC also signed a number of other agreements or MOUs for enhanced security cooperation. One was a 2005 MOU on bilateral defense cooperation that the PRC signed with Malaysia. The MOU established only limited bilateral military training, exchanges of defense officials, and some information exchange through bilateral dialogue. However, it represented an important shift in Malaysian defense policy, which had treated China as a serious ideological menace during the Cold War.[116] China also signed bilateral agreements with the Philippines and Singapore that include references to military cooperation.[117] They and other ASEAN states, including Indonesia, have increased defense cooperation with China, primarily through exchanges of officials and sometimes also through increased arms sales. In early 2010, Indonesia and China announced plans for a new strategic partnership that would include additional defense links.[118] The PRC's defense ties with a number of maritime ASEAN states are now approaching the level of limited alignments.

China's economic and political ties to its mainland friends have also strengthened more than its military links, but military ties have inched ahead. In 2002 the PRC tripled the modest volume of military aid it provided to Cambodia, signaling deeper (albeit still very limited) security ties between Phnom Penh and Beijing.[119] Periodic sales and donations of equipment, as well as exchanges of delegations and training opportunities, expanded the relationship slightly in the years following. In late 2008 the first visit of a Chinese warship to the southern Cambodian city of Kampong Sam was a symbolically meaningful step toward enhanced naval cooperation.[120] Laos and China have also maintained low-level security ties. The two states agreed in late 2009 to raise their bilateral ties to the degree of a "comprehensive strategic cooperative partnership," though the military aspect of the partnership is still quite modest, and the alignment is limited.[121]

Myanmar has continued to align with China throughout recent years but preserved modest security ties to India as well. China has consistently stood by the junta during times of severe international pressure, most notably after the junta's forceful repression of the monk-led Saffron Revolution in the fall of 2007 and woeful response to Cyclone Nargis in 2008. The resurgence of ethnic conflict along the Sino-Myanmar border in 2009 has complicated bilateral ties to a degree but has not fundamentally altered the two sides' interests in prioritizing stability and concluding economic deals that will supply China's energy-starved Yunnan Province with oil and gas exports from Myanmar.

Vietnam has edged toward China with greater caution than any of its neighbors. In 2005 the two countries agreed to settle on a border demarcation, and by late 2008 the landmines that had long divided them were largely removed.[122] Officials from Hanoi and Beijing have also engaged in a number of goodwill dialogues. Yet Vietnamese concerns have not evaporated. Vietnam and China have continued to spar diplomatically over the disputed Paracel Islands, most recently after China announced in early 2010 its plans to develop the islands for tourism. Hanoi has tried to multilateralize the negotiations over the Paracels and link them to China's disputes with other ASEAN states over the Spratlys, but Vietnamese leaders have also looked for ways to build their country's military defenses. In late 2009 Vietnam brought six submarines from Russia, a move widely interpreted as an effort to check Chinese ambitions in the South China Sea.[123] Vietnam's overall posture remains one of engaging China while hedging against it, largely through limited countervailing ties to Russia and other external powers.

ASEAN's Economic Diversification

Alongside its gains in the security arena, China has exploded onto the Southeast Asian scene as an economic force. During the 1980s Beijing's economic ties to the region were almost negligible compared to the region's massive trade and investment flows with Japan and the United States.[124] However, the PRC's commercial ties to its southern neighbors have increased dramatically since the end of the Cold War and now rival or exceed Japanese and American levels in many Southeast Asian states. Sino–ASEAN trade has exploded from less than $10 billion in 1980 to more than $200 billion today.[125]

Over the past several years, China has taken steps to open up its markets to Southeast Asian countries and build confidence. The most important was a 2002 ASEAN-China Framework Agreement on Economic Cooperation, which will give rise to a free trade area in 2010. Fears of Chinese competition have not dissolved, but Chinese diplomacy and strategic investments have helped position the PRC as an economic partner, not just an adversary.[126] China has also provided billions of dollars of investment and economic aid to a number of Southeast Asian states with few strings attached. China's economic clout has yet to result in a clear shift in alignment patterns, but it has clearly shifted the overall balance of great-power influence in the region.

The United States has also prioritized expansion of its own trade ties since 2002 through a free trade agreement (FTA) with Singapore, negotiations with Malaysia and Thailand for possible FTAs, and a U.S.-ASEAN Enhanced Partnership initiative. U.S. trade with ASEAN states now amounts to more than $175 billion per year, and America remains one of the top three trading and investment partners for most countries in the region.[127] Even after the Asian financial crisis, when America's response was roundly criticized, most Southeast Asian officials continue to see America as the leader of the international financial system and seek relations that will not only help ensure security support but also U.S. assistance in the event of an economic crisis. The desire in most Southeast Asian capitals to keep good overall relations with China and the United States, in part for economic reasons, has added another reason for governments to veer away from tight alliances in the post–Cold War era.

Normative and Institutional Efforts Continue

As part of a broad economic and diplomatic strategy to enmesh the great powers in a web of interdependence, ASEAN governments have continued to participate in an ever-larger array of multilateral forums. The most recent addition has been the East Asia Summit (EAS), which held its first summit in Kuala Lumpur in 2005 and excluded the United States. The ASEAN+3 forum—also an Asia-only grouping—has also expanded its activities, mostly in the financial area through the establishment of a network of currency swaps known as the Chiang Mai Initiative. Neither the EAS nor ASEAN+3 has offered a serious alternative to pre-existing security structures and bilateral defense relationships, but they have added to the dense institutional landscape that many Southeast Asian officials believe encourages peaceful change and thus, at least to a degree, reduces the need for protective great-power alignments. In that regard, China's accession to the Treaty of Amity and Cooperation (TAC) in 2003 and its expressed intent to accede to the Protocol on a Southeast Asian Nuclear Weapons Free Zone were welcomed by many Southeast Asian officials as signs of socialization. The 2009 U.S. decision to sign the TAC—an implicit acknowledgment of the success of China's charm offensive and the importance of the normative and institutional agenda in ASEAN eyes—was also a significant step.

ASEAN has continued to develop its own institutional features as well. In 2003 Southeast Asian leaders agreed to pursue an "ASEAN Security Community." That goal led to the launch of an annual ASEAN Defense Ministers' Meeting in 2006, which represents part of ASEAN's broader effort to take the edge off regional rivalries and promote security through dialogue. ASEAN's centrality to regional diplomacy was reinforced in 2007, when Southeast Asian leaders signed an ASEAN Charter giving the association a formal legal basis and fleshing out its goals and organizational features.

Confidence in regional security institutions has tended to be greatest in the governments of the original five ASEAN members, and especially Singapore, Malaysia, and Indonesia, which have usually driven the institutional agenda. Trust in regional institutions is generally weaker in the newer ASEAN members. Vietnam, Laos, Cambodia, and Myanmar lack deep historical experience participating in ASEAN and related forums, and all have felt the brunt of ASEAN criticism at some points in the past. Even mundane factors—such as a lack of travel resources for meetings and English-language skills—have prevented the new ASEAN states from becoming as centrally involved in multilateral forums as the ASEAN-6 countries. As Amitav Acharya asserts, the development of shared norms and institutions in the Asia-Pacific has been "cautious, pragmatic, informal, gradualist, and consensus-seeking."[128]

Institutions and informal multilateral groupings appear to have made greatest impact in dealing with nontraditional security challenges. One excellent example has been the naval cooperation led by Singapore, Malaysia, and Indonesia since 2004 to reduce the incidence of piracy in the Straits of Malacca through a multinational piracy patrol. To the extent that regional or institutional responses have addressed such security challenges, they have marginally curbed the need for great-power military support.

Regional Alignment Overview, 2002–2010

The regional alignment picture since 2002 has shown a return of stronger bilateral ties to the United States in Singapore and the Philippines (see table 3.3). Otherwise, however, the new international security environment created by the September 11 attacks and U.S.-led war on terror has not had a profound impact on alignment patterns in the region. China's steep economic rise also has not prompted a significant adjustment; most ASEAN states appear to have settled into comfortable limited alignment positions (table 3.3).

CONCLUSIONS ON THE EVIDENCE

Limited alignment has clearly been the dominant alignment strategy for Southeast Asian states during the post–Cold War period. After the Soviet withdrawal from Vietnam and Philippine closure of Subic Bay, only internationally ostracized Myanmar allied tightly with a great power, and that relationship ebbed as the costs of its de facto alliance with China became apparent. During the late 1990s no Southeast Asian government pursued tight alliance with a great power. Since September 2001 renewed American interest in regional security and a shared fear of terrorism have prompted a few ASEAN-6 states to increase their ties to Washington. However,

Table 3.3 Alignment Postures, 2002–2010

Country	Ally	Alignment Status
Brunei	USA	Limited alignment
Cambodia	PRC	Limited alignment
Indonesia	USA	Limited alignment
Laos	PRC	Limited alignment
Malaysia	USA	Limited alignment
Myanmar	PRC	Limited alignment
Philippines	USA	Limited alignment → tight alliance (2002)
Singapore	USA	Limited alignment
Thailand	PRC	Limited alignment
	USA	Limited alignment
Vietnam		No alignment

Source: Author's compilation

only the U.S.-Philippine security relationship has returned to a level that can be described as a tight alliance, and even that arrangement does not approach the depth of the two countries' Cold War–era defense pact.

The preceding narrative also suggests that Southeast Asian countries' alignment preferences were well reflected in the outcomes they achieved. No state in the region pleaded for a tight alliance and was refused by a great power. Although pressure to cooperate with the great powers was sometimes considerable—particularly from the United States after 9/11—no Southeast Asian state was coerced into a tight alliance. The sole nonaligned state, Vietnam, was not in that posture for lack of great-power suitors. On the whole, the dominance of limited alignments roughly reflected Southeast Asian leaders' preferences.

Figure 3.1 summarizes regional alignment behavior from 1992 to the present. Again, black boxes signify tight alliances, white refer to nonalignment, and grey denote limited alignment. Thailand has engaged in meaningful defense cooperation with both the United States and China. It is coded as engaged in limited alignment, though it is worth noting that its strategy differs somewhat from other states in the region that have tilted more clearly toward one of the two external giants in Washington or Beijing. Trends in the region suggest that other ASEAN-6 states are beginning to follow suit, building modest but consequential military ties to China alongside their links to the United States.

Taken together, the empirical data in this chapter and the preceding chapter support the claim that DCs generally prefer limited alignments when they are able to choose. Genuine nonalignment has occurred in a few cases, namely when Southeast Asian states have seen no great power as sufficiently credible to justify the establishment of significant security ties. Tight alliances have also occurred—particularly involving the Philippines and the frontline states in the Third Indochina War—but since 1975 only one new formal alliance with a great power has been

Black = tight alliance
Gray = limited alignment
White = no alignment

Country/Year	92	93	94	95	96	97	98	99	00	01	02	03	04	05	06	07	08	09	10
Brunei																			
Malaysia																			
Indonesia																			
Singapore																			
Thailand★																			
Philippines																			
Vietnam																			
Laos																			
Cambodia																			
Myanmar																			

Figure 3.1 Summary Data, 1992–2010

Source: Author's compilation

Note: ★ significant defense cooperation with both China and the United States (entire period)

created in Southeast Asia: the Soviet-Vietnamese pact. Few other tight alliances have existed for any extended duration. Even when Southeast Asian governments have allied tightly, they have always sought to place some meaningful limits on their security cooperation with great powers and have usually played down the closeness of their ties for both domestic and international audiences. Figure 3.2 aggregates the data from both periods.

The best way to count the data is to consider each country's alignment posture during each year as a single observation. Using calendar years as the operative time intervals makes sense, because shorter periods would expose the data to excessive

Black = tight alliance
Gray = limited alignment
White = no alignment

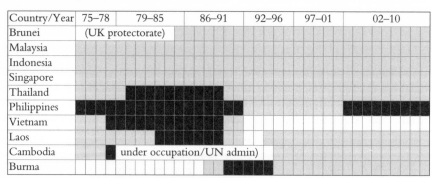

Country/Year	75–78	79–85	86–91	92–96	97–01	02–10
Brunei	(UK protectorate)					
Malaysia						
Indonesia						
Singapore						
Thailand						
Philippines						
Vietnam						
Laos						
Cambodia		under occupation/UN admin)				
Burma						

Figure 3.2 Aggregated Data, 1975–2010

Source: Author's compilation

month-to-month noise, while significantly longer periods would miss important shifts in alignment postures from year to year. Another key advantage to counting each country's alignment posture in each year as a single data point is that a long-lasting alignment should not carry the same weight in the data as a fleeting one. If a country spends ten years in a limited alignment and one year in a tight alliance, the former represents its dominant behavior, and the data should reflect that fact. Taking this methodological approach, Southeast Asian alignment behavior can be presented as follows (see figure 3.3).

Counting the data in this manner, one finds that Southeast Asian states pursued limited alignments in 239 observations—about 71 percent of the time. Governments allied tightly in sixty-one observed instances (roughly 18 percent) and pursued genuine nonalignment in thirty-five observations (about 11 percent). The preference for limited alignments has been clear.

The existence of significant data that defy the limited alignment hypothesis is no surprise. My argument is not that DCs always avoid tight pacts. Clearly, they do not. Rather, I contend that DCs generally prefer to do so, especially in the contemporary international system. Southeast Asian data since 1975 provide robust support for that hypothesis. Of course, these data are not absolute. They reflect empirical judgments about the nature of Southeast Asian states' security relations with the great powers at various times. Some analysts may differ with certain of the historical interpretations presented in this book. Even if one quibbles with some of my historical judgments and coding decisions, limited alignments have clearly been much more common than strict nonalignment or tight alliances in Southeast Asia since 1975.

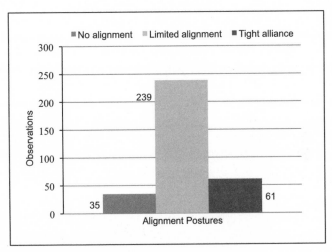

Figure 3.3 Tally of the Data, 1975–2010

Source: Author's compilation

Another way to tally the data would be to count an observation only when a new alignment was created or when an existing alignment shifted from one form to another. For example, one would count a single observation when two states move from a tight alliance to a limited alignment, regardless of the duration of the ensuing alignment. Stephen Walt used a similar methodology in his seminal book *The Origins of Alliances*.[129] This approach makes sense when analyzing the creation of alignments, but it has the significant drawback of weighing all alignments equally, whether they last for only a few months or for half a century. Brief aberrations—such as a short cancellation of military ties during a diplomatic row or a brief interlude of tight cooperation during a crisis—are thus treated that same as twenty-year stretches of behavior. Even taking this suboptimal methodological approach, limited alignments clearly come out on top. Counting only the changes in alignment postures reflected in figure 3.1, one arrives at the following breakdown: limited alignments = sixteen observations (60 percent); tight alliance = seven observations (26 percent); and nonalignment = four observations (14 percent).

The data also show that limited alignments tend to be more durable than tight ones. Since 1975 the average duration of limited alignments in Southeast Asia has been approximately fourteen years, whereas the average length of tight alliances has been roughly eight years. The longest tight alliances lasted between twelve and seventeen years, though a number of limited alignments have survived for the entire thirty-five years since the fall of Saigon. The risks of diminished autonomy, abandonment, and entrapment have not always deterred Southeast Asian states from entering tight alliances. The Vietnamese-Soviet alliance during the 1980s is perhaps the best illustration of that point. However, the data suggest that tight alliances often unwind quickly when threats recede because DCs seldom have much appetite for the risks of tight alliance when they do not have dire immediate need for external security support. The rapid distance that Vietnam and Laos placed between themselves and the USSR-Russia at the end of the Cold War is one example; Thai distancing from the United States in 1976 is another. The ebb of Myanmar's ties to China in the mid-1990s similarly reflects the general preference of the smaller Southeast Asian partners for limited alignments.

These findings represent an important challenge to existing theories, which focus overwhelmingly on how states choose sides and generally classify alignments as efforts to balance, bandwagon, or stay nonaligned. As this study suggests, DCs usually try to avoid those stark alternatives. That so many are pursuing limited alignments in the contemporary order makes the phenomenon especially important for scholars to acknowledge and understand. To explain accurately why individual countries pursue particular alignment options in specific instances, one needs to drill into governments' security perceptions in some depth. The following two chapters do precisely that, analyzing each of the ten Southeast Asian states in more detail.

Chapter 4

Maritime Southeast Asia

To EXPLAIN WHY SOUTHEAST ASIAN states have usually pursued limited alignments since 1975, I argue that alignment preferences and policies can be best understood as efforts to optimize the risks and rewards of alignment under conditions of strategic uncertainty. I first introduce some crosscutting risks and rewards that have influenced governments in the region and then show how assessments of risks and rewards have driven alignment preferences and strategies in specific Southeast Asian capitals. Governments consider myriad material and ideational factors as they weigh the pros and cons of various alignment options, and it is seldom possible to explain their decisions with a single independent variable. The best way to account for DC alignment preferences and policies is to present credible qualitative accounts of particular country cases. In this chapter I examine the five states of maritime Southeast Asia, and in the next the mainland country cases.

EXPLAINING PREFERENCES

Southeast Asian states have usually pursued limited alignments because they have seen that strategy as the most likely to optimize the risks and rewards of security cooperation. In short, they have sought the greatest degree of autonomy and flexibility consistent with their basic security needs. In most cases, genuine nonalignment has been unattractive because it provides too few rewards. In a relatively dangerous part of the world, Southeast Asian states have usually seen the need for at least some great-power security support. They have also welcomed the ancillary economic and political benefits of alignment.

Tight alliances have also been unappealing in most cases, however, because they carry added dangers of diminished autonomy, abandonment, or entrapment. Southeast Asian leaders have usually believed that limited alignments deliver sufficient security benefits and that the added risks of tight alliance outweigh the rewards. Sometimes threats have been comparatively modest, giving states in the region little incentive to ally tightly. In other instances governments have faced serious security challenges, but not the kinds that great powers are best at addressing. Leaders have also harbored concerns about the reliability and intentions of their great-power allies. Thus the expected rewards of tight alliance have often been modest and always uncertain. When Southeast Asian governments have believed they could protect their interests adequately alone or with limited security ties, they have usually tried to keep options open. They have allied tightly only when they have faced particularly grave threats and identified a capable and credible great-power ally.

Why Not Ally Tightly?

The risks of tight alliance have provided the disincentives for Southeast Asian governments to forge strong balancing or bandwagoning pacts. The first major risk of great-power alignment in Southeast Asia has been the danger of diminished autonomy. History has left leaders in the region sensitive to dominance and exploitation by imperial overlords. Southeast Asia has never been entirely free of the grip of great-power politics. China and India dominated or challenged local regimes for centuries. Western colonialism and a brief but bloody interlude of Japanese imperialism followed. Superpower intervention—especially during the Vietnam War—confirmed to many Southeast Asian officials that domineering great powers remained real threats to their survival and independent national identities. Indeed, Donald Weatherbee identifies the desire to maintain autonomy and maneuverability among the great powers as the central unifying theme of modern Southeast Asian foreign policies.[1]

Southeast Asian leaders have also shared a common concern that close identification with a great power would expose them to domestic backlash. For DCs, autonomy is not just about preserving policy flexibility; it is also about appearances. Most governments in modern Southeast Asia have suffered at least sometimes from haphazard and undemocratic governance, lackluster economic performance, and official corruption. Thus, they have not derived their public legitimacy from what Max Weber called rational/legal sources of authority. To justify their rule, most Southeast Asian governments have relied heavily on nationalist credentials and represented themselves as the anticolonial vanguards of national independence. No Southeast Asian leader has wanted to look like the puppet or stooge of a great power. Local populations, which in many cases spilled blood and treasure to forge independent national identities, would not be pleased.

A second major risk driving the preference for limited alignment has been the possibility of abandonment. Few if any leaders have believed that distant powers like the United States and USSR would always count Southeast Asia as a strategic priority. Even neighboring China has had bigger fish to fry in Northeast Asia and across the Taiwan Straits. During certain stretches of time—namely the eras of the Second and Third Indochina Wars—the intensity of superpower struggle made it less likely that either side would back down and leave its allies in the lurch. However, the U.S. withdrawal from Saigon in 1975 and crumbling in of the USSR in 1991 showed that reliance on an external protector was a dangerous affair. When possible, Southeast Asian governments have tried to reduce dependency on the great powers for their security. External security support could become a crutch, and leaning on great-power protector could stunt their countries' development of stand-alone strength and resilience. Without independent development, Southeast Asian states would become acutely vulnerable if left in the lurch.

A third major reason Southeast Asian states have generally disfavored tight alliance is a fear of being entrapped in conflict or antagonizing third parties. All leaders in the region witnessed the perils of embroilment in great-power conflict throughout the colonial period, World War II, and the eras of the First and Second Indochina Wars. The latter stages of the Cold War again raised the risk of being trapped in conflict fueled or instigated by the feuding great powers. Choosing sides in the midst of Soviet-American rivalry ran the risk that a spurned superpower would attack or undermine a Southeast Asian regime by funding local insurgents or political dissidents. The perceived risk of entrapment receded somewhat after the end of the Cambodian conflict, but the rise of China and episodic tensions and flare-ups between Washington and Beijing have again motivated Southeast Asian governments to avoid drawing unnecessary lines in the sand.

Why Not Avoid Alignment?

Despite the risks, Southeast Asian governments have usually sought at least some great-power security support because they face significant security challenges. Few have had enough confidence to rely entirely on their own means. Economic and political benefits have also flowed from security ties, providing important additional incentives in a number of regional capitals. Simply stated, the ample rewards of alignment explain why limited alignments have been much more common than genuine nonalignment in modern Southeast Asia.

To Southeast Asian leaders the clearest reward of great-power alignments has been help in defusing external military threats. In addition to providing combat support and deterrence, great-power allies have offered training and hardware to help states bulk up their own capabilities. Great-power assets have unsurprisingly been most attractive when Southeast Asian governments have faced dire, imminent threats involving foreign foes as well as local actors. It is no coincidence that most of the tight alliances in Southeast Asia since 1975 were related to intense armed conflict in Indochina. Serious threats during those conflicts drove up the expected rewards of tight alliance. In periods or zones of relative regional peace, limited alignments have been much more prevalent.

However, serious threats have not guaranteed tight alliances. Even if they have had the capabilities to help defend against external threats, great powers have sometimes lacked credibility, reducing the expected rewards of alignment. Indeed, when the great powers have become more or less attractive to their Southeast Asian allies, the reason has usually had more to do with perceived intentions than capabilities. Southeast Asian states have only allied tightly when they have believed that their great-power partner was solidly committed to defending their interests, at least in the short term. By contrast, when great-power credibility has weakened, Southeast

Asian states have favored limited ties or eschewed alignment altogether. When the United States lost credibility in the mid-1970s or early 1990s, or when the USSR's credibility waned in the late Cold War period, their close Southeast Asian allies tried to loosen their security relationships and take other measures to hedge their bets. Simply stated, questionable credibility creates uncertainty, and when they have had doubts, Southeast Asian states have usually seen little reason to ally tightly. When no great power has appeared reasonably credible, as in Burma in the 1970s or Vietnam in the 1990s, leaders have decided to pursue genuine nonalignment.

Another key reason to align with a great power has been help in dealing with domestic insurgencies and other internal security concerns. Ethnic guerilla movements—often communist or Islamist rebels in the ASEAN states and right-wing groups in Indochina—have been key concerns in a region where most governments rule diverse populations with varied allegiances to the state. The modern territorial boundaries in Southeast Asia—most of which were negotiated by the French, British, and Dutch during the late nineteenth and early twentieth centuries—often took little account of the ethnic composition of areas near national frontiers. Sometimes borders deliberately cut across ethnic lines as part of a divide-and-rule policy. The leaders of Southeast Asian states have therefore frequently faced the challenge of governing minority groups whose kinship allegiances lie across a border they view as arbitrary or illegitimate.[2] Centrifugal forces from separatist groups and insurgents have thus preoccupied most governments more than foreign military attack. Moreover, external and internal threats have been intertwined in the region, as foreign adversaries have funded local resistance movements to inexpensively (and sometimes deniably) undermine Southeast Asian regimes. With the exceptions of the wealthy microstates of Singapore and Brunei, Southeast Asian states have usually identified their principal threats from within their own borders or immediate neighborhoods.[3]

The need for support against internal threats has often encouraged Southeast Asian states to align, but it has seldom driven them to ally tightly. Officials in the region have sought great-power help in building the competence of their armed forces through training and technology transfer. They have also sought economic aid that often flows from friendly security ties. However, they have generally seen great-power capabilities as the wrong tools for addressing low-intensity threats to their states and regimes, such as domestic insurgencies or nontraditional security issues.[4] In managing such menaces, the military struggle is normally secondary to the political dispute. Great-power planes, tanks, and troops are only useful if they increase the government's effectiveness without compromising its domestic prestige or legitimacy. The militarization of conflicts and presence of foreign troops has usually been an unappealing way to address Southeast Asian resistance movements that usually have been rooted in local economic, political, and social deprivation. Limited alignments have often provided enough rewards for Southeast Asian states to meet internal challenges.

The Role of Uncertainty

Uncertainty has added to Southeast Asian preference for limited alignments. During the late 1970s the region was characterized by a high degree of strategic uncertainty as great power and regional dynamics shifted following the Vietnam War. The intentions of all three major external security actors—the United States, USSR, and China—came into question. That made it particularly important to keep options open, and limited alignments unsurprisingly predominated. When the Third Indochina Conflict exploded, the region re-polarized, making perceptions of friends and foes much clearer, at least to the frontline states. Securing protection became more important, and keeping options open became a less critical priority, in the face of such obvious military menaces. Several governments thus held their noses and entered into tight security cooperation with external protectors.

Toward the end of the Cold War, as doubts again arose about great-power commitments to Southeast Asia and the future evolution of regional affairs, most states veered back toward limited alignment strategies, attempting to position themselves in a way that would help them respond nimbly to whatever the post–Cold War order held in store. Since then uncertainty about the future roles of China and the United States in the region has continued to raise doubts about the wisdom of rigid alliances and encourage flexible security arrangements instead.

In sum, Southeast Asian states have allied tightly only when the expected rewards have been particularly great and particularly clear. Both dire threats and a capable, credible ally have been necessary precursors for tight alliance in modern Southeast Asia. Low levels of threat and weak great-power attractiveness have consistently led governments to limit their alignments and keep their options open.

Examining Individual States

The five maritime members of ASEAN—Indonesia, Malaysia, Brunei, Singapore, and the Philippines—have all tilted toward the United States since 1975. Largely for that reason, the United States has enjoyed relative primacy in maritime Southeast Asia throughout the period, challenged significantly only during the 1980s when Soviet forces began to assemble at Cam Ranh Bay. Nevertheless, maritime governments' individual alignment preferences have differed widely. The Philippines and Singapore are often described as strategic allies of the United States, whereas Indonesia and Malaysia (and to a lesser extent Brunei) have long declared themselves to be nonaligned.

In practice, distinctions have not been so sharp, especially since the end of the Cold War. When they have doubted American credibility or believed that limited security ties would suffice, America's closest strategic partners have pursued limited ties rather than tight alliances. The rhetorically nonaligned maritime ASEAN states have also tilted rather than pursuing genuine neutrality. The maritime states of Southeast Asia thus provide an excellent illustration of how much diversity exists on the spectrum between tight alliances and relative neutrality and why different governments veer toward one end of the spectrum or the other.

INDONESIA

Although Indonesia has often publicly declared itself to be nonaligned, it provides one of the clearest cases of limited alignment in modern Southeast Asia. Indonesia has pursued low-level security cooperation with the United States for almost the entire period since 1975. Indonesia's behavior is comparatively straightforward to explain in terms of the risk-reward calculus. External threats have been relatively weak because Indonesia has tended to face only modest menaces from abroad and manageable (if not insignificant) security challenges at home. The possible rewards of a tight alliance have also been unappealing because Indonesian officials generally have not believed that the United States and other great powers possess the tools and credibility to deal with Indonesia's domestic security challenges effectively.

Moreover, Indonesian officials have consistently viewed great-power alignment as a costly venture that undermines national independence and regime legitimacy and detracts from Indonesia's regional ambitions. Indonesia's tendency to avoid tight defense pacts is related to the long-standing priority its leaders have given to an in-dependent and active foreign policy and the country's prominent role in the NAM. Indonesia has not been truly nonaligned, but the limited nature of its tilt has allowed Jakarta to characterize its foreign policy as essentially independent, preserve do-mestic and regional prestige, and claim a leadership role in the NAM. As recently as March 2010 Defense Minister Purnomo Yusgiantoro gave a speech reemphasizing his country's independent and relatively neutral approach to relations with the great pow-ers.[5] Overall, Jakarta has favored limited alignment because its leaders have perceived the rewards of closer great-power support as modest and the risks as considerable.

Threat Environment

With the possible exception of the Philippines, Indonesia has devoted less attention to external security threats than any country in Southeast Asia.[6] Given its size and geography, Indonesia has historically felt relatively unthreatened by its immediate Southeast Asian neighbors. A 2003 defense white paper captured a long-standing view by declaring that "invasion or aggression from a foreign country [is] highly unlikely. . . . The majority of threats faced by Indonesia are estimated to root from non-traditional threats, both domestic and trans-national."[7] Ethnic fighting and do-mestic insurgencies—such as communist movements and struggles for indepen-dence in East Timor, Aceh, and Irian Jaya—have consistently been viewed as the principal threats to Indonesia's national security.[8] Indonesian security has not been unaffected by changes at the level of the international system—such as the rise and fall of Cold War competition or intensification of the worldwide Islamist challenge since 9/11—but the effects of those changes have been channeled through devel-opments at the domestic level.

Communism and the Ethnic Chinese Question

During the early years of the Cold War, as Indonesia sought to gain its independent footing after the departure of Dutch colonial masters, it was a mix of internal ethnic conflict and ideological rivalry that most seriously threatened the country. President Sukarno and his nominally nonaligned government faced mounting challenges from the left by the PKI, which drew heavily from the ethnic Chinese population. It also confronted rising pressure from the right, primarily from elements in the armed forces. That crescendo of ethnic and ideological conflict precipitated a violent and destabilizing series of events in October 1965, when the armed forces crushed an alleged PKI coup and took power, handing the reins to General Suharto. A brutal program of purges followed, and hundreds of thousands of suspected communists were executed.[9]

The shadow of the events of 1965 and 1966 hung over Indonesian security policy for decades. The Suharto regime generally perceived domestic communist groups as the principal continuing threat to regime security. China's explicit backing of those forces added to concerns. To a lesser extent, the Indonesian government was also wary of Soviet sponsorship of local communist groups.[10] Jusuf Wanandi argued in the early 1980s that "for the next ten years or so the challenge to [Indonesia's] security will stem from internal problems that must be solved by Indonesia's own national forces and leadership."[11]

The ethnic and ideological aspects of threat perception were closely related, because Indonesian leaders feared that communist insurgency and subversion would come via an ethnic Chinese fifth column. Relations between the ethnic Chinese and indigenous population were historically tense, owing partly to the prominent role that ethnic Chinese merchants had long played in the country. The ethnic Chinese population was small but economically dominant, owning an estimated 75 percent of the country's capital stock by the 1980s. To many Indonesian officials, that made the country highly vulnerable to Chinese (or Soviet) subversion.[12]

Tensions between the ethnic Chinese and indigenous (mainly Muslim) population—sometimes reinforced by government demonization of communists or discriminatory policies against ethnic Chinese—have not disappeared since the end of the Cold War. Those tensions exploded in a spasm of violence in Jakarta during the Asian financial crisis in May 1998, when gangs of *pribumi* (indigenous Indonesians) killed or raped more than 1,000 ethnic Chinese and pillaged their businesses.[13] No foreign army had exacted such a toll on the population since independence. Indonesian leaders remain concerned about the potential for economic turmoil to spawn ethnic bloodshed in the country. They also fear that any regional security crisis or economic maelstrom involving China could bring a wave of unwelcome Chinese immigrants to Indonesia and incite major domestic clashes.

The ethnic Chinese issue is not the only source of domestic ethnoreligious strife. Years of Christian-Muslim clashes, particularly in the eastern Maluku Islands, are another example. To head off these sources of insecurity, domestic and regional stability and economic development have consistently been higher

Indonesian priorities than preparedness for an interstate war using conventional defense forces.

Separatism and National Unity

Centrifugal threats from separatist groups have also preoccupied officials in Jakarta since the country's independence. Due to its sprawling geography and ethnic heterogeneity, Indonesia has displayed what Chin Kin Wah describes as an "obsession for territorial unity, expressed through a *wawasan nusantara* (unique archipelagic outlook) that considers the seas as the binding rather than dividing elements in its territorial environs."[14] Indonesia is one of the most diverse countries in the region, linguistically and otherwise, and leaders have feared that simmering conflicts in East Timor, Aceh, Papua, and other parts of the archipelago could lead to an unraveling of the modern state.

The nature of Dutch and Portuguese disimperialization added to the challenges from Jakarta's perspective. The Netherlands retained control over the western half of the island of New Guinea after Indonesia's independence and handed over control of the territory only in 1963, when the U.S. government applied pressure in an effort to forestall an Indonesian turn toward Moscow. Many in the local population, which called the area West Papua, have since resisted Indonesian rule. In addition to challenging the government's authority, they sit atop some of the country's most prized mineral resources—a source of much-needed foreign exchange and funds for Indonesia's elaborate military and civilian patronage networks. Testy negotiations for elements of local rule continue to the present day.

The preservation of Portuguese rule on the eastern half of the island of Timor had a similar effect. It was not until 1975 that domestic regime change in Portugal and foreign pressure led the Portuguese to relinquish colonial rule. The Timorese population, largely Catholic and Portuguese-speaking, sought independence and resisted Indonesia's harsh military occupation. Officials in Jakarta have seen the Timorese challenge both as an issue of territorial integrity and, at times, as an ideological threat due to the left-leaning nature of the resistance. Indeed, it became the subject of a major crisis in the late 1990s, as noted in chapter 3.

Islamist Threats

Closely related to the centrifugal threats above have been menaces from militant Islamist groups. Although the international attention given to such groups has risen dramatically over the past decade, violent religiously inspired resistance is nothing new in Indonesia. Shortly after independence in 1949, when the Muslim-majority province of Aceh was included in the largely Christian province of North Sumatra, the Acehnese protested. They rebelled in 1953 under the banner of *Darul Islam* (Islamic state), and the rebellion took years for the central government to bring to heel. In the 1970s Achenese frustration with perceived collusion between Jakarta and foreign companies exploring the area's oil and gas reserves contributed to an Achenese declaration of independence. The Free Aceh Movement (GAM) began a protracted struggle against local military forces that drew to a close only with the signing of a peace deal in 2005. Thousands of lives were lost.

A more extreme brand of Islamist resistance also took shape in the form of Jemaah Islamiyah (JI), an offshoot of *Darul Islam* founded in 1993. JI was initially active in ethnoreligious conflicts in the Malukus and other outlying areas, but after 9/11 it shifted focus toward tourist sites, foreign actors, and the central government. The threat of Islamic extremist groups grew significantly after the Bali bombings in 2002 and has remained high since the Jakarta hotel attacks of 2003 and 2009. In addition to threatening loss of life, JI poses a serious challenge to tourist industries and other businesses that provide much-desired foreign exchange and capital for the country's large, relatively poor population.

Even absent major terror attacks or crises like the 1999 affair in East Timor, domestic unrest challenges the government's legitimacy and threatens to encourage other groups in the huge, diverse country to revolt. In a 1997 white paper, the Indonesian Department of Defence and Security asserted that "in the medium-term instability will tend to be caused by internal rather than external factors."[15] That outlook remains intact today.

Weak External Menaces

Externally, Indonesian officials have usually not perceived serious short-term threats. Indonesia's sheer size relative to its neighbors has given it little to fear from neighbors beyond border disputes and other irritants. Indonesia's leading role in ASEAN and participation in a variety of related diplomatic forums have helped to reduce irritants in its relations with its immediate Southeast Asian neighbors.

Its distance from potential big-power foes has also shielded it from some of the traditional defense concerns that continental states may have. Even at the height of the Third Indochina War, Jakarta did not believe a large Soviet naval presence at Cam Ranh Bay gave Moscow the ability to project military power in maritime Southeast Asia at an acceptable cost.[16] Indonesian Armed Forces Chief Benny Murdani dismissed the importance of the Soviet naval expansion, saying, "The [American] Seventh Fleet is a very strong force. Why should anybody worry about [the Soviet naval build-up]?"[17] Indonesian Foreign Minister Mochtar Kusumaatmadja said, "We are non-aligned and we feel that if the Americans have base facilities in the Philippines, there could be no objections to the Russians having them in Vietnam. It is no threat to us. Communism never came to us in big ships. Big bases and big warships are manifestations of big-power rivalry, whether communist or not. How can you condone Subic and deny Cam Ranh? I feel no threat from either."[18]

Even this modest Soviet threat evaporated after 1991. Instead, since 1975 Indonesian officials have generally focused on the long-term strategic challenge from the PRC, in the South China Sea and beyond.[19] As Ralf Emmers argues, Indonesian leaders perceive themselves as the rightful leaders of a security complex within maritime Southeast Asia based on their country's size, history of overcoming colonial rule, strategic location, and abundant natural resources.[20] Even after the dramatic economic setbacks and political unrest of 1997 and 1998, that sense of purpose and entitlement remains. The rise of China therefore creates an incipient strategic rivalry that does not obtain to the same degree between the PRC and other ASEAN states.[21]

Indonesia has also expressed concern about the consequences of economic competition from China, as the PRC has increasingly absorbed foreign investment in the region and churns out unprecedented levels of exports ranging from electronics to textiles, some of which provide the lifeblood of Southeast Asian economies. President Suharto was blunt in characterizing China as a competitive threat to the economic well-being of its Southeast Asian neighbors, saying in 1996 that he "hoped China would not become a threat to Southeast Asia . . . [that] may dominate the global market with its economic power which is capable of producing low-priced goods."[22] Economic fears add to the strategic and historical reasons why Indonesia sees China as its greatest long-term threat. Nevertheless, Indonesia has not seen the need to seek strong U.S. alignment to balance against China. The absence of a dire near-term external threat is a key reason why Indonesia has not sought a tight alliance.[23]

Rewards of U.S. Alignment

In addition to manageable security threats, Indonesian perceptions of America's attractiveness as an ally have encouraged Jakarta to disfavor a tight defense pact. Indonesian leaders have seen America as a highly useful economic partner and provider of military goods and training, but they have been doubtful about U.S. capacity to solve domestic security problems. They have also harbored suspicion of U.S. motives and credibility. Ideational variables such as the lessons of history, modest ideological divergence, cultural sensitivities, and concerns about U.S. policy consistency have all contributed to those suspicions at various times.

Little Economic Incentive

During the Cold War era the principal attraction of the alignment was economic. Opening to the United States and Japan gave Indonesia's ailing economy access to much-needed markets for trade and investment in key sectors like oil, gas, and mining. Economic performance is intimately related to the Indonesian regime's performance legitimacy, and the *ketahanan nasional* concept implies that national economic development is as important to establishing security as the application of military means or the establishment of defense pacts.[24]

The economic benefits of a pro-American tilt were not just good for security and macroeconomic growth; they also enriched Suharto and his family and associates, who engaged in corruption on an unprecedented scale. The patronage networks that flowed from those lucrative contracts helped solidify the regime's position in power, and broader economic growth contributed to performance legitimacy. Indonesians called Suharto the father of development, and his ability to deliver strong GDP growth for over two decades owed partly to the benefits of being an American friend.

Economic factors have provided even less incentive to align tightly in the post–Cold War period. Development has been a critical policy goal; the Indonesian government's white papers on national defense and security have argued that security capabilities are not determined by military might but by the total of all components, including economic factors, that provide national resilience. The 1997 white paper also asserted that globalization and the post–Cold War era had resulted in a change of "stress from ideology to economic interest" as the most important factors driving "the relation[s] among countries."[25]

Yet tight alliance would do little to advance the aim of economic growth. Rather, a desire for diversified trade, aid, and investment has militated against tight alliance as China's economy has exploded in the post–Cold War era. Indonesia has not sought to balance against China outright, which it has seen as a strategically and economically unproductive strategy. It has instead maintained limited security links to the United States as a kind of insurance policy alongside its broader strategy of political and economic engagement with all of the major world economies, including China.

Questionable Payoffs

Indonesian officials have also seen little military rationale for a tight alliance with America. This owes primarily to the types of security challenges facing Indonesia. Leaders in Jakarta have consistently viewed military alliances as inappropriate tools for combating the predominantly domestic and nontraditional security threats they have confronted. Retired Indonesian General Wiranto has cited ethnic insurgencies as the greatest security threat to his country and has asserted that military tools are generally less effective than local political mediation in resolving insecurity.[26] Indonesian Foreign Minister Adam Malik put the matter bluntly in terms of the risks and rewards of alliance for a state besieged with a major insurgency: "Military alliances or foreign military presence does not enhance a nation's capacity to cope with the problem of insurgency. The price for such commitments is too high, whereas the negative ramifications for the state are too great."[27] Indonesian leaders have generally believed that they can best address internal threats with a combination of repressive techniques (often criticized by the West) and a hearts and minds campaign at local levels that would lose credibility if supported by foreign military forces.[28]

In fact, Indonesian officials have frequently argued that tight alliance with a great power could impede independent national development, both materially and ideationally. As early as 1969 Suharto said that "military pacts have not proven to be an effective form of defense, as they would weaken our national resilience and identity."[29] Indonesian policymakers prioritized developing the country's ability to stand on its own and rely on its own economic, political, and military resources to manage security threats. Achieving that goal requires some cooperation with outside powers but not excessive reliance upon them. Foreign policy advisor Dewi

Fortuna Anwar opined that "security must rest upon national and regional resilience rather than protection by foreign military patrons. The presence of foreign military interests in the region is viewed [by Jakarta] as an obstacle to the development of national and regional resilience."[30]

Doubts about U.S. Intentions

In addition to questioning U.S. capabilities in facing internal challenges, Indonesian leaders have usually been suspicious of American motives, diminishing the appeal of security cooperation with the United States. Part of the concern stems from Indonesia's postcolonial history. Indonesians have few fond memories of Dutch rule, and the bloody struggle for independence left residual distrust of great Western powers.

Ideology has also contributed to a degree. Even though Indonesia and the United States shared anticommunist outlooks during the Cold War, officials of the Suharto regime were concerned about the possible destabilizing effect of U.S. democracy promotion on their government. In 1986, after the People's Power revolution in the Philippines, President Reagan visited Bali and proclaimed that "the winds of freedom are blowing in Asia." Indonesian Foreign Minister Mochtar Kusumaatmadja summed up the concerns of some regional leaders by saying, "It is true the wind is blowing, but people are free to like it or not. . . . If a hurricane blows, people don't like it."[31] Many Indonesian officials saw perilous similarities between the crony capitalism of the deposed Marcos administration and the workings of Suharto's New Order regime.

Fears of U.S. motives have been even more apparent since the late 1990s, and they have not been without foundation. U.S. suspension of military ties after the 1991 Dili massacre suggested that when Washington was not compelled by a Soviet threat to look the other way, it would become much more critical of Indonesia's internal practices. Many Indonesian officials perceived the U.S. response to the 1997 financial crisis and push for East Timorese independence as serious betrayals and fear similar shifts in U.S. policy toward other separatist conflicts if they depend too much on Washington.[32] Indonesians saw the United States—not communist insurgents or ethnic separatists—as the force that overthrew the Suharto regime in 1998 after thirty-two years in power. The financial crisis had brought the Indonesian economy to its knees and required a U.S.-led international bailout. American Secretary of State Madeline Albright encouraged long-time leader Suharto to perform "a historical act of statesmanship for the democratization of Indonesia." Hours later Suharto announced his resignation, later saying that "a foreign power made me quit" using "economic weapons" at a time when Indonesia had dire need for foreign funding.[33]

The process of democratization in Indonesia after 1998 represents an ideological convergence of sorts between the two governments, but other factors have conspired against a dramatic increase in Indonesian confidence in American intentions. In particular, Indonesian leaders differed with key aspects of the U.S. campaign against terrorism after September 2001, and many Indonesians at both elite and public levels viewed U.S. policies as targeting or disadvantaging Muslims.[34] Added sensitivity to interfaith tensions generally offset the potential gains in mutual understanding as Indonesia emerged as a more robust democracy. Current U.S. President Barack Obama enjoys much higher levels of support in Indonesia, but there is little indication that his election is causing a significant shift in Indonesian alignment preferences. Weak external threats and doubts about U.S. commitment to their interests continue to lead Indonesian leaders to expect limited and uncertain rewards from tight alliance with the United States.

Perceived Risks

Although Indonesian leaders have generally seen the rewards of tight pro-American alignment as modest, they have perceived the risks as comparatively high. This owes less to systemic factors than to the country's identity and ambition as the largest state in Southeast Asia and its internal political environment.

Former Indonesian Foreign Minister Ali Alatas summed up the risks when he described Indonesia's policy of relative nonalignment as "a logical consequence of our struggle for independence and freedom from foreign domination or great-power entanglement."[35] This utterance bears a striking resemblance to the famous declarations by George Washington and James Madison early in U.S. history, when they too sought to avoid entangling alliances. Like early American leaders, Indonesian officials generally view their country as a rising power entitled to regional leadership due to its size and its anticolonial credentials. The United States avoided alliances to eschew entrapment, maintain flexibility and leverage, and limit the great powers' role in its own neighborhood (Latin America and the Caribbean). Indonesia has not issued a Monroe Doctrine for Southeast Asia, but its broad approach to alignment politics is quite similar, and the idea of a ZOPFAN was a small half-step in that direction.

Diminished Autonomy

Indonesia's government has sought to maintain that distance from the United States primarily to guard autonomy and leverage and avoid domestic backlash. Indonesian elites have believed that moving too close to the United States (or another great-power ally) would compromise national independence and foment domestic opposition.

Jusuf Wanandi summed up the view of most Indonesian officials by saying that "the absence of big-power domination means a decline in 'superpower-client' pressures and an increase in freedom to create societies that are in accordance with [Indonesian] cultural values and identities."[36] Indonesia has consistently been a leading proponent of both national and regional resilience, whereby Southeast Asian states would achieve the capability to manage their own security affairs and rely less on external protectors.[37]

The idea of national resilience relates to national pride and political psychology in Indonesia, which has long been vocal in opposing great-power intrusion into its sovereign sphere.[38] As stewards of the largest state in Southeast Asia, Indonesian leaders have felt a special sense of entitlement to regional leadership. They have also believed that the country can stand relatively well on its own. Indonesian officials have seen the need for external cooperation, particularly in the economic area, but have resisted being a follower in foreign policy. Pursuing the Indonesian ideal of an independent and active foreign policy means maintaining a high degree of autonomy in international affairs. By contrast, a passive foreign policy would lead to circumscribed independence and a loss of national self-respect. Indonesia's policy approach has not been inconsistent with a modest degree of alignment but has militated against a strong alliance that would bind Indonesia to a great power's agenda.

To many Indonesian officials, U.S. policies in the late 1990s reinforced the perils of dependency. The U.S. response to the Asian financial crisis, turn against Suharto, and shift in policy toward East Timorese independence all had major effects on Indonesia's internal politics and international image and standing. Although U.S. policies appear to have facilitated Indonesia's emergence as a more democratic state, many Indonesian officials instead focused on what they saw as a series of betrayals that destabilized and humiliated the country. In 1999, shortly after the East Timor intervention, Indonesian President Abdurrahman Wahid reflected that sentiment by saying angrily that Indonesia, India, and China should align to balance the "lop-sided power of the West."[39] At the time of that remark the U.S. congress had again sanctioned Indonesia for human rights abuses, cutting off military cooperation and providing a reminder of the danger of abandonment. Even when America became willing again to ramp up defense cooperation, Indonesia expressed interest in only a limited, flexible security relationship.

Domestic Backlash

If Indonesian leaders have had one eye on their country's position as a regional leader in Southeast Asia, they have always had to keep the other focused on domestic stability. Memories of colonial subservience loom large in Jakarta, and a government that appears to be a stooge for a foreign power would almost certainly lose domestic popularity and support. Since achieving independence from the Netherlands, Indonesian regimes have based their domestic legitimacy largely on the concept of self-reliance. The promotion of national resilience and a *bebas-aktif* foreign policy have been keys to domestic political legitimacy ever since.[40] The country's identity as the world's largest Muslim-majority state has also imposed pressures on its leaders not to be seen as kowtowing to the West.

Domestic pressures to avoid tight alliance are also partly due to what former Singaporean ambassador to Indonesia Barry Desker calls the "CNN effect."[41] The relative democratization of Indonesia in the late 1990s added to the importance of a foreign policy seen as compatible with Islam. The unpopularity of the U.S.-led wars in Iraq and Afghanistan has magnified the cost of close association with America considerably in recent years. The country's move toward democracy after 1998—a striking ideological development after the long tenure of the Suharto regime—has not fundamentally altered that dynamic, showing that the evolution of a DC's domestic political system does not guarantee a pronounced shift in alignment preferences.

Entanglement

Indonesian leaders were also wary of entrapment (or entanglement) during the Cold War, when they feared that tight alliance with the United States would unnecessarily antagonize Vietnam and the USSR. Sudjati Djiwandono of the influential CSIS think-tank in Jakarta described the rationale for Indonesia's policy as follows: "Geographically, Southeast Asia is not and will never be a vital link for Soviet security. . . . The Soviet power in the Pacific is not intended to go against us but to counter the U.S. military might in this region, which the Soviets consider a threat to their security. If we [Indonesia] favor President Reagan's call and enter into an alliance with the United States, the threats then become real because naturally the Soviet Union will consider us a U.S. ally."[42]

Shortly after the invasion of Cambodia, Indonesian Foreign Minister Mochtar Kusumaatmadja expressed similar concern about the alienation of third parties through alignment with the West, complaining of Washington's "attempts at drawing ASEAN into one certain side [of the conflict] and bringing about a confrontation between ASEAN and Hanoi."[43] In the post–Cold War period, a similar logic has encouraged Indonesia to avoid taking sides too decisively and stay out of any possible Sino-American crossfire. Entrapment concerns have receded, and worries about diminished autonomy, leverage, and domestic backlash have been increasingly dominant factors in Indonesian calculations of the risks of alignment.

Conclusions on Indonesia

Indonesia's preference for limited alignment is among the easiest to explain in Southeast Asia because it is in many respects overdetermined. Almost all the major factors that affect policymakers' risk and reward calculi have given Indonesia incentives to pursue only low-level security ties since 1975. One set of factors has to do with threat perceptions. Relative international peace in maritime Southeast Asia, even during the peak years of the Third Indochina War, has been an obvious factor shaping Indonesian preferences. Systemic changes have affected Indonesian security, but they have not changed the basic fact that most of the country's chief challenges are internal or nontraditional—not the types of issues that great-power protectors excel at addressing.

A number of other factors have contributed to the preference for limited alignment as well. Ideological affinity between Jakarta and Washington has ranged from weak to modest. It was less important than a shared disdain for communism in supporting the Suharto regime's limited alignment with America during the Cold War of recent years. The more democratic Indonesian government finds greater affinity with the form of the American political system than the substance of U.S. policymaking. Religion has also played a role. Indonesia's identity as the world's largest

Muslim-majority state has contributed to misgivings about U.S. foreign policy, especially in recent years.

Economic factors have influenced Indonesian alignment policy to a degree, though other factors may be sufficient to explain the country's preference for a limited alignment. Economic motives were a significant basis for Suharto's original tilt toward the United States in the 1960s because development was critical to head off a resurgent PKI and reduce security vulnerability.[44] Suharto's own financial motives also appear to have played a role: Western investment in natural resources and government-owned companies accrued directly to his family's benefit through an elaborate practice of corruption. Suharto's quest for U.S. aid and trade help explain why he preferred limited alignment to nonalignment. In the post–Cold War period, more balanced economic ties between China and the United States are an added reason to favor only limited alignment to avoid offending one by locking arms with the other.

Finally, Indonesia has invested greatly in institutional and normative alternatives to alignment. Its central role in the emergence of ASEAN has helped in the management of regional security and contributed to an attitude in Jakarta that Southeast Asia has little need for an external sheriff. Perhaps even more important is that Indonesian leaders have consistently marketed their country as a leading DC champion of the norms of national independence and nonalignment. Moving away from a limited security tilt toward tight alliance would therefore carry additional political costs, at home and in the region.

If Indonesia is an easy test for the proposition that DCs prefer to avoid tight alliances, it is a more difficult case for the claim that they usually prefer to avoid strict nonalignment as well. Indonesia's government has been one of the world's most outspoken advocates of nonalignment over the past several decades and has enjoyed a reasonably high degree of external security. Nevertheless, Indonesian leaders have accepted low-level security cooperation with the United States for most of the past forty years. The Indonesian case thus supports the notion that strict nonalignment is likely to be rare, because DCs usually prefer to have at least some access to great-power military aid, training, and support in the event of a crisis.

MALAYSIA

Malaysia has also favored limited alignment for most of the post-1975 period, tilting toward the United States but never approaching a tight alliance. Although Malaysia is much smaller than Indonesia and somewhat more vulnerable to external security challenges, it has formulated its preferences in a broadly similar manner. Many of the same factors help explain its desire to tilt but not to forge a stalwart pact. These include a focus on internal rather than external military challenges, concerns about U.S. friendliness to the governing regime's interests, and heavy investments in alternatives security strategies to great-power alignment. Like their colleagues in Jakarta, Malaysian officials have tended to see the rewards of tight alliance as questionable and the risks as significant, encouraging them to moderate their ties.

Menaces to Malaysia

Malaysia's history has inclined its leaders to focus on both great-power domination and fissiparous internal dynamics as the principal challenges to the country's unity and independence. The country gained its independence from British colonial rule in the late 1950s, and its birth involved a long and tortured struggle involving ethnic and ideological warfare. The 1948–1960 Malayan Emergency, pitted largely *bumiputera* (indigenous) government forces and British colonists against a festering communist insurgency that drew primarily from the ethnic Chinese population. British and allied Malayan authorities quelled the insurgency, partly by separating insurgents from the general population, but memories of that painful period would continue to stir ethnic tensions in the country.

After independence, Malaysia's early childhood was also marred by turbulence. From 1962 to 1966 Indonesia pursued an aggressive anti-imperial policy of *konfrontasi* to destabilize the British-backed government in Kuala Lumpur and bid for the disputed provinces of Sarawak and Sabah on north Borneo. Malaysian and UK forces repelled the attacks, and the provinces became part of the new Federation of Malaysia in 1963 (though the Philippines also laid claim to Sabah). However, Malaysian leaders continued to fear the strength of the ethnic Chinese population and expelled Chinese-majority Singapore in 1965.

Race and Communist Infiltration

Tensions with Indonesia subsided when Suharto took power, but the specters of ethnic unrest and communist insurgency remained foci of government security policies. Deadly racial riots between ethnic Malays and Chinese in Kuala Lumpur in May 1969 left hundreds (and by some accounts thousands) dead and drove home the danger of racial divides. Malaysian officials remained concerned throughout the ensuing decades and did not see the problem as entirely internal. They accused the PRC of cultivating relations with the country's large ethnic Chinese population for subversive purposes. Prime Minister Mohamad Mahathir later said that "the Communist Party of Malaya drew inspiration and support from the Chinese Communist Party, and . . . fears of a Chinese fifth column in Southeast Asia were strong."[45]

During the 1980s the Malaysian government suspected that the PRC's friendly overtures of economic and security cooperation were not only unreliable but also dishonest and intentionally subversive. Foreign Minister Tan Sri Ghazali Shafie described the Chinese government's diplomatic overtures in the midst of support for local communist groups as akin to "a policy of rotten fish being served in the specialized recipe of a sweet and sour dish." He added that "we in Southeast face a rather bizarre situation when our hands are being shaken by a government in the name of friendship, yet the political parties from which that government is formed declare openly to us in our faces, of its commitments to continue to support albeit morally and politically illegal and terroristic groups that are striving daily to overthrow by violent means our respective governments."[46] In 1985 Mahathir also alluded to his country's fears of an external threat from China, saying, "Anything that might make [China] too powerful might tempt certain Chinese leadership to take over and move towards expansionism."[47]

Malaysian leaders also feared the USSR's ability to foment domestic unrest. After the discovery of Soviet spy rings in Kuala Lumpur in 1976 and again in 1981, Foreign Minister Ghazali Shafie said, "Russia's objective is to bring the whole world under the ambit of Moscow while China resolves to place the whole of Asia under Beijing. So to us, both countries spell danger."[48] Ghazali Shafie emphasized that the USSR had ways to generate domestic insecurity: "The threat from the activities of the Soviet Union in pursuit of her own global design in this region is another possible source of insecurity. Like China, the Soviets too have their potential assets ready-made for conspiratorial exploitation with their specialized methods for deception, disinformation, manipulation, penetration and any specialized political action."[49]

Malaysia tended to take a more relaxed attitude toward the external military dimension of the Soviet threat. Despite its relative geographic proximity to the frontline of the Third Indochina War, Malaysia also expressed little apprehension of Vietnam. As Mahathir said, "Our concern is only the big powers. We don't think that a small power . . . will send its battleships against us. They can't."[50] He could have added that most small powers also lacked the resources to foment domestic rebellion by supporting local rebel groups.

Disputes with Neighbors

Although Malaysia's economic development has helped its government manage domestic challenges better than most of its Southeast Asian counterparts, the country's central position and unusual geography have rendered it vulnerable to frequent disputes with neighbors. Malaysia—which includes a peninsular lobe and the Borneo provinces of Sarawak and Sabah—shares either maritime or land borders with almost every other country in the region. Partly for this reason, Kuala Lumpur has long endured simmering disputes with its ASEAN neighbors.

Since 1975 protracted disputes with Brunei over the Limbang peninsula, with Thailand around the countries' shared land border, with Singapore over water rights and a host of other issues, and with several countries (including China) over maritime rights in the South China Sea have bedeviled Malaysia's regional relations. These disputes have had more than political importance; most of Malaysia's natural resources are taken from a 200-mile maritime exclusion zone surrounding its coastline, and officials have long made the protection of that exclusion zone a top defense priority.[51] Nevertheless, bilateral confidence-building measures, engagement through ASEAN, and Malaysia's own defense buildup have made it unlikely that any of its territorial or resource-related disputes would lead to large-scale armed conflict.

A China threat has also remained, especially in the context of the Spratly Island disputes. During the 1990s the chief of the Malaysian Navy and the head of Malaysia's Institute for Maritime Affairs voiced concerns that China would seek to "revive the Middle Kingdom mentality and expect tribute from Southeast Asia."[52] However, unlike Vietnam, Malaysia has not felt particularly exposed to a military menace from the PRC in the near term.

Facing a range of significant but nonexistential threats, Malaysian officials have generally seen a benefit of security cooperation with the United States and its Anglo-Saxon allies. Tilting toward Washington allows Malaysia to access advanced training and weapons systems to build its own security forces.[53] Low-level ties and facilitation of a U.S. role in the region have also helped to preserve maritime stability vital to Malaysia's economy and security interests. However, security threats to Malaysia since 1975 have not been severe enough to make tight alliance attractive.

Modest Expected Rewards

Although threats have not prompted Kuala Lumpur to align closely with the United States since 1975, modest expected rewards from the security relationship with America have also contributed to Malaysia's preference for limited alignment. Malaysia does see clear benefits to the U.S. relationship. The IMET program has offered more than 1,500 Malaysian military officers training in the United States. Since 1994 Malaysia has also participated in annual ten-day joint training with the United States under the CARAT program, under which U.S. forces share techniques on air and jungle combat, naval maneuvers, and diving and rescue operations.[54] Access to advanced weapons systems are a further bonus, and the alignment has served to facilitate the development of a robust economic relationship, whereby the United States has become Malaysia's largest trading partner.[55]

Doubts about America

Nevertheless, Malaysian officials have harbored concerns about U.S. intentions, relevant capabilities, and commitment. To some extent, those concerns stem from Malaysia's postcolonial legacy and general apprehension about great powers. Throughout the Cold War, Malaysia championed what Donald Emmerson calls a "strategically exclusive" concept of regional security, prioritizing ways to limit great-power interference in the region.[56]

Another concern (as in Indonesia) has been the limited effectiveness of American might in managing domestic threats. As Malaysian Defense Minister Najib Razak argued in 2003, a high degree of identification with an external power can undermine a domestic security campaign by making the government appear a puppet of foreign interests. Contemporary Malaysian security has been focused on economic well-being and ethnic relations, and foreign military power is not particularly helpful in dealing with either challenge.[57] Ghazali Shafie argued in 1975 that great powers are not very useful in quelling domestic insurgencies, and that "external support for internal insurgencies or for governments combating insurgencies, have the effect of raising the level of violence and complicating both conflict management and the peaceful resolution of conflicts through political means. Internal stability cannot after all be imposed from the outside."[58]

He spoke from a country with ample experience of confronting major armed insurgency throughout the emergency period and afterward. This partly explains why both Malaysia and Indonesia had rejected strong pro-Western alignments such as SEATO in their respective efforts to manage Cold War security issues. Malaysia has been particularly vocal in this respect since 2001, criticizing close Philippine-U.S. cooperation against Abu Sayyaf and other Muslim insurgents in the southern Philippines. The Malaysian government has consistently feared that the presence of American troops would increase the appeal of radical Islamic groups. Malaysian Foreign Minister Hamid Albar said in 2002, "We have always thought that the best way of handling internal or regional problems is between regional countries."[59]

Malaysia has long stressed the need to develop stand-alone capacity and to avoid reliance on great-power protection, especially when managing internal threats. The Malaysian concept of comprehensive security resembles the Indonesian principle of *ketahanan*. As Mahathir said in 1984, "Malaysia's first line of defense is not its military capability. The first line of defense lies in its national resilience."[60] Two years later, he added, "National security is inseparable from political stability, economic success and social harmony. Without these, all the guns in the world cannot prevent a country from being overcome by its enemies."[61]

Part of the reason for Malaysia's reluctance to rely on U.S. protection has been a fear that America lacks credibility when pledging to defend its Southeast Asian partners. Malaysian governments have been wary of relying too much on an uncertain U.S. security commitment to the region, fearing that dependence could be followed by abandonment.[62] Mahathir put the case most bluntly: "There is ample reason to doubt that the U.S. would come to our aid if we were under attack. It seems to me the Americans offer help only when they themselves feel threatened. . . . In short, a U.S. military presence here is no guarantee of security."[63]

Malaysian leaders have also been wary of placing too much trust in the United States for ideological reasons, because Washington has often criticized Malaysia harshly for human rights practices. In 1997 Mahathir complained of "a lot of pressures" from the United States and suggested that the American tendency to" impose things on others," such as human rights and democratic norms, was a greater threat to Southeast Asian stability than the rise of China.[64] Perceptions that the United States was slow to help Malaysia and its neighbors during the Asian financial crisis further undermined U.S. credibility, and the well-publicized exchange between Vice President Al Gore and Mahathir over human rights and the case of Anwar Ibrahim further soured relations.

With Mahathir's departure in 2003, public Malaysian spats with Washington have become much less frequent. In addition, as it has become more democratic, Kuala Lumpur has expressed a greater degree of ideological affinity for the United States—or at least a diminished sense of ideological threat from Washington. In 2005 Malaysian Foreign Minister Syed Hamid Albar cited ideological affinity as a growing reason for U.S.-Malaysian cooperation.[65] However, this sense of ideological convergence should not be overstated. Mahathir's less strident successors,

Abdullah Badawi and Najib Razak, and other Malaysian leaders remain cautious in their approach to the United States and continue to favor limited alignment.

Domestic and Regional Risks

The substantial perceived risks of alignment have given Malaysia further reason to keep America at arm's length. During the Cold War, Kuala Lumpur sought (like Indonesia) to avoid unnecessary embroilment in regional or superpower conflict. Following the Vietnamese invasion of Cambodia, Malaysia stressed the limits on its ties to the West so as to preserve frosty—but not openly hostile—relations with Moscow or Hanoi. Malaysian Foreign Minister Tengku Ahmad Rithauddeen was at pains to explain that disapproval of the Vietnamese occupation did not constitute anti-Soviet alignment. He wrote as follows: "Non-alignment is one of the principal cornerstones of Malaysia's foreign policy. Based on the need to be uninvolved or else become entangled with the major powers, Malaysia has adopted and consistently practiced a policy of balanced and equidistant relationship with the big powers.... Malaysia's stand on the Kampuchean problem is not influenced by any foreign power.... Malaysia's stand in fact is perfectly consistent with ZOPFAN and the non-alignment principles. Accusations that we are taking sides and that we are not neutral are untrue."[66]

Mahathir described his country's desire for relative neutralism clearly, saying, "We want to remain equidistant from the big powers, the United States, China, and the Soviet Union."[67] Malaysian officials also believed that a robust military alliance would provoke more aggressive behavior from Vietnam and increase both Thai and Vietnamese dependence on great-power allies.[68] Economics were also a factor. As a rapidly developing economy dependent on export of raw materials and manufactured goods for growth, Malaysia depended on having access to the world's largest markets.[69] Although the USSR was not an important trading partner in the 1980s, China was quickly becoming so.

Amitav Acharya argues that Malaysia has continued to pursue a "counterdominance" strategy in the post–Cold War era. With the uncertainties surrounding the rise of China, Malaysia has pursued a mix of engagement and containment techniques, but Kuala Lumpur has carefully avoided a policy approach that entails more than loose and informal security ties with the United States. "As a secondary state with considerable distrust of Western security guarantees.... Malaysia will do its utmost to avoid being seen as an American client."[70] Officials in Kuala Lumpur generally wish for neither the United States nor China to dominate the region and believe that a strong balancing alignment against China would give Washington too much influence.

Malaysia has been the most vocal of the maritime Southeast Asian countries in asserting the need for independence in the economic sphere. The Malaysian political system is dominated by a set of elites who depend largely on economic performance to preserve legitimacy and to maintain support at the mass level. Trade and financial relations with the West have been thus imperative throughout the country's independent history. However, Malaysia has been particularly critical of

Western policies in the economic sphere, as exercised through international financial institutions including the IMF and World Bank. UMNO leaders have feared that Western human rights, labor, and corruption standards would derail growth and undermine regime stability and legitimacy in Kuala Lumpur. The Anglo-American model of neoliberalism threatened to reduce the economic policy autonomy that UMNO enjoyed and to reduce the control that the regime had to manage national development, subjecting it more to the whims of market forces.[71] Mahathir expressed his fear of neoliberalism by saying in 1998, "We have seen that market forces can change governments. What is the need for national elections if the results have to be approved by the market?"[72]

Malaysia has also been outspoken in its desire to defend Muslim interests and values. Islam took on greater political importance in the country's domestic politics in the 1980s, as Middle Eastern influence in the country grew and as political participation led to the emergence of viable Islamist parties. During the Cold War era strains between the United States and the Muslim world occasionally bedeviled U.S.-Malaysian relations. In recent years, however, the role of religion in has become more obvious, making it more costly for the Malaysian government to be seen as an ally of America.

Since 9/11 Malaysia has been the most outwardly critical Southeast Asian state of the U.S. campaign against terrorism, distancing itself from numerous aspects of American foreign policy despite close technical cooperation. Malaysian leaders were also quick to emphasize that the Regional Centre for Counter Terrorism established in Kuala Lumpur in 2003 was a Malaysian, not an American, initiative.[73] "It is our policy not to allow foreign military bases or installations in our country," explained Foreign Minister Syed Hamid Albar.[74] Albar summed up Kuala Lumpur's position in a 2005 address in Washington: "On the campaign against terrorism, while Malaysia is committed to helping the U.S. in the war against terrorism, we are however very much against the unilateralist action of the U.S. and other countries with regard to Iraq."[75]

Special Advisor to the Malaysian Prime Minister Khairy Jamaluddin asserted that the 2003 war in Iraq tested the relationship more than any previous development but that the fundamentals of the relationship remained strong and that UMNO was not under as great a domestic political pressure to eschew Washington as some have argued. Despite political tensions on the surface, he noted, security and defense relations between Malaysia and the United States have gotten closer over the years.[76] That assertion, though true, has not resulted in anything approaching a tight alliance. The current government of Najib Razak has followed the same path as its predecessors, and Malaysian policy continues to be an excellent example of DC preference for limited alignment.

Conclusions on Malaysia
Many of the variables affecting Malaysia's alignment calculus are similar to those driving Indonesian preferences. A modest external threat environment has given

officials in Kuala Lumpur only modest need for the types of military rewards that a tight great-power ally can provide. That threat environment has varied somewhat according to global strategic conditions, as foreign sponsorship of local communist groups rose and receded and as China arrived on the stage, but the more important determinants have been regional or domestic. The country's location and relative success in managing neighborly relations since the era of *Konfrontasi*—largely through ASEAN and related cooperative ventures—have taken some of the edge off of regional threat perceptions. The maintenance of complementary defense ties with the ANZUK countries has also helped relieve a modest share of the external security burden. The country's main security concerns have remained internal— the types of concerns that great-power alliances are not ideally suited to address.

At the same time, Malaysia has seen considerable risks to tight alliance with America. This perception owes to the country's relatively recent history of colonial rule, episodic ideological tension between the "soft authoritarian" Malaysian regime and the U.S. government, doubts or misgivings about America's approach to international security, and some cultural sensitivities arising from perceptions of the U.S. government's disposition toward Islam. In short, without a strong threat vector pointing in the direction of a tight alliance, Malaysian leaders have seen ample reasons to avoid such an arrangement.

BRUNEI

Brunei's alignment policy can also be described as one of limited alignment, though the sultanate's small size and unusual political and economic constitution have inclined it to rely more heavily on external security support than Malaysia or Indonesia. The wealthy microstate was reluctant to assume full independence from Britain during the Cold War era because of its fears of predation by much larger, less affluent neighbors.[77] After gaining independence, Brunei's foreign policy placed it in the Western camp as a British ally. Bandar Seri Begawan also developed strong defense ties with Singapore, which faces a broadly similar set of external security concerns and possesses vastly greater military resources than Brunei. However, in its relations with the great powers, Brunei has tended to follow Malaysia's and Indonesia's lead and tilt toward the United States.

Threat Environment
One reason Brunei has avoided closer security cooperation with the United States is that the sultanate has not percieved serious enough security challenges to justify alignment with America. The economically advanced microstate has faced only limited organized dissent from within its borders, largely because strong Bruneian public welfare and education systems have contributed to a high standard of living and give the sultanate a high level of performance legitimacy. Leaders in Bandar Seri Begawan recall clearly that the traumatic 1962 Brunei Revolt occurred through local groups with Indonesian (and, to a lesser extent, Malaysian) sponsorship, but they

do not perceive close identification with the United States as an appropriate way to manage the possibility of renewed local dissent.

Like Singapore, Brunei has identified its immediate neighbors as the primary sources of external threat to the country and its governing regime.[78] Brunei is surrounded on land by the Malaysian provinces or Sarawak and Sabah and situated on the island of Borneo amid the sprawling Indonesian archipelago. With a very small land area and a population of less than 300,000, and with vast petroleum resources in its territory, the Sultanate has always been strategically vulnerable to its larger neighbors. Disputes over the Limbang territory and parts of Brunei Bay still obtain with Kuala Lumpur. Unlike Singapore, however, the Bruneian regime is ethnically Malay and Islamic, which has taken some of the edge off its fears of Malaysia and Indonesia.

Tensions in the South China Sea have become increasingly important during China's rise to power. Brunei is a claimant to some of the Spratly Islands and depends heavily on free maritime passage in the region for its export of petroleum. Like many of its neighbors, Brunei depends on the United States not only as an export market, but also as the dominant naval power that provides stability in the sea-lanes that facilitate trade. A disruption of sea-borne commerce in the South China Sea would be devastating for the Bruneian economy, which helps explain why the sultanate has facilitated a U.S. presence in the area, particularly after the closure of Subic Bay.

However, Brunei has generally faced less severe external and internal security challenges in the post–Cold War period, reducing its need for great-power allies. Communist groups have not presented a serious threat to the Bruneian government's interests, and neighborly menaces have generally waned. Bruneian leaders have believed that continuing ties to the UK government—and the presence of British Gurkhas to protect some of its most valued oil installations and government establishments—provide adequate protection against the principal external security challenges in its immediate environs. The risks of tight alliance with the United States have thus not been worth bearing.

The Shell Connection

The primary attractive forces between Brunei and the United States are also related to the sultanate's economic interests. The Brunei Shell Petroleum Company, a 50-50 joint venture between the Bruneian government and Royal Dutch Shell, is the chief oil and gas production company in the tiny, resource-rich country. It is intimately tied to the public coffers and the personal interests of the leadership, and it dominates the economy. At its peak level of dominance in the late 1970s and early 1980s, Brunei Shell accounted for nearly 99 percent of the country's exports.[79] Other companies have since carved out minority shares of Brunei's oil business, but they also operate closely with the government.

The United States, Japan, and other U.S. allies have long been key importers of Brunei's oil. Japan was easily the largest importer during the Cold War period, and other U.S. security partners such as Singapore, Taiwan, and South Korea are now major importers as well. Brunei's pro-Western and anticommunist foreign policy during the Cold War was thus motivated largely by economic considerations. These are closely tied to maritime security: America and its allies have promoted an open trading order and maritime stability that are critical for Brunei's continued wealth and regime stability. These economic and security interests have not led Bandar Seri Begawan to seek a tight military pact with America, but they have provided powerful incentives to maintain a loose, flexible alignment with the United States.

Islamic Legitimacy

In Brunei the legitimacy of the sultanate is only partly based on economic welfare. It is also premised on the sultan's identity as the last true Malay Islamic leader, which resonates deeply in Malay historical culture. The sultanate's Islamic credentials create incentives to keep Washington at arm's length, even while economic ties are close. In general, Brunei has been able to steer a pro-American policy without much public backlash, but the sultan's support for the 1990–1991 Gulf War generated domestic dissent and showed that his government's freedom of maneuver has limits. The government has more recently distanced itself from U.S.-led wars in Afghanistan and Iraq, and, as Roger Kershaw has argued, the sultanate is engaged in "a continuous balancing act between its external strategic interest (qua territory) and the requirements of domestic legitimation (qua regime)."[80] There is little doubt that the intercultural aspect of U.S. relations with Brunei has reduced the likelihood of a highly institutionalized alliance and increased the sultanate's propensity to favor an arm's-length security relationship.

Bruneian officials have also been wary of aligning with the United States or other Western powers to a degree that would cause unease in its much larger neighbors, Malaysia and Indonesia. As China becomes more powerful as a military player and as a trading partner, Brunei has also sought to avoid jeopardizing that relationship. Instead, leaders in Bandar Seri Begawan have pursued a multitrack approach to defending its security interests, relying partly on cultivating positive economic ties with China and other powers to moderate their behavior, partly on international organizations like the Organization of the Islamic Conference and ASEAN, and partly on limited fallback security arrangements with Western powers.[81] As a vulnerable microstate, Brunei has guarded its independence carefully, cooperating with Washington in various ways yet preserving a critical voice and its suspicious majority-Muslim population and neighbors that the regime is not subservient to U.S. interests.

SINGAPORE

Indonesia, Malaysia, and to a slightly lesser extent Brunei are all relatively straightforward and consistent examples of limited alignment behavior since 1975. The evolution of Singapore's alignment policy has been slightly more complex, shifting

from relative nonalignment during the Cold War period to a much more significant alignment with the United States since the early 1990s. Although Singapore
can be described as pursuing limited alignment for essentially the entire period
since 1975, it has come somewhat closer to allying tightly in recent years. The primary explanations are a sense of heightened threat from neighbors, international
terrorist groups, and uncertainty about China's rise in the region. Singapore has
nonetheless tried to manage the risks of alignment by downplaying the depth and
permanency of its defense ties with Washington. Always planning for the future,
Singaporean leaders have tried to keep open the possibility of changing course if
the balance of power in the region shifts or if relations with neighbors deteriorate
in unexpected ways.

Extreme Vulnerability

Singapore's threat perceptions are inextricably tied to its small territorial size and
vulnerability, as well as its identity as an island with a majority ethnic Chinese population in the midst of larger, predominantly Malay populations. Despite the city-
state's considerable military prowess, its government has usually viewed Malaysia
and Indonesia as the primary sources of threat to Singapore. Occupying an island of
just 632 square kilometers, Singaporean leaders have long been wary of becoming
a Chinese nut in a Malay nutcracker formed by its larger, predominantly Muslim
neighbors. Michael Leifer has described Singapore as "a state whose foreign policy
is rooted in a culture of siege and insecurity which dates from the traumatic experience" of the *Konfrontasi* and the city-state's expulsion from the Federation of Malaya in 1965.[82] As early as 1965 Lee Kuan Yew identified the centrality of geography
to Singaporean threat perception, saying, "we are in the heart of [the Malay/Indo-
nesian] archipelago which makes our position one of supreme strategic importance
and, at the same time, one of grave perils for ourselves if we overplay our hand."[83]
Singaporean officials have viewed the prospect of less secular governments coming
to power in Kuala Lumpur and Jakarta, or of spillover internal conflicts, as serious
ongoing dangers to Singapore, especially in the event of an economic downturn,
which could unmask latent instability.

Geography has also made Singapore more conscious than most Southeast Asian
countries of the broader strategic balance in the Asia–Pacific. Located along the
Straits of Malacca, one of the busiest sea-lanes in the world, Singapore derives its
wealth—and thereby much of its strength and political legitimacy—from trade.
During the Cold War, Lee Kuan Yew was the most outspoken leader in maritime
Southeast Asia in expressing fear of Soviet and Vietnamese power in the region,
exhorting the U.S. government to "ensure that the Soviet Union, either on her
own or through her surrogate, Vietnam, should not be allowed to dominate or intimidate Southeast Asia with her military might" or establish a hold on the Straits
of Malacca, which Lee called a "choke point" for regional trade and security.[84]
Although Singaporean leaders feared both Soviet-Vietnamese and Chinese plans to

dominate Southeast Asia, they perceived Hanoi and Moscow as more dangerous in the early 1980s, because as one senior official said, "they have the capacity" whereas "the Chinese [did not] have the capacity yet."[85]

In the post–Cold War period Singapore has again been concerned about the changing regional balance of power, focusing more of its attention on the uncertain consequences of the rise of China.[86] In 1996 Lee Kuan Yew asserted forcefully that all ASEAN countries shared a concern about Chinese growth:

> As China's development nears the point where it will have enough weight to elbow its way into the region, it will make a fateful decision—whether to be a hegemon, using its economic and military weight to create a sphere of influence in the region for its economic or security needs, or to continue as a good international citizen. . . . All countries, medium and small, have this concern: will China seek to re-establish its traditional pattern of international relations of vassal states in a tributary relationship with the Middle Kingdom? Any signs of this will alarm all the countries in the region, and cause most, not all, countries to realign themselves closer to the U.S. and Japan.[87]

Like many Southeast Asian officials, Singaporean leaders have viewed China's extraordinary growth through the lens of history, fearful of a return to the imperial rule they suffered under Chinese empires, European colonists, and the wartime Japanese army. Lee explained regional concerns in precisely those terms: "Many medium and small countries in Asia are uneasy that China may want to resume the imperial status it had in earlier centuries and have misgivings about being treated as vassal states having to send tribute to China."[88]

Parliamentarian Simon Tay linked the China threat directly to Singapore's increasingly tight relations with the United States, stressing that Singapore perceives threats to broader regional stability as a serious local concern: "It's no secret that Singapore believes that the presence of the U.S. military in this part of the world contributes to the peace and stability of the region. . . . We want the Yankees here . . . [The possibility of a two-pincer Chinese advance through Myanmar and the Spratlys] is quite a scary thought for those of us sitting here in the middle."[89] Singaporean leaders have enjoyed relatively warm ties with their PRC counterparts but have been remarkably candid in expressing their concerns about China's rise. In 2005 Lee Kuan Yew admonished China to teach its youth "to reassure the world that China will not turn out to be a disruptive force" and to warn tomorrow's leaders of "the mistakes China made [in the past] as a result of hubris and excesses in ideology."[90] Even if Chinese or other advances into the region do not reach Singapore's immediate environs, a disruption of commerce due to great-power conflict elsewhere in Asia would affect the tiny city-state's economy. In many respects Singapore is a developed country located in the developing world, and its concerns reflect its economic position.

Although Singapore's expressed concerns about China and the overall regional balance of power are not insincere, they help justify an American presence that also helps protect against more immediate and serious perceived threats to the city-state from its Malay-majority neighbors and terrorist groups. Singapore has long had tense relations with Malaysia and Indonesia, often over maritime sovereignty issues, and disagreements remain even after the International Court of Justice rendered an important decision on the matter in 2008.

External threats have always been present for the island city-state, but since its independence, no serious threat of force by any state has been directed against Singapore's territory. Given Singapore's military muscle, direct military attacks are unlikely. The greater fear in Singapore is that tensions with neighbors will result in the types of ethnic struggles that led to Singapore's expulsion from Malaysia in 1965. Such disputes could lead to a cut-off of Singapore's access to critical resources—above all water from Malaysia—or lead to renewed ethnic tensions within the city-state. Worse still, Singapore is a prime target for regional terrorist groups who could damage the country's stability and economy badly through a 9/11-style attack. Former Singaporean Secretary of Foreign Affairs Kishore Mahbubani has described Singapore's environs as "the Balkans of Asia" and cited the perpetual need to avoid ethnic friction.[91]

For much of the post-1975 period, Singaporean leaders believed that local and neighborly threats were best managed through a loose alignment or low-level cooperation with the United States, in addition to the FPDA and intraregional ties. However, the aftermath of the Asian financial crisis exacerbated Singaporean fears considerably. Malaysian and Indonesian leaders accused Singapore of failing to provide aid in a time of need. As late as 1999, racial tensions prompted Goh Chok Tong to assert that Singapore was still a fragile society and had not developed into a coherent nation.[92] The September 11 attacks reflected Singapore's nightmare scenario, and although Singapore's ethnic Chinese leaders have generally attempted to downplay the religious dimension of threat perception, they have come to identify Islamic terrorism as the primary short-term threat to their interests. In addition to concerns about the regional balance of power, the terrorist menace has given Singapore a reason to align somewhat more closely with the United States while sticking to a strategy that can still be best described as one of limited alignment.[93]

Rewards

In addition to increasingly strong external threats, Singapore has had incentives to align with the United States to secure high-tech weapons as it has developed and gone militarily up-market. Alignments with technologically advanced Western nations have long been critical for Singaporean security, because Singapore's geography prohibits a conventional land defense and compels the island city-state to rely on high-tech offensive weaponry and strategic preemption for protection. Through alignment with America, Singapore also gets access to state-of-the art hardware (such as F-16 fighter planes), advanced training for its air force in several American locations, R&D collaboration, and preferential access to American intelligence—which Singapore sees as increasingly critical in dealing with terrorism and other security threats.[94]

Singapore has been one of the most explicit Southeast Asian states in highlighting the attractiveness of America's raw military capabilities. As early as 1966, one year after independence, Lee Kuan Yew said, "In the last resort it is power which decides what happens and, therefore, it behooves us to always have overwhelming power on our side."[95] Singaporean Prime Minister Lee Hsien Loong also made the ancillary economic rewards of great-power military support clear. Since World War II, he said, the United States has "helped to keep the peace in the region, and to provide the stability and security that underpinned the growth and development of many countries in Asia. [The United States] defended the region not only with words but with action [and] bought fragile new countries precious time to consolidate and prosper."[96]

Derek Da Cunha, former senior fellow at the Institute of Southeast Asian Studies, describes the city-state's choice to align more closely with the United States over time as "placing a bet" on the superiority of American power and progressively "throwing in its lot" with Washington.[97] Singaporean Prime Minister Goh Chok Tong made his view of American power clear in 2003, saying, "[American] pre-eminence is the key geopolitical fact of the post–Cold War world. . . [and] is unlikely to be seriously challenged by any country or group of countries for a very long time."[98]

In addition to helping Singapore defend itself against external threats, U.S. capabilities can be useful in dealing with nontraditional security issues that have been increasingly important to Singaporean policymakers. Prime Minister Lee Hsien Loong cited the 2004 Asian tsunami, which devastated parts of Aceh and southern Thailand, as one such example. Although many countries contributed to the relief operation, Lee noted that "only the U.S. had the means to dispatch a carrier battle group" and that "neither China nor India can perform this security role of the U.S. in Asia for many years to come."[99] The U.S. Navy can help Singapore avoid security fallout from such crises, such as large-scale refugee flows.

The American military presence in Southeast Asia has paid considerable military dividends for Singapore, adding to the appeal of a strategic alignment. Singapore has also long cited strong trade and investment ties and compatible economic systems as part of the basis for solid security relations with the United States. In May 2003, when signing a free trade agreement with the United States (the first in Southeast Asia), Prime Minister Goh explained: "Today, we have one of the closest trans-Pacific relationships. Our relationship is multidimensional in defense, as well as economics, with a shared strategic vision."[100]

Cultural affinity has also served as a modest attractive force in Singapore-U.S. alignment. Singapore is an English-speaking country with strong ties to the West, based partly on its British colonial history. Most Singaporeans are ethnically Chinese but educated in English with a Western standard of living and high degree of access to Western media and consumer goods. Singaporean Foreign Minister S. Rajaratnam was frank about his country's cultural (and economic) reasons for alignment with the United States in the 1980s: "Though we want all powers to be present in Asia, we are closer and feel safer with the Americans than with the others. We make no bones about this. Our connections are close with America, our economic relations are with America. They can provide much more for our economic well-being, whereas Russia can give us very little. Our cultural orientation is towards the West, and we make no pretense about it."[101]

In theory, cultural ties should also establish a bond between Singapore and China. However, to avoid ethnic tensions, Singapore has repeatedly insisted that its economic cooperation with China is not based on ethnic affinity. Home Affairs Minister Wong Kan Seng described the perceptions of Singapore as a "third China" beside the PRC and Taiwan as "utter rubbish," describing his country's economic ties to Beijing as the products of "economic opportunities, not ethnic affinity."[102] For these reasons, the United States continues to have more appeal as a great-power ally from both material and ideational standpoints.

Regional Risks

Strong perceived threats and clear benefits of cooperation with America—largely through advanced arms systems and training—have meant that Singapore perceives great rewards from its alignment with the United States, particularly in the post–Cold War era. However, since 1975 Singapore has eschewed a tight alliance, and even as ties have strengthened, its leaders have been at pains to say that they are friends but not allies of America. The principal reason is that siding with Washington carries considerable risks for Singapore, particularly in its relations with regional neighbors.

The Singaporean government has been frank in its desire to avoid unnecessary embroilment in great-power and regional conflict. In 1999 Senior Minister Lee Kuan Yew emphasized the importance for smaller powers to avoid being seen as the pawns of greater powers. He said, "If we are not careful, we could get caught in a very big conflict; if there is no such thing as a balance of power in the Pacific, we are very much at risk. You know the saying, 'big fish eat small fish; small fish eat shrimps.' We are shrimps."[103]

Lee's remarks express long-standing fears about two layers of potential insecurity for the island city-state. The risk that big fish will eat small ones clearly refers to the risk that powerful countries like China, a remilitarized Japan, an emerging India, or the United States will clash and draw Southeast Asia into the fray. However, the smaller fish that Lee fears will eat the Singaporean shrimp are Indonesia and Malaysia.

During the Cold War Singapore was able to vocally support a strong U.S. presence in the region without aligning closely itself, mainly because other U.S. allies—namely Thailand and the Philippines—provided basing facilities and served as platforms for the projection of American power. Singapore could therefore maintain only loose security ties to Washington and avoid the risk of antagonizing the USSR, Malaysia, and Indonesia by being seen as an American client or outpost. Thailand's relationship with China also made it easier for Singapore to avoid developing security ties with China during the 1980s, despite a shared fear of the USSR and Vietnam.

The turning point for Singaporean alignment policy was the Philippine decision to close the U.S. bases at Subic Bay and Clark Air Field.[104] Singaporean leaders reacted more decisively than any other Southeast Asian state to provide an alternative platform for U.S. power. When other countries allowed Singapore to free ride to an extent on the American military presence in the region, the city-state did. However, when forced to assume more of the burden, the Lion City has done so despite the risks. Singaporean Permanent Secretary Bilahari Kausikan expressed Singapore's perception that only America can serve as a "strategic balancer."[105]

To avoid antagonizing its neighbors, Singapore has gone to considerable lengths to characterize the country's growing ties to America as limited and nonpermanent. As both Jürgen Haacke and Michael Leifer have argued, the U.S.-Singapore relationship has been a key to Singapore's policy of encouraging a strong U.S. role in the regional balance of power but has not amounted to forging a formal military alliance. Instead, Singapore has used a mix of bilateral, multilateral, military, and nonmilitary vehicles in attempting to influence the regional balance of power.[106] Prime Minister Goh has been explicit about the risk that cooperation with Washington could make Singapore appear a client state. He and other Singaporean leaders have carefully avoided referring to America as an ally, instead characterizing it as a friend with interests that coincide "in the short term, medium term, and in a strategic sense."[107]

Singaporean Prime Minister Lee Hsien Loong has also stressed his country's concern about being caught in the crosshairs of a great-power conflict. In late 2009 he repeated an assertion he had made throughout the preceding decade:"All countries would like to be friends with China, and all countries would also like simultaneously to be friends with America. We don't want to have to choose sides."[108] Singapore has thus been careful to stress that American access to the Changi naval facility does not amount to a permanent base and that the port is open to other countries as well.[109] Foreign Minister Jayakumar also pointed out that although Singapore has "excellent" relations with the United States, "that does not mean we are subservient to the U.S. or that we agree with everything that the U.S. does, or says, or requests, without regard for our own national interests."[110] As Naranyan Ganesan argues, Singapore has cautiously veered away from moves that would place it in a sandwich between rival powers.[111]

Economics have long been important factors in Singaporean strategic thinking as well, and the issue of choosing sides between China and the United States has presented an added dilemma for the city-state. During the late 1980s Singapore was the largest ASEAN investor in China, and by the late 1990s had more than $1 billion invested in the PRC. In 2001 Singaporean Foreign Minister George Yeo highlighted the potential advantages of China's economic growth by advising Singaporeans to "hitch a ride . . . to the coming Chinese economic juggernaut."[112] Engagement with China has thus been attractive on the economic level, encouraging Singapore to align loosely against the PRC in the defense arena, but not to balance against it aggressively. Moreover, Singaporean leaders have been frank in their view that an economically successful China is more apt to be a peaceful one.[113]

Domestic factors have likewise created incentives for Singapore to pursue limited alignment, especially since 9/11. Singapore has been as clear as any Southeast Asian state in citing terrorism as a serious, prolonged security threat. Given its location and demographic composition, the government has had to balance the competing aims of maintaining local political credibility while working closely with America in a war on terror that its leaders generally support. Shortly after the September 11 attacks Singaporean Prime Minister Goh announced that his country would stand with the United States in its campaign against terrorism and would be willing to "accept risks for the sake of a better world," but he cautioned that there were "regional and domestic sensitivities to manage."[114] Goh was explicit about the potential domestic risks of cooperation with American counterterrorism efforts: "Some Singaporean Muslims might mistakenly perceive [U.S.-Singaporean cooperation against Jemaah Islamiah], the global fight against terrorism and the United States' impending attack on Iraq as a conspiracy against their religion. This could turn them against the non-Muslim community. Worse it could radicalize some of them."[115]

A 2004 defense white paper, which treated terrorism as Singapore's overriding security concern, warned that Singapore's "strong stand against terrorism" and its part in the global campaign against terror would contribute to "the real prospect that a terrorist attack could occur" in the city-state.[116] The Singaporean government's concern with possible domestic and regional backlash help to explain why it sought to avoid looking like an American client and did not advertise the most important aspect of its cooperation: significantly increased logistical cooperation, which allowed larger numbers of U.S. aircraft and naval vessels to use facilities in Singapore.[117]

Ideology has also tended to place some limits on the Singapore–U.S. relationship. Washington has frequently accused Singapore of poor human rights practices and antidemocratic one-party rule. In 1988 Singapore accused U.S. officials of interfering in its domestic affairs, expelling an American diplomat alleged to have encouraged a high-profile political dissident to organize a bona fide opposition to the PAP. Senior Singaporean diplomat Bilahari Kausikan later asserted that there is "a natural tactical convergence of interests between the Western media and human rights activists and those aspiring Asian elites who are challenging established governments."[118] Lee Kuan Yew was a central protagonist in the Asian values debate of the 1990s and has resisted U.S. pressure for human rights and democratization.

In 2001 Lee warned that Washington's push to democratize Indonesia had pushed the country toward political chaos.[119] Singaporean perceptions of an overzealous American human rights and democratization agenda lead them to perceive a non-negligible domestic political risk of becoming too dependent on America.

Conclusions on Singapore

Overall, Singaporean officials have preferred a limited, flexible security alignment. When forced to choose between what they perceive as an inadequate U.S. presence in the region and a slightly stronger alignment, the Lion City has selected the latter but has attempted to minimize the domestic and regional risks of alignment by stressing the flexibility of the arrangement and insisting that it does not amount to an alliance.[120] As Bilahari Kausikan explained, Singapore hasn't signed a formal alliance with the United States, because it doesn't have to.[121] Singapore's leaders have carefully placed limits on the extent of their alignment with America, denying permanent bases, mutual security guarantees, or joint operations of broad scope. Singaporean leaders have been more explicit about the benefits of limited alignment than perhaps any other high-ranking officials in Southeast Asia. For a tiny state in a relatively dangerous neighborhood, a substantial but relatively flexible security arrangement with America has helped manage strategic uncertainty and provide elbow room for the city-state's striking economic development.

THE PHILIPPINES

The Philippines is in many ways the principal outlier in Southeast Asian alignment politics, allying tightly for a greater period of time than any other country in the region since 1975. The Philippine case is a powerful example of how factors other than power configurations and threat perceptions can drive DC's alignment preferences and policies. The Philippines has often allied tightly with the United States even though the country has generally not faced severe external military threats.

Tight Philippine alliance with America has owed partly to cooperation against domestic insurgents, but in most periods it can be better explained as a result of the secondary variables discussed in chapter 1. Perceptions of American friendliness, ideological and cultural ties, and ample experience in close cooperation have all served as more important glue for the pact than external threats. Economic support has also been important and was a major perceived benefit to Philippine leaders of the massive U.S. facilities at Clark Air Field and Subic Bay. Partly on the basis of the long-standing relationship between the two countries and the relative public popularity of America, Philippine leaders have also perceived the political risks of alignment with America as less severe than most of their neighbors. Taken together, these ideational and economic variables largely explain the Philippine anomaly.

Because of the country's geographic setting as an offshore archipelagic state, the Philippine government has tended not to be exceedingly concerned about military threats from its immediate Southeast Asian neighbors. The Philippine history of occupation by Japan and colonial rule by Western powers has contributed to the view that serious external challenges to the state are most likely to come from great naval powers. During the Cold War only the USSR developed the maritime might to pose a serious potential challenge, and even the possibility of Soviet attack was relatively remote, with or without the U.S. Seventh Fleet in Subic Bay. In the post–Cold War period China has become a more credible threat in the South China Sea, but it thus far lacks the blue-water naval capability to present an existential challenge requiring a tight countervailing alliance with America.

Most of the time, internal security menaces have preoccupied officials in Manila much more than external threats, and domestic considerations offer an essential part of an explanation for the country's alignment choices. For centuries the government in Manila has struggled to control an ethnically and religiously diverse population spread across a vast island chain.[122] Some key threats—such as the insurgency mounted by the NPA—emerged in the northern, predominantly Catholic island of Luzon, but many have arisen in the outlying southern portions of the archipelago. The sprawling island of Mindanao, with its large Muslim population and proximity to the outer provinces of Malaysia and Indonesia, has been an area of perennial concern to Philippine leaders.

Even during the peak years of the Cold War, as war raged in Vietnam, Philippine security concerns were largely domestic. President Ferdinand Marcos put the matter clearly in 1975, saying that external powers were most likely to challenge Southeast Asian governments and regimes by exploiting the latter's domestic weaknesses: "[We do not face] an open threat of aggression. [We face instead] exploitation of internal weaknesses, and exploitation of internal contradictions—lack of economic development and/or the lack of an even spread of the benefits of economic development, leading to guerilla insurgency."[123]

Marcos made a similar point the following year, saying that "Asian nations, including the Philippines, will always be facing the danger of subversion. The principal threat, however, is internal not external."[124] Tight alliance with the United States helped manage such threats directly and indirectly—bases provided billions of dollars of needed government revenue, security cooperation helped the Philippines obtain bilateral aid, and U.S. soldiers trained many of the their Philippine counterparts. Still, those rewards did not preclude Philippine leaders from trying to create some room for maneuver. After the end of the Second Indochina War, Manila began to pull away slightly from the American embrace.

The Cold War Era

By 1975 the Philippines had been a relatively close U.S. ally for more than a quarter century. The alliance had always had limits, however. The Philippines leased the bases at Clark Air Field and Subic Bay to the United States, and the Philippine government had restricted the types of U.S. operations that could be conducted from its territory during the Vietnam. Even when Filipino soldiers went to Vietnam, the U.S. government paid a heavy price in aid and material support. For Philippine leaders, cooperation with the United States served practical ends in securing aid and other forms of support, but it also carried risks of antagonizing foreign powers or stirring domestic unrest.

With one eye toward domestic nationalists and rebels, and the other eye toward Moscow and Beijing, President Ferdinand Marcos argued after the end of the Vietnam War that the Philippines had become too dependent on Washington and had "fought the wars of other nations and allowed others to fight its wars." He asserted that dependency on America had benefited the country's oligarchic elite but had damaged Manila's relations with other developing countries and the socialist world.[125] The Philippines expedited the phase-out of SEATO and participated more actively in the NAM. Manila's shift in policy was not dramatic—a relatively tight formal alliance remained intact, and the move was largely done to increase Filipino leverage. However, Marcos's rhetoric signaled that Philippine policy was headed in that general direction, mainly due to the risks of domestic backlash or entrapment in America's feud with the Soviet Union and other communist powers.

Marcos's critique of the alliance was partly an effort to bolster his own domestic legitimacy; after the imposition of martial law in 1972, Marcos came under steady fire from domestic political opponents on the left, and distancing himself rhetorically from Washington was one way to blunt those attacks. Critics argued that the alliance helped the authoritarian Marcos regime cling to power and repress its opponents by providing a guaranteed source of aid and revenue, no small portion of which went directly into the family coffers.[126] The alliance also helped shield the government somewhat from Western human rights critiques and helped Marcos co-opt the armed forces and suppress political opponents. Marcos believed that it was essential to maintain U.S. support as backing for his autocratic governing regime but endeavored to project a more independent and nationalist character.[127] In renegotiating the 1947 Military Bases Agreement after the Vietnam War, Marcos did not seek to expel American troops, but he insisted that the bases be considered sovereign Philippine territory.

Philippine leaders also became more concerned that close identification with America would provoke ire from Moscow and Beijing. The victory of Vietnamese communists shifted the correlation of forces in the region and made the Soviet Union, China, and allied local groups somewhat more formidable threats to Philippine interests. The Marcos regime took steps toward accommodation. Shortly after the U.S. evacuation of Saigon, Ferdinand Marcos normalized ties with China and the USSR and said that the region had reached "the end of the Cold War as far as the Philippines were concerned." He added that the "post-colonial pattern of Philippine foreign relations which relied almost exclusively on relations with the United States was over" and stressed his determination to break down "ideological barriers in international relations."[128]

Marcos and other Philippine officials had long worried that large U.S. bases were targets that could provoke a nuclear attack from the USSR or even China.[129] Much more likely was that if the United States retreated from the region, the Philippines would be vulnerable to China and the Soviet Union. If those giants perceived the Philippines as an enemy, they could undermine the regime in Manila by funding expanded operations by NPA guerilla forces. The Philippine government sought to reduce these risks of entrapment or abandonment by mending fences with old adversaries and establishing a bit of public distance between itself and Washington.

Concerns about U.S. credibility also caused the Marcos regime some consternation and increased Philippine interest in developing slightly greater autonomy. As U.S. forces pulled out of South Vietnam, a senior Philippine official described the reason for his country's reevaluation of its military relationship with Washington, citing a loss of U.S. credibility and fears of antagonizing the communist powers: "We are disturbed by an emerging view that commitments made by U.S. presidents are nothing more than statements of intent that do not bind the American people or Congress. . . . we have to ask ourselves, whether we can continue to be involved in conflicts and animosities engendered by policies not our own."[130]

In May 1975 Singaporean Prime Minister Lee Kuan Yew privately put the matter more delicately to President Gerald Ford, saying simply, "You are doing a reassessment so [Marcos] has to do one."[131] Philippine Foreign Minister Carlos Romulo said that American credibility further suffered in 1979, when the U.S. government announced that it would abrogate its treaty with Taiwan following the normalization of relations with Beijing.[132] The Carter administration's proposal to withdraw combat forces from South Korea also magnified fears that Washington was turning away from its commitment to defend the noncommunist states of the Pacific Rim.[133] Some of these expressions of concern were doubtlessly instrumental, but they did provide an indication that Philippine certainty about U.S. commitment to the region was not quite as solid as in the past.

Why Did the Alliance Survive?

These factors all provide reasons why the U.S.-Philippine alliance could have weakened considerably after the Vietnam War, but it did not. The alliance did not dissipate as quickly as American ties to Thailand because Philippine leaders continued to see ample rewards from the alignment and perceived lower risks than their Thai colleagues.

The rewards of the U.S. alliance to the Philippines continued to be substantial. As his critics claimed, President Marcos was able to use the alliance to secure the allegiance of the military and underscore his rule, partly by channeling American aid and rental income to his associates. The Armed Forces of the Philippines (AFP) had been largely built with U.S. assistance, creating a strong interest among military officers in the extension of the status quo. American assistance improved the quality of the AFP and helped the Philippine army increase threefold in size and tenfold in budget between 1972 and 1985. Philippine Foreign Secretary Raul Manglapus made the case for U.S. military support clearly: "We can't pretend that we can take care of ourselves. We still have to deal with outside powers."[134] The AFP remained quite weak and ineffective, but U.S. support had provided extensive training and weapons. In addition, an external American security umbrella enabled the AFP to focus more closely on fighting the NPA insurgency and Muslim resistance groups in the south than it otherwise would have been able to do. The Marcos regime's close ties to America tended to fuel the communist insurgency, which in turn gave the government a continued incentive to ally tightly and pursue U.S. support.

The Philippines also continued to receive substantial development assistance from the United States. During the Marcos era, that aid helped prop up an increasingly unpopular presidency. After the People's Power revolution brought Corazon Aquino to power, the same aid helped a new democratic regime find its footing. In 1986 the United States provided emergency grants and led a multibillion dollar multilateral bailout package for the Philippines that helped the new government restore stability. For both countries, the alliance continued to serve key national interests. It served strategic interests for the United States, which sought a regional outpost, R&R and training facilities, and the like. It also provided a critical foundation for aid and political support for the new Aquino regime.[135] The United States continued to serve as the largest destination for Philippine exports and a key source of investment funds. Public money also continued to pour into the country. By the late 1980s the United States provided nearly $1 billion of bilateral aid to the Philippines annually through its military assistance program and a variety of development channels. The United States also channeled another roughly $1 billion per year though multilateral assistance, the Overseas Private Investment Corporation, the U.S. Export-Import Bank, and compensation for the bases at Clark Air Field and Subic Bay.

Rent for the American bases was a key source of foreign-currency income for the Philippines throughout the 1970s and 1980s, providing a considerable part of the glue holding the alliance together. Even more importantly, the bases generated a tremendous level of economic activity for the surrounding area. By the late 1980s American bases housed more than 30,000 U.S. personnel, employed more than 68,000 Filipinos, and generated roughly $500 million to the local economy, far above any other nongovernmental employer in the country.[136] Directly and indirectly, the bases generated an estimated 3 percent of Philippine GDP. At the same time, the presence of friendly U.S. forces reduced the need for Philippine leaders to spend heavily on external defense. Dependency was dangerous, but in the short term it often saved a great deal of money.

In addition to military and economic aid, ideological and cultural forces continued to encourage alliance between Manila and Washington. Although most Filipinos are ethnically Malay in the broadest sense of the term, and 4 million Muslims reside in the country, the Philippine government represents a constituency that is more than 90 percent Roman Catholic, leading some observers to characterize the former Spanish and American colony as a part of Latin America in the western Pacific. The Philippines' colonial history also contributes to strong cultural links to America. The central pillars of the Philippine governing regime—which have remained relatively intact for nearly sixty years—include rule by powerful landed families, strong ties to the Catholic Church, and close identification with the United States. Frequent immigration, high levels of intermarriage, and widespread use of American English and adoption of American popular culture also accentuated the U.S. connection.

Cultural and ideological bonds were not the principal reasons for Philippine interest in the alliance. A desire for economic and security support and fears of communist expansion were stronger driving causes. However, ideational forces made it less costly for Philippine leaders to embrace America at home. Even Filipinos who resented the U.S. role in the country showed ambivalence about America, captured in the humorous but telling expression that some displayed on placards near the U.S. Embassy: "Yankee, go home ... but please take me with you." Most Filipinos continued to support the alliance in the 1980s, and in Southeast Asia's most democratic state, their views mattered. Public attitudes in the Philippines helped the United States reposition itself as an ally of the President Corazon Aquino administration even as America's erstwhile ally, Ferdinand Marcos, fled to a sunny exile in Hawaii. Filipinos' comfort with U.S. ideology and culture did not stop the alliance from weakening at the end of the Cold War but helped the alliance from dissipating sooner.

Finally, the U.S.-Philippine alliance survived during the 1980s because the risks of that alliance appeared lower. Marcos did see the need to appear more autonomous in the late 1970s, but public pressure to loosen the alliance was generally concentrated on the left; most Filipinos accepted the alliance as a source of income and national security. By 1986 the United States managed to reposition itself adroitly, partly by helping the Aquino government get rid of Marcos, and won general public acceptance as a friend of the emerging democracy. The Philippine government also faced lower risks of entrapment or abandonment. Unlike Thailand, the Philippines was not likely to be drawn into direct conflict with a muscular Vietnamese army, which was still a sea away. As a maritime state, the Philippines also had a greater degree of trust in the credibility of U.S. security guarantees. Although U.S. forces had visibly disengaged from mainland Southeast Asia, the American Seventh Fleet remained clearly committed to defense of the maritime sea-lanes of the Pacific Rim.

End of the Cold War

Despite considerable rewards and comparatively moderate risks, a desire for autonomy began to weaken the alliance toward the end of the Cold War. A divergence in threat perception also contributed; some Philippine leaders argued that American forces were ill equipped to deal with the most pressing threats to national security. U.S. officials were most concerned about Soviet naval expansion in the South China Sea, whereas leaders in Manila oriented their military and security apparatus toward the looming domestic menace of NPA rebel groups. A significant number of officials in Manila—especially in the nationalistic legislature—argued that the American military bases contributed little to the country's security but gave

Washington undue influence in Philippine politics.[137] In short, they contended, the sacrifices in autonomy were not worth the gains in security. In 1990 the Philippine government issued an official statement on the matter, expressing the view that "the Philippines faced no external enemies or threats and [believed] that threats arising from both communist insurgency and the right-wing military rebels could not be addressed by U.S. military presence in the country."[138]

To make matters worse, American officials informed the Philippines in the mid-1980s that the United States did not consider its obligations under the Mutual Defense Treaty to extend to defense of contested areas in the South China Sea. The fear that Washington would abandon Manila in the most likely theater for an external military challenge considerably undercut Philippine and ASEAN confidence in the U.S. commitment to Southeast Asia and weakened the U.S.-Philippine alliance.[139] To an increasing number of Philippine officials, the rewards of the alliance were declining, but the risks were on the rise, as dependency remained an issue, and the collapse of the USSR made abandonment more likely.

The Early Post–Cold War Period

For a country that had identified itself so closely with its former colonizers and protectors, the decision to shut the bases was an arduous one. In the event, it was a narrow Senate decision—and not a choice by executive branch policymakers—that led to the closure of the bases and a weakening of the alliance. Public and official ambivalence about the strong U.S. role in the country surrounded the highly charged negotiations over U.S. military bases. Although the Senate vote was close, opponents to the bases expressed their objections as issues of national sovereignty and independence.[140] Between 1986 and 1992, as Philippine democracy got off the ground, the bases became a hotly contested political issue.

To some extent, opponents of the bases were posturing in an effort to secure significant increases in the rental income paid by the United States for the bases. When the Philippine government asked for roughly a doubling in annual rent, America balked.[141] Concerns about Clark Air Field after the eruption of nearby Mount Pinatubo in July 1991 also lowered U.S. enthusiasm for the bases, and Clark was dropped from the talks. The negotiations ultimately fell through, providing reasonably clear evidence that Philippine officials put a price on the alliance. If the United States was willing to provide sufficient rewards—primarily in the form of dollars—the Philippines would be willing to assume the risks of dependency, entrapment, and abandonment. When America chose not to pay that price, the cost-benefit calculus shifted just enough in Manila to cause the Senate to close the bases.

After the closure of Subic Bay and Clark Air Field, the U.S. government took a further step of declaring that without the bases, it could not guarantee the Philippines against attack.[142] This announcement reduced the perceived rewards of the alliance to the Philippines, and the alliance reached its weakest point in decades. Some Philippine officials also stressed that reliance on American military aid had its drawbacks. Excessive reliance on U.S. military might throughout the Cold War helped insulate poorly organized and underdeveloped armed forces against reform. Despite decades of American aid, a Philippine undersecretary of defense lamented in 1993 that his country "would not last 24 hours" in a naval and air battle with one of its neighbors.[143] Some Philippine officials argued that the AFP's weakness was a reason for the Americans to stay; others contended that a looser alignment would remove the crutch and force the AFP to develop stronger independent capability.

The economic incentives to limit the U.S. alliance also increased in the post–Cold War period. Once an economic backwater, a booming Chinese economy increasingly became a place where Philippine businesses could turn a profit. The PRC also emerged as a significant potential investor in the Philippines. The economic price of shunning China during the Cold War had been negligible, but during the 1990s opening to commerce with the PRC was more attractive. From 1975 to 1991 annual PRC-Philippine trade had increased sharply from roughly $40 million to more than $350 million, but trade exploded after the Cold War's end. In recent years China has rocketed ahead to become the Philippines' largest trading partner at more than $25 billion per year, surpassing the United States and Japan.[144] Trade linkages to China do not guarantee limited alignment in the security sphere (as Japanese, Taiwanese, and South Korean behavior attests). However, PRC-Philippine trade provides one additional incentive for the Philippines to avoid a stalwart pro-U.S. alliance that would look to Beijing like a new form of containment.

Some of China's economic attraction was offset in the security sphere. From a military standpoint, China surfaced as a growing external threat in the eyes of some Filipinos. The Mischief Reef crisis and a number of other incidents during the mid-1990s, including the Taiwan Straits crisis, led some to view China as a creeping menace in the South China Sea. It was China's assertiveness in that theater that most directly contributed to a restoration of stronger Philippine-U.S. security cooperation. President Fidel Ramos, a former military general with a pro-business orientation, also contributed to a rebound in Philippine interest in the alliance after taking power in 1992. In 1995 Ramos made it clear that he believed only an ally with America's power would be useful vis-à-vis Beijing: "Only with U.S. help, only with America's leadership, are we to have lasting regional stability. . . . Over the next quarter century, China will unavoidably press—politically and militarily—on East Asia."[145]

Ramos also said that the United States "must continue to be the fulcrum of East Asia's balance of power" to provide "lasting regional security" in the context of China's rise.[146] A 1998 defense white paper made the same point: "The United States must continue to be the main prop, the fulcrum of the East Asian balance of power in order to preserve the bubble of stability that keeps East Asia's economic miracle going. America's presence provides a measure of certainty during periods of tension and strife."[147] At the same time, Philippine officials were quite explicit in identifying a China threat in the late 1990s, and China's military modernization efforts exacerbated that threat perception. The 1998 white paper specifically cited a lack of transparency in China's military modernization as a source of continuing uncertainty.[148]

Nevertheless, a major military attack by China was regarded as highly unlikely. Sino-Philippine links in the economic and diplomatic spheres continued to increase at an impressive clip. Even hawkish officials in Manila did not advocate breaking ties with China or pursuing a tight, highly confrontational countervailing alliance. Without a more definite perception that China had the will and intention to undermine Philippine interests, limited alignment was a way to take out an insurance policy yet enjoy generally positive relations with Beijing.

The Philippines' main security challenges during the period continued to stem from domestic communist and Islamist insurgents, a point emphasized in the 1998 defense white paper. The communist NPA was waning, and the government signed a 1997 peace agreement with the Moro Islamic Liberation Front (MILF)—the leading source of the Islamist resistance in the southern island of Mindanao. However, the NPA still had thousands of active members scattered in villages around the country, and the MILF truce appeared fragile, eventually unraveling in 2000.

Stronger Ties since 9/11

After the attacks of September 11 it was the domestic threat from terrorist groups—more than fears of PRC ambitions in the South China Sea—that drove the Philippines to embrace tighter alignment with America again. The George W. Bush administration's hard-line approach to the war on terror alienated many constituencies in Southeast Asia but restored perceptions of U.S. credibility. The American campaign against terrorism was clearly grounded in America's own sense of security vulnerability, and that self-interest lent credibility to U.S. promises that it would back its allies in their struggles against radical Islamic groups.

During the same period, Islamic groups resisting central government authority became increasingly serious challenges to Manila. The radical Abu Sayyaf—a group with apparent links to both the MILF and al-Qaeda—staged high-profile kidnappings and bombings in 2002 and 2003 that threatened both the security of large Philippine cities and the fragile economy, which depends considerably on tourism and foreign investment. Many Philippine officials viewed the war on terror as a common cause with America, and most of their electorate agreed. Although few wished for U.S. forces to deploy widely on their soil, many Philippine leaders perceived U.S. training and arms as useful devices for facing the terrorist threat. Thus the appeal of tight alliance with America rebounded in Manila.

The Philippine government's decision to embrace tight alliance with America after 2001 and to preserve those close bonds can be explained largely as an effort to secure additional aid for the weak and obsolete AFP. In recent years the U.S. military has been a key partner to the Philippine government in combating armed elements of the MILF and Abu Sayyaf group in the south of the country. (The struggle against Islamist groups has stayed on the front burner of Philippine security affairs, most notably in 2007 when Islamist militants beheaded a number of Philippine marines on the southern island of Basilan, promoting a massive AFP response.) U.S. forces trained Philippine troops in jungle combat operations and contributed to the so-called hearts and minds strategy by building roads, bridges, and other infra-structure. In 2003 President Bush also pledged to participate in a five-year plan to "modernize and reform" the AFP through "technical expertise and field expertise and training."[149] The Philippines has tried to preserve some independence, however, partly to increase the AFP's leverage in securing better weaponry and training from the United States. President Arroyo made that point obliquely by saying that the Philippines would not be a "pawn" in Sino-American competition and might find "additional leverage" in that context.[150]

For Manila the risks of alignment with Washington have tended not to be ex-treme. Deep cultural, historical, and ideological ties mean that Washington typically has not pushed Manila to adopt policies or measures that the government deemed anathema. Public support for the alliance has been strong for decades despite rou-tine protests over U.S. visa policies, occasional military mishaps, and other subjects of controversy. Some Muslim communities in Mindanao resent the alliance in-tensely, but they are politically marginalized. Most Filipinos have supported a tough line against Islamic militants, and the governing class has close familial and financial ties to America that moderate their criticisms of the alliance. Regionally, other ASEAN states have generally accepted the restoration of Philippine-U.S. ties pro-vided that American troops do not become heavily involved in combat operations or seek out large new basing privileges.

Nevertheless, the risks of the alliance are far from negligible. In recent years, as the Philippine government has sought to rebuild ties, it has kept a watchful eye on domestic public opinion and has cautiously designed joint security programs that officials perceive as consistent with independence and national sovereignty. For example, the Visiting Forces Agreement prohibits permanent bases and limits U.S. troops to training missions. President Arroyo rejected a 2003 request by President Bush to deploy American forces in a combat role against Abu Sayyaf.[151]

As recently as August 2009 U.S. commanders were at pains to deny allegations that they were engaged in combat operations against Philippine militants in south-ern Mindanao.[152] To the extent that such operations may have occurred, they have been kept as secret as possible to avoid political and legal challenges to the two governments. The Supreme Court's 2010 affirmation of the VFA's constitutionality was a victory for the alliance, but nationalists such as former Senate president Jo-vito Salonga—who led opposition to U.S. base renewals in 1991—have continued to attack the VFA as a breach of Philippine sovereignty. Senator Miriam Defensor Santiago has been one of the most outspoken critics, arguing that the alliance sub-ordinates Philippine policy autonomy to U.S. strategic interests. Status as a major non-NATO ally, she said, has not stopped the United States from "treating us like a shabby country cousin."[153] Such political sensitivities have placed an important limit on the alliance, which today is far from its Cold War apex.

In addition to vigorous left-wing and nationalist campaigns against the Arroyo government, there have also been tactical reasons to limit the alliance. Philippine officials have feared that a visible American presence in Mindanao would incite local resistance and possibly drag U.S. forces and their Philippine allies into escalating armed conflict.[154] A visible escalation of the U.S. role in the Philippines could also attract unwanted foreign fighters into the country, as occurred in Iraq and Afghanistan after the deployment of American forces to those countries.

The China factor has given Philippine leaders a further reason to avoid a return to a Cold War-level alliance. Since the late 1990s, when Manila approached Washington for stronger military ties, and especially since 9/11, when Philippine-U.S. security cooperation took on a new sense of urgency, China has periodically expressed angst about the alliance. China's suspicion of the relationship may represent the most significant risk of the alliance to the Philippines. Partly for that reason, and partly to assure neighbors and domestic constituencies that Manila would not retreat entirely into America's security orbit, President Arroyo has been clear about the Philippines' intent not to reestablish permanent U.S. bases in the country.[155]

The U.S.-Philippine alliance has become closer since 2002, but it no longer involves major bases or significant joint combat operations. Renato Cruz de Castro argues that Manila prefers limited alignment with the United States rather than a robust defense pact, because "there's simply no point to confront China."[156] Avery Goldstein similarly argues that the Philippines "like other ASEAN states[157] . . . has not embraced a simple-minded strategy that treats China as an implacable foe to be balanced at all costs." Fortunately for the Philippines, the United States has taken a measured approach in its own relations with China and has not pressed Manila hard for the creation of an overtly antagonistic anti-PRC alliance.

Conclusions on the Philippines

Philippine behavior does not square well with the limited alignment hypothesis for much of the period since 1975, even though Philippine leaders have often expressed concerns about the tightness of their alliance with America. One important reason for Philippine divergence from limited alignment behavior is that highly institutionalized alliances are difficult to unwind. Large bases and substantial military bureaucracies create stakeholders in the status quo. The relative inflexibility of such alliances is one key reason most DCs try to avoid them. DCs usually prefer to keep their options open.

In the Philippine case, the country's creation as an independent state was closely tied to its relationship with the United States. Large U.S. bases had existed in the country for most of the period since the Spanish-American War, and, as in West Germany and Japan, the United States played a major part in creating and supporting the new Philippine political regime. The bases became a key source of revenue and helped bolster regime security as much as national security. By the late 1970s President Marcos expressed an interest in limiting the alliance, but it was many years before a narrow legislative decision made that a reality.

Another reason the Philippines has aligned more tightly than most of its Southeast Asian neighbors is that cultural (and, to some extent, ideological) affinity makes the public more accepting of close identification with the United States. These factors are messy to consider from a theoretical standpoint, but they are too important in the Philippine case to be ignored. Officials in Manila have indeed perceived threats from communist insurgents, terrorist groups, and external powers (namely, China and the USSR) since 1975, but so have their ASEAN neighbors. The Philippine decision to ally more closely with the United States than other ASEAN states owes partly to the lesser political risks that Philippine leaders have incurred by participating in what critics can easily describe as a patron-client relationship.

The unique path-dependence of Philippine-U.S. relations and the two countries' deep bonds have not eliminated the risks of tight alliance. Consequently, Philippine leaders have placed significant limits on their security ties to America to minimize the risks of diminished autonomy and continued dependency. In recent years, continued threats from terrorist groups, a revived NPA, and a growing China have given the Philippines ample security concerns. However, to manage the risks of rebuilding its alliance with America, the Philippines has espoused a policy broadly similar to Singapore's. It has welcomed close security cooperation but has attempted to reassure neighbors and the public that the alliance will not return to its Cold War level and that U.S. troop deployment in the Philippines is both temporary and limited.

CONCLUSIONS

Since 1975 great-power alignment in maritime Southeast Asia has meant developing security ties to the United States. The USSR was never able to present itself as a credible friend to the noncommunist states in the region, and it won no ASEAN allies. Malaysia, Indonesia, and Brunei explicitly rejected the atheistic communism of the Soviet Union, as did many of their predominantly Catholic neighbors in the Philippines and Buddhist counterparts in Thailand. Anemic soft power forced the USSR to rely heavily on hard power in Southeast Asia, which further alienated governments in the region.[158] Chinese relations with the maritime ASEAN states have improved dramatically since their nadir in the 1960s and 1970s, when China openly supported communist insurgents throughout the region, but the PRC continues to suffer from ethnically, ideologically, and historically based suspicions. Consequently, when it comes to great-power security support, alignment with the United States has been practically the only game in town in maritime Southeast Asia.

For its security partners, the rewards of alignment with the United States have included training and aid to bolster their security capabilities and help in meeting predominantly local threats. At the same time, pro-American alignments of various degrees have helped to preserve what maritime Southeast Asian governments have perceived as a healthy balance of influence among the great powers in Southeast Asia since the fall of Saigon. The same governments have perceived significant risk in aligning with the United States, however. They have feared that tight alliance would reduce their independence and subject them to unwanted American political pressure. They have also been sensitive to the danger that identification with

America could stoke the flames of domestic communist or Islamist resistance or antagonize other great powers.

Since 1975 four of the five states of maritime Southeast Asia have consistently pursued limited alignment with the United States. The most powerful factors affecting their alignment calculi have been the relatively low levels of external military threats and concerns about the appeal of the United States as a security partner, usually based on misgivings about U.S. policies and more general aversion to great-power intrusion after emerging from colonial rule. Only the Philippines has been a significant exception for much of the period—a phenomenon attributable to the sum of second-order variables such as historical experience and cultural and ideological affinity, which have driven up the expected benefits of close alignment and driven down the anticipated risks.

Collectively, the maritime states have sought, to varying degrees and not without disagreement, to preserve a relatively unobtrusive American "over the horizon" presence in the region through a general policy of "places not bases." Although they have not pursued identical alignment strategies, their overarching aims have borne important parallels. Despite their many differences, the five maritime states have operated in a broadly similar strategic environment characterized first by communist threats and more recently by the challenge of a rising China and global terrorism. Limited alignments have reflected an effort to achieve an American security blanket without incurring excessive risks—particularly the dangers of excessive dependency and compromised regime legitimacy.

The United States has enjoyed a kind of "primacy by invitation" in maritime Southeast Asia during the post–Cold War period. By aligning with Western powers and granting U.S. forces continued access to military facilities, states in the subregion have effectively promoted American primacy in the region.[159] U.S. primacy signifies Washington's ability to project overwhelming and decisive force in maritime Southeast Asia, which gives the United States a significant degree of influence over other actors in the region by shaping their risk-reward analyses.[160] Although U.S. forces do not need a great deal of assistance to project power, they do need access to military facilities in the region, enabling Washington to maintain an active territorial presence and credible capacity to deploy and support forces quickly in the event of a crisis.

The maritime states have continued to align with the United States in the post–Cold War era to balance against more pressing perceived threats, but even old security partners in Singapore and Manila have not wanted to serve as permanent bases for U.S. forces, because among other things, they have concluded that the hub-and-spokes system gave Washington too much control and placed too much reliance on an uncertain U.S. security commitment. Nevertheless, the perceived risks have tended to be lowest in the Philippines and Singapore, which partly explains why those countries have generally aligned more openly with America, especially in recent years.

Chapter 5

The Mainland Peninsula

THE FIVE STATES OF MAINLAND SOUTHEAST ASIA—Burma, Vietnam, Laos, Cambodia, and Thailand—present a somewhat stiffer test for the hypotheses advanced in this book. It is more difficult to summarize their alignment strategies than the policies of their maritime ASEAN neighbors. All the mainland states save Burma were deeply embroiled in the Third Indochina War. Vietnam and Thailand formed relatively tight alliances for considerable periods during the peak years of the conflict, and each of their mainland neighbors has also entered into tight alliances at various points since 1975. Moreover, unlike the U.S.-led maritime subregion, three great powers have extended their reach into the mainland peninsula—China, the United States, and the Soviet Union. Nevertheless, a shared desire to avoid too much dependence on the great powers and to minimize further conflict has made limited alignments attractive to the mainland states when intense security threats have not required immediate and extensive great-power succor. The result has been a strong collective tendency toward limited alignment and relative neutrality since the end of the Third Indochina War.

BURMA/MYANMAR

As much as any other Southeast Asian country, Burma has historically prioritized independence and nonalignment in its foreign policy. For most of the Cold War period, despite significant internal security threats, Burma was the most genuinely nonaligned country in the region, tilting only slightly toward Beijing. The upheaval that followed the rise of the SLORC regime in 1988 resulted in a harsh international sanctions program and the threat of Western efforts to destabilize the regime, temporarily driving the new Union of Myanmar into temporarily tight alliance with China. However, Yangon soon reasserted its traditional priority on independence and has pursued a limited pro-PRC alignment for most of the post–Cold War period.

Burma was born into a relatively dangerous neighborhood, and its tendency to avoid alignment has not been because of any lack of security threats. Although relations with China and India have been perennial security concerns for Burma, Burma's leaders have tended to focus even more on internal, centrifugal threats.[1] Burma is the second largest country in Southeast Asia, and its diverse population—comprising ten major ethnic groups speaking more than 100 dialects—includes large numbers of ethnic minorities who live in the country's dense and mountainous northern and eastern jungles. Minority groups have frequently received external support in their struggles against the Burman-dominated central government, and the country's long, winding borders with China, India, and Thailand are extremely difficult to police effectively. The disproportionate economic power of Burma's ethnic Indian and Chinese minorities has added to a sense of vulnerability to Chinese or Indian-inspired subversion.

Neutrality under Ne Win

Throughout the Cold War era, Burma was a champion of nonalignment, primarily because of the perceived risks of great-power alignment. In 1960 U Nu had articulated the reason why developing countries should moderate their cooperation with great powers in striking terms during the era of the Bandung Conference: "Whatever ideologies they have, whatever policies they outline, whatever resolutions they pose, whatever slogans they shout, in actual practice, whenever there is a conflict with their interests, they are not ashamed to discard their policies, to shelve their resolutions, and to change their slogans as easily and quickly as a woman of no character changing her lovers. Since these great powers are not acting for the interests of anybody else but their own, do not let yourselves be their stooges . . . never trust them completely to the extent of leaving all in their hands."[2]

Sovereignty has been a core driver of Burma's long-standing efforts to preserve relative neutrality. Colonial domination by Great Britain has been a key in shaping the country's strategic culture and has created a hypersensitivity to perceived threats of foreign interference and neocolonialism.[3] Sino-Indian rivalry has also been a perennial concern and Burmese leaders have sought to avoid antagonizing either colossus.

During the 1970s geography and Burma's relative military and economic weakness made it difficult to defeat the BCP and disrupt their supply lines from China. In addition, porous borders and dense jungles enabled some of Burma's insurgent groups to fund themselves though a massive drug trade. Testy exchanges with India and historically frictional relations with Thailand—where many rebel groups were based—also contributed to security problems for the Burmese government. These threats were by no means inconsequential, but nor did they seriously challenge the ascendancy of the Ne Win regime.

Even if Burma had sought to align itself during the Ne Win era, it would have been hard-pressed to find an appealing ally. Alignment with the United States was particularly unattractive because of the country's colonial legacy and anti-imperial regime credentials, as well as its adherence to a modified socialist economic program. Tilting toward America could also have provoked both China and India without necessarily helping to defuse local threats. Given the communist menace posed by the BCP, China and the Soviet Union were also unattractive allies, and alignment with either risked the antagonism of Burma's neighbors.

Burma also had concrete economic reasons for avoiding tight alliance with a socialist country. In 1976 Ne Win and the Burmese leadership decided to seek massive aid from the World Bank to revive its ailing economy. The World Bank agreed to an annual program of grants, loans, and investments amounting to well over $200 million per year.[4] That sum was nearly an order of magnitude larger than the regime's largest previous request for $30 million in the early 1950s. Aid from the multilateral institutions provided vital budget support and funded critical development projects, and any alignment that alienated America could have jeopardized those programs. Burma had only to look at the Vietnamese predicament to see the economic perils of antagonizing America. In sum, the absence of existential security threats, the lack of attractive allies, and the high perceived risks of alignment were a recipe for a nonaligned Burmese position under Ne Win.

Sino-SLORC Alignment

The country's strategic outlook changed abruptly in 1988. The military coup that brought the SLORC regime to power quickly led to Western recrimination and a program of political and economic sanctions. China gained appeal as a security partner, as the troubled new SLORC regime faced much more serious threats. SLORC leaders considered themselves to be the victims of neo-imperial Western pressure and developed a siege mentality. They saw China as a country in a similar predicament.[5] The June 1989 Tiananmen Square massacre brought the two countries closer for that reason, and enhanced trust was one of the underpinnings of the stronger Sino-Myanmar alignment in the years that followed. By the late 1980s the PRC had also essentially ceased to support the BCP, removing a key barrier to alignment.

One of the most obvious rewards of the alignment to Myanmar was military. During the 1980s Burma had spent enormous sums in a failed effort to quell insurgencies and preserve national unity. Ironically, these high military expenditures—which ranged from a staggering 40 to 60 percent of the Burmese budget—had prevented government funds from use in the economic development desperately needed to provide greater welfare and reduce domestic strife.[6] Between 1988 and 1992 large Chinese aid packages helped the *tatmadaw*'s strength grow by 50 percent in material terms. The PRC became the largest source of arms and other military equipment to Yangon, supplying more than $1.5 billion in weapons and other military equipment to Myanmar during the early 1990s. China also upgraded Myanmar's naval bases in the Andaman Sea. Chinese aid certainly did not turn Myanmar into an economic juggernaut, but it did reduce the budgetary pressure from the SLORC military buildup.[7]

Trade with Yunnan Province and large PRC aid packages were also key rewards of the alignment, enabling the Myanmar regime to survive increasingly stringent

Western sanctions for nearly two decades. The SLORC regime was much more concerned about domestic challenges than foreign military attack, and the economy was a major, obvious vulnerability. The internal threats Burma faced were difficult to combat in large part because of economic weakness. Failed economic policies had brought about the partial overthrow of the Ne Win regime in 1988, when a summer of nationwide pro-democracy demonstrations was followed by harsh repression and a coup by hard-line elements of the *tatmadaw*. After 1989 stringent Western sanctions exacerbated Myanmar's economic plight, contributing to an explosion of public debt after the SLORC regime took a series of disastrous economic reforms that included the demonetization of all bank notes of over K. 15 ($2.50).[8]

Witnessing the breakdown in administrative capacity and human rights abuses of the new SLORC regime, the United States, Asian Development Bank, World Bank, and other U.S. allies—namely Japan, Germany, and the United Kingdom—suspended their foreign assistance programs. The country's desperate need for aid was perhaps the decisive factor that propelled Myanmar into a much closer alignment with China. The junta essentially struck a bargain with Beijing—Myanmar would align more closely with China and help the PRC build its economic and military presence in the eastern Indian Ocean in exchange for large-scale economic and political support.

The scale of Western opposition to the SLORC regime also meant that alignment with China carried only modest risks. The United States and its allies were resolutely opposed to the new regime, especially after the imprisonment of Aung San Suu Kyi, and tighter links to China did not jeopardize much economic aid or trade that the West and Japan did not already intend to curtail. The country's deviation from a limited alignment strategy can thus be explained as a result of stronger perceived threats to the regime, enhanced Chinese credibility, and a diminution of the economic and political opportunity costs of alignment.

Limiting the Relationship with China

By allying closely with China after 1988, Myanmar abandoned decades of a relatively nonaligned foreign policy, but SLORC leaders soon developed misgivings about its loss of independence as Beijing came to exercise an uncomfortable degree of influence in the country. Myanmar's decision to keep China at a greater distance after the mid-1990s was based more on the risks of alignment than any reduction in the threat environment. Ethnic insurgencies and separatist movements have continued to challenge Myanmar, making the *tatmadaw* focus primarily on internal challenges.[9] The principal external threats perceived in Yangon have all been closely tied to internal security, as officials fear that foreign economic and military penetration will encourage separatist groups along the country's long, relatively porous borders.[10] ASEAN Secretary-General Ong Keng Yong expressed Myanmar's worst nightmare—and the region's—by citing the possibility that an unstable and ethnically diverse Myanmar could erupt into "another Yugoslavia, multiplied many times over."[11]

Continuing Threats

Throughout the post–Cold War period, Myanmar's leaders have described the United States and its domestic allies as their most serious threats. They view the U.S.-led campaign for democracy and human rights as a fig leaf for regime change in countries the West disfavors. An official statement made that fear explicit: "At present, we keep hearing two overworked clichés. Those are the terms human rights and democracy. The Western nations are using these two clichés at every turn in order to indoctrinate the people of developing nations to suit their ulterior motives, in what could be termed a form of psycho-colonialism."[12]

The junta continues to view the United States very much through the prism of its colonial experience and to perceive American policies as levers for reasserting imperial control over the country through Aung San Suu Kyi's NLD and pro-Western dissidents. Internally, Myanmar officials have consistently identified the NLD as the most serious threat to their regime, frequently accusing NLD officials of terrorist acts and other subversive activities. The Myanmar junta also accuses Washington of funding dissident groups to destabilize the country and raise tensions in the region. Than Shwe said in December 1999, "Neo-colonialists and their subservient negativistic internal axe-handles wearing the cloaks of human rights and democracy are violating all kinds of laws, moving to incite anarchy and interfering in the internal affairs of the nation and are even perpetrating terrorist acts transgressing the sovereignty of the state."[13]

The Myanmar leadership—which renamed itself the State Peace and Development Council in 1997—often refers to Aung San Suu Kyi as an "axe-handle" to signify that she is the instrument through which the West chops away at the regime. In Myanmar, perceptions of the security of the state are intimately tied to the fate of the *tatmadaw*-backed political regime; great priority is placed on territorial integrity, order, and national unity.[14]

In 2004, after the U.S. Congress recommended that the UN Security Council consider sanctions against Yangon, the Myanmar government accused Washington of "promoting poverty, instability, drugs, and armed conflicts" in the country.[15] Than Shwe and his colleagues have consistently characterized U.S. sanctions as a security problem, arguing that they exacerbate the economic woes that make drug trafficking and associated ethnic conflicts such widespread problems in Myanmar.

Myanmar officials have even feared an external American military threat in recent years. American economic sanctions against Myanmar and overt support for Aung San Suu Kyi have left little doubt of hostile U.S. intentions toward the regime. Myanmar officials watched with trepidation at the announcement of the Bush administration's doctrine of preemption and 2003 displacement of the Iraqi Ba'athist regime. The decision to move the government capital to Naypidaw owes at least partly to a fear that the United States will go to considerable lengths to bring about regime change and establish a ring of containment around China. In 1998, an official military report argued that "Myanmar could be deemed the weak link in the [U.S.] regional China containment policy. . . . The [U.S.] attempt in creating Myanmar as a Client State is quite obvious in their blatant interference in Myanmar's internal affairs."[16] From Myanmar's perspective, Western governments, human rights organizations, and the NLD combine to present an existential challenge to national security. The 2007 Saffron Revolution appears to have reinforced that perception. In 2009 and 2010 the Barack Obama administration began to explore possibilities for engagement, but the extent of the U.S. policy shift and its likely effects on Myanmar's threat perceptions remain uncertain.

Despite the regime's rhetorical focus on enemies from the West and the NLD, some of its most serious security challenges have come from continuing ethnic insurgencies and nontraditional threats. The effects of Cyclone Nargis in 2008 were potentially highly destabilizing for a regime that already lacks performance legitimacy. The tatmadaw continues to confront the Kachin Independence Army, United Wa State Army, and Shan rebels. In 2009 Burmese troops also clashed with ethnic Chinese Kokang insurgents, putting strain on ties with Beijing.

Risks of Alliance with China

Although Myanmar's leaders have perceived some need for external support to meet real security threats, the tight Sino-Myanmar alignment weakened after an initial honeymoon period in the early 1990s. By the mid-1990s officials in Yangon became concerned about the unpredictability of Chinese assistance because Beijing often failed to fulfill its pledges and certain military hardware has been poorly functional or obsolete. Questions about China's reliability as a security provider have lessened the regime's interest in tight alliance.[17] Myanmar's relationship with China owes less to a sense of trust than to a lack of alternatives for the embattled junta, and over time the Myanmar generals have gently loosened security cooperation to reduce their reliance on the PRC.

By the mid-1990s many Myanmar officials also began to consider the risks of pro-PRC alignment to be excessive. Trade with the PRC served elite financial interests by providing large kickbacks to officials, and it also supplied the broader economy with much-needed foreign currency reserves. By 1995 China accounted for roughly $800 million of Myanmar's trade, or 40 percent of its worldwide total. Exploding trade also enabled the PRC to wield much greater economic and political clout, however, which cut against decades of Burmese commitment to avoiding foreign domination.[18]

SLORC officials began to resent Chinese economic domination and feared political subservience to the PRC or even territorial encroachment along the country's northern border. Myanmar leaders were also sensitive about the risk that tight alliance with China would provoke ethnic tensions in areas where ethnic Chinese traders were becoming rich beside poverty-stricken Burman and minority communities.[19] Thus Myanmar described the alignment of the 1990s as "a temporary measure only" and took steps to avoid becoming a Chinese client state, such as pursuing better relations with India and joining ASEAN.[20] Myanmar also diversified arms sales to include Russia, India, Ukraine, Israel, Singapore, and others to avoid the undue reliance of the early 1990s on the PRC. Myanmar officials also declared that they would not permit foreign bases in the country, which would violate their "independent and active" foreign policy.

Myanmar's leaders have seen that great-power alignment carries risks of regional antagonism. Although China has provided much-needed military and economic aid, the SLORC regime's de facto alliance with China coincided with a sharp downturn in Indo-Myanmar relations and frustrated ASEAN ties. India openly supported the NLD and offered refuge and material support to a number of insurgent groups along Myanmar's borders.[21] Without a viable U.S. option to play, Myanmar moved toward ASEAN membership as a means to balance its external relations and has improved ties with India markedly during recent years, despite the presence of NLD activists on Indian soil. The junta also remained resolute that it would not allow any foreign troops on Myanmar soil.[22] Sino-Myanmar ties have remained significant; since 1997 the PRC has provided well over $3 billion in combined military and economic development assistance.[23] However, Myanmar has diversified its relations and placed clearer limits, especially in security affairs, to salvage some autonomy and leverage and to keep doors open.

Conclusions on Burma/Myanmar

Burma/Myanmar has often been something of a strategic and political oddball in Southeast Asia. Burma was a leading voice for neutralism throughout the Cold War era and often found common cause with Indonesia and Malaysia in promoting the norm of nonalignment. In general, its policymakers have perceived tight alliances as carrying excessive risk of dependency and the danger of offending larger, more powerful neighbors. Shortly after the rise of the SLORC regime, the junta veered significantly away from its tradition of relative neutralism and embraced a strong alignment with China for a period of years, when most of the international community shunned it. That choice was largely driven by a perception of vastly increased threat from the United States, Europe, and to a lesser extent India, all of which favored regime change and contributed to a tough regime of political and economic sanctions. Strong, interrelated internal and external threats to the junta are the best explanation for Myanmar's temporary foray into a relatively tight alliance relationship during the early 1990s. As the SLORC leadership gained its footing, it moved to reassert its autonomy vis-à-vis China. For the past decade, Myanmar's junta has tilted toward Beijing to secure arms and aid in the face of international condemnation and sanctions. Nevertheless, the Burmese generals have kept the relationship limited, mainly to guard national independence but also to avoid poking their other neighbors with a stick.

VIETNAM

Like their colleagues in Burma/Myanmar, Vietnamese officials have traditionally placed great importance on the notion of national independence. The VCP endured staggering losses of life and other sacrifices between 1945 and 1975 to achieve the aim of an independent, unified nation. However, Vietnam's fierce brand of independence did not prevent the country from becoming one of the most tightly aligned Southeast Asian states during the latter years of the Cold War. The threat of Chinese attack or encirclement and the demands of occupying Cambodia sent the newly independent Socialist Republic of Vietnam (SRV) hurtling back into the arms of the USSR for more than a decade. The tight Soviet-Vietnamese alliance is an important reminder that even DCs intensely sensitive to diminished autonomy sometimes do agree to enter stalwart defense pacts when doing so appears to be the only viable way to deal with dire perceived security challenges.

Vietnam initially sought to avoid a deeply embedded alliance, refusing to join COMECON despite Soviet pressure in 1976. Even as late as 1978 the VCP leadership refused to endorse Moscow's vision for Asian security, which had anti-China overtones.[24] However, with the onset of the Third Indochina War, Hanoi became steadfastly allied with Moscow, swapping arms for loyalty and base access for roughly a decade. Only after the end of that conflict and reduction in great-power Cold War competition did Vietnam drift toward relative nonalignment.

For Vietnam, like most Southeast Asian countries, threats have been defined in large part by geography, which has presented a formidable challenge to the establishment of national unity and contributed to an ever-present fear of Chinese intervention. The country's serpentine shape has meant for centuries that authorities near the head of Vietnam, in the fertile lowlands of the Red River Delta, would be hard pressed to exert control over the population residing nearer to the country's tail, where the Mekong River empties into the South China Sea. Rugged mountains and thick jungles separate the two areas, which helps to explain why Vietnamese leaders have traditionally believed that at least some control over neighboring Laos and Cambodia is essential to ensuring the country's security. The division of the country along the 17th parallel in 1954 provided a powerful reminder of this reality, choking the long and lean country and dividing north and south at its narrowest point.

At the same time Vietnam shares a border on its north with China, the colossus that has virtually defined Vietnamese history through repeated efforts to invade or control the country. Like Indonesian leaders, Vietnamese officials tend to perceive themselves as the rightful leaders of their surrounding subregion and a corresponding responsibility to defend it against perceived Chinese efforts at domination. The shadow of history has been evoked frequently to summon fears of a Chinese menace to Vietnam. Even though China and North Vietnam were allied during the Second Indochina War, VCP officials feared excessive Chinese influence and published articles about the history of Chinese efforts to dominate Vietnam from the legendary Trung sisters' uprising in 39 CE to the present.[25] Although common Western adversaries tamed Sino-Vietnamese suspicions for much of the twentieth century, the three decades since the fall of Saigon have witnessed a return toward traditional threat perceptions in Hanoi.

Soviet-Vietnamese Alliance

Immediately after the fall of Saigon, the victorious VCP leadership sought to mend fences with the United States and other capitalist states to develop sources of economic aid, consolidate their rule of the south, and reconstruct their war-torn state. However, by 1978—after a rebuff from Washington, deteriorating relations with China, and escalating Khmer Rouge border attacks—Vietnam abandoned its effort to steer a middle course and entered into a strong alliance with the USSR. After the PAVN allied with Khmer rebels to invade Pol Pot's Cambodia and China launched a punitive counterattack from the north, the SRV found itself in an even more menacing environment on all sides. The 1979 war had shown that the Chinese armed forces were a threat to be feared on Vietnam's northern border, and the budding alignment between China and Thailand was a pincer-like menace similar to the one that developed when China became the principal supporter of the Khmer Rouge regime.[26] The Vietnamese decision to accept—and perhaps even welcome—tight military alliance with the Soviet Union was due primarily to the intensity of external security threats that VCP leaders perceived from 1978 onward.[27]

In addition to the obvious threat of Chinese troops along Vietnam's border, VCP leaders saw prominent economic and internal dimensions to the China threat. Officials Nhuan Vu and Thien Nahn described the military's outlook, emphasizing Chinese efforts to sabotage Vietnam's industrial efforts and bring about an economic collapse and precipitate political chaos.[28] In 1983 SRV Foreign Minister Nguyen Co Thach also cited internal threats to VCP rule, asserting that "China has still not abandoned its plan to divide our country" by stirring up resistance in "indisciplined" southern Vietnam.[29]

On an ideological plane the VCP described the PRC as counterrevolutionary and reactionary. It cited the Sino-American and Sino-Japanese rapprochements and Deng Xiaoping's modernization campaign as evidence that Beijing was selling out the revolution to collude with imperialist forces.[30] China also joined the United States, Japan, the ASEAN states, and many others in participating in a suffocating international regime of political and economic sanctions. Few states in the Global South faced such a dire security environment during the 1980s, which pressed Vietnam into its close military alliance with the Soviet Union.

In the context of the highly polarized and dangerous Cold War period in Indochina, the Soviet Union was a valuable if not ideally suited great-power ally. Moscow supported almost all areas of Vietnamese military and economic development. The 1975 Soviet aid package to Hanoi was worth roughly $500 million and paid for more than forty capital projects throughout the war-torn country. By 1978 after China canceled its cooperation, Soviet and Eastern European aid to Vietnam was five times what the impoverished state received from the rest of the world. The USSR alone provided half a billion dollars in food aid to Vietnam in 1978 to head off mass starvation, and by 1979 the Soviet Union funded roughly 60 percent of the Vietnamese budget. After the formation of the alliance and the PAVN invasion of Cambodia, Soviet support rose dramatically to roughly $1.5 billion per year, and by 1983, annual bilateral aid exceeded \$2.2 billion.[31] Soviet aid gave Vietnam the most potent army in the region. Vietnam's armed forces totaled nearly 1.5 million, compared to an ASEAN total of slightly more than 800,000. The material rewards of the alliance were great indeed.

The ideological dimension of the Soviet-Vietnamese relationship grew along-side expanding military ties, leading scholar Muthiah Alagappa to argue that "geo-political considerations and ideological affinity were the two main pillars of the Soviet-Vietnamese alliance."[32] SRV Premier Le Duan described his country's alli-ance with Moscow by asserting that "linking ourselves closely and cooperating in all domains with the USSR is for us a principle, a strategy and at the same time a revolutionary sentiment."[33] Vietnam's affinity for the Soviet model should not be overstated as an attractive force, as there were also obvious power-political reasons for security cooperation, but the similarity of regime types did play an important role in establishing Moscow's credibility and trust until the glasnost and perestroika reforms of the mid-1980s created a rift. Reaping the rewards of Soviet aid meant following Moscow's political lead, even though many VCP conservatives did not support the new doctrines of glasnost and perestroika. Ideological compulsion be-came a source of Vietnamese resentment for the USSR.[34]

Costs of the Alliance
Vietnam's experience with the Soviet Union after 1978 shows the tremendous risks that tight alliance can entail for a DC. VCP leaders welcomed massive assistance but soon came to resent the tremendous sacrifice in autonomy that their tight alli-ance with the USSR entailed. Vietnam's loss of independence was painfully ironic, because its people had fought for more than thirty years and sacrificed millions of lives to achieve precisely that aim. During the late 1970s the country's domestic and international struggles left it progressively more dependent on Soviet aid. Initially the country's primary needs were economic. By 1977 dire fiscal conditions forced Vietnam to consider pragmatic factors alongside ideological ones in its alignment posture. At Moscow's urging, Vietnam joined COMECON in June 1978, further reducing the possibility of robust trade with the major noncommunist economies and pushing Vietnam into the less promising communist trading bloc.[35] By that time Moscow was supplying Hanoi with roughly \$1.5 billion in annual assistance, half of Vietnam's worldwide total.

The yoke of dependency frustrated VCP officials. *Doc Lap* (independence) has been a major theme in Vietnamese politics since the August 1945 revolution, and Vietnamese have traditionally viewed themselves as the protagonists in a struggle to preserve political and cultural independence vis-à-vis great powers, especially China. Even near the height of Hanoi's need for great-power support in 1978, a few months before signing an alliance treaty with the Soviet Union, Pham Van Dong said, "Whenever in our four-thousand year history Vietnam has been reliant on one large friend, it has been a disaster for us."[36] Strains in the alliance began to mani-fest themselves quickly, as the VCP leadership resented the strong policy control exercised by Moscow, as well as the USSR's moves to challenge Vietnam's political dominance in Laos and Cambodia. Vietnam's attack on Thai border forces in 1980 was an example of Vietnam's effort to assert autonomy; the USSR had recently promised ASEAN states that such attacks would not occur.[37]

Officials in Hanoi showed other signs of frustration with the nature of Soviet economic aid and policy advice, but they had little leverage because of their hostile relations with China, the United States, and the ASEAN countries. As Donald Zagoria and Sheldon Simon argued, "Such an extraordinary degree of dependency on a European power [could not] be easy for the fiercely independent Vietnamese leaders, who have struggled for more than three decades against foreign domination."[38] Vietnamese Foreign Minister Nguyen Co Thach made it clear that his country's dependency on the USSR owed much to a lack of alternatives: "We have gone through many difficult times and during these difficulties it was the Soviet Union that helped us the most. Others closed the door against us. It is not our crime to be dependent on the Soviet Union. We open the door to everyone ... but it is the policy of the U.S. and China to blockade us economically."[39]

Hanoi thus leaned heavily on the Soviet Union largely because China, the United States, and their allies gave it little choice. By 1982 roughly 65 percent of Vietnam's worldwide trade was conducted with the Soviet Union, which supplied up to 30 percent of the country's rice, without which mass starvation would have likely occurred. The USSR also funded more than half of the VCP's Five-Year Plan at a cost of $3.2 billion, supplied all of its military hardware, and sent thousands of technical advisors to Vietnam.[40]

Vietnam tried in vain to seek economic aid from western European countries and to begin opening to China, espousing a more flexible approach to the Cambodian conflict.[41] However, Vietnam's scope for substantive policy maneuver was very small. Moscow clearly expected firm Vietnamese loyalty in return for its arms and money. A joint declaration by Le Duan and Mikhail Gorbachev in 1985 asserted that Hanoi and Moscow shared "a complete identity of views" on international issues of concern.[42]

The slow thaw in Sino-Soviet relations during the mid-1980s added to Vietnamese concerns about the degree of their dependence on Moscow. Hanoi feared being abandoned by the Soviet Union if the two communist behemoths reconciled, and VCP officials imagined a nightmare scenario of facing a vengeful China without Soviet support. There was little doubt in Hanoi that Soviet commitment to the alliance was primarily instrumental and that the USSR saw Vietnam mostly as a pawn on a strategic chessboard.[43] However, VCP leaders had little flexibility to distance themselves from the USSR given their dire need to feed the population and offset the immediate Sino-American and insurgent threats surrounding Indochina. By the late 1980s Soviet aid to Vietnam exceeded $2 billion annually, excluding enormous military aid and a large program of technical assistance. Vietnam's nonconvertible currency debt to the USSR and its Eastern European allies exceeded $6.5 billion, further ensuring deep dependency on Moscow.[44]

Antagonizing China, America, and Their Allies

Hanoi's alliance with Moscow also carried great external costs, adding to animosity from China, the United States, and some ASEAN countries. The alignment virtually eliminated the SRV's chance of mending fences with the United States and China, arguably putting Vietnam in even more danger than it would have faced without Soviet support. As Vietnam joined COMECON and drifted toward a Soviet alliance, the PRC canceled what had become a $300 million annual economic aid program to Hanoi.[45] Sour relations with America also limited Vietnam's access to much-needed investment and access to the international financial institutions, which could otherwise have aided in the country's economic reconstruction.

Although Vietnam depended heavily on the USSR after the invasion of Cambodia, leaders in Hanoi sought to moderate the form of alignment to reduce the suspicions of China and ease pressure from ASEAN and the West.[46] Even after the invasion of Cambodia and Sino-Vietnamese border war, Premier Pham Van Dong said in May 1979, "We regard the visits to our ports and airfields of Soviet ships and planes as a normal practice. . . . We are, however, a sovereign nation and Soviet bases are an entirely different matter. There are no [Soviet] bases here now and none are planned for the future."

Foreign Minister Nguyen Co Thach later presented a slightly different view, saying, "There are no foreign bases in our country at the present time. As for the future, we must leave all doors open. If there is a serious threat to our country we can take many options."[47] By 1983 Cam Ranh Bay had become one of the largest Soviet military installations in the world and easily the largest outside of the Warsaw Pact countries. Nevertheless, Thach was at pains to deny that the Soviet Navy had a base at the former American naval hub and assert (somewhat incredibly) that the "Soviet-Vietnamese relationship will never become a military alliance."[48]

To help minimize the effect of its alliance on relations with China, the United States, and ASEAN, Hanoi would almost certainly have preferred a more limited alignment, but dire economic and strategic needs gave the Soviet Union tremendous leverage. Moscow favored a formal pact and long-term basing privileges to provide a durable encirclement of China and reliable post for expanding Soviet influence in Asia.

China continued to remind its smaller neighbor of the dangers of occupying Cambodia and allying with the USSR. In addition to funneling aid to the Khmers Rouges and other rebels, the PRC became more aggressive in shelling Vietnamese positions as retaliation for Vietnamese moves in Cambodia. The PRC also bolstered its forces near the Sino-Vietnamese border in early 1984. China timed the escalation to coincide with Ronald Reagan's visit to Beijing, reminding Vietnam of the tacit Sino-U.S. alignment and suggesting that Hanoi's ties to Moscow would not intimidate the PRC.[49] The Chinese army was still a force to be reckoned with.

Although the risk of another Chinese invasion could not be discounted after 1979, the economic costs of the Viet-Soviet alliance arguably contributed most to a change in Vietnam's security policy.[50] As the capitalist Asian Tiger countries of the

Pacific Rim enjoyed rapid growth, Vietnam's dire poverty, stagnation, and weaker regime legitimacy prompted the VCP to pursue a foreign policy that would promote Vietnamese integration into the world economy. In 1987 the VCP Politburo adopted a secret new national defense policy called Resolution 2 that aimed at "achieving close coordination and intimate attachment between the economy and national defense."[51] In 1988 the Politburo secretly passed Resolution 13, which overturned Hanoi's previous alignment strategy and called for a "multidirectional" foreign policy.[52]

Nguyen Co Thach was one of the architects of Resolution 13 and attributed the shift in policy to scientific and technological changes that blurred the distinction between the socialist and imperialist camps and made economic interdependence the key to national development and security.[53] In alignment terms, this meant reducing dependence on the USSR, opening to other trading partners, and wooing commerce from China and the West. Vietnam was only able to distance itself from the Soviet embrace after the resolution of the Cambodian problem but did so quickly after the PAVN withdrawal, seeking to normalize ties with China and the United States after 1989.

Relative Neutrality since the Cold War

After the signing of the Paris Peace Accords, for the first time since the French colonial period, Vietnam enjoyed a period of relative external peace. One of the key strategies of the new era was to pursue a more neutral foreign policy. As one Vietnamese foreign ministry said, Vietnam had learned the lessons of the past. Its relatively one-sided policy during the 1980s antagonized China and the United States, and Vietnamese officials learned that they need to pursue a more balanced approach.[54] Membership in ASEAN and other organizations has helped Vietnam engage its neighbors and the great powers, relieving some of the pressure on traditional power politics as a guarantor for national security.

Vietnam's relative neutrality since 1991 has been based largely on an abiding suspicion of both China and the United States. After withdrawal from Cambodia, the leadership in Hanoi became much less concerned about external military menaces but remained wary of internal threats and outside support for a "plot of peaceful evolution."[55] As one of the poorest nations on earth, Vietnam faced massive economic challenges when Soviet aid declined. Poverty exacerbated the long-term fear in Hanoi that social conditions would result in challenges to the positioning of the governing regime and that Vietnam would fall like the communist regimes of Eastern Europe. Vietnam's minister of national defense, General Doan Khue, did not name external adversaries but asserted that the imperialist forces would use "unarmed and armed measures against us to undermine in a total manner our politics, ideology, psychology, way of living, and so on. . . . They have been trying to seek, build and develop reactionary forces of all kinds within our country; at the same time to nurture and bring back groups of armed reactionaries . . . and to combine armed activities with political activities. . . . They may also look for excuses to intervene, to carry out partial armed aggression, or to wage aggressive wars on various scales."[56] The Vietnamese defense ministry expressed a similar concern in a 1998 white paper, which cited plots of peaceful evolution by ideological and economic means as "great menaces to Vietnam's security and national defense."[57]

Despite resumption of diplomatic relations and trade, many Vietnamese officials continued to harbor suspicions of American ideological designs, even perceiving the 2001 bilateral trade agreement as a Trojan horse designed to bring about peaceful evolution.[58] In 1998 the Vietnamese government released its first defense white paper and explicitly referred to the ideological dimension of its threat perception as being "plots to take advantage of such pretexts as 'human rights' or 'democracy' in order to interfere in Vietnam's internal affairs, the intrusion into this country by means of culture and ideology and through various attempts and maneuvers of the wicked forces, the actions of lending a hand to violent disturbances, activities of subversion and destabilization for the purpose of replacing the current political and social system of Vietnam, are all great menaces to its security and national defense."[59] Nayan Chanda notes that an internally circulated VCP paper in 1999 even warned of the possibility of a "Kosovo-like U.S. intervention in southern Vietnam."[60]

Russia has continued to be friendly, but its influence in the region has plummeted, and Moscow has little to offer beyond outdated arms and some training. Many Vietnamese officials see China as a continuing threat due to lingering disputes in the South China Sea and memories of past friction between the two countries.[61] Even during the friendlier post–Cold War period, Vietnam has not been eager to align with China, fearing a loss of independence. Historically, the relationship between the two countries has never been equal, and partnership has generally occurred through a tributary relationship that Hanoi is not willing to enter unless strategic imperatives leave it little other choice.[62] The United States is also unattractive given residual fears of a plot of peaceful evolution, as described earlier. The Vietnamese belief that both China and the United States present meaningful threats helps to explain why the country has taken a middle path in the post–Cold War Era.

Since the end of the Cold War, Vietnam—which spent over a decade at loggerheads with both Beijing and Washington—has been particularly keen to avoid getting caught in the middle of a Sino-American strategic rivalry. Privately, some Vietnamese officials express a desire to establish cooperation with America to prevent China from exercising too great an influence in the region. However, to avoid antagonizing Beijing, officials have been careful not to make that wish public and to calibrate relations with the United States carefully. Thus, after Vietnam agreed to modest new defense ties with the United States in 2005, officials downplayed the anti-Chinese aspect of the alignment. "Everyone knows we have to keep a fine balance," said Ton Tu Thi Ninh, a leading member of the National Assembly's Foreign Affairs Committee. Vietnam has been careful, he said, not to "bow" to China or "lean over" clearly toward the United States.[63]

Instead, Vietnam has pursued a course of relative neutrality. The Vietnamese government has outlined a vision of security remarkably similar to the *ketahanan* idea in Indonesia and comprehensive security concept in Malaysia. A 1994 article in a government defense journal explained it this way: "National defense must be a general strategy in which *national defense* is closely combined with *security* and *foreign relations*; and even national defense, security, and foreign relations themselves must be *closely combined with economic development and national construction in all respects*. [The new environment demands a] *modern model of national defense* and the abandonment of the classical thinking on and model of national defense based solely on military forces."[64]

Vietnam's strategy in the post–Cold War period has focused on building robust trading relationships with China, the United States, and other regional neighbors. During the 1980s, Chinese and American trade with Vietnam was negligible, and Hanoi received little assistance from the international financial institutions. By 2008 two-way trade with China was more than $21 billion (roughly 23 percent of GDP), trade with the United States was roughly $16 billion (about 17 percent of GDP), and Vietnam was one of the largest recipients of multilateral development aid in the region. Trade and aid have helped Vietnam achieve unprecedented real GDP growth of roughly 8 percent per year during the post–Cold War era, second in the world only to China. The relative economic rewards of Vietnamese nonalignment support the argument that to preserve access to aid and trade, it is arguably more important not to align against a great power than to align with it. Relative neutrality may not secure massive bilateral aid packages, but it can help ensure that most or all major markets are open to one's exports.

Conclusions on Vietnam

Vietnam's behavior early in the post-1975 period was consistent with the hypothesis that DCs usually try to limit their great-power alignments. The serious external threats that VCP leaders perceived after 1978 drove Hanoi to veer from that strategy and embrace close ties with Moscow. Still, the immense costs of that relationship appear to have reinforced Vietnam's desire to avoid overly tight alliance. During the post–Cold War period, Hanoi has pursued a much more neutral position among the great powers, continuing in limited alignment with Russia and avoiding serious security ties to both China and the United States. Its effort has been to achieve what one official called an "optimal position" by striking a kind of "dynamic balance" between the external powers, rather than against any one of them.[65]

LAOS

Lao alignment policy since 1975 has been more consistent with the hypothesis that DCs usually prefer limited great-power security ties to tight ones. The long-standing fraternal relationship between Hanoi and Vientiane has helped Laos avoid close, subordinate relations with the great powers by providing an alternative source of security support. Threats were pressing during the Cold War period, and Laos did ally closely with the Soviet Union during the mid-1980s. However, Vientiane pulled back as soon as threats began to recede, perceiving that close pro-Soviet alignment carried significant costs by antagonizing China and Thailand. In the post–Cold War period, Laos has existed in a much less menacing security environment and has gently tilted toward China to help manage security without closing its doors to aid and commerce from other sources.

Lao security has traditionally been influenced by three larger neighbors surrounding the small, sparsely populated, and landlocked country: Vietnam, China, and Thailand. For centuries Siamese and Vietnamese empires encroached upon Lao territory until French colonial demarcations arrested their advance. However, Siamese conquests left a majority of ethnic Lao peoples in modern Thailand, accentuating the challenge to Vientiane of controlling its western border. The presence of more than sixty ethnic groups in outlying areas of the country and the weakness of the military and central state add to internal vulnerability.[66]

After the Victory Celebration

After the end of the Second Indochina War, Laos perceived many of the same risks of alignment that Vietnam perceived. However, by virtue of its lesser strategic value to the Soviet Union and less hostile relations from China, it was able to keep its ties to the USSR quite limited for much of the 1975–1990 period. Shortly after the Lao communist victory in 1975, Prime Minister Kaysone Phomvihane made clear the Pathet Lao perception that the United States and its domestic allies had represented the clearest threat to the revolutionary movement. He said: "People in the areas controlled by the U.S. and its lackeys, unable to tolerate living as slaves any longer, have resolutely mutinied and fought dauntlessly and vigorously and have successfully overthrown the dominating yoke of U.S. neocolonialism."[67]

In a 1975 joint communiqué, Lao and Kampuchean officials also declared that "as long as there are U.S. military bases and the Lao traitors and Cambodian traitors in Thailand, the threat to peace and security of Laos and Cambodia will always exist."[68] Like Vietnam, Laos was emerging from years of divisive war, and the new regime's overwhelming priority was to engage in reconstruction and pacification of areas under the control of right-wing rebels.

Ideology accounted partly for the Lao attraction to the USSR during the 1970s and 1980s; Kaysone described the USSR as the "bulwark and hope of the world's revolutionary and progressive forces."[69] Material support was also critical. After 1975 and especially after 1979 Laos enjoyed considerable Soviet assistance that propped up the weak Lao armed forces and anemic national economy. Hundreds of Soviet diplomats and technicians poured into Laos in 1975, and the two countries signed an aid agreement worth hundreds of millions of dollars in early 1976. The USSR provided substantial direct budgetary aid, filling the chronic fiscal gap for the Lao government. Soviet experts also helped Lao authorities develop five-year economic plans in line with communist economic principles. Soviet technicians led the construction of a major hospital, bridges, a polytechnic institute, and many other public works projects.[70]

By late 1978 Laos became caught up in Sino-Vietnamese rivalry. Prime Minister Kaysone expressed his fear of Chinese ideological subversion, warned of "Lao traitors in exile," and accused China of "very wicked and dangerous propaganda aimed at sowing bedevilment and anxiety among our people to make them lose confidence in the line and policies of our country and . . . sabotage our revolution."[71] After the punitive 1979 Chinese invasion of Vietnam, Lao Prince Souphanouvong also launched a public attack on China, accusing the PRC of "pursuing a counterrevolutionary policy of regional hegemony and big-nation expansionism . . . ruthlessly carrying out schemes to swallow up our country as well as Vietnam and Kampuchea." Souphanouvong added that the Chinese "now pose a grave danger to our people and to the whole of Southeast Asia," and Kaysone stoked old ethnic sensitivities by attacking PRC policies as evidence of Han chauvinism.[72]

Lao leaders also attacked China for allying itself with the American imperialists. Kaysone wrote in 1985 that "the direct and most dangerous enemy of the three countries' revolutions at this new stage is Chinese big-nation expansionism which is colluding with the U.S. imperialists and other ultra-rightist reactionary forces to oppose the revolutions of the three Indochinese countries—a main obstacle to China's scheme of conquering all of Southeast Asia."[73] As relations between China and Laos worsened, the LPRP also began to view the PRC-backed Communist Party of Thailand, which it described as Maoist reactionaries, as a considerable ideological and military menace, especially when allied with ethnic Lao rebels loyal to Beijing.

The 1980s

Lingering concerns about U.S. Special Forces and allied Montagnard ethnic rebels also remained. Kaysone explicitly described his country's alliance with Vietnam and the USSR as a response to a U.S.-led capitalist threat: "U.S. imperialism still stubbornly refuses to renounce its global strategy, [so] Laos and Vietnam as well as fraternal Cambodia need to always heighten their revolutionary vigilance and . . . our country very much now needs the assistance of all fraternal and friendly countries, first of all Vietnam."[74]

Thailand presented a related menace to the LPDR. Although LPDR officials sometimes described the Thai and Lao peoples as brothers in culture based on their close religious and linguistic ties, Bangkok and Vientiane became bitter adversaries during the era of the Third Indochina War. To the Lao communist regime, cultural affinity gave Thailand levers to influence Lao domestic affairs, and the Thai monarchy presented a dangerous alternative model of government deeply rooted in local historical culture. Many Lao citizens regarded the Thai king as their rightful monarch after communist troops jailed the Lao royals in 1975, and many Lao Theravada Buddhists took spiritual guidance from Thai religious leaders.[75] Lao fears were reinforced after the 1988 border war with Thailand by the words of former Thai Prime Minister Kukrit Pramoj:

It is now 200 years since [our last war with Laos]. We should cross over and burn Vientiane once more. There is no need to declare war; just go across and burn it; when it's done come back. I don't think friendly relations can happen between the Thai and Lao. . . . If we want to be countries like elder and younger brother, the elder brother must be strong, to make the younger brother fear. There is no use being too compliant like this. If you go to war, do it properly, break them completely. . . . Associating with the Lao is like keeping gibbons as pets. You never know when they will bite. . . . The Lao have a long-standing inferiority complex [that will] always cause trouble.[76]

Lao officials also deeply resented the common Thai reference to the relationship as *ban phi muang nong*, which implies a fraternal relationship between an older and younger brother.[77]

The high degree of threats during the 1980s explains why Laos briefly tipped away from a limited alignment strategy and accepted a relatively strong alliance with the USSR. By the mid-1980s roughly 1,500 Soviet political, economic, and military advisors lived in the country. The USSR also provided artillery, light weaponry, airplanes, helicopters, and other military hardware to Laos and set up a variety of transportation, logistics, and communications centers throughout the country. Kaysone wrote, "At all stages of our revolutionary struggle the CPSU and the government and people of the Soviet Union have constantly rendered us tremendous support and effective aid."[78] At its peak in the early 1980s, Soviet aid comprised roughly two-thirds of all foreign aid to Laos. Even as late as 1990, the USSR provided about 50 percent.

Laos was nonetheless eager to avoid being seen as a puppet regime. Its officials feared angering its colossal northern neighbor and erstwhile ally, the PRC, and relying on uncertain foreign military pledges of protection. In a letter to the secretary-general of the United Nations, Lao officials reacted with anger to China's "calumnious allegations affirming that Laos is tailing after Vietnam and the Soviet Union."[79] For a small country like Laos, the fear of abandonment was strong, and the country's leadership tried to move toward a more nonaligned posture. In December 1985, on the tenth anniversary of the Pathet Lao victory, Kaysone said, "We want the Southeast Asian region to be free from external interference."[80] The diminution of Soviet aid and need for aid from others was the key driver of Laos' more neutral foreign policy at the end of the Cold War.[81]

The Post–Cold War Period

Since 1989, Lao leaders have seen their regional neighborhood as more benign, and relations with China have improved dramatically on both the political and economic fronts. The country's mountainous jungle borders continue to generate security concerns, however. Insurgents along the Thai border, mostly Hmong tribesmen, have been a continuing problem, and Vientiane has always believed that the highlanders could not have operated at such levels without Thai complicity.

Border demarcation problems have remained, and Laos has continued to perceive modest threats from guerillas, bandits, and drug runners near the Thai border.[82]

The LPDR has also remained fearful that capitalist countries would use economic levers to pry apart the Lao socialist political system. The loss of material support from the USSR and Eastern Europe, together with Kaysone Phomvihane's death in November 1992, exposed the Lao regime to serious problems of domestic legitimacy and economic vulnerability. The Lao politburo expressed its fears of ideological and economic attack in a formal statement:

> The imperialists have concentrated on carrying out a strategy of effecting change through peaceful means with the hope of doing away with our party's leadership and moving our country into their orbit. They carry out sabotage and subversive schemes through armed activities while creating problems regarding the implementation of the democratic and multiparty system as well as human rights in our country. They have also taken advantage of economic difficulties, problems, in daily life, and various negative phenomena to sabotage and change our country in accordance with their warfare strategy of peacefully effecting change in the same way as they have already done against the former Soviet Union and other socialist countries in eastern Europe.[83]

In October 1999 an unprecedented student rebellion broke out in Vientiane. Six of the student leaders escaped arrest and traveled to Thailand, where the United States granted them asylum, infuriating the LPRP. Lao officials decried the American "interference in the internal affairs of Laos" and expressed their ongoing concern that Washington intended to effect regime change through "peaceful evolution."[84]

Although Lao officials certainly do not perceive a level of threat comparable to the Cold War period, they have remained guarded in their relations with the United States and other capitalist countries, especially Thailand. Economic and low-level military aid from China, as well as a degree of ideological affinity, has encouraged Vientiane to align very loosely with the PRC. China became the largest foreign investor in Laos by 2004, overtaking Thailand, and continued to jockey with Vietnam for influence in Vientiane. However, Lao authorities continued to harbor concern about China's growing power and tended to veer toward traditional allies in Hanoi to establish a rough equilibrium.[85] Lao avoidance of tight alignment owes largely to historical learning. Authorities learnt a painful lesson in the 1980s of the perils of identification with China's foes. The Cambodian saga also reinforced the danger of allying tightly against Thailand or Vietnam. Today's Sino-Lao ties barely rise to the level of an alignment as defined in this volume.

CAMBODIA

Tracing Cambodia's alignment policy since 1975 is challenging because the nature of the governing regime in Phnom Penh and the country's strategic environment have changed dramatically from period to period. The Khmer Rouge regime came to power espousing a xenophobic form of nonalignment but gradually veered toward closer ties with China. After the Vietnamese invasion of December 1978, Cambodia spent over a decade in a semi-sovereign state, followed by a period of international governance by UNTAC. Only after the UNTAC-supervised elections of 1993 did the country return to a normal level of autonomy. Since the mid-1990s Phnom Penh has tilted toward the PRC but has not aligned strongly with Beijing. During both the Khmer Rouge and post-UNTAC periods, Cambodian leaders have shown a preference for limited alignment.

Cambodia has long been vulnerable to territorial encroachment by Thailand and Vietnam, and Cambodian officials have tended to focus on perceived threats from those two adjacent states. Arbitrary colonial frontiers have added to Cambodia's long-standing sense of territorial insecurity, particularly along the eastern frontier, where the French division of Indochina left a large population of ethnic Khmers in southern Vietnam and significant numbers of ethnic Vietnamese in eastern Cambodia.[86] Cambodian officials and many among the general population are intensely aware that modern Cambodia is just a fraction the size of the once-expansive Khmer Empire. Neighboring states and empires gradually chipped away at Khmer territory, and perceived encroachment remains a very sensitive issue in Phnom Penh to this day. Cambodia and Vietnam have clashed on numerous occasions over the Brévié Line, which France used to divide Cochinchina from Cambodia in 1939. After gaining independence, Cambodia enjoyed only a brief respite before great-power competition contributed to a new round of regional conflict. Vulnerability to larger, more powerful neighbors—and to distant imperial powers—lies at the heart of Cambodia's foreign policy, which has placed great emphasis on sovereignty. The same vulnerability helps explain why the country's leaders have pursued limited alignments when they can.

The Pol Pot Period

The Khmer Rouge leadership—hardened by years of war, distrustful of neighbors, and intensely resentful of great-power intrusion—sought to remove foreign influence and pursue an intensely xenophobic form of nonalignment.[87] Days after capturing Phnom Penh, the new state of Democratic Kampuchea announced that it would not allow any foreign power to exert undue influence in Phnom Penh or use its territory for bases. The message was widely interpreted as one directed at Hanoi, which still held an estimated 20,000 troops on Cambodian soil. Vice-Premier Khieu Samphan announced to the Cambodian people that "Cambodia will not allow any foreign bases on its territory . . . and will cooperate with the peoples of Asia, Africa, and Latin America as well as with certain Americans who really love peace and justice. . . . With these peoples, we must work together against the new and old imperialists, against the former colonialists and neo-colonialists, to achieve true independence, peace, justice, and development."[88] This principle became an explicit part of the DK constitution and represented part of a policy to "cleanse" the country of foreign influence by all means necessary. The Khmers Rouges closed all but a few embassies and expelled nearly all foreigners in Cambodia, reinforcing perceptions that the new regime would follow a policy of isolationism.

The DK regime quickly paid a price for nonalignment, however. During the *Mayaguez* incident in May, when DK forces seized an unarmed American freight vessel in international waters in the Gulf of Thailand, China was unwilling to embroil itself in the crisis. Deng Xiaoping declared, "If [the Americans] intervene, there is nothing we can do." He did not even suggest that the PRC would support Cambodia diplomatically in the dispute, and when the United States applied deadly force to recapture the crew, Beijing offered no public condemnation.[89] Harsh economic and strategic realities compelled Phnom Penh to seek PRC support shortly thereafter, but the Khmers Rouges put limits on that alignment. King Sihanouk assured the UN in October 1975 that Democratic Kampuchea would "never allow any foreign country to set up military bases on its land or in its territorial waters."[90]

The vociferous Khmer Rouge regime was explicit about the threat of domination by foreign powers states, drawing a close connection between lost territory and independence. An official 1977 broadcast outlined Phnom Penh's threat perception, "Never again [will we] allow any enemies—near or far, big or small—to rule the roost and do with us as they formerly did. Our brothers and sisters unanimously hold that they will not allow the U.S. imperialists, their lackeys or any other land-grabbing bandits to come back and violate our national sovereignty and territorial integrity as before."[91]

However, until Khmer-Vietnamese border tensions escalated in late 1977 and 1978, the Khmer Rouge regime saw its main security threats as internal. DK officials described the country's "enemy situation" as including a military threat from Thailand but asserted that domestic subversion and sabotage presented the gravest challenges.[92] Above all, the country's decrepit economy threatened the regime's survival. The Khmer Rouge ideology was intensely xenophobic and disfavored any alignment with a foreign power, but it quickly became obvious that the regime needed foreign succor.

The United States was openly hostile to Democratic Kampuchea, particularly after the *Mayaguez* incident of May 1975. To the Khmers Rouges, the Soviet Union was also unappealing as an ally. To the Pol Pot clique, the USSR was an industrial northern power and center of "white imperialism." Moscow had betrayed local communists at the 1954 Geneva Settlements, sought détente with Washington at the height of the Cambodian civil war, and even attempted to cut another deal with the United States toward the end of the Second Indochina War. Ideology added to antipathy for the USSR. An extreme brand of Maoist agrarianism—characterized first and foremost by the mass collectivization of agriculture—lay at the heart of the Khmer Rouge vision for a proud and independent nation.

China was the only great power that possessed reasonable credibility in the eyes of the Pol Pot regime. Although the leaders of Democratic Kampuchea believed their comrades in Beijing were not radical enough, they clearly drew inspiration from Maoist principles, tellingly referring to their plan for advancement as a "Super Great Leap Forward." Thus, despite the obvious xenophobic streak in Khmer Rouge ideology and the regime's fear of ethnic Chinese and other minority groups, Beijing represented the most attractive external protector from an ideological standpoint.[93] Given Democratic Kampuchea's extreme poverty and weakness, any great power possessed sufficient material resources to provide rewards to Phnom Penh.

In late 1975 China committed to providing Democratic Kampuchea with $1 billion of aid over several years, which was a lifeline for the cash-strapped regime.[94] China was also an important source of military support, training, and materiel for the Khmer Rouge regime. Beginning in mid-1975 China reportedly supplied Democratic Kampuchea with MiG 15 jets, 130-millimeter artillery, tanks, weapon carriers, and transport and communications equipment, which the impoverished and technologically handicapped Khmers Rouges would have been hard-pressed to obtain from any other source.[95]

The dominant impetus for Kampuchea's move from a limited alignment to a tight one with China in 1977–1978 was the escalating border conflict with Vietnam. As Pol Pot said in September 1978, "Our strategic duty is to protect our territory with total mastery [and] to protect our territory and our Kampuchean nation forever. . . . [We] will not allow Vietnam to swallow Kampuchean territory without putting up a fight."[96] China provided much of the backing for Khmer military and industrial forces and had an estimated 14,000 to 20,000 military and technical advisors in Cambodia at the peak of Sino-DK cooperation in 1978.[97]

The PRK and UNTAC Periods

After Pol Pot was overthrown and the Hanoi-backed PRK was established, Cambodian leaders remained sensitive to external domination. During the PRK period, Cambodia did not have enough autonomy to make independent alignment decisions and its foreign policy was shaped largely by Hanoi. The PRK regime overwhelmingly depended on Vietnam and the Soviet Union for its survival, but even when relations were at their peak and cooperation was greatest, Kampuchean officials were resentful of the degree of Vietnamese control over their country. Prince Sihanouk, who remained influential in the nation's politics despite his dealings with China and the Khmers Rouges, expressed fear of the tide of Vietnamese settlers, whom he described as "hundreds of thousands of Vietnamese who threaten to turn Cambodia into another Vietnam."[98]

Many PRK officials began to share Sihanouk's concerns. The presence of roughly 180,000 PAVN troops and thousands of Vietnamese advisors added to the quiet resentment in Phnom Penh because many Khmers perceived the occupation as akin to colonization.[99] During the late 1980s, PRK leaders like Chea Sim and Hun Sen attempted to wean themselves away from the Vietnamese and Soviet embrace, concerned about the high political price of such dependence.

Cambodia also forfeited much of its autonomy in foreign policy matters after the signing of the Paris Peace Accords in 1991, when the country became a ward of the international community and entered into a period of UN administration. During that period, the Cambodian desire to put distance between themselves and Vietnam was also obvious, though international pressure for the Vietnamese withdrawal was the more determinative factor in changing relations between Phnom Penh and Hanoi. The Hun Sen government had little scope for foreign policy decision-making during the 1980s, but over time the intent of policymakers in Phnom Penh to pursue a somewhat more neutral course became evident.

The Post-UNTAC Period

Cambodia emerged from the shadow of Vietnamese occupation and the UNTAC administration with general elections in 1993. The two-headed government—under Co-Prime Ministers Hun Sen and Norodom Ranariddh—had as its primary aim the maintenance of internal stability. The most serious threats to national security and stability emanated not from Thailand and Vietnam but from tension between the two leading parties, the royalist Funcinpec and the CPP of Hun Sen, and from the continuing existence of Khmer Rouge rebels in the densely forested Cardammon Mountains in the west of the country.[100] Rebels were able to survive government forces for years under the cover of the jungle by selling precious stones and timber to Thai buyers across the border. Only in the 1996–1998 period did Khmer Rouge defections diminish this internal menace to the government in Phnom Penh.

Cambodia's security focus thus shifted away from combat operations toward other nontraditional threats that could jeopardize the country's development. A 2000 defense white paper cited possible economic spillover from sparring in the South China Sea as an issue of "primary concern" and cited criminal networks and maritime and land border disputes as other important security issues.[101] A 2002 strategic defense review and 2006 white paper added international terrorism to the list of security issues that could affect Cambodia—most likely via indirect effects on trade and tourism.[102] Like most of its ASEAN neighbors, Cambodia has voiced little concern over direct foreign military menaces. The most noteworthy exception has been minor sparring between Thai and Cambodian armed forces on the border around the disputed temple of Preah Vihear in 2008 and 2009. Even that dispute has not posed a major military menace. Leaders from both states have issued invective, but neither side has mobilized for war, and Hun Sen has pressed his case diplomatically through ASEAN channels.

The Cambodian government has stressed its willingness to seek aid from international partners in building its security forces, but following the colonial experience, the period of U.S. intervention, a decade of Vietnamese military occupation, and UN administration, the Cambodian government has been unsurprisingly vehement about opposing foreign domination. The Cold War period had made the risks of tight alliance abundantly clear. Hun Sen said in 1995 that Phnom Penh would be grateful for external assistance in the country's development but would frown upon any relationship that would jeopardize its independence: "[Cambodians] should join hands to work to prevent foreigners from interfering excessively in our internal affairs. If you are happy you can give aid, but you should never talk about my affairs. . . . What I have done is defend the country's independence and sovereignty. . . . If you interfere too much, it is time for you to get out."[103]

There was a legal basis for a policy of nonalignment written into the country's 1993 constitution.[104] The Cambodian government's militant position on foreign interference was also related to its contentious domestic politics. Hun Sen and the CPP were focused on solidifying control against their old royalist adversaries, led by Ranariddh. The CPP also saw a threat from the upstart liberal political leader Sam Rainsy, who gradually won Western backing as the party of urban liberals. China was content to do business with the authoritarian CPP and became more attractive than America as a security partner, largely for that reason. The PRC shared Cambodian resentment of the American human rights and democratization agendas and was much less critical of the Hun Sen government.[105]

Relations between Cambodia and the United States became increasingly sour, especially after the alleged coup of July 1997, when Hun Sen marginalized Ranariddh and seized the reins of power more firmly. The U.S. government accused Hun Sen of antidemocratic practices and human rights abuses and cut off most forms of bilateral aid to Phnom Penh. A war of words ensued, making serious security ties between the two states highly unlikely. By contrast, in 2001 Hun Sen publicly expressed his admiration for China's "neutrality" and Beijing's policy of "not interfering in another country's affairs."[106] Since 1995 low-level Sino-Cambodian defense cooperation had existed, and Cambodia continued to tilt toward Beijing.

China has also provided attractive economic aid, because it comes unencumbered by restrictions relating to environmental standards, corruption, and the like. Hun Sen announced in 2006 that the Chinese government had offered Cambodia $600 million of loans with "no strings attached."[107] In doing so, China has won increasing trust from many Cambodian officials.[108] The PRC has made considerable economic inroads into Cambodia, accounting for more than 40 percent of all foreign investment by 2009 and emerging as the largest provider of external aid.[109] Chinese construction and mineral extraction companies are becoming increasingly influential in outlying areas of the country, where Western companies have been unable or unwilling to establish operations. China has reportedly been granted rights to develop some of the newly discovered oil fields off of the Cambodian coast and has expressed interest in assisting with the modernization and deepening of the maritime port of Sihanoukville.[110] Many analysts perceive the latter project as an effort by the Chinese government to gain access to a valuable naval port in the South China Sea.

Cambodian officials have nevertheless been wary of the risks of their country's tilt toward Beijing in the post–Cold War period. Military and economic aid carry the risk of dependency or subservience, and ties to the economically influential ethnic Chinese community in Phnom Penh give the PRC an added lever for domestic influence. Prime Minister Hun Sen and other Cambodian leaders have remained privately ambivalent about the PRC. As one senior official said, "China is like fire. If you get too close you get burnt, but if you are too far you feel the chill."[111] This metaphor helps explain why Cambodia has pursued limited security ties with China rather than inviting a strong alliance.

Another reason is that the Cambodian economy depends increasingly on exports (mainly textiles) to the United States. Private trade between the two countries has risen dramatically in recent years, and nearly 60 percent of official exports from Cambodia have gone to the United States, mostly from the garment industry.[112] That trade did not motivate the Hun Sen government to build extensive defense ties with Washington but exerts influence on Cambodia's foreign policy and gives Phnom Penh an important incentive not to adopt a more overtly anti-American posture. In addition, Cambodia relies on grants and subsidized loans from the World Bank, Asian Development Bank, and other sources to pursue its development agenda. Antagonizing the U.S. government, which exercises considerable power on the boards of those institutions, could jeopardize Cambodia's access to multilateral funding.

Finally, Cambodian officials remain ever cognizant that close alliance with China could alienate its Southeast Asian neighbors, which fear Chinese encroachment through the establishment of naval bases in the Gulf of Thailand. Other ASEAN countries now provide a significant amount of trade and investment for Cambodia, which could fall if Cambodia returns to its erstwhile status as a regional pariah. Worse still, tight alliance to Beijing could undermine relations with Vietnam, as it did during the Cold War period.

Summary on Cambodia

Cambodia's preference for limited alignment has remained reasonably consistent during periods in which it has been able to formulate a meaningfully independent foreign policy. Systemic changes in the international system have affected those preferences by contributing to the intensity of regional conflict in and around Indochina. Perceived threats from neighbors, relative ideological friendliness between Phnom Penh and Beijing, and economic aid have been the key pull factors encouraging alignment. During the late 1970s, steep security challenges thus pushed the Pol Pot regime to set its fears of diminished autonomy aside and seek a tight military pact with China. Whether the PRK regime shared this preference for tight alliance is difficult to discern due to the commanding role of the Vietnamese army in Cambodia during the 1980s.

Evidence from the post–Cold War period is more clear. A desire for some training and military equipment, a new variety of ideological affinity, and booming economic ties have all encouraged Cambodia to tilt toward Beijing. However, these pull factors have not been enough to tempt Phnom Penh toward a tight alliance that would jeopardize autonomy and likely offend larger, much mightier neighbors.

THAILAND

Thai alignment policy since 1975 has evolved in large part because of changing strategic conditions in the region. After the fall of Saigon, Thai officials took steps to dilute their long-standing alliance with the United States and build a limited alignment with China to accommodate a new balance of power in Indochina. The Vietnamese invasion of Cambodia prompted the Thai government to veer away from a limited alignment strategy and ally more tightly with both the United States and China. When the Vietnamese military threat to Thailand's eastern border receded, Thailand returned toward limited alignments with both Washington and Beijing, which it has maintained with some modest variation throughout the post–Cold War era.

Like other Southeast Asian countries, Thailand has long faced the twin perils of external and internal insecurity. Located in the center of the Southeast Asian peninsula, with many of its frontiers running through lowland plains, Thai strategists have historically feared land-based incursions and prioritized defense against immediate continental neighbors.[113] Thailand and Vietnam have struggled for control over the trans-Mekong region for much of modern history, and particularly during the nineteenth century, because both sides have long believed that the area surrounding the great river is vital to their security and economic prosperity. Burma and Thailand also share a long history of military conflict, and after the rise of the militarized SLORC regime in Yangon, the two countries again engaged in fighting along the border. Interminable ethnic wars between the Myanmar government and rebel Mon, Wa, Kachin, and Karen groups also persisted along the Thai-Myanmar border.[114]

Geography has made Thailand vulnerable to certain internal threats as well. Some parts of Thailand are flat and lie exposed to foreign armies, but several of its border areas are mountainous and covered in dense jungle, making them extremely difficult to police and control. Many were also arbitrary colonial demarcations that cut across ethnic groups, such as the Lao people in the northeast and the Karens and Shans in the west.[115] Geography and the presence of ethnic minority groups along Thailand's borders also made the country vulnerable to infiltration by PRC-backed communist insurgents, who constituted the primary menace to Bangkok throughout the 1970s.[116] Since 1975 Thailand has supported the Karen National Union in its struggle against Yangon, the Hmong tribes against communist Laos, and the Khmers Rouges in the war against Vietnam. Because Thailand's principal perceived threats have almost always come from its immediate neighborhood, Bangkok has traditionally taken a tough line toward other peninsular Southeast Asian states neighbors and sought friendly, balancing relations with large external powers.[117]

The Interwar Period, 1975–1978

Anticommunism had been the principal ballast of Thai security policy throughout the early stages of the Cold War period. Subversive leftist groups were a genuine concern for Thai leaders who sought to protect their king and their Buddhist faith from the grip of atheistic and antimonarchical communism. At the same time, the specter of communism enabled the military to justify a strong role in national politics—and to come out of the barracks on more than one occasion—to steer the country along a path that favored the status quo. During the latter years of the Vietnam War, Thai activists agitated for an end to military dominance and for closure of the large U.S. bases that supported many U.S. operations in Indochina. The bases were, both substantively and symbolically, linchpins in a tight alliance that had helped to solidify a generation of conservative, relatively authoritarian governments in Thailand. As North Vietnamese forces marched toward victory, the U.S.-Thai alliance came under strain for strategic and domestic political reasons.

The Thai government certainly did not cease to see a threat from communist insurgents and an emboldened VCP leadership in Hanoi. In 1976 the Thai National Reform Council essentially extended the Anti-Communist Activity Acts of 1952 and 1969, legally identifying communism as the principal threat to the nation's security.[118] At around the same time, the CPT reached its apogee, fielding up to 14,000 guerilla soldiers, controlling 400 villages, influencing thousands of others, and operating actively in more than half of Thailand's seventy-one provinces.[119] An increasing number were funded by the Soviet Union and Vietnam rather than China. Thai policymakers interpreted the withdrawal of American troops from South Vietnam in April 1975 with great concern, believing that the United States would not again introduce ground forces for the defense of mainland Southeast Asia.[120] This diminished Thai confidence in the United States as a credible defense partner, precisely when the sweeping victory of communist forces in Indochina exposed ASEAN countries to an increased external threat.[121]

In 1975, when U.S. Defense Secretary James Schlesinger said that America had a moral obligation to defend Thailand, Thai Foreign Minister Chartichai Choonhavan responded, "Moral? The United States does not have any morals at this point. They have already pulled out from Cambodia and South Vietnam, so we are going to depend on ourselves."[122] Thailand faced three hostile communist regimes to its east and a simmering domestic communist insurgency supported largely by China. During the heyday of the U.S. alliance in the 1960s and early 1970s, Washington essentially guaranteed Thailand against external military attack, and the Thai armed forces had become underdeveloped.[123] After 1975 the Thai military worked to become less dependent on the United States. In particular, Thailand moved toward security ties with China. Singaporean Prime Minister Lee Kuan Yew privately explained the logic of the Thai decision to President Ford, citing his own conversations with senior Thai policymakers: "The credibility of U.S. aid being sustained over a long period is not good. Thailand will fight for 3 to 5 years with your help, but won't want to go through the Phnom Penh and Saigon mangling machine. They will come to terms with China . . . China is their insurance agent."[124]

Thai officials were also concerned about the effects of their tight alliance with America on Thailand's regional relations. Unauthorized American use of the U

Tapao Air Base in Thailand during the *Mayaguez* affair—in which U.S. warplanes bombed Khmer Rouge facilities—strained the U.S.-Thai alliance significantly for that reason. Prime Minister Kukrit Pramoj described the U.S. use of the base for positioning Marines as a violation of Thai sovereignty and said that Thailand would not permit its territory to be used for any American attacks on Cambodia.[125] Pramoj later accepted an American apology, but reiterated his public commitment to secure the withdrawal of all U.S. forces by March 1976. The episode had shown Thai officials the potential peril of hosting U.S. armed forces, which could embroil the kingdom in regional conflict by staging attacks from Thai soil. The Thai government thus emphasized its independence from the United States and temporarily improved relations with Democratic Kampuchea and Vietnam.

Finally, the tight U.S.-Thai alliance carried added domestic perils after the U.S. withdrawal from Vietnam. The American defeat provided ammunition for Thai politicians and activist groups on the left—including Prime Minister Pramoj—to argue that the tight alliance had produced insufficient gains for Thailand to justify their domestic and regional costs. Domestic political resentment of the military's strong hand in government became more acute. As in the Philippines, the U.S. bases became associated with a period in which Thailand lacked national autonomy and suffered under authoritarian rule justified by Cold War imperatives. The Thai decision to move toward a more independent foreign policy, closing U.S. bases in 1976 and edging toward alignment with China, quite clearly reflected a sense of decreasing rewards and increasingly high risks of tight Thai-U.S. alliance. By the late 1970s China appeared the most likely great power to help defend Thai security interests in mainland Southeast Asia. The Thai military thus reached out to the PRC and began to pursue limited security cooperation. Thailand's strategy of "bending with the wind"—or aligning in a manner that accommodates the most influential external power in mainland Southeast Asia—had served it well during the age of the European empires, helping Thailand become the only Southeast Asian state to avoid colonization.[126] In part, the Thai-PRC alignment represented a continuation of that strategy and effort to turn a Chinese foe into a great-power friend.[127] Improved Sino-Thai links after 1975 had an economic dimension as well. The two sides set up a joint trade committee and witnessed growth in bilateral commerce of nearly 200 percent between 1978 and 1980 alone.[128]

The Third Indochina War

The alliance between Thailand and the United States became strong again—and Sino-Thai alignment increased—when the Vietnamese invasion of Cambodia magnified the threat from Indochina. The Vietnamese threat was the critical factor that drove Thai officials to deviate from their limited alignment strategy of the late 1970s. Thai Deputy Prime Minister Thanat Khoman explained it this way:

> The fact that Vietnam had sent its troops outside of its borders and installed by force of arms a government of its choice in place of another one, obviously

removes any doubt that if it can intervene militarily in Kampuchea it can also get mixed up elsewhere. This kind of threat is not imagined or perceived; it jumps into the eyes of people willing to look. . . . Vietnam is obviously a tiger which is squatting at our doorsteps backed by another tiger, one not far behind [the USSR], while the other potential tiger [China] still lies hidden in the woods.[129]

By 1980 the Royal Thai Army sought to fend off increasingly formidable PAVN adversaries that had advanced all the way to the Thai border. The Vietnamese and Lao challenges to Thai security had a strong domestic component as well. Few expected that Vietnam would attack Thailand directly, but Thai leaders did fear that PAVN incursions in pursuit of Cambodian rebels would destabilize Thai borders, resulting in a refugee crisis and fomenting rebellion among local dissident groups.[130] Others feared that a struggle between pro-Hanoi and pro-Beijing factions in the CPT could erupt into a broader conflict in the north of the country.[131] The Thai government accused the PAVN and Lao military of fomenting unrest in the ethnically Lao areas of northeastern Thailand.

In the context of stronger external security threats from the PAVN, the rewards to Thailand of alignment with America were also clear during the 1980s. Thailand received access to military and financial assistance, as well as the intangible but undeniable security blanket conferred by close ties to Washington. The deterrent effects of annual Cobra Gold exercises and other military cooperation were difficult to measure, but Thai officials perceived them as critical in moderating Vietnamese and Soviet designs on Thai territory. The American alliance also gave Thailand much-valued political support in the UN, where U.S. and ASEAN diplomats bludgeoned Hanoi and subjected the SRV to a harsh regime of economic sanctions.

Facing a serious military threat along its eastern border, Thailand sought an infusion of advanced defense hardware, and Washington was the obvious place to shop. By the mid-1980s, when resistance to the Vietnamese occupation of Cambodia neared its zenith, the United States was granting Thailand almost $2 billion per year in FMS credits—funds earmarked for purchases of American-made military hardware—and other forms of military assistance.[132] Thailand purchased F-5E fighters, tanks, armored personnel carriers, and light weapons to defend against possible PAVN incursions.[133]

In 1981 Thai Foreign Minister Siddhi Sawetsila made the appeal of America's military capabilities explicit by saying that "at the root of the Indochina problem today is the issue of power balance."[134] By 1986 American port visits had become much more frequent, and joint Cobra Gold exercises had expanded. The United States also provided advanced F-16 fighter aircraft, long-range artillery, and other hardware that helped to repel Vietnamese incursions.[135] The U.S. military also trained Thai forces in counterinsurgency techniques, which Sukhumbhand Paribatra cites as perhaps the most critical reward of the alliance to Thailand.[136] Military prowess was thus a major attractive force leading the Thai government to expect—and derive—rewards from a strong alliance with the United States during the 1980s.

The Reagan administration's more aggressive posture toward communist expansion and its demonstrated intent to establish closer ties with key U.S. allies, including Thailand, also gave Bangkok a margin of greater confidence in the credibility of the American commitment to Thai defense.[137] Reagan pledged his support to Thailand in a letter to Thai Prime Minister Prem Tinsulanonda, and a series of high-level visits resulted in stepped-up American military and economic aid. Thai leaders believed that the American Vietnam syndrome was on the wane and that they could count on U.S. commitment to Thailand as long as a staunch anticommunist occupied the White House.[138] In October 1985 Prem and Defense Secretary Caspar Weinberger signed an MOU on logistics supplies. Malaysia also began defense cooperation with the United States during this period.

Security cooperation with China also increased markedly, though Bangkok was careful to limit that alignment and keep Chinese forces from using Thai air and naval facilities. Thai officials characterized the pro-PRC alignment as a necessary deviation from relative neutrality to deal with pressing security threats from Indochina. One high-ranking official described the country's alignment with China in the early 1980s as "a matter of necessity" to confront a menacing PAVN.[139] China helped provide a strategic deterrent to Vietnam after the border war in 1979 by leaving troops at the border and forcing the PAVN to devote large numbers of troops to border defense.[140] High-level military meetings between Chinese and Thai officials in 1984 showed that the relationship had reached a new zenith, but Bangkok still did not permit the PRC's armed forces to use Thai military airspace or port facilities. By the mid-1980s some Thai officials believed that Bangkok risked provoking wider conflict with Vietnam by playing too closely into China's hands.[141]

China's modest power capabilities limited Beijing's appeal as a great-power ally and the rewards it could provide. Thailand received added security from alignment with Beijing, but China had too little power-projection capacity to influence events at the Thai-Cambodian border decisively. The PLA's defeat at the hands of the PAVN in March 1979 had shown that Chinese armed forces were not a failsafe defense against a muscular Vietnam.[142] China could supply cheap arms to Thailand but was unable to furnish the state-of-the-art systems that the Royal Thai Army sought for its modernization program. Consequently, Thailand tended to look for relatively cheap, plentiful, and unconditional arms from Beijing and pursued high-tech systems from the United States.[143]

China's credibility was one of its principal assets, even if it lacked America's raw power capabilities. This was especially true after the brief Sino-Vietnamese War of 1979. According to former Thai Foreign Ministry official Sukhumbhand Paribatra, "The credibility of China's contribution is based on the demonstration in February–March 1979 that alone among the great powers involved in the affairs of Southeast Asia it is prepared to use force, and suffer great losses, to contain Vietnam's expansion."[144]

Deng Xiaoping told Thai officials in no uncertain terms that the PRC would "stand on the side of Thailand if Vietnam attacks it," a pledge most Thai officials believed.[145] The relationship also facilitated a boom in economic exchange. Chinese investments in Thailand also boomed in the 1980s, rising from less than 1 million baht to 100 million baht in only five years.

Alignment with China was not without perceived risks, however, which explains why Thai officials placed limits on the alignment. Thai officials continued to fear Chinese subversion despite the PRC's reduction of support to local communist groups under Deng Xiaoping. By the early 1980s some Thai officials believed their country had moved too close to the PRC, exposing themselves to subversion or dependence.[146]

Overall, Thailand clearly welcomed a tighter alliance during the Third Indochina War but did not seek a return to a relationship as rigidly institutionalized as the U.S.-Thai alliance of the pre-1975 period. As Leszek Buszynski has argued, "The experience of alliance with the United States during the Vietnam War and what was seen as the sudden American decision to withdraw from Indochina had taught the Thais the dangers of being drawn into a dependent relationship with a single great power that could reinterpret priorities with little regard to Thai susceptibilities."[147]

At the same time Thai Deputy Foreign Minister Thanat Khoman said in 1981 that Thailand did not "bow to the Chinese."[148] Thai officials saw their dependence on China to fight Vietnam as a temporary divergence from a more balanced foreign policy and spoke throughout the 1980s about an "omnidirectional" approach to foreign affairs. As the Cambodian stalemate moved toward resolution in the late 1980s, Thai leaders were eager to reduce some of the risks of their security ties to Beijing and Washington and edged back toward more limited security relationships.

The Post–Cold War Era

In the post–Cold War period, Thailand has seen a significant diminution of external military threats and the threat of communist subversion. Internal and nontraditional security threats have persisted, however, such as a flourishing drug trade, illicit human migration and trafficking, and resistance from ethnic minority groups in the south of the country.[149] Thailand has generally perceived its principal security challenges as arising from its border areas.[150] Border skirmishes with Laos and Cambodia continued.[151] Increased cooperation between Myanmar, Laos, and Cambodia during the 1990s raised new Thai fears of encirclement by a mini-bloc of authoritarian nationalist regimes.[152] Troubles with rebel groups and the Myanmar army on the western Thai border remained, precipitating a heavy build-up of Thai and Myanmar troops along the border in early 2001.[153] Thai officials cited Yangon-backed drug cartels and ethnic Wa guerillas near the border as the chief threats to national security.[154] Domestically, separatist Malay factions in southern Thailand have been a rising concern since 2001. The magnitude of perceived security threats has diminished overall, however, diminishing the expected rewards of great-power alignment.

Weaker American credibility has also reduced Thailand's expected rewards from the Thai-U.S. alliance in several periods. Thailand allowed U.S. forces to use its bases for staging operations during the 1990–1991 Gulf War, but after the military crackdown on pro-democracy demonstrations in 1991–1992, the U.S. Congress suspended military ties with Thailand. That move, which some Thais saw as a betrayal, prompted Thailand to put distance between itself and America, in part by joining the NAM.[155] Many officials in Bangkok doubted the long-term U.S. interest in Southeast Asian security and believed that when possible, Washington should not be counted on.[156] Nevertheless, the alliance has continued to produce considerable rewards through advanced weapons systems and access to defense training and doctrine and advanced weapons systems, and Cobra Gold remains intact as the largest U.S. joint exercises in the region. In addition to being a major recipient of foreign military sales credits for F-16 fighter aircraft and other state-of-the-art systems, Thailand has been one of the most active participants in the IMET program over the past few decades, with tens of thousands of officers participating.[157]

The Thai government has generally seen China as credibly committed to a strong security relationship in the post–Cold War era, and China's proximity made Thai officials see its interest in Southeast Asia as less fleeting than America's.[158] In addition, ethnic issues have not bedeviled Sino-Thai relations as they have other parts of Southeast Asia. Many of Thailand's political and military elites are part of the country's well assimilated ethnic Chinese population, which has generally reduced any cultural perception of threat and contributed to strong economic bonds.[159] However, the nature of security challenges that Thailand faced in the early post–Cold War period made it unclear how China could provide major security rewards. With the PAVN no longer stationed near Thailand's borders, weaker external threats contributed to a somewhat more limited Sino-Thai alignment.

As traditional security threats waned, Thai foreign policy in the 1990s came to focus primarily on economics and leadership in multilateral forums. A 1994 Thai national defense strategy white paper emphasized the increasing importance of economic security in the post–Cold War era, asserting that "there are no friends or enemies as in the past" and that the country's security forces should "focus and concentrate more on protecting national economic interests."[160] Many Thai officials perceived the 1997 financial crisis as the most serious threat to Southeast Asian security since the end of the Cold War.[161] Many Southeast Asian officials believed that the financial crisis resulted from an effort, either planned or tacitly accepted by U.S. officials, to curtail the dramatic economic growth of Pacific economies.[162] Whether that allegation is true or not, Thai leaders viewed the episode as another reason to avoid undue dependence on Washington and build more diverse foreign relations.

Much of Thailand's diplomacy has focused on building economic bridges, which Thai officials see as a key way to promote peace and stability in the region. More than its mainland neighbors, Thailand has been an engine for the development of initiatives in ASEAN and beyond. Thailand hosted the first leaders' meeting of the ASEAN Regional Forum in 1994 and an ASEAN-UN Summit in 2000 to help the region regain its footing after the Asian financial crisis. Thailand also played a lead-ing role in the establishment of the most successful ASEAN+3 initiatives to date—the Chiang Mai Initiative, featuring a network of currency swaps, and the Asian Bond Market Initiative. Prime Minister Thaksin Shinawatra also introduced the Asian Cooperation Dialogue (ACD), in which officials from east, west, and central Asia discuss issues of common concern.

Thai officials have seen limited alignments with external powers as a way to help Thailand exercise subregional and regional leadership. As one senior Thai official said, Thai success in launching new initiatives like the ACD owes to its balanced approach to the great powers. He argued that Thailand is seen by the major powers as moderate. Its track record shows that Thailand tries to balance the interests of the key powers, which enables Thais to gain their diplomatic support.[163] That former Thai Foreign Minister Surakiat Sathirathai was a credible candidate for the position of UN secretary-general before the 2006 Thai military coup testifies to the merit of a post–Cold War alignment policy that has preserved favorable relations with the United States, China, and other great powers.

The Thai government's priority on economic growth has similarly encouraged it to limit security allegiance to both Washington and Beijing to keep both doors open to finance and commerce.[164] In addition to the strategic perils of taking sides, the antagonism of large trading powers—including Japan, India, and the European Union as well as China and the United States—can also have dire economic con-sequences. Southeast Asian countries that depend heavily on exports for economic growth—including Thailand—have been particularly keen to avoid alignments that put economic opportunities at risk.

The U.S.-Thai alliance rebounded to a degree after the attacks of September 11, when southern Islamic insurgents and international terror groups created stron-ger push factors encouraging Thailand to build on its security ties with Washing-ton. However, Prime Minister Thaksin Shinawatra immediately noted his concerns about tight alliance with the United States after the September 11 attacks, saying his country would remain "strictly neutral." Deputy Prime Minister Isarangkul na Ayuthaya was more explicit: "We would not want to help the U.S. in perpetrating a war," he said, pointing out that "Thailand could become vulnerable to foreign ter-rorists if it showed a strong alliance to the U.S."[165]

Thai officials were also concerned about domestic Muslim separatists. Indeed, allowing the United States to use the U Thapao air base and naval port of Satta-hip to support operations in Afghanistan and Iraq and sending a small contingent of troops to Afghanistan gave rise to popular resentment in Thailand's troubled, Muslim-majority provinces.[166] Consequently, although Thaksin accepted designa-tion as a major non-NATO ally of the United States in 2003, he asked the U.S. government not to name his country as part of the U.S.-led coalition of the will-ing. In addition to the risks, the rewards of tighter alignment have been unclear, as U.S. military or counterterrorism support may not be able to help greatly in the government's management of the insurgency in the south.[167] An alliance also offers little succor for Thailand's dominant recent challenge of resolving domestic political disputes between supporters of the ousted Thaksin and supporters of the traditional ruling class.

Like most other Southeast Asian states, Thailand has seen limited alignment as the most effective way to both reap rewards and manage the risks of security engagement with the United States and China. The Thai government's ability to maintain strong links with both China and the United States keeps supplies of arms and training coming from both sides and gives officials in Bangkok some added leverage.

CONCLUSIONS

As the mainland states demonstrate, DCs do not always pursue limited alignments. Some choose to ally tightly when confronted with strategic opportunities, or simply because they face dire threats and see little other choice. Seismic changes in the balance of power on the peninsula and episodes of war and peace have pushed all five of the mainland states toward tight pacts at some points in the past three decades. The most obvious reason for a number of tight alliances in mainland Southeast Asia has been the existence of serious, external armed threats to countries on the peninsula.

DCs that do form tight alliances sometimes come to regret it, because great-power protectors sometimes use their leverage to exploit their weaker partners economically or as pawns in broader security strategies. The three states of Indochina suffered woefully in that respect during the Cold War, becoming embroiled in a series of conflicts partly instigated and significantly escalated by rival great powers. All three states appear to have learned a painful lesson, veering toward limited alignment or relative neutrality in the post–Cold War era to avoid the perils of dependency, entrapment, and abandonment that can flow from tight alliances with an unworthy great-power partner. Thailand and Myanmar were able to survive their periods of tight defense pacts with somewhat less sacrifice in autonomy, but they too sought to loosen their security relationships with their protectors when the period of clear and present danger had passed. Overall, the mainland states have shared a consistent desire to assert their independence vis-à-vis the great powers and neighboring states. Consequently, during the more peaceful post–Cold War period, all five states have tended to pursue limited alignments or relative neutrality.

New alignment postures since the 1990s have given rise to an entirely different strategic topology. Whereas Indochina was the focal point of division in the region throughout the 1970s and 1980s, it has since become much less polarized and limited alignments have helped soften the impact of resurgent Sino-American strategic rivalry. The United States still has a formal security treaty with Thailand, but Thai governments have maintained a delicate balance in their relations with Washington and Beijing. The parallel Thai relationships with China and the United States were forged in a period of Sino-American cooperation against Vietnam and the USSR in the early 1980s, and Thailand has been able to preserve limited alignments with both countries even when the Third Indochina War ended and Sino-American relations became more competitive.

Vietnam has been another major factor, adopting a position of carefully calibrated neutrality that limits both Chinese and American leadership in Indochina. Laos, Cambodia, and Myanmar have been friendliest to the PRC, but even they have limited their exposure to Beijing, and it would be inaccurate to depict the overall subregional alignment structure as oriented clearly toward China or the United States. Instead, the mainland states appear collectively quite neutral; if the sum of their security ties now slightly favor China, the two most important states—Vietnam and Thailand—have left themselves plenty of room for maneuver if one great power or the other becomes too domineering.

Chapter 6

The Prevalence of Limited Alignments Today

ONE REASON LIMITED ALIGNMENTS deserve careful study is that the practice is particularly common today. This chapter explains why Southeast Asian countries—like other states in the Global South—have had added incentives to pursue loose, flexible security arrangements in the post–Cold War era. I also discuss why that trend is apt to continue in Southeast Asia in the near term. Thus, where the last two chapters pulled apart individual case studies, this chapter takes a big-picture approach. I attempt to show how the structure and nature of the contemporary international system have affected Southeast Asian alignment calculations.

In chapter 1, I laid out my basic theoretical arguments for why DCs are even more likely than usual to prefer limited alignments in the post–Cold War context. Part of the explanation relates to the distribution of power in the international system. The greater concentration of capabilities in a single country (the United States) has driven up some of the risks of tight alliances. It is particularly dangerous to balance against the United States assertively when U.S. forces enjoy such overwhelming might. Unrivaled U.S. power also adds to the possibility that the United States will either dominate its allies or abandon them, simply because its unrivaled capabilities make it easier to do so.

Perhaps even more importantly, American primacy has contributed to relative peace among the major powers, as none has the capabilities to easily challenge U.S. leadership. This Pax Americana of sorts has reduced some of the perceived need for major external defense support in many parts of the Global South. Second-order powers are simply seen as less likely to disturb the status quo in ways that would invite American wrath.

The nature of the contemporary international order also helps to explain why DCs are more likely to favor limited alignments. The character of U.S. and other great-power policies—and in particular the convergence toward more pragmatic engagement and away from ideological feuds—has facilitated a vast expansion of economic, diplomatic, and institutional linkages. Regional institutions have sprung up around the world and assumed an increasing share of the international security burden alongside traditional alliance structures and self-help remedies. These

developments, like the existence of clear U.S. primacy, have led many DCs to perceive lesser external threats and contributed to lower expected rewards from tight
alliances.

As I have argued throughout this book, DCs pursue limited alignments in an
effort to strike the best possible balance between the risks and rewards of alignment
in a fluid security environment. The structure and nature of the post–Cold War
order make limited DC alignments even more likely than at other times in history,
primarily because many DCs have simply seen less need for robust alliances. Without serious threats of attack, the rewards of tight alliance seldom justify the risks.

Southeast Asian behavior supports my claim that limited alignments are particularly appealing in the contemporary international order. Clearly, they have been
more common since 1990 than they were in Southeast Asia during the Cold War.
Almost all instances of tight alliance in the region since 1975 occurred during the
Third Indochina War, when the mainland peninsula was wracked by ideological
and strategic polarization and military conflict. Since the end of that struggle, limited alignments have been thoroughly dominant in the region. Figures 6.1 and 6.2
illustrate the shift.

In the next section I elaborate on the reasons why limited alignments have been
so dominant in Southeast Asia since the end of the Cold War and why that trend is
likely to continue in the near term.

HIGHER RISKS UNDER RELATIVE UNIPOLARITY

One reason limited alignments have been so common in the post–Cold War era—
and tight alliances so rare—is that some of the risks of tight alliance are higher in

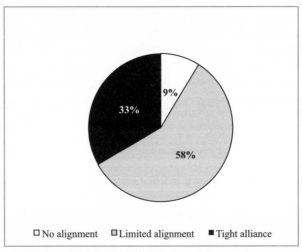

Figure 6.1   Cold War Alignment Behavior

Source: Author's compilation

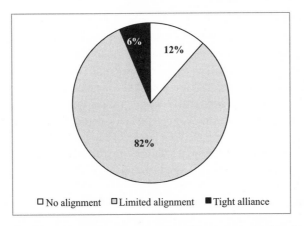

Figure 6.2 Post–Cold War Alignment Behavior

Source: Author's compilation

a relatively unipolar system. During the Cold War, the dangers of allying tightly with any of the feuding external powers were certainly substantial. A state could lose the independence it had just fought off colonial powers to obtain. Worse still, it could cast its lot only to be abandoned in an hour of need. Further, it could become entrapped in ideological and strategic conflict instigated by its stronger ally. However, to many governments in Southeast Asia, the risks of outright balancing or bandwagoning strategies have been even more acute since the demise of the USSR. Many of America's allies have perceived heightened dangers of dominance or abandonment by the mighty United States, which faces no serious counterweight in the international system. At the same time, the huge U.S. lead in military capabilities and influence in global economic and political institutions has made tight anti-American alignments more dangerous than before.

Rising Concerns about U.S. Dominance

The danger of diminished autonomy has long provided a powerful incentive for Southeast Asian leaders to pursue flexible arrangements rather than allying tightly with the great powers. Once the Soviet specter was gone, American allies often believed that they had even less leverage in their asymmetric relations with the United States than they had during the Cold War. When the Soviets were breathing down America's neck, U.S. officials constantly had to worry about losing allies to the USSR. The removal of Cold War imperatives gave the U.S. government more leeway to bully DCs, which often had nowhere to turn if they resented American pressure. Malaysian Prime Minister Mohamad Mahathir pointedly said during the 1992 conference of the NAM that a "unipolar world is every bit as threatening as a bipolar world." Indonesian President Suharto added that "the new world order to which leaders of industrialized countries often refer [must] not turn out to be but a new version of the same old patterns of domination of the strong over the weak."[1]

After the Cold War America could advance its democratization and human rights agendas with less fear of adverse strategic consequences. During the 1990s U.S. and European promotion of those norms led to the highly publicized "Asian values" debate featuring Mahathir, Singaporean Prime Minister Lee Kuan Yew, and others, who claimed that Asian culture and tradition pointed in a different direction that some analysts call the "soft authoritarian" model. Many Southeast Asian citizens and activists agreed with the Western push for democracy, but governing elites in most capitals in the region have seen America's focus on pluralism and respect for opposition rights as dangerous challenges to the status quo. Most Southeast Asian states are still dominated by a single political party.

The U.S. response to the Asian financial crisis reinforced the view that that too much dependency on America can be perilous for Southeast Asian regimes. When several economies were prostrate, the U.S. government used its leverage to help ease out the Suharto regime, promote East Timorese independence, and impose painful economic reforms, especially in Indonesia and Thailand. The American emphasis on democracy, human rights, and liberalization may have been advantageous for the afflicted states in the long run, but Southeast Asian elites bitterly resented having their hands forced. The fate of Suharto, a long-time U.S. ally, was particularly concerning to some, who feared that they could be next on the chopping block. Frequent U.S. pressure for controversial domestic reforms has contributed to a general reluctance to pursue tight security alignment with America lest they follow in the footsteps of Suharto.[2]

For some Southeast Asian leaders, the importance of asserting autonomy vis-à-vis the United States has risen again in recent years, as unpopular U.S. policies since 9/11 have added to the domestic risk of allying tightly with America. This has been particularly in the Muslim-majority states of Malaysia, Indonesia, and Brunei. Local Islamic parties, who oppose the secular regimes in Kuala Lumpur and Jakarta, have attacked their governments' cooperation with Washington and accused their leaders of allowing America to exercise dominance over Muslim countries.[3] The general public has often voiced similar misgivings about seeing their governments cooperate closely with the "crusading" Bush administration.

Potential for Chinese Domination

As China becomes more influential in the region, some PRC allies in mainland Southeast Asia have also become sensitive to the possibility of domination by Beijing. Since the era of the Four Modernizations, and especially since the mid-1990s, pragmatism has helped China mend damaged fences and become less menacing, especially in mainland Southeast Asia. Vietnam and Laos have feared the kind of "peaceful evolution" that disposed of communist regimes in Eastern Europe. The dominant Cambodian People's Party fears Western support for opposition leaders like Sam Rainsy, and the junta in Myanmar always has one eye on the iconic Aung San Suu Kyi. In that context, China has been a less threatening great-power ally in some respects than the United States. Nevertheless, the mere possibility that China will use its rapidly rising economic and strategic clout to boss around its friends in Southeast Asia is enough to make regimes in Myanmar, Laos, Cambodia, and Thailand nervous.

Geographic distance has had some impact on the levels of risk perceived. America's distance has generally reduced fears of U.S. domination at the margins, and China's proximity has clearly added to concerns that it could wield unwanted influence over its mainland Southeast Asian allies. Overall, as Amitav Acharya has argued, individual and collective Southeast Asian foreign policies have emphasized the importance of counterdominance vis-à-vis external giants.[4] Limited alignment has been a way to reduce the scope for foreign domination.

Heightened Fears of Abandonment

Rising or resurgent fears of abandonment have provided a second key incentive for Southeast Asian leaders to favor limited alignments in the post–Cold War era. Concerns about abandonment are nothing new in the region. Few officials in the region have trusted that the great powers would look out for Southeast Asian interests out of sheer loyalty or benevolence when their own interests pointed in a different direction. In international security, as any policymaker knows, depending heavily on allies is a dangerous business. Amid Cold War competition, Southeast Asian leaders sometimes feared that the great powers would sell out their friends to achieve détente or other objectives. Most saw superpower rivalry in the region as a means for each to achieve broader global objectives. Few officials labored under the illusion that the superpowers saw the region as a critical end in itself. Still, superpower feuds made abandonment somewhat less likely, because neither the United States nor the USSR wanted its opponent to run the table in Southeast Asia. After the collapse of the USSR, abandonment fears returned to the fore.

Cold War

Cold War concerns about abandonment were strongest in the late 1970s and receded thereafter. To communists in Vietnam, Laos, and Cambodia, the Soviet deal with America to neutralize and partition Indochina at the 1954 Geneva conference and the superpowers' 1972–1973 peace talks showed that officials in Moscow would sacrifice allies' interests to advance their own. After 1975, Soviet allies were fearful that they could be left to fend for themselves against China or the United States if the Kremlin decided to pursue broad rapprochement with its chief nemeses. Cultural factors contributed to an underlying distrust of the USSR as well; Vietnamese and Lao officials never became quite comfortable with the alien style of Soviet diplomacy and communication.

U.S. allies also worried about being left to fend for themselves. The enunciation of the Nixon Doctrine and Vietnamization of the Vietnam War had generated serious concerns, and uncertainty about America's commitment to Southeast Asia rose after the U.S. withdrawal from Saigon. Thailand lowered its expectations of a future American commitment to the defense of mainland Southeast Asia, and governments in the maritime subregion feared that the Vietnam syndrome in Washington would reduce U.S. willingness to defend the vital waterways of Southeast Asia as well.

During the 1980s, however, intense superpower competition reduced fears that the superpowers would simply pack up and leave. It was clear that neither American nor Soviet leaders wanted to forfeit the struggle in Indochina or see their allies switch sides due to conquest or revolution. Although U.S. credibility had waned after the withdrawal from Vietnam, it rebounded after the Vietnamese invasion and the arrival of the sternly anticommunist Reagan administration. To ASEAN officials' relief, the United States also abandoned the "swing strategy" under which some parts of the Pacific fleet could be moved to Europe in the event of a crisis. Buildup of U.S. naval forces in the Indian Ocean, cancellation of plans to withdraw troops from South Korea, and rapid increases in military and economic aid to key U.S. allies throughout Asia added to perceptions of rebounding American credibility.[5]

Thailand similarly had little doubt about Chinese support against Vietnam after the PRC invaded Vietnam in early 1979. Vietnam also had reason to believe that the Soviet Union would not abandon Indochina easily, because doing so would tilt the overall balance toward China and the United States. Only after Mikhail Gorbachev introduced sweeping reforms and pursued rapprochement with the West did concerns about Soviet abandonment begin to increase sharply. The increased confidence in superpower credibility and corresponding reduction in fears of abandonment helps explain why frontline states to the Third Indochina War allied tightly for significant periods.

Post–Cold War

For many Southeast Asian states, the end of the Cold War revived old fears of being abandoned. In most capitals, those concerns have been relatively high ever since. The crumbling Soviet Union was making a hasty exit from Indochina, leaving its impoverished former allies to face the perils of a new regional order on their own. In the maritime subregion, the United States accepted the closure of Subic Bay with a degree of nonchalance that suggested a lesser commitment to the defense of the region after the Soviet menace was gone. Almost every Southeast Asian government scrambled to diversify its foreign relations to come to terms with the smaller superpower footprint in the region. The reminder to most Southeast Asian officials was clear: a great-power protector cannot always be counted upon to stay the course when its own strategic interests change.

Expectation of abandonment encouraged Vietnam, Laos, and newly independent Cambodia to move away from Russia after the Soviet implosion reduced the Kremlin's credible capacity and willingness to defend Indochinese interests. Leaders in Hanoi still harbored serious concerns about China after spending a decade at loggerheads with Beijing, but there was no appealing ally in sight. Relations with America were still frosty, and distrust of U.S. intentions was strong. Vietnam's decision to pursue relative neutrality in the early 1990s was based partly on the diminution of a China threat as bilateral relations improved, but its inability to align loosely against the PRC was more a function of the lack of a credible great-power partner.

Relative unipolarity also added to the perceived risk that America would leave its allies in the lurch, because the United States needed each of its Southeast Asian allies somewhat less to preserve a commanding lead in global security affairs. U.S. credibility rebounded somewhat after September 2001, when American interest in regional security visibly increased in the hunt for al-Qaeda and its affiliates, but America's Southeast Asian allies have continued to harbor concerns about the reliability of U.S. support.[6] The United States has often sought to address this concern—as Hillary Clinton did by stressing renewed U.S. commitment to Asia in a January 2010 speech and asserting that "the United States is back in Asia . . . to stay."[7] Nevertheless, doubts have been difficult to dispel in the ASEAN region.

The sheer distance of the United States and its interests elsewhere in the world generate perennial fears that the U.S. government puts little priority on Southeast Asia. U.S. policy toward Southeast Asia has usually appeared to be subsidiary to larger goals—such as global containment of communism during the Cold War or the worldwide campaign against terror since 9/11. That perception is strong in Southeast Asia, leaving many officials with the fear that shifts in overall U.S. foreign policy or even changes in administrations could have significant adverse consequences for their own relations with America. Abandonment concerns have encouraged U.S. allies to avoid strong defense pacts even as they have taken bilateral and multilateral initiatives to keep the United States engaged in regional security.

The Risk of Entrapment

The third major risk of alignment relates to entrapment and the alienation of third parties. In the post–Cold War period, America's power capabilities give it the capacity to act more unilaterally than before. For example, many key states vehemently disagreed with American proposals to invade Iraq in 2003, but unrivaled power enabled the U.S. government to override their objections and lead an invasion anyway. America's security partners in the Global South have generally avoided tight alliances that could entrap them in conflict by obligating them to support controversial U.S.-led campaigns or policies.

Cold War Entrapment Concerns

In the context of Cold War confrontation, Southeast Asian governments were sensitive to the possibility that aligning too closely with any great power would alienate neighbors and rival great powers. At times leaders feared direct entrapment in interstate military conflict, but more often they believed that tight alliance would make them the objects for domestic subversion funded by rival great powers.

Immediately after the fall of Saigon, Vietnam, Laos, and Cambodia all sought to pursue limited alignments—albeit without much success. They did so largely to reduce the risk that adversarial great powers would attack them or provide guns and butter to domestic insurgents and hostile neighbors. Frigid Sino–Soviet relations gave Vietnamese and Lao leaders an incentive to shy away from embracing the USSR too closely. Indochinese fears were later validated; Vietnam's decision to ally tightly with the USSR after 1978 resulted in serve punishment, both in military and economic terms.

Entrapment also concerned Thai officials, who edged gently away from America to lower the likelihood of conflict with the communist regimes of Indochina. The U.S. military's use of Thai bases to rescue the *Mayaguez* from Khmer Rouge forces in May 1975 was a classic case in which Thailand could have been entrapped in conflict not of its choosing. Maritime ASEAN governments were also sensitive to the danger of antagonizing the Soviet Union, China, and the Indochina states. None believed it was likely to suffer direct military attack from a communist state, but all feared Chinese or Soviet support for domestic insurgents. China in particular had links to local communist groups that could wreak havoc, especially in Malaysia, Indonesia, and the Philippines. Maritime ASEAN governments had little desire to provoke Chinese or Soviet anger, which was part of the reason why they generally stressed that their security arrangements with America were both temporary and consistent with full local sovereignty and freedom of choice.[8]

Contemporary Concerns

In the post–Cold War period, entrapment in a major military conflict has appeared unlikely for Southeast Asian states, except to the extent that they are asked to contribute troops to American-led conflicts. However, the possibility of alienating key economic or political partners has taken on greater prominence. Most Southeast Asian governments have sought to preserve sufficient distance from both China and the United States, wary of being caught in the crosshairs of an emerging regional rivalry.[9] The George W. Bush administration's early characterization of China as a "strategic competitor" added to concerns in some Southeast Asian capitals that governments in the region would increasingly have to choose sides.[10]

Although many ASEAN leaders have come to perceive a growing China as a potential threat, they have avoided balancing against the PRC too overtly, which most view as impracticable and unduly provocative.[11] Antagonizing China would encourage the PRC to become more defensive and perhaps aggressive, which no ASEAN government wants to happen. It would also jeopardize important economic opportunities (discussed below). Most Southeast Asian states now have considerable economic and political incentives to avoid alienating China by allying tightly with the United States. As the Thai ambassador to the United States Tej Bunnag said in 2001, even America's allies in the region would not be willing to take actions that risked offending China.[12]

To date, most Southeast Asian officials have not feared a direct military clash between the United States and China in their neighborhood, but Sino-American conflict over Taiwan or on the Korean Peninsula has not been beyond the pale of possibility. No Southeast Asian government has wanted to have to choose between

Washington and Beijing in such a context. Even if China and the United States were unlikely to attack their rival's allies, they might penalize adversaries economically or politically, or undermine governments by supporting local rebel groups or dissidents.

Tight alliance with the U.S. government has also carried added domestic risks in the post-9/11 era, especially in states with large Muslim populations. Voters could punish leaders seen to be in bed with America, or extremist groups could use alignment to drum up violent opposition to the government. For example, Jemaah Islamiyah leader Abu Bakar Bashir has called Indonesian antiterrorism officials both "tools of America" and apostates.[13] Finally, small Southeast Asian countries have sought to avoid alignment decisions that unduly antagonize larger, potentially menacing regional neighbors. Singapore's caution in approaching the United States and Cambodian and Lao caution in establishing security links with China are perhaps the best examples.

Summary on Heightened Risks

The risks of diminished autonomy, abandonment, and entrapment have not uniformly risen since the end of the Cold War, but relative unipolarity has generally magnified concerns about the possibility that the United States will either become too dominant or too disengaged. The higher perceived risks of tight alliances do not alone explain why limited alignments have been so dominant in the post–Cold War period, but they are an important part of the explanation. They provide the incentives for Southeast Asian states to pursue limited ties or genuine nonalignment unless they need and expect immense rewards from tight security cooperation.

DIMINISHED REWARDS IN THE POST–COLD WAR ERA

During the Cold War period, most of the risks described in the previous section were present, but the high expected rewards of tight alliance encouraged some Southeast Asian governments to forge close security ties. In the post–Cold War period, external military threats and domestic insurgencies have presented less existential challenges to most states in the region, giving leaders less incentive to veer from limited alignment strategies. Security threats and uncertainty about the future intentions of neighbors and external actors have still given Southeast Asian leaders reasons to seek some security support. However, they have overwhelmingly pursued limited alignments while hedging their bets through increased diplomatic and economic engagement of erstwhile adversaries.

External Security Threats

Structural changes in the international security system have influenced Southeast Asian alignment patterns largely by affecting the overall level of external military threats perceived in the region. Stephen Walt's balance-of-threat theory implies that the magnitude of external threats a government faces is the primary determinant of the tightness of the countervailing alignment that state will pursue. Threat perceptions, which depend on a complex bundle of material and ideational factors, certainly cannot explain alignment preferences alone—as this book emphasizes, perceptions of prospective allies and the risks of alignment also matter. However, the magnitude and nature of security threats is a key factor in governments' risk-reward calculi. Southeast Asian alignment preferences have clearly changed in response to shifts in their external threat environments, and the general diminution of external threats after the Cold War is one reason for the dominance of limited alignments since 1990.

Cold War

After the U.S. withdrawal from Saigon, most Southeast Asian governments perceived a significant level of strategic uncertainty. The Vietnam War was over, implying that superpower-sponsored confrontation would subside, but it was unclear how China, the United States, and the USSR would adjust to the new strategic landscape. In the context of that uncertainty, limited alignment strategies were attractive. Vietnam and Laos saw less need to ally tightly with the USSR and China, and they also sought to stay out of a fight between Moscow and Hanoi. The ASEAN-6 states were concerned about communist gains, but none believed that a direct Soviet or PRC attack was likely. Local threats had been brought under relative control in the maritime subregion, except for the Philippines, where communist rebels were gaining ground against the Marcos regime. With the U.S. bases in the Philippines intact, Indonesia, Malaysia, and Singapore saw little need to ally tightly with America. Their basic security interests were adequately protected by limited cooperation.[14]

Nevertheless, intense strategic and ideological competition between the United States and USSR and their allies continued. As détente began to unravel and Sino-Soviet acrimony persisted, superpower feuds encouraged armed conflict, subversion, and large-scale insurgency in parts of Southeast Asia. By the late 1970s the Soviet Union achieved rough military parity with the United States in the Pacific, in part by seeking bases in Southeast Asia. The USSR's rising power in the Pacific made the prospect of Soviet ties to Vietnam particularly menacing to anticommunist regimes, especially in Thailand, which would be the likely frontline state in the event of Vietnamese expansion. The Sino-American rapprochement contributed to a crystallization of the conflict and gave officials in Bangkok, Manila, and Singapore added confidence in opposing Soviet-Vietnamese encroachment. Relative bipolarity thus encouraged a process whereby local tensions in Indochina spilled over into a broader regional rivalry.

Mounting military tensions in Indochina and the Third Indochina War were the proximate causes for tight Kampuchean alignment with China in 1978 and tight Thai and Vietnamese alignments with their respective superpower protectors from the late 1970s to the late 1980s. The frontline states of Vietnam and Thailand faced threats that they simply did not believe they could meet without extensive great-power backing. The structure of the international system did not make the Third Indochina War inevitable, but it clearly contributed to the onset of hostilities and thus to deviations from limited alignment behavior. The ongoing Cold War also clearly contributed to the preservation of the U.S.-Philippine alliance in the 1980s, largely because China and the USSR had continued incentives to fund NPA rebels and undermine the Philippine regime. In all those instances, the systemic environment made tight alliances more likely by contributing to the conditions for armed conflict and serious domestic resistance to Southeast Asian political regimes.

By contrast, the states that could more easily afford to limit their alignments generally did so. Burma was the most genuinely nonaligned for most of the 1980s, whereas Indonesia, Malaysia, Singapore, and newly independent Brunei all pursued limited alignments. Uncertainty was a key factor, because those governments all harbored at least some concerns about American staying power and about the wisdom of drawing China more fully into regional security affairs at a time when the PRC still funded local communist movements. Without more direct military challenges that only great-power support could meet, those governments saw no reason to ally tightly with the United States or the PRC.

Post–Cold War

The end of the Third Indochina War reduced the most intense interstate threats in Southeast Asia, thus ushering in a period in which fewer states saw the need for tight alliances. After Vietnamese forces withdrew from Cambodia, almost all Southeast Asian governments felt capable of defending their near-term security interests without robust great-power alliances. Vietnam turned inward to rebuild its economy after years of armed conflict, and the Soviet Union quickly receded as a player in the region. China flexed its growing military muscle in the South China Sea during the 1990s but found assertive tactics largely counterproductive, and the PRC's well-documented charm offensive in recent years has taken some of the edge off of short-term ASEAN suspicions of China.[15] Uncertainty still clouds Southeast Asian relations with the PRC, but China generally is not seen as an immediate and incorrigible menace.

The withdrawal of the USSR and transformation of China into an increasingly capitalistic state also removed fears of communist insurgency and an ethnic Chinese fifth column in the capitalist states of the region. The ideological fault line in regional threat perceptions has blurred, and most Southeast Asian leaders like it that way. Without a clear strategic standoff and competition between two alternative political models, it has been marginally easier for most Southeast Asian governments to avoid allying tightly with China or the United States.

Continued U.S. military primacy along the region's vital sea-lanes has also moderated fears of China, and America's allies have seen modest, nonpermanent ties as sufficient for a stable maritime balance of power. Fears of terrorism and residual concerns about Chinese assertiveness have more recently contributed to a Philippine decision to veer away from its limited alignment strategy, but even its relationship with America has been limited, barely crossing the threshold of what this book considers a tight alliance. For the Indochina states and Myanmar, the United States has remained threatening, but more from a political than military standpoint. Even officials fearful of a U.S. attack have seen that possibility as comparatively remote. Limited alignments have remained the norm, in no small part because Southeast Asian officials believe that a modest amount of external support gives them enough tools to provide adequate security. Thai Prime Minister Thaksin Shinawatra summed up this attitude after 9/11 by saying, in respect to terrorist threats, "We can look after ourselves."[16]

Opinions on the desirability of U.S. primacy vary, but most analysts agree that America's strategic superiority in the Asia-Pacific region has been a significant deterrent to any would-be revisionist powers. U.S. military primacy, aided by key alliances in Northeast Asia and elsewhere, has thus contributed to a relative peace that obviates the need for tight alliances. The systemic distribution of power matters, but so does the nature of the leading power and its relations with other major states. If the United States had used its might to aggressively contain China or instigate armed conflict in Asia—over Taiwan, North Korea, or Myanmar, for example—the region could easily have become more polarized, and tight alliance would have been more common. Conversely, if America had retreated into complacent isolation, some current U.S. allies might have pursued more neutral alignment postures for lack of an American option.

Since the end of the Cold War, the United States has remained engaged enough in Asia to reassure its allies and preserve relative stability, particularly in Northeast Asia. The U.S. government has also generally avoided belligerent acts that would provoke conflict in the region or result in a rapid deterioration of Sino-American relations. The United States has not always stood behind the principles of economic liberalization and multilateral diplomacy, but as the leading power, it has generally driven, facilitated, or at least condoned a dramatic rise in trade and investment among former adversaries in the Asia-Pacific region, as well as a boom in multilateral diplomacy.

The relatively liberal character of the post–Cold War order has helped reduce some of the tensions that give rise to tight alliances. China has also contributed, scrapping the revolutionary Maoism of the past, ceasing support for communist rebels in Southeast Asia, and joining a more constructive web of economic and diplomatic relations in the region. As noted, the more open nature of the international economic order has given all states in the region more incentive to diversify and avoid drawing unnecessary lines in the sand. Security threats remain, but most have been internal or transnational, primarily relating to ethnic separatism and terrorism. As Mely Caballero-Anthony and numerous others have emphasized, Southeast Asian governments have increasingly focused on nontraditional security issues such as fighting transborder crime and piracy and improving crisis response in the event of natural disasters and mass dislocation.[17] Most believe they can manage such menaces without great-power pacts. Indeed, many believe that tight alliances would undercut the independence and flexibility needed to tackle internal or non-traditional threats effectively. They prefer to deal with a range of bilateral partners and institutions depending on the specific contingency. In a period of relative peace among major powers and diffuse security challenges, most Southeast Asian leaders see little reason to forge tight defense pacts.

A New Economic Order

Economic aid and trade can be significant benefits of alignment and offer another potential explanation for alignment choices, especially for poor countries. Economic aid has been an important part of the justification for a number of Southeast Asian alignments, but more often during the Cold War era, when overall levels of national wealth were lower, and bilateral and multilateral foreign aid generally funded a greater share of national budgets. In the post–Cold War era, diversification of trade and investment ties has given most states in the region less need for the aid that flows from tight alliances and more incentive to avoid drawing lines in the sand.

Cold War Economic Aid

No Southeast Asian country save Brunei entered the modern era with great wealth, and the struggle to provide for growing populations has been a pervasive concern among governing elites. During the Cold War era, most political regimes in Southeast Asia depended heavily on economic development for legitimacy and to fight homegrown unrest. For the Marcos and Suharto regimes, alignment with the United States brought economic rewards for the countries as a whole and for corrupt elites, who used some of the funds they diverted from public projects and grants to solidify their holds on power. In Brunei, alignment with the West was linked to the country's peculiarly strong nexus to the Shell Oil Corporation, which dominated the economy. For Malaysia, Singapore, and Thailand, pro-Western security alignment helped solidify positive relations with major capitalist trading partners. In the impoverished states of Indochina and Burma/Myanmar, alignment brought much-needed aid packages, as well as occasional sweetheart deals for unscrupulous government officials. In some of Southeast Asia's poorest countries, foreign aid funded much of the government budget in the 1970s and 1980s.

Few Southeast Asian countries allied tightly with economic benefits foremost in mind. Economic aid was perhaps most important as a contributor to the tight Philippine–U.S. alliance during the Cold War. Even in that case, military support against communist rebels was a similarly important, if not more important, basis for tight alliance. Still, trade and investment were key rewards that countries in the region sought from great-power protectors when they did elect to ally tightly. The Pol Pot regime, Vietnam, and Laos were all destitute by the late 1970s, and that reality gave them added reasons to assume some of the risks of tight security relationships with China and the USSR, respectively.

Post–Cold War Diversification

After the end of the Cold War, regional trade and investment with external powers flourished. The three states of Indochina were no longer locked into a set of trading relationships centered on Moscow and could reach out to erstwhile adversaries. The other states of Southeast Asia could also diversify their economic ties by engaging with China. Vietnam, Laos, and Cambodia all suffered economic starvation during the 1980s, when a punishing U.S.-led international sanctions regime cut them off from global markets. Their relative contemporary success in economic development owes largely to diversified trade and investment and bilateral and multilateral aid. Each country has other, more important reasons not to align closely with China against the United States, or vice versa, but keeping the doors open to commerce adds another marginal reason to avoid tight alliances. They need only look at Myanmar for a reminder of the perils of ostracism by the West.

With the exception of the calamitous 1997 to 1999 period, the ASEAN-6 economies and Vietnam have achieved impressive growth over the past two decades. Even Laos and Cambodia have enjoyed stints of solid economic expansion. Growth and market liberalization have reduced the importance of great-power economic aid to most Southeast Asian states but made it more critical to keep doors open to commerce with a variety of foreign powers. As Southeast Asian states have increasingly plugged into the global economy, they have also become more vulnerable to external market shocks, making diversification a key to stability and regime security as well as growth. In the context of the current global financial crisis, efforts to pursue economic and financial diversification are only likely to rise. The new ASEAN+3 reserve pooling fund is just one example of a continued effort by Southeast Asian states to forge strong economic links in surrounding Asia, as well as with their major Western trading partners.

In general, Southeast Asian governments have found limited alignment strategies compatible with their post–Cold War economic interests. Tight alliances could generate more aid and base-related revenue—as in the Philippines during the Cold War—but would also carry the risk of adverse responses from third parties, as occurred to Vietnam during the 1980s. Most Southeast Asian states are now less concerned with development aid than open markets, and most see diversification as the key to achieving growth and resilience. Limited alignments provide a margin of security protection that gives most Southeast Asian governments the confidence to engage in robust economic engagement with a variety of states outside the region, even ones that appear threatening from a strategic or political standpoint.

For American allies, China's economic boom has added somewhat to the risk of close alignment with the United States. During the 1970s China's economic relationships with most Southeast Asian states were miniscule compared to the region's massive trade and investment flows with Japan, the United States, and their wealthy Western allies.[18] China's newfound might as an aid provider and trade and investment partner has made a tight balancing posture against China economically unattractive to Southeast Asian states.[19] The volume of PRC aid and trade now rivals or exceeds

Japanese and American levels in many Southeast Asian countries. China has even offered aid to traditional U.S. allies, giving the Philippines billions of dollars of preferential loans and other aid over the past several years.[20] Meanwhile, Sino-ASEAN trade
has risen meteorically from less than $10 billion in 1980 to more than $200 billion
today. A 2002 Sino-ASEAN preferential trade agreement and a number of bilateral
deals, such as a 2005 deal with Indonesia worth an estimated $20 billion over the next
fifteen to twenty years, have further increased economic links.[21] C. P. Chung argues
that "if ASEAN states are engaging in a form of pragmatic 'hedging' behavior, this
is principally motivated by the need to optimize economic benefits and minimize
security risks in response to an environment of uncertainty, primarily driven by the
rise of China as an economic and military power. The region hopes to maximize
economic opportunities with China, but is uncertain as to its future foreign and
security policy orientation."[22] In general, Southeast Asian governments have sought
security backup from America but tried to avoid sending the message that they are
balancing in an overt and hostile manner against China.

The same economic logic encourages China's friends in the region to not offend
the United States, Japan, and their allies. Cambodia and Laos have tilted slightly toward the PRC in security affairs but have strong economic incentives not to alienate the U.S. or Japanese governments, which are responsible for large shares of trade,
investment, and multilateral and bilateral aid. Even ostracized Myanmar receives
considerable aid from Japan and has held out the hope of resumed trade with the
West and the multilateral development institutions.

The economic motives for limited alignments certainly should not be exaggerated. After all, South Korea, Japan, and Taiwan are all engaging the PRC economically while preserving alliances with America. Economic ties give China an extra
lever of influence in ASEAN-6 states, and U.S. engagement has added to America's
influence in Indochina, but the volumes of trade and aid that Southeast Asian states
enjoy with the great powers are not reliable predictors of their alignment postures. Cambodia sends a higher percentage of its exports to America than any other
country in the region (roughly 60 percent in recent years) but is hardly a stalwart
U.S. ally, while Singapore is among China's closest economic partners but tilts toward Washington in security affairs. The most that can be said about economic
trade and aid after the Cold War is that the interest in diversifying economic ties has
provided an extra incentive for Southeast Asian governments to avoid steps in the
security sphere that appear hostile to any particular outside power.

Complements to Alignment Politics

A final factor that has diminished the need for tight alliances in the post–Cold War
era has been the development of other security options. Self-help is the most obvious such option, and the importance attached to the concept of national resilience
in the region is evidence that all Southeast Asian states would prefer to rely primarily on independent power resources to defend and prosecute their security interests. During the Cold War era, even if they could manage homegrown unrest, most

Southeast Asian states were hard pressed to meet serious external security challenges on their own. In general, they lacked the wealth, technology, and accumulated expertise to develop formidable military machines without great-power sponsorship. Regional defense ties and multilateral institutions are other alternatives to great-power alignment.

Regional Defense Cooperation

After ASEAN was established in 1967, members led a drive to develop regional cooperation, norms and institutions to supplement military defense and promote peace and security in the region. The Five-Power Defense Arrangements also tied the ANZUK states of Australia, New Zealand, and the United Kingdom to the region after 1971. Regional defense cooperation and confidence-building measures also became common during the era of the Third Indochina War, when ASEAN-6 states cooperated to deal with problems related to communist insurgency, ethnic separatism, and piracy.

Singaporean officials have described the development of regional security ties alongside great-power alignments as a process of "adding extra strings to the bow."[23] Intramural ASEAN-6 cooperation helped participants ease conflict with one another and enabled each government to focus on quelling local communist and separatist challenges. Regional defense ties also provided a modicum of extra leverage in ASEAN-6 relations with Washington; as Acharya has argued, they helped enhance "regional cohesion and clout."[24] Nevertheless, regional and multilateral vehicles for security cooperation were relatively embryonic during the era of the Third Indochina War, leaving much of the external security load in Southeast Asia to be borne by alignments with the great powers.

In the post–Cold War period most Southeast Asian states have become somewhat less reliant on great-power alignments because they have built their own capabilities and developed new avenues for regional cooperation. As Shaun Narine has argued, Southeast Asian countries have been among the most successful in the Global South at establishing multiple lines of defense to provide greater security and complement great-power ties.[25] Modest defense cooperation with a number of external powers has helped ASEAN-6 governments strengthen their defenses. Cooperation with the ANZUK states in particular has provided access to weapons and training as well as serving as both a complement and partial alternative to alignments with America. In a sense, the FPDA and related bilateral ties to the ANZUK states are alignments by proxy that help bind the United States to the region. For example, an attack on Malaysia or Singapore could elicit assistance from Australia or New Zealand under the FPDA, which in turn could invoke U.S. defense obligations or at least make U.S. support more likely.[26]

Regional Institutions

Regional institutions and multilateral diplomacy have also complemented alignment politics in securing the regional environment. Southeast Asian governments—especially in Malaysia, Singapore, and Indonesia—have invested tremendous energy in promoting the ASEAN Way of diplomacy and helped build institutions like the ARF, APEC, EAS, ASEAN+3, and ASEM to socialize larger neighbors and set up structures for peaceful dispute management and resolution. A related result of that movement has been the expansion of ASEAN itself, which grew from six members to ten between 1995 and 1999. These new members have not become parts of the spiderweb of ASEAN-6 alignments, but their entry into ASEAN and regular participation in forums such as the ASEAN Defence Ministers' Meeting has diminished the perceived threats that they pose and limits the ability of any great power to pursue a divide-and-conquer strategy in the region.

Regional institutions do appear to have reduced Southeast Asian states' dependence on tight great-power alignments to a degree, because they have helped reduce some of the interstate tensions that could spill over into broader conflict. Amitav Acharya has thus argued that "Asia is increasingly able to manage its insecurity through shared regional norms, rising economic interdependence, and growing institutional linkages."[27] As some scholars have emphasized, institutions and their associated norms can help to socialize potentially problematic actors and enmesh great powers in a way that makes aggression less likely.[28] These interests have provided an added incentive for governments not to enter hostile balancing coalitions when they don't need to do so.

Nevertheless, it would be an exaggeration to argue that multilateral institutions and related diplomatic norms offer the most powerful explanation for Southeast Asian states' preference for limited ties. Even if Southeast Asian states had spent less time and treasure promoting diplomatic practices and forums, limited alignments would probably have been the norm in the region. ASEAN-inspired forums have had a short time to develop and considerable hurdles to overcome, and Southeast Asia has not yet achieved what Karl Deutsch idealized as a "security community," in which unifying habits, values, and institutions provide security by generating durable shared expectations of peace.[29] Even if such a security community did emerge, it would not preclude tight alliances. The region that best approximates a security community today is western Europe, where most countries have long been NATO members.

The cultivation of multilateral institutions is not inconsistent with limited alignment strategies; on the contrary, the two coexist quite naturally. Rosemary Foot and Evelyn Goh describe this dual-track approach as a salient feature in the contemporary security strategies of a number of Asian states.[30] If alignments do not provide for stable security relations, norms or institutions can pick up some of the slack, and vice versa. Each aspect of a country's security strategy thus serves as an insurance policy against failures in the other. Yuen Foong Khong also links alignment policy with the institutional agenda, describing limited pro-U.S. alignments and institution building as two key features of the Southeast Asian security landscape since the end of the Cold War.[31] Limited alignments represent one important dimension of the ASEAN Way of conducting foreign policy, which emphasizes informality, the avoidance of unnecessary confrontation, and the preservation of future options.

Evolution of Regional Norms

A further factor in Southeast Asian alignment politics has been the influence of relevant norms, such as the norm of nonalignment, the norm of peaceful dispute resolution, and the distinctive regional ZOPFAN principle. Rather than treating alignment decisions as the products of rational cost-benefit calculations, one could explain outcomes as the products of socially constructed habits, values, and standards of behavior. A number of states in the region played key roles in the NAM, and the ZOPFAN principle was a regional expression of a similar norm. ASEAN's creation and development has been related to the idea of nonalignment and the ZOPFAN concept. As Michael Leifer argued, the concepts of alliances and conflictual balances of power were "excluded deliberately from [ASEAN's] corporate philosophy and declaratory vocabulary from the outset."[32]

The avoidance of tight alliance with great powers has emerged as a salient regional norm, particularly in the post–Cold War era. Most Southeast Asian officials see stalwart alliances as too confrontational and provocative, associating such policies with an overly legalistic Western approach to security. Some analysts have even argued that tight alliances cut against the grain of Southeast Asian strategic culture, which has tended to view robust alliances as unwise and even morally disfavored, because they implicitly single out others as enemies.[33] In 1993 Indonesian Foreign Minister Ali Alatas referred to nonalignment as the "moral alternative" to polarizing alliance blocs.[34]

An extensive debate exists among scholars about the independent effect of norms on Southeast Asian foreign policies, particularly in the security sphere. There is no question that leaders in the region have frequently appealed to the norms of nonalignment and the ZOPFAN principle, but it is less clear whether norms can be described as the causes of their resulting alignment choices. Assessing normative inputs into international behavior is always difficult, partly because norms often prescribe behavior that is also (at least arguably) in a state's rational interest. In the case of DC relations with the great powers, the norm of nonalignment and ZOPFAN principle came about at least partly as a result of strategic calculi by the leaders of small states and middle powers, which sought to reduce the very risks of alignment discussed in this book.

The question for this analysis is whether norms offer powerful stand-alone explanations for alignment behavior in Southeast Asia. Thus far, they do not. Two of the countries most closely identified with the norm of nonalignment and ZOPFAN principle—Indonesia and Malaysia—actually can be better described as tilting during the post-1975 period. Most other Southeast Asian states have invoked those principles, but their actual alignment behavior has varied considerably. When push has come to shove, quite a number of states in the region have deviated significantly from the norms they profess in diplomatic forums. This does not make their espousal of such norms insincere, but it does suggest that norms are merely one consideration in a more complex decision-making process that underlies alignment choices. Like cultural or ideological differences, norms do appear to raise the domestic and psychic costs of tight alliance (or even limited alignments toward the strong end of the spectrum) in Southeast Asia, but they do not represent independent variables that can explain most alignment outcomes.

Conclusions on Limited Alignment Behavior

During the post–Cold War era, limited alignments have become much more preponderant in Southeast Asia. The risks of tight alliance with or against the United States have increased somewhat since the collapse of the Soviet Union, but the main reason for the increased prevalence of limited alignments has been the change in the overall external threat environment in the region. Southeast Asia has been more peaceful and less ideologically polarized since the collapse of the Soviet Union and rise of more pragmatic leadership in Beijing. Instead of seeing clear, ideologically defined threats to their states and regimes, leaders have sought to keep options open in the context of uncertainty about the future intentions of China and other rising powers as well as the United States. Southeast Asian states have not allied tightly, because most simply have not needed massive external security support to confront the largely domestic and nontraditional security threats they face. They have also had less need to ally tightly for economic reasons, as diversified trade and aid relations have provided them with multiple channels of commerce and finance.

An element of learning has also contributed to the prevalence of limited alignments in the post–Cold War period. DC governments don't always strike the optimal balance, and, as Dan Reiter has argued, they often learn from experience in formulating their alignment policies.[35] Nothing provides a sterner lesson to a government than following a risky policy and getting burnt. Vietnam, Laos, and Cambodia probably learned the potential perils of tight alliance more than any other countries in Southeast Asia, experiencing the animosity of neighbors, protracted conflict, diminished independence, and relative economic isolation. The contemporary order has given them a much-welcomed chance to steer a less confrontational course in security affairs.

THE FUTURE OF SOUTHEAST ASIAN ALIGNMENTS

Southeast Asian alignment choices will continue to affect regional security in the future. As China rises, will limited alignments continue to be the norm? The United States remains the world's leading military power, but its power resources are thinly stretched in the broader Middle East and elsewhere. The Chinese and Indian economies are growing rapidly, and China in particular appears poised to play a greater role in Asian security affairs in the coming decades. For the time being, Japan appears poised to maintain relatively strict limits on the extent of its own offshore military activities, and India is only beginning to develop the ability to project meaningful conventional military power in Southeast Asia through improved air and blue-water naval forces. Consequently, the near-term strategic question of utmost importance to Southeast Asian governments will be how to adjust to uncertainty about the future roles of China and the United States.

Opinions about the course of Asian security differ widely, but essentially all ob-servers view regional responses to the rise of China as a key. Aaron Friedberg has argued that Asia is "ripe for rivalry" and that Europe's past could be Asia's future as a rising China comes to challenge existing great powers, as Germany did in the late nineteenth century.[36] In a recent debate about the future of Asian security, John Mearsheimer argued that China is likely to attempt to dominate Asia as it gathers the strength to do so, because it is "better to be Godzilla than Bambi." Zbigniew Brzezinski countered that China is a power bent more on economic development and acceptance as a major player in world affairs.[37] Still, there is broad agreement that the changes under way are potentially destabilizing and have potentially sweep-ing security implications. How Southeast Asian states align will be important fac-tors in determining whether shifts in great-power influence occur peacefully or give rise to dangerous levels of strategic competition in the region.

A Range of Options

The question of how Southeast Asian governments will align between China and the United States has rightly drawn considerable attention in the literature. Re-gional alignment patterns could unfold in myriad ways. In theory, Southeast Asian governments could flock toward alignment with China to offset superior American power or move en masse toward the United States to keep the PRC down. Finally, ASEAN members could declare their collective neutrality and seek to minimize security ties to both China and the United States. All three of those stark options are extremely unlikely. Virtually all scholars agree that the Southeast Asian security landscape will be more complex. Individual states will pursue different alignment policies to bring about a desired balance of influence among the great powers. Nevertheless, scholarly predictions vary considerably. The sections that follow cri-tique some prevailing approaches and offer a rough forecast based on the lessons learned from this study.

The Balancing Thesis

According to the logic of classical realism, as China becomes mightier or more threatening, many Southeast Asian governments will rally to the side of the United States and form stronger balancing alignments. Robert Ross offers the most com-pelling account of how realist balance-of-power principles could apply to Southeast Asian alignment politics in the future. He argues that traditional power-balancing politics are alive and well in the region and emphasizes the security dilemma: even if China is not hostile today, it may become so in the future. That possibility encour-ages Southeast Asian governments to build their defenses and ally with the United States to contain China's expansion when they can. Only when they have no other choice—as China develops enough power to fundamentally affect their security—do Southeast Asian states fall into line and accommodate Beijing.[38] Mearsheimer agrees, arguing that "China cannot rise peacefully" and that "most of China's neigh-bors ... will likely join the United States to contain China's power."[39]

To Ross, military power and geography are the keys. He envisions China and the United States competing for primacy in Southeast Asia through control of key land areas and waterways along the Pacific Rim. A belt of countries in the maritime subregion will tilt toward the dominant naval power, the United States, to help it preserve its naval ascendancy. Peninsular Southeast Asian countries will increasingly bow to China's military might, making the PRC a continental hegemon.[40] This vision of Southeast Asian preferences is based on a compelling assessment of the interests of each great power in the region—for China, which shares borders with fourteen countries, a key to security is to stabilize its frontiers and avoid land-based threats that contribute to centrifugal forces in the huge, diverse country. For the United States and Japan, securing vital sea-lanes for the flow of trade and resources is paramount, leading them to prioritize naval dominance.

However, there are serious problems with the neorealist approach. Ross discounts the roles of economics and cultural affinity and boldly asserts that "domestic politics and intention-based threat perceptions are unnecessary variables" to explain Southeast Asian alignments.[41] That claim is difficult to reconcile with reality. The ability of the United States to preserve alignments in the maritime region, even during a period when it has overwhelming power, is based largely on Southeast Asian perceptions that American intentions are comparatively benign. Domestic politics also cannot be brushed aside so easily; they help explain why Indonesia and Malaysia are more constrained than the Philippines and Singapore in promoting U.S. strategic influence in the area. By focusing too exclusively on the material and geographic determinants of ASEAN alignment behavior, Ross gives short shrift to the significant differences in alignment behavior among different mainland and maritime states.

Overall, even close maritime friends of the United States have considerable disincentives to balance assertively. In addition to the risk of overdependency on America—with its associated dangers of diminished autonomy, abandonment, and entrapment—that strategy would push China into a corner, which no Southeast Asian states wants to do. Chinese leaders already perceive their country as the object of an American strategy of neocontainment. If Southeast Asian countries appear to be tightening the noose, the PRC could intensify its efforts to project military or subversive influence in the region, as it did during the Cold War. Michael Green, a former special advisor to President George W. Bush, has described the possibility of a "maritime versus continental divide" as "a specter that concerns everyone in the region," because "a hardening of camps . . . could be destabilizing."[42]

Bandwagoning and Accommodation Theses

Other scholars forecast very different alignment behavior in the region. They expect most Southeast Asian governments to accommodate or bandwagon with the PRC as it gathers steam, either to reap the rewards of its friendship or because they simply have no viable balancing option. Most such analysts give more weight to economics, soft power, and cultural factors. For example, David Shambaugh stresses China's growing soft power in the region through gentler and more multilateral diplomacy, aid, and cultural and social exchanges. He argues that "concerns about a looming 'China threat' are still occasionally heard among regional security specialists in Hanoi, New Delhi, Singapore, Tokyo, and certainly Taipei. Yet overall these voices increasingly reflect a minority view. Even though some countries remain unsure of China's long-term ambitions, and are thus adopting hedging policies against the possibility of a more aggressive China, the majority of Asian states currently view China as more benign than malign and are accommodating themselves to its rise."[43]

David Kang agrees that Southeast Asian states are generally pursuing broadly accommodative strategies toward China, largely because "Asia has different historical traditions, different geographic and political realities, and different cultural traditions" than the West, where realist international relations theories were born. Contrary to Ross, he argues that China's neighbors are generally bandwagoning rather than balancing and that China is becoming the "gravitational center" of an East Asian order that could become more hierarchical in the future.[44] He contends that Asian concepts of order may incline governments in the region to be more accepting of hierarchy than their Western counterparts.

Martin Stuart-Fox broadly concurs, contending that Southeast Asian foreign policy cultures—defined as established sets of beliefs, values, and practices regarding the conduct of foreign affairs—and historical learning incline mainland Southeast Asian states to avoid balancing coalitions that could provoke Chinese ire. Instead, culture and history promote "bilateral regimes" under which Southeast Asian states gain security by entering into tributary-style arrangements. He argues that in a great-power conflict, even Vietnam would likely accommodate China with great reluctance, largely because "history and culture predispose the countries of Southeast Asia to draw on their own experience of the benefits of due deference to status in working out their relations with China."[45]

These authors imply that over time many ASEAN governments are apt to view the PRC either as an irresistible force to be accommodated or as the wave of the future offering them potential gains. None is specific about the degrees of alignment to be expected in various ASEAN states; each author implies only that some will form tighter alignments with China than others. However, to the extent that they are correct, and most Southeast Asian states choose to accommodate China as it gathers steam, the region will have a very different future than balance-of-power models suggest.

There are a few reasons to question these accommodation theses, however. First, it is not clear that Southeast Asian strategic or foreign policy culture favors accommodation. Although the ten members of ASEAN may share certain common historical experiences, the region's diversity militates against broad cultural claims. Laos is not Singapore, and Myanmar is not the Philippines. In many capitals, foreign policy cultures have been shaped more by European, American, or other forces than the Chinese Confucian tradition. In fact, China's soft power gains in Southeast Asia appear to owe largely to the PRC's respect for traditional Westphalian sovereignty. As Kang and Stuart-Fox acknowledge, the country with the closest cultural ties to China is Vietnam, which has a deeply rooted strategic self-conception as a state that has successfully resisted Chinese domination.

Strategic culture did not prevent Vietnam or Laos from hugging the Soviet Union and spewing invective at China during the era of the Third Indochina War. When push has come to shove, and when an ally has been available, Southeast Asian states have sometimes been willing to stare down and fight the colossus to the north. Stuart-Fox makes the case for strategic culture most convincingly when he focuses on the general Southeast Asian preference for avoiding antagonistic alliances. Indeed, no Southeast Asian state wants to confront China aggressively and later be left in the lurch. DCs generally prefer to avoid drawing lines in the sand. As this book has argued, a preference for limited alignments is by no means distinctively Southeast Asian.

A second reason to question the accommodation thesis relates to the behavior of the maritime states, some of which have compelling strategic reasons to remain at least loosely allied with the United States. They also have considerable historical and domestic political reasons to avoid moving too close to China in the security sphere. C. P. Chung rightly asserts that despite talks of forging various strategic partnerships with China, ASEAN governments are unlikely to bandwagon with China "given their sensitivity as small countries and as mostly post-colonial creations . . . over the preservation of their sovereign independence and autonomy in foreign policy orientation."[46] In addition, U.S. officials would likely see pro-PRC alignments as a hostile move aimed at limiting America's role in the region. In the near term, it is unlikely that many maritime states will be willing to take the risk of quickly switching sides as long as they are able to preserve the status quo. Change is apt to be incremental, and not all countries will move toward China as its might rises; some are apt to cling more tightly to the blanket of U.S. protection.

A More Nuanced Picture

These widely differing forecasts for Southeast Asia's future show how powerfully theories of alignment behavior affect scholars' expectations about the evolution of regional security systems. The findings in this book suggest that most ASEAN states will continue to favor limited alignments in the years ahead, in effect blurring the lines of strategic competition in the region and creating a more nuanced security environment.

Despite increased intraregional defense cooperation, few ASEAN countries are likely to rely entirely on their own resources or Southeast Asian neighbors for protection. ASEAN has never been a defense community, and a number of its states will continue to rely partially on alignment with friendly outside powers for security. Not all Southeast Asian states will pursue the same alignment policy. Individual postures are likely to be diverse, with some veering more toward neutrality and others tilting toward China or the United States. A number of leading analysts of regional affairs—including Acharya, Evelyn Goh, C. P. Chung, and others—have come to broadly similar conclusions. As Gaye Christofferson and Shannon Tow have argued, most Southeast Asian countries will likely seek to establish a middle ground and preserve a stable strategic balance between China and the United States.[47] Both expect that Southeast Asian states will tend to avoid tight alliance with either power to maximize their room for maneuver and prevent any external giant from dominating the region.[48]

Vietnam and Thailand will be key factors in determining the overall strategic orientation of mainland Southeast Asia. Vietnam has historically resisted Chinese efforts to dominate Indochina and will likely do so again, if only by pushing for neutralization of the subregion rather than forging a hostile balancing coalition against the PRC. Thailand's future alignment policy is more questionable. Its traditional policy of "bending with the wind" suggests that it could become a closer ally of either Beijing or Washington as regional dynamics change. Its size, central location, and large armed forces make Thailand a key to the entire peninsula, and although many analysts believe the "bamboo is now swinging" toward China, Thai alignment policy is difficult to predict.

Myanmar appears to be the most promising ally for the PRC, but its leaders have historically been wary of too much exposure to Chinese influence, and Myanmar officials increasingly have an alternative card to play as India becomes more powerful. Laos and Cambodia may also fall increasingly into China's strategic orbit, partly because a lack of American strategic interest in those countries leaves them no option of a limited alignment against China. Even if they do cooperate more closely with China in security affairs, Cambodia and Laos will both try to preserve a local balance of influence between the PRC and their larger neighbors, Thailand and Vietnam. Tight alliance with China would be an invitation for tension with Vietnam and could jeopardize relations with other ASEAN states and the West, which are vital providers of aid, trade, and investment for the weak Lao and Cambodian economies. These factors make it likely that Lao and Cambodian security ties to China will be limited unless Vietnam or Thailand becomes much more domineering or armed conflict threatens to erupt.

As long as the United States is perceived as less threatening than other powerful states in the area, key governments will continue to support American primacy in maritime Southeast Asia. As Philippine President Fidel Ramos said, "This is the consensus in ASEAN."[49] Singapore appears to have built a relatively durable alignment with the United States, and, given its neighbors' sensitivities, it is unlikely to move toward alignment with the PRC unless Indonesia or Malaysia becomes more threatening and American support is lacking. Singapore has often possessed the most forward-looking and cerebral strategic policy in the region, and it is most likely to adjust its ties with America to achieve a stable distribution of great-power influence in Southeast Asia. Prime Minister Lee Hsien Loong has repeatedly urged the United States to remain "a major element in the power balance of Asia" to help manage the "tectonic forces" associated with the rise of China and India and other developments.[50] The Philippines also appears likely to remain a relatively close ally of the United States for long-standing cultural and political—as well as strategic— reasons. President George W. Bush expressed a similar expectation when he described the U.S.-Philippine alliance as a key node for future American engagement in Asia and "rock of stability in the Pacific."[51]

None of the three Muslim-majority countries in Southeast Asia is likely to ally tightly with either China or the United States. They have remained relatively faithful to their long-standing emphasis on the ZOPFAN principle and sought to limit opportunities for great-power domination. Strong domestic constraints on foreign policy add to the likelihood that Indonesia, Malaysia, and Brunei will stick to limited alignment strategies unless they face a major unforeseen security crisis. Siding closely with either great power would likely produce serious domestic strife in those Muslim-majority countries, either inflaming Islamist parties or stoking old resentments against the ethnic Chinese community. Instead, those countries are likely to continue to invest with vigor in the development of regional norms, institutions, and intramural cooperation that decreases dependence on the great powers. In fact, the original formulation of the ZOPFAN concept—which emphasized limiting the influence of external powers in Southeast Asia—could regain strength if China's rise leads to increased great-power tension and more aggressive efforts by China and its rivals to carve out spheres of influence in the region.

Almost all ASEAN officials hope that China and the United States will continue to enjoy peaceful relations in the coming decades. The vast majority also views the U.S.-Japan alliance as a key element in preserving regional stability and preventing Japanese remilitarization. If great-power relations remain stable, ASEAN governments will find it relatively easy to maintain limited alignments, even if separatist or extremist groups continue to present serious domestic challenges. Modern Southeast Asian experience confirms the obvious—that DCs find it easier to be relatively nonaligned during times of peace and regional stability. However, if relations deteriorate between the United States and China, or if Japan or India becomes a serious strategic player in the region, pursuing limited alignments will become more difficult and complicated, as rival great powers may put more pressure on prospective developing country partners.

The Overall Pattern of Alignments

Karl Mueller has outlined a number of ideal-type alignment patterns that tend to form when DCs exist between two competing powers.[52] Southeast Asian states could form *satellite belts*, aligning with the most geographically proximate great powers, either by choice or compulsion. They could establish a *buffer zone*, attempting to stay as neutral as possible. They could create a kind of *checkerboard*, aligning with relatively distant powers to protect them against adjacent states. By bonding closely with one another but not with the great powers, they could pursue *independent aggregation*. Finally, they could create an *alignment balance* by maintaining different but complementary alignments with the great powers, individually threatening to tilt away from an ally if it becomes too menacing.

This study suggests that the future of Southeast Asian alignments between China and the United States will most closely resemble the ideal-type of an alignment balance. As Rosemary Foot has argued, the priority that Southeast Asian governments have generally placed on internal security challenges, and their lack of a shared external threat perception, makes it difficult to present a "neat strategic depiction" of the region.[53] In the near term, as long as great-power relations remain relatively peaceful, the overall pattern of Southeast Asian alignments is likely to remain relatively stable, featuring a degree of accommodation of China on the mainland, strong nodes of American naval power in the Philippines, Singapore, and perhaps elsewhere, and a number of states that continue to pursue relative neutrality and focus on developing institutions and intra-ASEAN defense ties. Occasional bilateral flare-ups between ASEAN members or serious domestic challenges to regimes in the region could result in tight alliances from time to time, but such arrangements are apt to be temporary.

Predictions in the medium term are much more difficult to make. One reason DCs favor limited alignments is that international security is characterized by uncertainty. As China and other Asian powers develop added military power, as great-power relations evolve, and as domestic politics evolve in places such as Washington, Tokyo, Beijing and New Delhi, one cannot dismiss the possibility of a return to a more polarized international system. In that context, tight alliances could become more appealing. However, this study suggests that many Southeast Asian governments will hold out and try to avoid taking clear sides unless the strategic imperatives to do otherwise become quite strong.

Positioning themselves as a fulcrum can help ASEAN states preserve both independence and influence. As in bilateral alignments, moving too close to any of the great powers can diminish their collective independence and antagonize other great powers.[54] Conversely, moving too far from the American pole may be problematic for ASEAN states, exposing them to an unacceptable level of strategic vulnerability.[55] The desire to remain pivotal helps explain why most ASEAN states have pursued U.S. alignments but refused permanent American bases and taken consistent measures to avoid unduly antagonizing China.[56] ASEAN leaders have generally balanced their desire for independence and influence with their need for security. Small powers can punch well above their weight if they manipulate their strategic relations well, but they can also be knocked out easily if they strike the wrong balance between influence, flexibility, and protection.

The Balance of Great-Power Influence

Thus far, limited alignments have contributed to a great-power military balance in Southeast Asia that resembles neither a neo-suzerain hierarchy centered on China nor rigid, competing alliance blocs in the style of nineteenth-century Europe. The mainland peninsula more closely resembles a buffer zone, where both China and the United States enjoy limited military influence. In the maritime area, America remains preponderant but not hegemonic, enjoying enough access to military facilities to project overwhelming naval and air power. Overall, the military balance in contemporary Southeast Asia is characterized by a soft form of U.S. primacy that reaches its apex around the Philippines and the Straits of Malacca and recedes in the parts of the mainland subregion that border on China.

Alignments are critical in shaping the security architecture of the region, but they certainly do not determine the distribution of great-power influence alone. China and other great powers have made substantial inroads in Southeast Asia through economic and other nonmilitary means. Economically, they have diversified. All Southeast Asian governments have been glad to trade with all of the great powers, even if a few (like Myanmar) have been frequently rebuffed. The collective idea has been to give each great power a stake in regional peace and stability. As Fidel Ramos said, Southeast Asian leaders have gradually tried to "replace the balance of power with the balance of mutual benefit."[57] Diplomatically, Southeast Asian officials have tried to spin a complex web of multilateral forums and institutions that begin to socialize China and other external powers to play by ASEAN's rules of the game.

The result has been what a few scholars have termed a "complex balance of influence" in which the great powers become enmeshed in (or bound through) a network of interdependence.[58] Collectively, Southeast Asian governments have tried to stake out middle positions in areas other than the politico-military arena. Institutionally, they have been driving forces in establishing an alphabet soup of regional forums with ASEAN at the core. Ideologically and normatively, they have also hedged their bets, trying to maximize their security, leverage, and independence by avoiding undue identification with any particular outside power or bloc. Southeast Asian alignment strategies have been a critical part of this overarching strategy to diversify ties, promote warm relations with all outside powers, and achieve the conditions for growth and security in the region.[59]

Are Limited Alignments Good for Southeast Asia?

Opinions differ on the desirability of limited alignment strategies and other options. To some analysts, balancing alignments will be important pillars of stability in Asia during a period of power transition. Michael Leifer was a well-known advocate of balance-of-power policies as ways to promote security and growth in the region. Ross characterizes his version of the balance of power, roughly dividing mainland and maritime states into different great-power camps, as a "geography of the peace." He suggests that if each great power has its rightful sphere of influence, they can preserve a relatively stable strategic balance along the Pacific Rim in the twenty-first century.

Critics of balance-of-power politics argue that stern balancing alignments against China (or the United States) could polarize the region and lead to dangerous standoffs reminiscent of the Cold War. They point to the flare-ups in Indochina and the domestic upheaval associated with superpower rivalry as evidence that great-power standoffs often have serious adverse consequences for DCs stuck in the middle.

Scholars advancing the accommodation thesis tend to suggest that gradual realignment of regional security affairs in favor of China will be more likely to deliver peace to Southeast Asia than contentious balancing strategies. Kang presents a relatively sanguine view of the security order that could emerge if most Asian countries bandwagon with China, arguing that Asian tolerance for hierarchy would lend itself to a relatively stable and peaceful form of Chinese primacy. He may be correct about the future for Asian security if China becomes the dominant external player in regional security affairs, as the United States has been for decades in Latin America. However, there is no reason to assume that the mechanism for China's ascendance to primacy will be smooth. Tighter alignments between China and some ASEAN states could precipitate domestic ethnic conflict in the region. It could also encourage Japan, the United States, and maybe India to flex more military muscle and assert their positions in Asia, making the region ripe for conflict.

In the near term, the Southeast Asian preference for limited alignments probably adds to regional security, because by tilting, DCs avoid drawing lines in the sand and provoking a cycle of retaliatory measures by jealous great powers. Limited alignments also give Southeast Asian governments more wiggle room to adjust their positions as conditions evolve, which gives the great powers an incentive to tread carefully in the region. Moreover, limited alignments will probably facilitate continued economic diversification and institutional expansion. Michael Leifer argued that the viability of the ARF and other regional security institutions "seems to depend on the prior existence of a stable balance [of power in the region]."[60] However, this study suggests that a major reason for developing multilateral norms and security organizations is to reduce dependency on great-power alignments and to provide mechanisms for gradual and peaceful realignment as the distribution of power changes.[61] Institutions and limited alignment strategies can thus serve complementary and largely reinforcing roles in absorbing some of the shocks that occur when great-power capabilities and intentions change.

It is more difficult to determine whether limited alignments will be good for Southeast Asia in the medium term. If China becomes militant and aggressive at a later date, ASEAN members may wish they had embarked on a robust containment strategy to arrest the PRC's expansion. Conversely, if China becomes powerful but friendly and America becomes menacing or undependable, officials in the region may wish they had declared their allegiance to Beijing. The problem is that no Southeast Asian leader has a crystal ball. Even the most careful assessment of a great power's past behavior and current capabilities and intentions provides only a rough indication of its likely future behavior. Unless serious conflict erupts and repolarizes Southeast Asia, strategic uncertainty will continue to encourage limited alignments in the years ahead.

Conclusion

Key Findings and Implications

THE IMPORTANCE OF ALIGNMENT POLITICS of Southeast Asia and other regions of the Global South may become even more important in the future than they have been in the past. At the end of World War II, the countries of the Global South (including China) amounted to roughly 70 percent of the world's population. They now account for more than 85 percent, and that figure is rising. As demand for scarce resources increases—and as the world becomes more genuinely multipolar in the years ahead—competition among the great powers for economic and strategic influence in the developing world is more likely to intensify than diminish.

Many of the most important theaters for great-power strategic rivalries will be in the Global South. Resource-rich regions and areas around key transportation nodes—like the Straits of Malacca, Suez Canal, and Persian Gulf—have always been sites of major power competition, and they will continue to be. In that context DCs will often be asked to choose sides, and great powers will burnish both carrots and sticks to secure their allegiance. How DCs respond to those overtures, and whether they seek out security ties themselves, will play a major role in shaping international security.

Most DCs will face at least some traditional security challenges from avaricious or predatory neighbors. They will also face perennial concerns stemming from domestic sources and significant nontraditional threats ranging from terrorism or piracy to environmental crises or natural disasters. Governments will have more mouths to feed, and economic development will continue to be a ubiquitous policy priority with important security implications. The yawning gap between living standards in the industrialized north and the Global South, as well as within many DCs, will at least occasionally stir serious public discontent. Struggles related to ideological discontent, ethnic feuds, and self-determination struggles may subside in some areas but show little sign of evaporating. Technological change and changing networks of substate and transnational actors will complicate the business of policing transnational crime and uprooting terrorism. In their efforts to meet these and other challenges, DCs will have plenty of reasons to seek or accept aid and support from friendly great powers.

However, they will also have powerful incentives to guard their autonomy and maintain policy flexibility. In a world where some military threats remain, they have reasons to try to stay out of harm's way and avoid making unnecessary foes. Keeping doors open will also be important as DCs try to address many emerging nontraditional security threats, which usually span many borders and often strike unexpectedly. DCs will need to position themselves to work with a wide range of foreign states and multilateral institutions to address such threats and contingencies. The ever-increasing imperatives of economic development give them cause to protect themselves from subordinate status and exploitation. Last but not least, the governments of DCs will need to protect their independence and domestic legitimacy. Even as colonial experiences recede into time, anti-imperialism (or counterdominance) resonates strongly throughout the Global South and is likely to remain a powerful consideration as leaders formulate their security policies.

The question for analysts of international security is how states in the Global South will try to obtain valued great-power security assistance without making undue enemies, locking themselves into subordinate relationships, or jeopardizing their legitimacy at home. This book has suggested that they will usually do so by pursuing limited alignments. This concluding chapter reviews some of the key findings of this study and discusses the broader implications of those findings for international security going forward.

KEY FINDINGS

This book suggests a number of key conclusions about alignment policies and preferences in the Global South. First, modern Southeast Asian experience supports the proposition that DCs usually favor limited alignments and attempt to pursue them. Since 1975 Southeast Asian states have usually tilted toward one or more great powers, seeking and obtaining limited, flexible security cooperation with great-power partners about 70 percent of the time. They have allied tightly only in about one-fifth of observed instances. Genuine nonalignment has been even rarer, occurring only about one-tenth of the time.

Southeast Asian behavior between 1975 and 1990 suggests that DCs often favor limited alignments even in times of turmoil. Despite ideological polarization, intense superpower rivalry, and interstate war during that period, states in the region pursued limited alignments in roughly 60 percent of observed instances. This is an important finding because it confirms that limited alignments are not flash-in-the-pan phenomena or products of the particular features of the contemporary world order. They reflect a general preference among states throughout the Global South to limit the scope of their security ties to the great powers when they can do so without incurring unacceptable levels of vulnerability.

These preferences matter partly because they constrain great-power policy choices. When the stakes are high enough, great powers sometimes override DC preferences and compel their allegiance. However, the Southeast Asian cases examined support the view that DCs usually do have a significant say in the matter. Even great powers do not have infinite money or manpower, and they cannot compel a large number of DCs to do their bidding all of the time. This is especially true in an era when DC populations are larger, the norms of sovereignty and anticolonialism are relatively strong, and nationalist forces abound. Forcing DCs to ally tightly is politically costly, resource-taxing, and difficult to sustain when the DC is not compliant.

Evidence that these observed outcomes diverge widely from Southeast Asian preferences is scant. In Indochina, Thailand, and the Philippines great powers did not impose tight alliances by force. The Philippine alliance with America did grow out of a constrained postcolonial relationship, but when the Philippine Senate voted America out, U.S. forces peacefully departed. In a few cases DCs preferred tighter alliances but were rejected or abandoned. China's rejection of Pol Pot's request for PRC troops in November 1978 is one example. The Soviet withdrawal, somewhat in advance of Vietnamese preparedness at the end of the Cold War, may be another. By and large Southeast Asian alignment preferences and outcomes have corresponded quite closely since 1975.

Second, modern Southeast Asia confirms the notion that limited alignments are particularly dominant in the post–Cold War era. States in the region have pursued limited alignments with the great powers more than 85 percent of the time since 1991. Part of the explanation lies in the relative unipolarity of the contemporary order. Allying against the leading power is dangerous, whereas siding with an unrivaled giant can carry special risks of dependency and abandonment. However, the nature of U.S. primacy has also been a critical factor encouraging DCs to limit their ties. The United States has occasionally instigated conflict, but its comparatively liberal form of primacy has had a pacifying effect among major powers through enabling erstwhile cold war adversaries like China and Russia to come in from the cold. The relatively liberal contemporary order has made it possible for would-be revisionists to pursue economic and political gains without resorting too frequently to military saber rattling or ideological subversion. The diminution of military tensions among major states has made it easier for many DCs to avoid stalwart pacts because they face fewer threats requiring great-power military succor.

Third, Southeast Asian behavior supports the argument that DCs pursue limited alignments in an effort to optimize the risks and rewards of alignment under conditions of uncertainty. Southeast Asian leaders have usually perceived the need for some great-power security support but concluded that the risks of tight alliance outweigh the rewards. They have forged tight alliances only when pressing threats have required a military response and when a suitable great-power ally has been available. When threats have been less pressing, or when great-power allies have had limited capabilities or credibility, Southeast Asian states have merely tilted. Limited alignments are simply sound diplomacy to most policymakers in the region, who perceive tight alliances as too rigid, too conducive to great-power dominance, and too likely to sow divisions rather than resolving them. If a state in the Global South can get adequate security at a moderate risk, there is little reason to forge strong defense pacts.

Fourth, the Southeast Asian cases examined support the claim that the risks of dependency, abandonment, and entrapment provide the principal incentives to limit alignments. Southeast Asian leaders have been particularly concerned about dependency and curtailed policy autonomy because of the strong colonial and imperial legacies in the region. Abandonment has also been a consistent concern in a region where officials have often felt peripheral to the core interests of the great powers. Fears of entrapment in military conflict or nonmilitary great-power feuds have provided a further reason for Southeast Asian states to limit their security ties. The perceived risks of alignment vary across times and places, but hazards always exist and provide strong incentives for DCs to favor flexible security arrangements and keep their options open.

Fifth, this book's analysis of Southeast Asia suggests that the expected rewards of alignment are determined primarily by perceived security threats and a great-power ally's perceived capabilities and commitment. In general, states in the Global South willingly bear the risks of tight alliance only when they have dire need for great-power support. When they face modest or uncertain threats, their interest in tight alliances usually recedes, because in such cases the rewards of tight alliance rarely justify the risks. Thus the magnitude of threats that a government perceives often provides a good indication of its likely alignment preferences. However, that variable is usually not enough. The availability of a suitable protector also matters. When powerful allies lack the apparent means or will to help advance their security interests, DCs have little incentive to align at all.

Sixth, a range of material and ideational factors infuse policymakers' calculi of risks and rewards. The most important factors identified in this study are the magnitude and nature of threats that a DC faces and the perceived credibility of its prospective great-power ally. Those variables are in turn affected by changes in the distribution of power, ideational factors, economic links, and alternatives to great-power protection (such as self-help measures, small-power pacts, and institutions).

Modern Southeast Asia suggests that the relative importance of these factors shifts considerably from case to case and over time. For example, ideology was generally more important during the Cold War than it is today in shaping perceptions of friends and foes. Economic aid became a less crucial spillover reward of security cooperation to some states as they built up stronger sources of domestic growth and revenue. Cultural considerations have risen since 9/11 in a few Southeast Asian countries. The effects of norms such as noninterference and institutions such as ASEAN have also varied considerably across the region and over time. No single independent variable can reliably explain decisions by DCs to pursue particular alignment options across all times and places. The best way to treat these various material and ideational factors is to consider them as roughly weighted inputs into the scorecard of risks and rewards that determines a government's preferences.

Finally, this study strongly confirms that a great power's policies matter. Great-power policies are not wholly responsible for DC alignment preferences, but in any given security environment, a great power has some latitude for choice in how it responds. Those choices have alignment consequences. In general, DCs that are friendly to a great power because of shared threat perceptions or ideational bonds tend to reward tough great-power policies, because tough words and deeds often convey added commitment and credibility. Hard-line U.S. policies in the early 1980s and the post-9/11 period thus encouraged stronger ties to Manila, Bangkok, and Singapore. Vietnam also moved closer to the USSR as it saw Moscow adopt a more assertive stance toward China in the late 1970s.

Tough policies also tend to drive unfriendly states to look for protection elsewhere. The opposing alliances in Indochina during the late 1970s fed off of one another in this way. Another example is America's hard line toward Myanmar after 1989, which encouraged Yangon's close alignment with China. When great powers menace one another or the DCs in between, they usually have a polarizing effect on alignments in the Global South.

Assertive great-power policies do not always favor tight alliances, however. When they are unpopular—as the U.S.-led war on terror has been in many countries—they raise concerns about the great power's intentions and drive up the domestic political risks of alliances for their DC partners. Friendly DCs thus have added reasons to limit their ties. Indonesian and Malaysian relations with the United States in recent years may be the best Southeast Asian cases in point.

Comparatively passive great-power policies also affect DC alignment preferences. Friends tend to see its support as less credible, and adversaries see it as a threat less in need of balancing. Periods of relative U.S. pullback have generally led Southeast Asian states to invest less in U.S. security guarantees, but Southeast Asian states did not flock en masse toward another protector. The general effect of relative U.S. withdrawal, most notably in the late 1970s and early 1990s, was to add to the prevalence of limited alignments. The same argument applies to Soviet policies. When the USSR began to withdraw support in the mid-1980s, Indochina gradually depolarized.

For a great power the best way to win closer DC allies is to pursue foreign policies that appear muscular but normatively justified. Such a policy maximizes the expected rewards of alignment to a DC and reduces some of the risks. However, achieving those ends is easier than it sounds. Any strong policy is likely to be welcomed by some DCs and seen as threatening by others. Some DCs will view great-power restraint as a sign of weakness; others will see the same behavior as an indication of a benign, nonintrusive approach to world politics. Even the most effective great-power messaging and diplomacy cannot make everyone happy in the Global South. The optimal great-power strategy thus depends on context.

This book has not attempted to discuss great-power behavior in detail. It has merely emphasized that DCs respond to great-power policies as well as capabilities, and illustrated some important effects that different policies are likely to have. The two major external actors most active in Southeast Asia today clearly believe that to be the case. China continues a charm offensive designed in no small part to diminish views of the PRC as a threat and head off any potential ring of containment.

Thus far, that policy has been quite effective. The Barack Obama administration has countered with a reassertion of U.S. interest in Southeast Asia and efforts to boost America's image in ASEAN capitals though steps like the 2009 signing of the Treaty of Amity and Cooperation. Whether the latest shifts in U.S. policy will have the desired effect on regional alignment preferences remains to be seen.

WILL LIMITED ALIGNMENTS CONTINUE TO BE THE NORM?

The behavioral patterns identified in this study are hardly confined to Southeast Asia. In many parts of the world, DCs are undertaking the same basic balancing act: attempting to procure security support from great-power allies while preserving as much autonomy, flexibility, and leverage as they can. If limited alignments were happening only in peaceful, out-of-the-way places, they would not be such critical objects of study, but they are occurring in many of the most volatile and strategically contested parts of the globe.

There is little reason to expect that the prevalence of limited alignments will decline dramatically in the near term. Genuine nonalignment will continue to be a dream deferred in most parts of the Global South. As emphasized earlier in this book, nonalignment in the developing world has been more a statement of aspiration than a description of actual practice. In the 1950s leaders such as India's Jawarhalal Nehru, Egypt's Gamal Abdel Nasser, Indonesia's Sukarno, Yugoslavia's Josip Broz Tito, and Ghana's Kwame Nkrumah created a vision of third world solidarity that would keep imperialism at bay and increase the stature and security of postcolonial states. In fact, the NAM was composed of a diverse lot of states, most of which were actually engaged in limited alignments.

Then and now, solidarity in the Global South has been tough to muster. In addition to vast cultural and ideological differences, most DCs lack the hardware to provide for one another's security, especially when it comes to military defenses. Standing together on certain political and moral issues offers DCs some shield against unwanted intrusion, but few leaders would wager their entire security fortunes on the types of support that the NAM can offer. In a dangerous world, most DCs will still seek out various forms of great-power military and economic aid if they can do so at an acceptable price.

Tight alliances are also apt to be the exceptions rather than the norm. For at least the next decade—and possibly for a much longer period—the United States will possess a decisive military edge over its potential rivals, driving up the risks of strong balancing or bandwagoning strategies. Allying tightly against the United States will remain unattractive because most DCs will see little to achieve by poking America in the eye. Moreover, few will trust that another great power—like China or Russia—will willingly bear the brunt of U.S. forces on their behalf. Unless a future U.S. government becomes widely perceived as belligerent, confrontational balancing against U.S. power is likely to be rare.

Tight bandwagoning alliances with the United States are also likely to be uncommon in the global South. First, the United States will likely put less pressure on DCs to ally tightly. As long as it enjoys clear military primacy, the United States will have less strategic incentive to spend blood and treasure locking up blocs of allies against an equally powerful foe.

Second, the risks of pro-American pacts will continue to be high. U.S. military primacy will make it relatively easy for Washington to abandon its allies. The ability of U.S. leaders to act unilaterally or with weak multilateral support will also heighten dangers of entrapment in undesired conflicts such as the 2003 Iraq War. With inferior power and no credible option to defect to a rival bloc, most DCs will also have limited leverage over America, raising concerns about diminished autonomy. In an era in which the United States is held largely responsible for many of the features of the contemporary international order, DCs will often face resistance from disaffected populations if they cling to America too tightly.

Third, the perceived need for tight pro-U.S. alignments will probably also be modest. U.S. military primacy will not guarantee international stability, but if the past two decades are any guide, it will induce caution in potential revisionist states. As long as America is seen as a credible defender of the status quo, its rivals are unlikely to launch major military invasions. American hard power will thus diminish the types of military threats to the status quo that typically serve as the impetus for tight alliances.

This does not mean that serious security threats will be lacking. Technological advances and resentment of the dominant world order have added to the importance of nontraditional threats such as terrorism, drug trafficking, illegal migration, and the dispersal of nuclear and biological weapons. Managing these types of challenges requires cooperation with a wide range of partners and international institutions depending on the threat or contingency. Building relationships among law enforcement agencies and humanitarian relief organizations will often provide better protection against such threats than traditional defense arrangements. Overt military pacts could actually backfire, antagonizing and cutting off cooperation with some important partners.

The same is true with respect to the local security threats facing many DCs from insurgents, violent criminal groups, or others. Defense pacts with great powers may help deliver desired military support but can just as often mobilize added resistance to the government, magnify casualties, and frustrate the advancement of political solutions.

Rajan Menon has stated the case even more bluntly, arguing that the twenty-first century will see an end of alliances in both the industrialized world and the Global South. He maintains that rigid or formal military alliances are inherently transient, citing Lord Palmerston's famous quote that nations do not have "permanent friends, only permanent interests." States will return to a more traditional model of "agile and creative statecraft that looks beyond—but does not exclude—traditional

friends and solutions, and that musters alignments and coalitions that vary according to the context."[1] His argument is a bit overdrawn; some tight alliances will
likely prove durable, perhaps including the Anglo-American or U.S.-Israeli alignments, and new alliances will likely form as the architecture of the international
security system changes. Nevertheless, the basic thrust of Menon's argument is consistent with the lessons learned from this study. When they are not compelled by a
domineering great power or the prospect of imminent conflict, DCs will usually
opt for limited, flexible security ties.

The most important and interesting cases of limited alignment may take place
in hotly contested and insecure regions such as the Middle East, Eurasia, and Central and South Asia. Benjamin Miller expects many Arab governments to continue
cooperating with the United States to obtain military and economic aid, but they
will limit those ties because of domestic political pressure and a desire to avoid undue identification with disfavored U.S. policies.[2] In a trip to the Arab Gulf states in
early 2008, President George W. Bush found that traditional U.S. allies are seeking
to hedge their security bets by reaching out to other possible friends and keeping
America at arm's length lest they be entrapped in conflict with Iran or inherit future burdens from America in Iraq or the Palestinian territories.[3]

Ariel Cohen predicts that the strategic environment in Central Asia and the
Caucasus will also remain complex and fluid, avoiding the polarization that sometimes accompanied the Great Game in the nineteenth century or Cold War era. He
anticipates that the DCs of that region are "unlikely to align in clear-cut coalitions,
unless a major confrontation between great powers takes place" and "polarizes
the region."[4] There is little sign that DCs in South Asia, Africa, or Latin America
will flock toward tight alliances any time soon. Some small European members of
NATO and a handful of close contemporary U.S. allies—such as Israel, Australia,
and perhaps South Korea—will probably continue to engage in strong defense
pacts, but they will be the exceptions rather than the norm.

Whether tight alliances occur in large numbers will depend much on the evolution of great-power capabilities and relations. Evidence in this book suggests that
tight alliances are considerably more likely to form (or survive) when there are two
or more major poles in the international system around which to organize. Bipolarity or multipolarity is not a necessary condition for tight alliances, but systems
characterized by intense strategic rivalry among major powers put more pressure
on DCs to choose sides clearly. As they do so, they make friends and enemies,
which sometimes encourages them to seek further protection from the former.

Most analysts now agree that the period of clear U.S. primacy is gradually giving
way to a more diffuse power structure. Some foresee the reemergence of a relatively
bipolar order and a rising China as the second pole in the system. More anticipate
multipolar order in which states or groups including China, Russia, the European
Union, and others will gain influence. A shift away from unipolarity could result in
a higher incidence of tight alliances. In the past, great powers have often failed to
manage multipolar orders peacefully. The possibility of renewed military threats has

motivated many DCs to take out insurance policies in the form of limited align-ments. If major-state tensions rise or proxy wars begin to flare, fear of external at-tack could trump the desire for flexibility and autonomy and prompt DCs to veer toward tight alliance pacts.

There are nevertheless reasons to expect that limited alignment behavior will survive the shift toward multipolarity, at least in the near term. As this book has emphasized, the distribution of power is not the only systemic factor bearing on alignment outcomes. The nature of the system is also critical. Complex interde-pendence characterizes the current world order and constrains great-power poli-cies even more than in the past. Interdependence is not a perfect prophylaxis to conflict—a lesson learned painfully in World War I—but it does give major powers and DCs alike a powerful incentive to resort to diplomacy first, maintain flexibility, and avoid rock-ribbed defense pacts.

Technology, population growth, and other changes during the past century make it almost certain that the world will remain highly interconnected and in-terdependent from a security standpoint. Nontraditional transnational threats will remain major priorities in DCs' security strategies. Addressing them will require working with numerous partners and assembling relevant ad hoc coalitions to deal with specific menaces or contingencies. They will thus have a lasting reason to seek the tactical and political flexibility that limited alignments offer.

Certain of the political constraints on alliance behavior are also likely to be stronger than they have been. Many of the governments that formed tight alliances during the Cold War era, in Southeast Asia and elsewhere, now have higher levels of public accountability even if they are not perfectly democratic. Populations that are often galvanized or assuaged by appeals to nationalism will usually oppose defense arrangements that undercut their states' independence. This adds to the likelihood that DCs' preference for limited alignments will survive shifts in the global power structure, at least for some time.

Finally, institutional evolution will be important. Bodies like the United Nations or the ASEAN Regional Forum are not likely to develop into ideal-type collective security organizations, but they do need to adapt as the power configuration shifts. Strong multilateral institutions have the potential to facilitate peaceful diplomacy and smooth the rough edges of a future multipolar order, curbing threats of war and reducing the incidence of tight, antagonistic defense pacts.

LIMITED ALIGNMENTS AND THE FUTURE OF INTERNATIONAL SECURITY

When DCs pursue limited, flexible security arrangements instead of allying tightly or staying neutral, they affect international security in several important ways. First, their alignment postures affect regional and systemic power balances. Allies in the Global South can bolster or constrain a great power's ability to project its strength far from home, react quickly in times of crisis, and mount campaigns with the ap-pearance of broad legitimacy. By resisting tight alliances, DCs deliberately constrain a great power's capacity to drive the international security agenda, with respect to both military and nontraditional issues. Further, limited alignments help DCs keep their options open—diplomatically, economically, and in security affairs. This at least arguably creates space for international cooperation that transcends the zero-sum logic of traditional balance-of-power politics and straightforward balancing and bandwagoning strategies.

The Balance of Military Power

In the near term, limited alignments by states in the Global South—with or against America—will not prevent the United States from sitting atop the global security order and exerting strong influence in most parts of the developing world. Tight allies in the Global South can certainly augment U.S. power, but to keep its decisive military edge in most regions, America needs only a modest number of close friends. As long as the United States maintains strong defense pacts with several key first-world partners—such as the United Kingdom, Germany, South Korea, Japan, and Australia—those countries can provide adequate platforms for American forces to maintain a clear upper hand in systemic terms.

Those allies also have vast economic resources, political influence, and military muscle to contribute to U.S.-led coalitions if they choose to do so. Bases in those countries enable U.S. forces to deploy overwhelming power in many parts of the globe. Small U.S. or British territories such as Guam, Diego Garcia, and Guantanamo Bay, coupled with even a handful of facilities in other places, such as Southeast Asia and the Persian Gulf, can also help the U.S. armed forces stretch deep into the developing world.

From a systemic viewpoint, limited alignments by DCs are unlikely to prevent American primacy from continuing for some time. Still, primacy is not the same as outright, unbridled domination. U.S. leadership of international security affairs will be softened by the need to negotiate with friendly states in the Global South over base access, coalition partnership, and other matters when crises arise. As David Lake contends, hierarchy is a basic feature of the international security system, but not all hierarchies are equal.[5] Hedley Bull offered a classic distinction between three forms of hierarchical relationships: dominance, hegemony, and primacy. At one end of the spectrum is dominance, in which one or more DCs essentially concede their independence to a great power. At the other end is primacy, which implies contractual arrangements imposing limited restrictions on the weaker state's sovereignty.[6] Limited alignments represent one important way that states in the Global South seek, individually and collectively, to bring about great-power primacy but not hegemony or dominance in their environs.

If most of America's friends in the Global South resist tight defense pacts, they will not prevent America from exercising military primacy at the global level. However, similar behavior by the DCs tilting toward other great powers may delay the rise of serious systemic rivals to the United States. Emerging giants such as China, India, Russia, or even the European Union currently lack broad networks of bases overseas. If those countries seek to project their conventional military power globally, they will need some stalwart allies in places far from home. As long as DCs avoid tight alliances, they will find it difficult or impossible to become real military forces in far-flung areas like Africa and the Western hemisphere. To challenge American military might seriously on a global scale, a competing great power would need to cultivate a number of devoted allies in the developing world that would provide bases, launching pads for nuclear weapons, and troops and hardware for coalitions. That prospect is unlikely given the difficulty of assembling a group with enough resources to rival the U.S. military and the dangers of antagonizing America.

More important will be the effects of limited alignments by DCs on regional balances of power in various parts of the Global South. In Latin America the United States may only need a few key bases in places like Panama to perpetuate military dominance. By contrast, if American forces begin to draw down in Iraq, basing privileges and other forms of support from friendly DCs will affect the extent to which America maintains its commanding military position in the turbulent Middle East. If access to military facilities dries up, Iran, Russia, or other players could become more significant rivals for regional leadership. The same is true in Central Asia: without base access, mutual defense commitments, and the like from regional allies, the United States will have a less decisive edge vis-à-vis other major powers that are competing for military influence.

Great Power Crisis Response Capacity

The alignment choices of DCs will also affect great powers' ability to wage war or respond quickly to crises. As Robert Art argues, strong existing alliances enable a great power to project power much more quickly and effectively than hastily arranged ad hoc coalitions.[7] This point is important, because it underscores that the strength of a DC's alignment is relevant even in times of peace, before push comes to shove and military conflict erupts. If a great power needs to scramble to arrange assets in a region and respond to a gathering security crisis, it may lose much of its ability to shape the outcome. A vulnerable DC may be bombed or overrun before its protector can come to its defense, or an opportunity to seize a strategic opportunity may be lost. The United States still has semipermanent military bases, joint combat arrangements, and other mechanisms for force projection around the world. However, the choice of some countries to close or discourage those bases—such as the Philippines in 1991, Saudi Arabia in 2003, and Uzbekistan in 2005—has forced American military strategists to adapt in those regions. Limited alignments means more limited great-power military options.

DCs can also help or undermine their great-power partners from political or economic standpoints. Allies make a campaign multilateral, help foot the bill, and give it a greater appearance of legitimacy. The importance of legitimacy helps explain why the United States has been so eager to host even small groups of ill-equipped personnel from DC allies in many of its campaigns since World War II.

The U.S. experience in waging the campaigns in Iraq in 1990 and 2003 provides a striking example of the importance of legitimacy. During the 1990–1991 Gulf War, relatively strong backing from Saudi Arabia, Kuwait, Turkey, and other allies helped make the U.S.-led victory relatively inexpensive and contributed to the conflict's international legitimacy. By contrast, limited alignments have driven up the political and economic costs of the current war in Iraq.

DC Security Cooperation

Although the foregoing discussion focuses on military cooperation and armed conflict, limited alignments will affect international security in the context of lower-level, day-to-day security cooperation between DCs and the great powers. In the coming decades, the diffusion of technology and other social and political factors make it likely that many of the most critical threats to international peace and stability will not take the form of armies marching across borders. Terrorism and nuclear proliferation are serious concerns, as are criminal activity, environmental abuse, natural disasters, and myriad other nonmilitary security challenges. Although tight alliance does not guarantee a DC's fidelity to great-power interests, it does make their assistance more likely, because tight allies depend more on their protector's support and stand more to lose from a falling out. Countries that resist tight pacts do so partly so they can decide whether and when to cooperate on such requests.

At times, limited alignments can help governments in the Global South defuse threats of concern to their great-power allies. For example, Osama bin Laden got much mileage out of the presence of U.S. troops on Saudi soil during the 1990s. Many analysts believe that the closure of U.S. bases from Saudi soil removed a significant thorn from the side of U.S.-Saudi relations and took at least a bit of steam out of local extremist movements. Extremist groups in Central Asia and the Caucasus have also drummed up recruits by painting local regimes as Russian, American, or other great-power lackeys. In that context, DCs can sometimes reduce terrorist or other nontraditional threats by insisting on a reduction in a great power's military footprint.

In other instances, limited alignments are a way DCs try to avoid doing a great power's bidding. Governments in the Global South often have incentives to pass the buck in dealing with external security challenges by distancing themselves from great-power allies and forcing the latter to clean up the mess. Domestically, DCs sometimes have incentives to avoid cracking down on criminal and extremist groups to save their own skin, allowing those groups to operate outside the country with relative impunity.

The U.S. government routinely requests that its allies track down and arrest affiliates of al-Qaeda, freeze their bank assets, and take other measures to weaken their organizations. Doing so often entails domestic political risks for the allied governments in question, especially in majority-Muslim countries. Key U.S. security partners like Turkey, Saudi Arabia, and Pakistan have limited their alignments partly to increase their leverage and give them the ability to resist American requests to crack down on domestic extremist groups. Doing so can have good or bad outcomes, depending on the context. For example, many observers believe that Pakistan's unwillingness to form a stalwart alliance with America against the Taliban is sure to enable terrorist camps to flourish along the country's northwestern frontier. Others argue that for Pakistan to join hands with U.S. forces and pummel Taliban strongholds would help radicals recruit waves of young jihadists and be a recipe for disaster.

America is not the only great power asking for help from security partners. For example, Russia asks neighboring Eurasian and Central Asian states to find and detain Chechen rebels, and China asks Myanmar and North Korea to clamp down on drug runners operating on the borders with Yunnan Province and Manchuria. Sometimes those allies comply, and sometimes they do not. In each of these cases, tight alliance would make it somewhat harder for a DC to say no, because the weaker ally's overall security dependence would be greater. Whether one deems their resistance to great-power control desirable largely depends on where one sits.

Broader International Relations

The foregoing sections all highlighted the likely effects of limited alignments in the security sphere. However, security and defense relations obviously do not take place in a vacuum; they are related to the patters of economic and political cooperation and conflict that emerge among nations. DCs' alignment choices will thus contribute to the course of international relations well beyond the realm of security and defense.

Balances of Influence

Perhaps most important, limited alignments by DCs will affect the aggregate influence that great powers enjoy in particular regions. Even if the global distribution of military might remains lopsided in America's favor, China, Russia, India, Brazil, Iran, and others will be more able to develop influence in their neighborhoods if they do not face stalwart U.S. allies on their periphery. If America's friends in the Global South generally resist close allegiance and veer toward relative neutrality, U.S. rivals will have more opportunities to build clout through diplomatic and economic channels.

To many analysts, that is precisely what has been occurring. Parag Khanna argues that the United States is "waving goodbye to hegemony" as China and the European Union use trade, aid, and diplomacy to build their influence "without firing a shot." He focuses on a group of large DCs that he describes as "swing states" and rightly asserts that "[Egyptian President Hosni] Mubarak, Musharraf, Malaysia's Mahathir, and a host of other second-world leaders have set a new standard for manipulative prowess: all tell the U.S. they are its friend while busily courting all sides."[8] In a nutshell, they are tilting toward America in the security arena but hedging their bets. Thus, even if America retains a large military lead, its economic and political rivals have ample opportunity to build their relative influence.

In strategic crossroads throughout the Global South—in the Middle East, Africa, Latin America, and Asia—economic development and resource scarcity are major (if not primary) concerns driving big-picture foreign policy decisions. The Shanghai Cooperation Organization is an excellent example of a group with a strategic purpose but economic focus. Limited alignment strategies help some of the organization's smaller players stay on sufficiently warm terms with the major participants—namely China and Russia—to advance their economic and political interests. In the meantime, both Russia and China develop clout without relying on extensive military ties and traditional competition for allies.

Institutions and Interdependence

As scholars like Robert Keohane and Joseph Nye have long argued, international security and related goods can be advanced not only through conflictual power politics but also through enhanced international cooperation and interdependence. This study suggests that limited alignments can help DCs keep the doors open to productive diplomacy and commerce. Southeast Asia has not yet evolved into a genuine security community as idealized by Karl Deutsch, but it is further along than most other regions of the Global South. One reason is that most Southeast Asian governments have been able to avoid polarizing or antagonistic foreign policies that shut off avenues for economic and diplomatic cooperation.

Limited alignments provide no guarantee that economic ties or institutionalization will flourish, but they do diminish the likelihood that rigid, antagonistic blocs will form. Multilateralism can certainly evolve behind high strategic walls (witness NATO and the European Union). However, the development of truly global interdependence is likely to be easier in the absence of highly polarized alignment structures. Since the end of the Cold War, countries once hidden behind Iron or Bamboo Curtains have been able to plug into global institutions. Their engagement in forums such as the IMF, World Bank, and World Trade Organization builds bridges to old adversaries and gives them added incentives to avoid antagonistic defense pacts. The avoidance of tight alliances may in turn help maintain space for further diplomacy and institutional evolution. Efforts to build global institutions and maintain flexible, limited alignments can thus be mutually reinforcing.

Regional institutions and alignment politics are also closely related. A variety of new multilateral forums have arisen over the past twenty years, often as ways to project great-power influence without resorting to confrontational defense pacts. The United States has promoted forums such as the Asia-Pacific Economic Cooperation forum and the ASEAN Regional Forum in part to project peaceful diplomatic influence and reinforce existing alignment structures. Other major powers have built alternative institutions such as the Shanghai Cooperation Organization, East Asia Summit, and ASEAN Plus Three as ways to build influence and constrain America without having to undertake risky counterbalancing alliances. New forums with different members and specialties give DCs options. Again, institutional evolution and alignment policies can reinforce one another. When DCs find value in using multiple diplomatic forums to prosecute their interests, they have added incentive not to alienate the leaders of any key institution allying tightly with its rival. In institutional spaces, as in alignment politics, preserving tactical flexibility will remain a major priority for DCs and other states as they plan for future contingencies.

Are Limited Alignments Good or Bad?

Limited alignment can sound like a dirty phrase in international relations because it implies a measure of caution or even distrust. For reasons enumerated above, great powers prefer stalwart allies. In public rhetoric, great-power leaders demand unflinching support from their allies and promise to reward it. No leaders stand behind podiums to heap praise on their security partners for keeping them at arm's length. Privately, great-power officials acknowledge the strategic and political dilemmas of DCs, but they still try to entice as many as possible to ally tightly in security affairs. When DCs try to place limits on security cooperation, their great-power protectors criticize them—sometimes openly, and sometimes behind closed doors—for being fair-weather friends or fence-sitters.

Great-power governments usually seek tight allies through one of two means: outright compulsion or a strategy of appearing as low-risk and high-reward as possible. The first option is exceedingly costly, both materially and politically. Even great powers with the willingness to shed blood and to incur international opprobrium usually cannot exercise coercive hegemony over a large number of allies in the postcolonial age. The United States has sometimes availed itself of that option, but in addition to material costs, imposition of hegemony runs against the grain of espoused national values. In any event, this book suggests that tight alliances are quite difficult to sustain over long periods.

Securing stalwart allies through friendliness is also fraught with difficulty. Military resources and credibility are important attractive forces for a great power, contributing to the expected rewards of alignment. However, the line between showing allies one's willingness to use force and appearing to be a loose cannon is a fine one. A great power may win kudos for strong rhetoric and tough policies against a common enemy, but weaker allies may simultaneously become more fearful of entrapment. A DC's preferred option will often be to pass the buck, convincing its great-power ally to bear the brunt of an adversary's attack while coyly staying out of harm's way. The more a great power assures a DC partner of its support—thus reducing concerns about abandonment—the less leverage it may have in negotiations with its weaker partner over basing rights, financial support, and the like.

From the standpoint of a great power, the downsides of DCs' preference for limited alignments are clear. When DCs offer only limited support, they hamper a great power's efforts to advance a particular security agenda in the Global South. Ambivalence by key Middle Eastern, Asian, and European governments has already contributed to the high cost and limited success of the U.S.-led wars in Iraq and Afghanistan and the failure to achieve greater progress against terrorist groups and nuclear proliferation. As another example, this book has shown that limited alignment by states like Cambodia and Myanmar has hampered China's ability to develop leadership in mainland Southeast Asia.

However, when DCs limit their ties, they do not necessarily undermine international security. Sometimes great-power ventures are misguided and deserve no allied support. In some cases, the best allies in the Global South may be states that preserve flexibility, protecting local and regional credibility while quietly supporting the main pillars of a great power's foreign policy agenda. Writing a blank check to a corrupt, ineffective, or odious third world regime may provide real security dividends, but over time that strategy can backfire badly. U.S. support for the shah of Iran during the 1950s and 1960s developed an ally that was a linchpin of America's strategy in the Persian Gulf, but his oppressive domestic tactics and monomania contributed directly to the Iranian Revolution of 1979, which has since spawned countless security challenges for the United States.

The best outcome for a great power is to cultivate allies that develop a deep sense of trust and shared purpose but manage their own domestic and foreign affairs astutely. Obsequious allies can deliver immense short-term security benefits but can quickly become liabilities. Strong, legitimate states are more reliable and effective security partners, even if they often insist on more policy independence than full-fledged client states do. Consequently, a DC that limits its ties is not necessarily a bad ally; on the contrary, it may be the type of state that adjusts well to international currents and proves to be a durable partner.

Ultimately, whether one judges DCs' preference for limited alignments to be a good or bad thing depends largely on one's beliefs about what type of international security order best promotes peace, stability, economic growth, and other desirable ends. Opinions on this matter vary widely. Some theorists believe that hegemonic systems are the most stable and peaceful when a relatively benign leading power provides collective public goods, such as establishing workable norms and institutions. According to this logic, a global policeman needs strong, loyal allies to help it keep misbehaving rivals in check and to put out fires quickly when they arise. In the contemporary context, advocates of continued U.S. primacy tend to advance this view.

Others, including Kenneth Waltz and many structural realists, believe that bipolar systems are inherently more stable, because no single state can exert its will with impunity on other members of the international system. According to this line of reasoning, without a serious rival to keep them honest, U.S. leaders are liable to use force to promote national interests, sometimes at the expense of international security writ large. Many opponents of American foreign policy or ideology take the view that a more genuinely bipolar or multipolar security order would be more desirable.

Limited alignments by DCs do not clearly support either of these outcomes; instead, they make both robust unipolarity and antagonistic bipolarity somewhat less likely. At their best, limited alignments can serve as shock absorbers and ease tensions among major states. They can also help provide an enabling environment for the growth of economic interdependence and multilateral diplomacy. By contrast, rigid alliances can seal off those avenues of cooperation, making conflict more likely. At their worst, limited alignments can become a way of buck-passing that results in a failure to meet grave gathering menaces to world peace, like Nazi Germany in the late 1930s. This book has shown that limited alignments very often serve the near-term interests of DCs. The broader effects of the practice on international security are somewhat less clear and represent an important subject for further study. For better or for worse, limited alignments will continue to be a salient feature of international security affairs in the years to come.

Notes

Introduction

1. For similar definitions, see Snyder, *Alliance Politics*, 4; Walt, *Origins of Alliances*, 1, 13–14; and Liska, *Nations in Alliance*, 12–13.

2. Bush, Address to Joint Session. See also "You are either with us or against us," *CNN Newswire*, November 6, 2001.

3. See, e.g., Walt, "Testing Theories," 278; Walt, *The Origins of Alliances*, 17–21; Schweller, "Bandwagoning for Profit," 72–87, 99–104; and Schweller, *Deadly Imbalances*, 83–91. Schweller, Kenneth Waltz, and Quincy Wright all use the term bandwagoning to signify alignment with the stronger or more promising of two rival coalitions. See Wright, *Study of War*, 1258–59; and Waltz, *Theory of International Politics*, 126.

4. Waltz, *Theory of International Politics*, 105–6, 121–28; and Waltz, "International Politics," 57.

5. See, e.g., David, "Explaining Third World Alignment," 235–38; David, *Choosing Sides*, 6–18; Larson, "Bandwagon Images," 86–95; and Barnett and Levy, "Domestic Sources," 370–79.

6. See Walt, *Origins of Alliances*, 17–22, 27–38, 149, 263; and Walt, "Alliance Formation," 51–56. For similar theses, see Liska, *Nations in Alliance*, 13; and Labs, "Do Weak States Bandwagon?" 385–406.

7. See Schweller, "Bandwagoning for Profit," 72–104; and Schweller, *Deadly Imbalances*, 83–91.

8. See Walt, "Testing Theories," 282, 315–16; and Walt, *Origins of Alliances*, 13.

9. Schroeder, "Historical Reality," 117.

10. Rothstein, *Alliances and Small Powers*, 30–32.

11. See Pape, "Soft Balancing," 36–43; Paul, "Soft Balancing," 58–70; and Paul, "Introduction," 3. A few studies have referred to soft balancing more as a limited form of countervailing security alignment. See, e.g., Khong, "Coping with Strategic Uncertainty"; and Roy, "Southeast Asia and China." These definitions accord somewhat better with the traditional understanding of balancing behavior in international security, but most scholars now use the term to refer to diplomatic strategies.

12. For similar critiques, see Press-Barnathan, "Managing the Hegemon," 272–73; and Brooks and Wohlforth, "Hard Times for Soft Balancing," 76–78.

13. Schroeder, "Historical Reality," 117.

14. Goh, "Meeting the China Challenge," 2–5.

15. See Art, "Europe Hedges Its Security Bets"; Heginbotham and Samuels, "Japan's Dual Hedge," 110–13; and Foot, "Chinese Strategies," 77–94. On China, see also Shambaugh and Inderfurth, "China and the U.S."; and Lampton, "Paradigm Lost," 67–75. Lampton refers to China as pursuing a strategy of "hedged integration."

16. See Wohlforth, "Revisiting Balance of Power Theory"; Miller, "International System;" Markey, "A False Choice"; "Problem with Pakistan," *New York Times*, February 28, 2007; and Serge Trifkovic, "Pakistan, A Questionable Friend," *Front Page Magazine*, January 2, 2003. On Saudi Arabian hedging, see Muqtedar Khan, "Saudi Arabian-U.S. Relations at Crossroads,"

Foreign Policy in Focus, August 13, 2003, 1–2; and Flynt Leverett, "Prince Turki comes to Washington," *New York Times,* July 27, 2005.

17.   See, e.g., Medeiros, "Strategic Hedging," 145–164; Chung, "Southeast Asia-China Relations," 35; and Roy, "Southeast Asia and China," 306–13.

18.   See Wohlforth, "U.S. Strategy," 103–06; and Wohlforth, "Stability," 5–41.

19.   See, e.g., Ikenberry, "Institutions, Strategic Restraint, and Persistence," 43–47; and Owen, "Transnational Liberalism," 242–57.

20.   Waltz, "Evaluating Theories," 915. See also Press-Barnathan, "Managing the Hegemon," 273–81; and Posen, "European Union Security," 155–59.

21.   On the breadth versus depth debate, see King, Keohane, and Verba, *Designing Social Inquiry,* 212, 229; and Gaddis, "History, Science and International Relations," 34–44.

22.   Eckstein, "Case Study and Theory," 80–127.

23.   Roger Mitton, "Man behind the Vision," *Asiaweek,* March 31, 1997. See also Walt, *Origins of Alliances,* 15, making a similar point on methodology.

24.   For key works on the Southeast Asian region, see Leifer, *ASEAN and the Security;* Acharya, *Quest for Identity;* Neher, *Southeast Asia;* Ellings and Simon, *Southeast Asian Security;* Johnston and Ross, *Engaging China;* and Alagappa, *Asian Security Practice.*

Chapter 1

1.   See Handel, *Weak States,* 30–46, 131–48; Rothstein, *Alliances,* 28–36; and Fox, *Power,* 180–82.

2.   Kennan, *Fateful Alliance,* 238.

3.   Warren Hoge, "Bogotá Begins Seeking 'New Partners' among Non-Aligned," *New York Times,* January 9, 1983, E5.

4.   See Inter-American Treaty of Reciprocal Assistance, signed in Rio de Janeiro, August 15–September 2, 1947; and Oelsner, *International Relations,* 84–85.

5.   Atkins, *Latin America,* 77–78.

6.   Schoultz, *National Security,* 171; see also Blaiser, "Security," 528–29.

7.   See Laïdi, *Superpowers,* 42–43; and Lefebvre, "Moscow's Cold War," 209–10.

8.   See Laïdi, *Superpowers,* 9–10, 35–43, 64–69, 180–93.

9.   See Schraeder, "Removing the Shackles," 192; and Laïdi, *Superpowers,* 15–17, 126–31.

10.   See Wohlforth, "Revisiting Balance of Power Theory," 226–32; Allison, "Military and Political Security," 31–57; Rashid, *Jihad,* 77–83; Kasenov, "Central Asia," 190–205; Goncharenko, "Ukraine," 121–32; Tymoshenko, "Containing Russia," 69–70; and Paznyak, "Belarus," 163–70.

11.   Schoultz, *National Security,* 171–73.

12.   Keohane, "Big Influence," 161–82; see also Bercovitch, "Superpowers," 17–19; and Vital, *Survival,* 190–91.

13.   See Kegley and Raymond, *When Trust,* 55; Walt, *Origins of Alliances,* 282; Gaddis, *We Now Know,* 150; Atkins, *Latin America,* 73–78; and Simon, "Davids and Goliaths," 305–06.

14.   See Horn, *Soviet-Indian Relations,* 123–59; and Walt, "Testing Theories," 297–303.

15.   Snyder, "Security Dilemma," 461–95.

16.   See Snyder, "Mearsheimer's World," 161–67; Mearsheimer, "False Promise," 11; Osgood, *Alliances,* 20–21; Kegley and Raymond, *When Trust,* 57–59; and Snyder, "Security Dilemma," 466–67.

17.   See Sabrosky, "Interstate Alliances," 161–98.

18.   Markey, "A False Choice," 86–94; see also Bhutto, "Pakistan's Foreign Policy," 150–51; and "Al Qaeda Resurgent," *New York Times,* February 25, 2007, 13.

19.   Lake, "Escape," 62–63.

20.   See Snyder, *Alliance Politics*, 48; and Morrow, "Alliances and Asymmetry," 904–33; see also Altfeld, "Decision," 523.

21.   Seligson, "Costa Rica," 460–61.

22.   George Washington, "Farewell Address to the People of the United States," *Independent Chronicle*, September 26, 1796.

23.   Schroeder, "Historical Reality," 117–25.

24.   See Blaiser, "Security," 534–38; and Gilderhus, *Second Century*, 200, 217–18.

25.   Schoultz, *National Security*, 238–49.

26.   Dent, "Ecuador," 378–79.

27.   Ayoob, *Third World*, 6–9.

28.   Kechichian, "Trends," 233–47.

29.   See, e.g., Ryan, "Jordan"; and O'Reilly, "Omanibalancing."

30.   See Liska, *Alliances*, 20; and Rothstein, *Alliances*, 34.

31.   See Arreguín-Toft, "How the Weak," 99–109; De Wijk, "Limits," 83–87; Simon, "Davids and Goliaths," 306; and Cassidy, "Why Great Powers," 41–53.

32.   Lyall and Wilson, "Rage," 67–106.

33.   Larson's study focuses on the relationship between small central and eastern European states and Hitler's Germany during the 1930s. See "Bandwagon Images," 102–03. Such aid-seeking alignments can also be viewed as efforts to manage internal threats to the regime. See David, "Explaining," 236.

34.   See Cooper, "State-Centric," 311–18.

35.   See Gowa and Mansfield, "Power Politics," 412–17.

36.   See Liska, *Nations in Alliance*, 26–27; Morrow, "Alliances and Asymmetry," 910–11; Rothstein, *Alliances*, 49–53; Liska, *Alliances*, 23–26; Schroeder, "Alliances," 227–62; and Dibb, "Australia's Alliance," 4.

37.   See Morgenthau, *Politics among Nations*, 201; Snyder, *Alliance Politics*, 45; Morrow, "Arms versus Allies," 207–33; and Kegley and Raymond, *When Trust,* 57.

38.   Mearsheimer, *Tragedy*, 269.

39.   Wohlforth, "Revisiting Balance of Power Theory," 226. For a similar argument, see Rothstein, *Alliances,* 28.

40.   Wohlforth, "U.S. Strategy," 103–8; and Wohlforth, "Stability," 5–15; see also Walt, "Keeping the World," 128.

41.   Layne, "Unipolar Illusion," 13–14.

42.   Aziz, "Post–Cold War Era," 63.

43.   Fujimori, "Peru," 140–41.

44.   Kenneth Waltz has argued that this feature of a relatively unipolar environment makes it inherently unstable. See Waltz, "Evaluating Theories," 915; Press-Barnathan, "Managing the Hegemon," 273–81; and Posen, "European Union Security," 158–59.

45.   Rajan Menon argues that in the contemporary era, without a pressing threat like the Soviet Union, America's friends see less reason to be bound to U.S. policies. See Menon, *End*, 67, discussing European states in particular.

46.   See Walt, *Origins of Alliances*, 21–26, 33–49, 181, 218; Liska, *Nations in Alliance*, 13; Walt, "Why Alliances Endure," 21–26; Snyder, "Alliances, Balance, and Stability," 123–25; and Walt, "Testing Theories," 308.

47.   See Christensen and Snyder, "Chain Gangs," 138–47.

48.   Weitsman, "Alliance Cohesion," 82 (emphasis in original); see also Lake, "Escape," 72–73.

49.   Buchan, "Problems," 295.

50. See Waltz, "Structural Realism," 42–51; and Menon, *End*, 57.

51. See Posen, "Struggle," 43–54.

52. See David, "Explaining," 233–56; David, *Choosing Sides,* chap. 1; Ayoob, "Security Problematic," 211–32; Barnett and Levy, "Domestic Sources," 369–95; Harknett and VanDenBerg, "Alignment Theory," 115–28; Singer and Small, *Resort to Arms*, 92–99; and Clapham, *Third World Politics*, 18.

53. See Osgood, *Alliances,* 21–22; and Scott, "Patron-Client Politics," 411–25.

54. Reagan, Address before a Joint Session.

55. See Eban, "Statement to the Security Council"; see also Walt, *Origins of Alliances*, 3–5; and Walt, "Testing Theories," 278–79; and Schweller, *Deadly Imbalances*, 48.

56. See Larrabee, "Turkey Rediscovers the Middle East," 105–11.

57. On the Latin American cases, see Palmer, "Peru," 262–65; Oelsner, *International Relations*, 89; and Sigmund, "Chile," 177. On Iran, see Chubin and Zabih, *Foreign Relations*, 77; Zabih, "Iran's International Posture," 312–14; and Ramazani, *Iran's Foreign Policy*, 312–28.

58. For similar definitions, see Russett, Starr, and Kinsella, *World Politics*, 168; and Holsti, "Belief System and National Images," 244–52. In this book, communism, democratic capitalism, authoritarian capitalism, and political Islam are treated as examples of relatively distinct ideologies, although each is far from monolithic. Many states fall in between these ideal-types, and qualitative judgments are inescapable.

59. Kegley and Raymond, *When Trust,* 58; see also Walt, *Origins of Alliances*, 33–38, 203; Walt, "Testing Theories," 313; Morgenthau, *Politics among Nations*, 183–84; and Holsti, Hopmann, and Sullivan, *Unity*, 61–64.

60. Mearsheimer, *Tragedy*, 48.

61. Walt, *Origins of Alliances*, 203.

62. On the importance of ideology in establishing trust, see Hermann and Kegley, "Rethinking Democracy;" Liska, *Nations in Alliance*, 61–62; Osgood, *Alliances,* 20; and David, *Choosing Sides,* 5.

63. MacFarlane, *Superpower Rivalry*, chap. 5. Brian Lai and Dan Reiter conducted an extensive study of alliance patterns between 1816 and 1992 and found that democracies were more likely to align with one another than nondemocratic countries, but only after 1945. They also found that ideology exerted a greater attractive force among nondemocratic states after 1945. See "Democracy," 221–24. For a similar finding, see Siverson and Emmons, "Birds," 292–305.

64. Morrow, "Alliances and Asymmetry," 917.

65. Cha, "Ideational Dimension," 41–70.

66. Dibb, "Australia's Alliance," 3; see also Haas, "Ideology and Alliances," 34–79; Kaufman, "To Balance," 426–30.

67. Warner Levi has argued that the effect of ideology is apt to be particularly great in highly centralized or authoritarian regimes, in which the individual biases of particular leaders are most apt to exert a major effect on policy outcomes. See "Ideology," 25; see also Siverson and Starr, "Regime Change," 148–50, 158–60.

68. Snyder, "Concept," 4.

69. See Huntington, *Clash*, 231–35.

70. Buzan, "Civilizational *Realpolitik,*" 182; Dupont, "Is There," 18–19; Walt, "Building Up," 184–86; and Welch, "'Clash of Civilizations' Book," 200–06.

71. See Liska, *Nations in Alliance*, 12, 21; and Barnett, "Alliances and Identity."

72. Bennett, "Testing Alternative Models," 855–56, 874.

73. Ross, "Balance of Power," 366.

74. Walt, *Origins of Alliances*, 221. See also Burns, *Economic Aid*, 208.

75.   See Mastanduno, "Economics and Security," 825–26, 839–43; and Brand, "Economics," 393–413.

76.   Albert Hirschman referred to Machiavelli's classic work on statecraft, arguing that a modern edition of *The Prince* would need to include "extensive new sections on the most efficient use of quotas, exchange controls, capital investments, and other instruments of economic warfare." *National Power*, 15–18. As E. H. Carr rightly argued, the "illusion of a separation between politics and economics has ceased to correspond to any aspect of current reality . . . military and economic weapons are merely different instruments of power." *Twenty Years' Crisis*, 117–20. See also Mastanduno, "Economics and Security," 826.

77.   Brand, "Economics," 393–413. See also Clapham, *Third World Politics*, 39–43; and Ryan, "Jordan," 136.

78.   For recent data, see World Bank, *Indicators*.

79.   John Mearsheimer argues that "institutions have minimal influence on state behavior." "False Promise," 7. See also Kennan, *Realities*, 47–50.

80.   Grieco, "Anarchy," 498–500; Grieco, "Realist International Theory;" and Mearsheimer, "False Promise," 18–19. For a series of essays debating this long-standing issue in international relations theory, see Keohane, *Neorealism*. For a strong constructivist view, see Wendt, "Collective Identity Formation," arguing that "anarchy is what states make of it" and placing priority on how governments formulate their norms and interests in the security sphere.

81.   See Lipson, "International Cooperation," 12–19; and Axelrod and Keohane, "Achieving Cooperation," 232–33.

82.   See Mohan, *Crossing the Rubicon*, 34–39, 48–56, 113–14; and Thomas, "South Asian Security Balance," 313–28.

83.   See Medeiros, "Strategic Hedging," 146; and Paul, "Introduction," 3.

84.   For an argument that ententes or flexible security arrangements sometimes deliver greater security payoffs than rigid alliances, see Kann, "Alliances versus Ententes," 611–21.

85.   See Schweller, *Unanswered Threats*, 11–15; and Schweller, "Unanswered Threats," 159–60.

86.   Posen, "European Union Security," 155–57.

87.   See Walt, "Alliances in a Unipolar World," 95–100; Waltz, "Structural Realism," 40–42, 53–54; and Huntington, "Lonely Superpower," 42.

88.   See Mueller, *Remnants*.

89.   See Menon, *End*, 67.

90.   See Ikenberry, "Democracy," 213–38.

91.   See Owen, "Transnational Liberalism," 242–57.

92.   See Papayoanou, "Interdependence," 43–50.

93.   Walt, *Origins of Alliances*, 13.

Chapter 2

1.   See Heder, "Kampuchean-Vietnamese Conflict," 27–30.

2.   See SRV Foreign Ministry, "Border Question," 126; "Statement of the Government," 81.

3.   See Poole, "Cambodia 1975," 28–29; Quinn, "Cambodia 1976," 47–48; and Acharya, *Quest for Identity*, 109.

4.   Edith Lenart, "Indochina: Each to His Own," *Far Eastern Economic Review*, June 13, 1975, 25–26.

5.   *Chinese Rulers' Crimes*, 76–86; and Burchett, *China, Cambodia, Vietnam Triangle*, 165–68.

6.   Heder, "Kampuchean-Vietnamese Conflict," 44–45. See also "Further Reportage on Cambodian Delegation Activities," *FBIS-PRC*, August 18, 1975, A5.

7. Amer, "Sino-Vietnamese Normalization," 362, 369; Turnbull, "Regionalism and Nationalism," 297; and Porter, "Vietnamese Policy," 82.

8. Storey and Thayer, "Cam Ranh Bay," 454.

9. On the "stab in the back," see Porter, "Vietnamese Policy," 73–75; and Yahuda, *International Relations*, 203. On the Spratly clashes, see Snitwongse, "Soviet-Vietnamese Alliance," 48, Amer, "Sino-Vietnamese Normalization," 358–59; and Porter, "Vietnamese Policy," 80–82.

10. See Amer, "Sino-Vietnamese Normalization," 359–63, 368–76; "Assessing Sino-Vietnamese Relations," 325–26; and Ross, *Indochina Tangle*, 62–70, 125–33, 148–55, 176–89, 202–07.

11. Ross, *Indochina Tangle*, 56–62, 118–23; and Simon, "Peking and Indochina," 403.

12. Simon, "Davids and Goliaths," 313; Snitwongse, "Soviet-Vietnamese Alliance," 48–49; Pike, "Vietnam 1977," 74; and Lau, "ASEAN," 555–56. See also Elliott, "Third Indochina Conflict," 17–18.

13. See Thayer, "Laos and Vietnam," 251–55; and Brown and Zasloff, "Laos 1977," 172.

14. "LPDR Anniversary Celebrated in Vientiane," *FBIS Asia-Pacific*, December 2, 1976, A5. See also Stuart-Fox, *History of Laos*, 176–77; and Brown and Zasloff, "Laos 1976," 112.

15. Evans, *Short History*, 186; and Porter, "Vietnamese Policy," 79–80.

16. Stuart-Fox, *History of Laos*, 177–78. See also Brown and Zasloff, "Laos 1976," 113; Brown and Zasloff, "Laos 1975," 199; Stuart-Fox, "National Defence," 230–31; and Evans, *Short History*, 189–90.

17. Yahuda, *International Relations*, 90–91; Leifer, *Indonesia's Foreign Policy*, 178; and Buszynski, "Thailand," 1045.

18. Acharya, *Quest for Identity*, 96; interview with Kwa Chong Guan, Singapore, March 29, 2004; and Buszynski, "Thailand," 1039–41.

19. Acharya, *Quest for Identity*, 68.

20. See Acharya, *Constructing a Security Community*, 47–62; *Quest for Identity*, 83–98; Turnbull, "Regionalism and Nationalism," 287–89; Leifer, *ASEAN*, 1–9; and Wanandi, "Conflict and Cooperation," 503–04.

21. Horn, "Southeast Asian Perceptions," 681–82; Solidum, "Philippine Perceptions," 538; Nathan, "Malaysia and the Soviet Union," 1063–64; and Yahuda, *International Relations*, 88–91.

22. See, e.g., Acharya, *Constructing a Security Community*, chaps. 2–4; "Ideas, Identity," 323–32; and Busse, "Constructivism," 2.

23. "Treaty of Amity and Cooperation in Southeast Asia," signed in Denpasar, Bali on February 24, 1976, art. 2(b) and art. 11.

24. "Zone of Peace, Freedom and Neutrality Declaration," signed in Kuala Lumpur, November 27, 1971, art. 1.

25. Adam Malik, "Towards an Asian Asia," *Far Eastern Economic Review*, September 25, 1971, 29–33. For a similar view, see Tengku Ahmed Rithauddeen, "Seeking Security without Interference," *Far Eastern Economic Review*, August 29, 1975, 3.

26. Turnbull, "Regionalism and Nationalism," 312; Indorf, "ASEAN," 93; and Simon, "China, Vietnam, and ASEAN," 1172.

27. Weatherbee, "U.S. Policy," 413.

28. Cited in Buszynski, "Thailand," 1041.

29. "Troops Ordered to Be Ready for Worse after U.S. Pullout," *Bangkok Post*, January 31, 1976, 1–3.

30. Buszynski, "Thailand," 1038–39; and Neher, *Southeast Asia*, 275.

31. See Wheeler, "Thai-Vietnamese Relations," 8; Emmerson, "Indonesia, Malaysia, Singapore," 66; Ross, "Geography," 84–85; and Zimmerman, "Thailand in 1975," 169.

32. Communiqué of Thai Prime Minister Thanin Kraivichien and Philippine President Marcos, December 20–22, 1976, cited in Buszynski, "Thailand," 1043.

33. "Thais Hold Communist Suspects," *Straits Times*, July 6, 1977, 1.

34. Viraphol, "Thai-American Relations," 135–43.

35. V.G. Kulkarni, "Timor Issue Widens China-Indonesia Split," *Christian Science Monitor*, January 28, 1976.

36. See "Panggabean Accuses Peking," *Straits Times*, February 24, 1978, 1.

37. Singh, "The Soviet Union," 280.

38. See Suryadinata, *Indonesia's Foreign Policy*, 140; Emmerson, "Indonesia, Malaysia, Singapore," 67–68; and Simon, "The Superpowers," 76.

39. Acharya, *Quest for Identity*, 70; Leifer, "ASEAN Regional Forum," 10; and Acharya, "New Regional Order," 58.

40. Nathan, "Malaysia and the Soviet Union," 1064–65.

41. Leifer, *ASEAN*, 56–58; and Indorf, "Malaysia in 1977," 192–93.

42. Neher, *Southeast Asia*, 156; and Yahuda, *International Relations*, 204.

43. Leifer, *ASEAN*, 58; and Shee, "Singapore in 1977," 198–99.

44. Liang, *Burma's Foreign Relations*, 59–65; Martin, "Burma in 1975," 173; Buszynski, "ASEAN's New Challenges," 562; and Than, "Myanmar and China," 191–93.

45. Neher, *Southeast Asia*, 205; Haacke, "Myanmar's Foreign Policy," 16–17; and Than, "Myanmar and China," 193.

46. Liang, *Burma's Foreign Relations*, 92–94; Martin, "Burma in 1975," 173–74; Than, "Myanmar and China," 193; and Scully and Trager, "Burma 1979," 173.

47. *The Guardian* (Rangoon), September 21, 1979, cited in Scully and Trager, "Burma 1979," 172.

48. Chandler, *History of Cambodia*, 216–22; Jackson, "Cambodia 1977," 82–83; and Jackson, "Cambodia 1978," 72–81.

49. See Kiernan, *Pol Pot Regime*, 376–85; Chandler, *History of Cambodia*, 221–22; Heder, "Kampuchean-Vietnamese Conflict," 49–51; Chanda, "China and Cambodia," 4; Ross, *Indochina Tangle*, 135–38; and Heder, "Kampuchean-Vietnamese Conflict," 58–60.

50. Scobell, *China's Use*, 129–130.

51. See Elliott, "Third Indochina Conflict," 10–12; Yahuda, *International Relations*, 205–06; and Amer, "Assessing Sino-Vietnamese Relations," 320–21.

52. Storey and Thayer, "Cam Ranh Bay," 455.

53. Elliott, "Third Indochina Conflict," 12–14. See also Leifer, *ASEAN*, 102; and Singh, "Singapore's Perspectives," 64–66.

54. Henry Kamm, "Laos Backs Vietnam in Dispute Despite Chinese Troops in North," *New York Times*, July 23, 1978, 3.

55. Stuart-Fox, *History of Laos*, 197–98; and Brown and Zasloff, "Laos 1977," 174.

56. Neher, *Southeast Asia*, 256. Moscow provided much of the weaponry and almost entirely funded the operation. See also Kintner, *Soviet Global Strategy*, 188–89.

57. Simon, "Superpowers," 66; Simon, "Davids and Goliaths," 311–12. See also Heder, "Kampuchean-Vietnamese Conflict," 60–61; Leifer, *ASEAN*, 102; and Lau, "ASEAN," 558–59.

58. Alagappa, "Soviet Policy," 331–32; Storey and Thayer, "Cam Ranh Bay," 457; and Snitwongse, "Soviet-Vietnamese Alliance," 49–55; and Amer, "Sino-Vietnamese Normalization," 362–63.

59. Leifer, "Kampuchea 1979," 40.

60. Hun, "Kampuchean Foreign Policy," 29.

61. Chinh, "Big Powers," 181; Stuart-Fox, "National Defence," 238–39; and Bedlington, "Laos in 1980," 106–07.

62. Thayer, "Laos and Vietnam," 255–57, 260–61; Brown and Zasloff, "Laos 1979," 103–04; Bedlington, "Laos in 1981," 91–92; and Thayer, "Laos in 1983," 57.

63.   See Zagoria, "Strategic Environment," 6; and Walt, *Origins of Alliances*, 35–36, describing communism as a divisive ideology.

64.   See Nathan, "Malaysia and the Soviet Union," 1070–72; Suryadinata, *Indonesia's Foreign Policy*, 144–45; Zagoria and Simon, "Soviet Policy," 169; and Alagappa, "Soviet Policy," 342.

65.   Savetsila, "Thailand's View." See also Van der Kroef, "Hanoi and ASEAN," 171.

66.   See Turley, "Thai-Vietnamese Rivalry, 157–59.

67.   Copper, "China and Southeast Asia," 55; and Emmers, *Cooperative Security*, 99.

68.   Simon, "Superpowers," 67–68; Paribatra, "The Challenge," 16–19; and Teo, "New Omnidirectional Overtures," 755–56.

69.   Lau, "ASEAN," 551; and Buszynski, "Thailand," 1046. Small-scale Lao incursions added to the Thai threat perception.

70.   Buszynski, "Thailand," 1045; and John J. McBeth, "Thailand's Rush to Re-Arm," *Far Eastern Economic Review*, October 19, 1979, 28–29.

71.   Lau, "ASEAN," 558; and Emmers, *Cooperative Security*, 99.

72.   Teo, "New Omnidirectional Overtures," 755; Samudavanija and Paribatra, "Development," 201; and Buszynski, "New Aspirations," 1067.

73.   See Goodman, "Are Asia's."

74.   Schier, "Indochina Conflict," 227–28; Singh, "Singapore's Perspectives," 73–78; and Neher, *Southeast Asia*, 173.

75.   *Mirror* (Singapore), April 15, 1981, cited in Singh, "The Soviet Union," 288.

76.   Interview reprinted in "Don't Let the Soviets Dominate Southeast Asia," *U.S. News & World Report*, February 8, 1982, 37.

77.   Koh, *The Quest*, 189.

78.   Emmerson, "Indonesia, Malaysia, Singapore," 70.

79.   See Wanandi, "Conflict and Cooperation," 504, 509–10; Leifer, *Indonesia's Foreign Policy*, 168–70; Nathan, "Malaysia and the Soviet Union," 1068; Acharya, "New Regional Order," 8; Gordon, "Asian Angst," 52–53; Scalapino, "Political Influence," 86–87; Simon, "ASEAN's Strategic Situation," 73–83; and Singh, "Soviet Union," 283.

80.   Wanandi and Soesastro, "Indonesia's Security," 83–102.

81.   See "Mochtar on Restoration of Relations with PRC," in *Jakarta Domestic Service*, in FBIS, March 12, 1984, N2; Leifer, *Indonesia's Foreign Policy*, 179; Neher, *Southeast Asia*, 156; and Sukma, "Recent Developments," 37–38; Ganesan, "ASEAN's Relations," 260–62; and Storey, "Indonesia's China Policy," 146–47.

82.   Simon, "Two Southeast Asias," 527–28; and Simon, "ASEAN's Strategic Situation," 80.

83.   *The Business Times* (Kuala Lumpur), November 27, 1981. See also Chang, "Sino-Vietnam Rift," 546–47; Simon, "ASEAN's Strategic Situation," 77–80; Wanandi, *Security Dimensions*, 36; Wanandi, "Conflict and Cooperation," 514; and Khong and Abdullah, "Security Co-operation," 133.

84.   Gordon with Vasey, "Security," 41. See also Mahathir's remarks to Secretary of State Shultz, quoted in Bernard Gwertzman, "Malaysia, Seeing a Threat, Urges U.S. to Stop Building Up Power of China," *New York Times*, July 10, 1984.

85.   *New Straits Times*, July 29, 1983, cited in Horn, "Southeast Asian Perceptions," 683.

86.   Suryadinata, *Indonesia's Foreign Policy*, 150.

87.   See Wanandi, "Conflict and Cooperation," 513; Susumu Awanohara, "The Spurned Hosts," *Far Eastern Economic Review*, October 12, 1983, 14–15; and Weatherbee, "Indonesia in 1984," 193–95.

88.   James Clad, "Warning to Washington," *Far Eastern Economic Review*, September 20, 1984, 14–15.

89.   See Emmers, *Cooperative Security*, 74–81; and Singh, "Brunei in 1985," 169–71.

90. See Ahmad, "Oil and Security," 188–89; Mulliner, "Brunei in 1984," 216–17; and Menon, "Brunei Darussalam in 1987," 257–58.

91. Alagappa, "Regional Arrangements," 280; and Bessho, "Identities and Security," 42.

92. Acharya, *Constructing a Security Community*, 56; Simon, "ASEAN's Strategic Situation," 77; and Wanandi and Soesastro, "Indonesia's Security," 96.

93. Leifer, "Indonesia and the Dilemmas of Engagement," 98.

94. See Segal, *Great Power Triangle*, 6; Chen, *Strategic Triangle*, 8–10; and Stryker and Psathas, "Research on Coalitions," 23.

95. Maranan, "China and the Philippines," 266–67.

96. "NPA Threat," *Hong Kong AFP*, in FBIS, April 15, 1983, P1; Mediansky, "New People's Army," 1–2; Barnds, "Political and Security Relations," 244–45; and Villegas, "The Philippines in 1986," 198.

97. Acharya, "Association," 164–68 and appendix 1; Alagappa, "Asian Practice of Security," 635; Acharya, *Quest for Identity*, 134–43; and Simon, "ASEAN's Strategic Situation," 86–88.

98. Haacke, "Myanmar's Foreign Policy," 15. See also Than, "Myanmar and China," 193–95; Malik, "Sino-Indian Rivalry," 139; and Liang, *Burma's Foreign Relations,* 226–34.

99. Than, "Myanmar and China," 193–94; and Haacke, "Myanmar's Foreign Policy," 17.

100. Thayer, "Vietnamese Foreign Policy," 2.

101. Thayer, "Vietnamese Foreign Policy," 2–3.

102. Pike, "Vietnam in 1990," 84; Pike, "Vietnam in 1991," 80; and Susumu Awanohara, "Withdrawal Symptoms," *Far Eastern Economic Review*, February 1, 1990, 8.

103. Stuart-Fox, "Foreign Policy," 197–99.

104. Stuart-Fox, "Laos in 1988," 83–87; and Gunn, "Laos in 1990," 91–92.

105. Pike, "Vietnam in 1990," 85.

106. Khong, "ASEAN's Post-Ministerial Conference," 44; and Acharya, "New Regional Order," 13, 41–52

107. Huxley, "Insecurity in the ASEAN Region," 57–58; and Mak, "Chinese Navy," 150.

108. Anwar, "Indonesia: Domestic Priorities," 507.

109. Vatikiotis, "Indonesia's Foreign Policy," 365.

110. Leifer, "ASEAN Regional Forum," 7–8; and Huxley, "Insecurity in the ASEAN Region," 23.

111. *The Straits Times*, Weekly Overseas edition, September 2, 1989.

112. Ganesan, *Realism and Interdependence*, 16, 44, 52.

113. Menon, "Brunei Darussalam in 1986," 86.

114. Buszynski, "New Aspirations," 1059–60.

115. Barnds, "Political and Security Relations," 231.

116. Bertil Lintner, "SLORC Salvation," *Far Eastern Economic Review*, October 3, 1991, and *Jane's Defence Weekly*, September 13, 1990. See also Than, "Myanmar and China," 195; and Neher, *Southeast Asia*, 205.

117. Than, "Myanmar and China," 195; and Buszynski, "ASEAN's New Challenges," 562.

Chapter 3

1. Stubbs, "Subregional Security Cooperation," 398–99.

2. "U.S. Exit Poses Problem for Philippine Defense," *Reuters News Service,* March 3, 1992.

3. Kirk, *Looted*, 8.

4. See Fisher, "Rebuilding the U.S.-Philippine Alliance"; Kirk, *Looted,* 192; and Novicio, "South China Sea Dispute," 44–45.

5. Neher, "Post-Cold War Security Issues," 167–72; Whiting, "ASEAN Eyes China," 314; and Rüland, "ASEAN," 434.

6. Simon, "Parallel Tracks of Asian Multilateralism," 21.

7. Elaine Sciolino, "With Thai Rebuff, U.S. Defers Plans for Navy Depot in Asia," *New York Times*, November 12, 1994, A6.

8. See Haacke, "Myanmar's Foreign Policy," 28; and Malik, "Sino-Indian Rivalry," 139–40; and Lee, "China's Expanding Maritime Ambitions," 554.

9. Leifer, "Indochina and ASEAN," 274–75; and Acharya, "New Regional Order," 41.

10. See Chang, "Vietnam and China," 138–39; and Amer, "Sino-Vietnamese Normalization," 366–67.

11. See Thayer, "Beyond Indochina," 28; Williams, *Vietnam at the Crossroads*, 62; Johnson, "Laos in 1991," 86; Gunn, "Laos in 1989," 84–85; and Acharya, "A New Regional Order," 45.

12. Gunn, "Laos in 1989," 81; Johnson, "Laos in 1991," 86–87; and Johnson, "Laos in 1992," 81.

13. Shawcross, "Cambodia's New Deal," 5–10, 71.

14. Muni, "China's Strategic Engagement," 36; Cheng, "Sino–ASEAN Relations," 423–24; and Chanda, "China and Cambodia," 4.

15. Leifer, "Indonesia and the Dilemmas of Engagement," 125. See also Zakaria, "Culture Is Destiny," 122–23; and Acharya, "New Regional Order," 14, noting similar concerns from Indonesian Foreign Minister Ali Alatas.

16. Valencia, "China and the South China Sea Disputes," 3–14; Leifer, "ASEAN Regional Forum," 17; and Yahuda, *International Relations of the Asia-Pacific*, 274.

17. Khong, "Singapore," 115–16; and Goldstein, "Great Expectations," 39–55.

18. See Paul Jacob, "China, India and Japan 'Are New Military Powers,'" *Straits Times*, November 22, 1995.

19. General Dato' Che Mohamad Noor bin Mat Arshad, cited in Acharya, *Quest for Identity*, 132.

20. Valencia, "China and the South China Sea," 6–7, 12–24; Cheng, "Sino-ASEAN Relations," 424–25; Leifer, "ASEAN Regional Forum," 16–18; and Lam, "A Short Note," 459–60.

21. Huxley, "Insecurity in the ASEAN Region," 23; and Acharya, "A New Regional Order," 57.

22. Ganesan, *Realism and Interdependence*, 52; Emmerson, "Indonesia, Malaysia, Singapore," 76; and Goh, "Singapore and the United States," 4.

23. See also Acharya, "New Regional Order," 58; and Emmers, *Cooperative Security*, 111, 150.

24. Emmerson, "Indonesia, Malaysia, Singapore," 76; Cheng, "Sino-ASEAN Relations," 428; and Acharya, *Quest for Identity*, 139–40. See also "Tightening Security Bonds: A Malaysian View," *Asia-Pacific Defence Reporter*, August 1991, 19.

25. Huxley, "Insecurity in the ASEAN Region," 22–24. See also Nayan Chanda, "U.S. Maintains Broad Asian Military Pacts," *Asian Wall Street Journal*, April 8, 1992.

26. Defense Minister Najib, Address to the Malaysian International Affairs Forum, *Asian Defence Journal*, February 1993, cited in Huxley, "Insecurity in the ASEAN Region," 24.

27. Leifer, "Indonesia and the Dilemmas of Engagement," 87, 90, 95–96, 101; and Gallagher, "China's Illusory Threat," 173–74.

28. Anwar, "Indonesia," 486; and Storey, "Indonesia's China Policy," 156–60.

29. See Paul Jacob, "Indonesian Military Exercises 'Includes China Factor,'" *Straits Times*, August 21, 1996; and Leifer, "Indonesia and the Dilemmas of Engagement," 103.

30. Smith, "Reluctant Partner," 5; Huxley, "Insecurity in the ASEAN Region," 25; and Suryadinata, *Indonesia's Foreign Policy*, 142.

31. Philip Shenon, "Non-Aligned Bloc Seeks New Reason for Being," *New York Times*, September 2, 1992, A9.

32. Quoted in Acharya, "New Regional Order," 56–57; Alatas, "The Emerging Security Environment in East Asia and the Pacific: An ASEAN Perspective," Address to the NUS Society, October 28, 1992, reprinted in Alatas, *Voice for a Just Peace*, 83–95.

33. Emmerson, "Indonesia, Malaysia, Singapore," 72–78.

34. See Acharya, "New Regional Order," 58; Leifer, "ASEAN Regional Forum," 15; and Kershaw, "Partners in Realism," 47–48.

35. Thayer, "Beyond Indochina," 31; and Novicio, "South China Sea Dispute," 10–11.

36. See *Sunday Chronicle,* October 29, 1995, cited in Whiting, "ASEAN Eyes China," 316; and Buszynski, "Realism, Institutionalism, and Philippine Security," 496; and Storey, "Creeping Assertiveness," 97–100.

37. Kirk, *Looted,* 192–93.

38. Press conference, Malacañang Palace, September 24, 1997, cited in Kirk, *Looted,* 194. See also Novicio, "South China Sea Dispute," 46.

39. See Acharya, "New Regional Order," 55–95; Huxley, "Insecurity in the ASEAN Region," 66; and Simon, "Parallel Tracks of Asian Multilateralism," 25.

40. See Sukma, "Indonesia's Bebas-Aktif Foreign Policy," 231 and note 17; Weinstein, *Indonesian Foreign Policy,* 161; and Leifer, "Indonesia and the Dilemmas of Engagement," 101–02. See also Hasnan Habib, "Remarks by General Hasnan Habib, May 22, 1996," *KOMPAS,* May 23–24, 1996.

41. See Leifer, "ASEAN Regional Forum;" and Khong, "Making Bricks without Straw," 290–91.

42. Simon, "Realism and Neoliberalism," 20–21; and Simon, "ASEAN's Strategic Situation," 75.

43. Lee, Speech to the Nixon Center.

44. Interview transcript printed in Michael Richardson, "Asian Security and the Evolving U.S. Role," *International Herald Tribune,* July 19, 1993.

45. Leifer, "Indonesia and the Dilemmas of Engagement," 139. See also Khong, "ASEAN's Post-Ministerial Conference," 46.

46. Whiting, "ASEAN Eyes China," 300–13.

47. Haacke, "Myanmar's Foreign Policy," 26. See also Buszynski, "ASEAN's New Challenges," 562–63; and Than, "Myanmar and China," 195–98.

48. Muni, "China's Strategic Engagement," 28–29, 79; and Haacke, "Myanmar's Foreign Policy," 26.

49. Badgley, "Myanmar in 1993," 157–58; Steinberg, *Burma,* 238; and Haacke, "Myanmar's Foreign Policy," 27.

50. Dommen, "Laos in 1994," 90; and Johnson, "Laos in 1992," 79–80.

51. Johnson, "Laos in 1992," 80–81.

52. Thayer, "Laos in 1999," 45.

53. Bourdet, "Laos in 1995," 93; and Bourdet, "Laos in 1996," 74–75.

54. Shawcross, "Cambodia's New Deal," 44–45.

55. Peou, *Cambodia after the Cold War,* 4–7; Lizée, "Cambodia in 1996," 66–70; "Cambodia: Dancing with the Dragon," *Far Eastern Economic Review,* December 11, 1997; and "Cambodia: New-Found Generosity: China Offers Phnom Penh Military Aid," *Far Eastern Economic Review,* May 9, 1996.

56. Goodman, "Vietnam in 1994," 98–99; Pike, "Vietnam in 1991," 80–81; and Buszynski, "ASEAN's New Challenges," 558–60.

57. Thayer, "Beyond Indochina," 56–57.

58. See Patrick E. Tyler, "Vietnamese Hint the U.S. Could Use Port Again," *New York Times,* November 24, 1994, A12; and Charles Fenyvesi, "Thanks, but No Thanks: U.S. Navy

Rejects Hanoi Invitation to Return to Cam Ranh Bay," *U.S. News & World Report*, November 4, 1991, 31. See also Storey and Thayer, "Cam Ranh Bay," 457.

59. See Paul Cleary, "Vietnam: Hanoi Observed—Old Enemies Locked in a Delicate Balancing Act," *Australian Financial Review*, December 21, 1994.

60. Thayer, "Beyond Indochina," 60, citing ITER-TASS, *World Service*, June 16, 1994.

61. See, e.g., Huntington, *Clash of Civilizations*, 229–38; and Kang, *Culture, Hierarchy and Stability*.

62. For a fuller discussion, see Ba, "China and ASEAN," 635–38.

63. Emmerson, "What Do the Blind-Sided See?" 7–8.

64. Mohan Srilal, "Singapore-Indonesia Ties Sink to Chilly Depths," *Asia Times*, March 5, 1999.

65. Lee, "ASEAN Must Balance," 20–21. See also Goh, "Singapore and the United States," 4; and "U.S. Carrier to Make First Port Call to Singapore," *Weekly Defense Monitor* 5:12 (2001).

66. See Doug Struck and Rajiv Chandrasekaran, "Nations across Asia Keep Watch on China," *Washington Post*, October 19, 2001. See also "U.S. Aircraft Carrier Makes First Call to Singapore's Changi Naval Base," *People's Daily*, March 24, 2001; and Tan and Cohen, News Briefing.

67. See Doug Struck and Rajiv Chandrasekaran, "Nations across Asia Keep Watch on China," *Washington Post*, October 19, 2001; Storey, "Creeping Assertiveness," 98, 104–05; and Novicio, "South China Sea Dispute," 11–14.

68. Rigoberto Tiglao, "Seaside Boom," *Far Eastern Economic Review*, July 8, 1999, 14; and Rigoberto Tiglao et al., "'Tis the Season," *Far Eastern Economic Review*, December 24, 1998, 18–19.

69. Quoted in Vatikiotis, *Political Change*, 193.

70. Novicio, "South China Sea Dispute," 48–49; and Rigoberto Tiglao, "Growing Up: Manila's Military Pact with U.S. Signals New Maturity," *Far Eastern Economic Review*, 3 June 3, 1999, 27.

71. Cited in Baker, "China-Philippines Relations," 4.

72. Steinberg, *Burma*, 234–350; and Seekins, "Burma in 1999," 21–22.

73. Haacke, "Myanmar's Foreign Policy," 35–36; and Than, "Myanmar (Burma) in 2000," 154–55.

74. Thayer, "Beyond Indochina," 21–22.

75. See "Sino-Vietnam Relationship to Smoothly Develop-New Vietnamese Party Leader," *Xinhua News Agency*, April 22, 2001; and "Political Report of the CPV Central Committee, Eighth Tenure, and the Ninth National Party Congress," cited in Thayer, "Vietnam in 2001," 87.

76. Storey and Thayer, "Cam Ranh Bay," 465–67. See also Sidel, "Vietnam in 1998," 95–97.

77. Hung, "Vietnam in 1999," 108; and Thayer, "Vietnam in 2000," 187.

78. Ang, "Vietnam," 348–49.

79. Ibid., 351.

80. Abuza, "Laos," 160–62.

81. Thayer, "Laos in 1998," 42; and Thayer, "Laos in 1999," 45–47.

82. Bertil Lintner and Shawn W. Crispin, "Brothers in Arms: Vientiane Looks to Vietnam and China as It Battles Economic Stagnation and the New Threat of a Revived Hmong Insurgency," *Far Eastern Economic Review*, May 11, 2000.

83. Bourdet, "Laos in 2000," 168–69; and Bourdet, "Laos in 2001," 112.

84. Un and Ledgerwood, "Cambodia in 2001," 103.

85. "Cambodian Leader says China 'Most Trustworthy Friend' Despite Grim History,"

Associated Press, July 22, 2003. See also Mark Mitchell and Michael Vatikiotis, "China Steps in Where U.S. Fails: Jiang Zemin Visits Indochina in a Broader Push to Improve Ties with Southeast Asia," *Far Eastern Economic Review*, November 23, 2000; and Julio Jeldres, "China-Cambodia: More Than Just Friends?" *Asia Times Online*, September 16, 2003.

86. Buszynski, "ASEAN's New Challenges," 555–77; and Acharya, "Concert of Asia?" 84–90.

87. Khong, "Making Bricks without Straw," 296–99. See also Yahuda, *International Relations of the Asia-Pacific*, 274; Emmers, "Influence of the Balance of Power," 275–92; Khong, "ASEAN's Post-Ministerial Conference," 50–53; and Leifer, "ASEAN Regional Forum," 51–59.

88. Zakaria, "Culture Is Destiny," 122.

89. Simon, "President Bush," 72.

90. Interview with Bilahari Kausikan, Singapore, September 22, 2003.

91. See Office of the Press Secretary, "September 11, 2001." See also Capie, "Hegemon and a Hard Place," 233–34.

92. See "The Philippine Connection: Manila Is America's Natural Ally in the War against Terror," *Asian Wall Street Journal*, September 30, 2001; "Arroyo Defends U.S. Troops' Presence," *CNN Report*, January 17, 2002; and Banlaoi, "Role of Philippine-American Relations," 294–95.

93. "U.S. Troops Move to Guerrilla Stronghold," *CNN Report*, February 15, 2002; Novicio, "South China Sea Dispute," 51–52; and "Philippines Debates More U.S. Troops," *CNN Report*, January 11, 2002.

94. Rogers, "Beyond the Abu Sayyaf," 15.

95. See de Castro, "Revitalized Philippine-U.S. Security Relations," 167–68; Baker, China-Philippines Relations," 3–8; "RP Now Biggest U.S. Military Aid in East Asia," *Manila Standard*, March 6, 2004; Capie, "Hegemon and a Hard Place," 234; and Ross, "Balance of Power Politics," 391.

96. "Philippine Supreme Court Rules U.S. Visiting Forces Agreement Legal," *Philippine Inquirer*, March 3, 2010.

97. See Natalie Soh, "S'pore a Friend of the U.S., Not a Client State, Says PM," *Straits Times*, November 28, 2002. See also Goh, "Meeting the China Challenge," 25–26.

98. Lee, Speech to the U.S.-ASEAN Business Council.

99. Emmerson, "What Do the Blind-Sided See?" 11; Huxley, "Singapore's Strategic Outlook," 146; Ganesan, *Realism and Interdependence*, 52–53; and Ross, "Balance of Power Politics," 390–91.

100. Medeiros, "Strategic Hedging," 151; and Neher, *Southeast Asia*, 14.

101. Limaye, "Minding the Gaps," 85.

102. For a similar view, see Goh, "Meeting the China Challenge," 15, 19.

103. Mahathir, Speech at Opening Session.

104. Cited in Mak, "Malaysian Defense," 148. For a similar view, see Capie, "Hegemon and a Hard Place," 231–32. See also Razak, "U.S.-Malaysia Defense Cooperation."

105. *KOMPAS*, December 1, 1999, and October 26, 1999, cited in Sukma, "Indonesia and Regional Security," 83.

106. Limaye, "Minding the Gaps," 82; Sukma, "Indonesia and Regional Security," 84; Smith, "Reluctant Partner," 3; Capie, "Hegemon and a Hard Place," 224–30; Emmerson, "Whose Eleventh?" 118–21.

107. "U.S. Policy on Indonesian Military Hampers Bilateral Relations: Minister," *Xinhua News Agency*, July 21, 2003.

108. See Medeiros, "Strategic Hedging," 152; Ross, "Balance of Power Politics," 390; and "U.S. Warships Arrive for Exercise with Indonesian Navy," *Associated Press*, May 17, 2001.

109. Anwar, "Southeast Asian Perspective," 215.

110. Kershaw, "Partners in Realism," 46–47; Horton, "Brunei in 2004," 185; and Sulaiman, "Negara Brunei Darussalam," 78.

111. Storey and Thayer, "Cam Ranh Bay," 404–05; and Jane Perlez, "U.S. Competes with China for Vietnam's Allegiance," *New York Times*, June 19, 2006.

112. See Kang, "Getting Asia Wrong," 58; and Shambaugh, "China Engages Asia," 85–89.

113. ASEAN Secretariat, "ASEAN-China Strategic Partnership."

114. Storey, "China and Thailand," 4–5.

115. Greg Torode, "Beijing, Bangkok, and the Great Game," *South China Morning Post*, March 15, 2009.

116. Thayer, "China's International Security Cooperation Diplomacy," 9; and Jamaluddin Muhammad, "Malaysia-China Sign MOU on Defence Cooperation," *Bernama Daily Malaysian News*, September 2, 2005.

117. Thayer, "China's International Security Cooperation Diplomacy," 14–21 (providing a detailed account of Sino-ASEAN military cooperation between 2002 and 2006); and Kang, *China Rising*, 57–62.

118. "Indonesia to Seek to Enhance Economic, Defense Ties with China," *Jakarta Post*, March 20, 2010.

119. Un and Ledgerwood, "Cambodia in 2002," 117; and Chanda, "China and Cambodia," 2.

120. "Chinese Navy Ship Makes First Ever Visit to Cambodia," *Xinhua*, November 5, 2008.

121. "Laos Vows to Advance Bilateral Ties with China," *Xinhua News Agency*, March 20, 2010.

122. "Chinese Soldiers Nearly Done with Landmine Sweeping on Sino-Vietnamese Border," *BBC Monitoring Asia Pacific*, December 31, 2008.

123. Edward Wong, "Vietnam Quietly Seeks Partners against China in Island Feud," *International Herald Tribune*, February 6, 2010; Greg Torode, "Building Tension," *South China Morning Post*, January 26, 2010.

124. For a discussion of China's economic ties to Southeast Asia during the latter stages of the Cold War period, see Herschede, "Trade between China and ASEAN," 179–93.

125. Data from Asian Development Bank, *Asian Development Outlook*.

126. Ba, "China and ASEAN," 638–44. Bilateral deals have also been important. For example, in 2005 China signed trade and investment agreements with Indonesia worth $20 billion over the next fifteen to twenty years. See "Indonesia, China Sign $20 Billion Worth of Trade, Investment deals," *Xinhua Financial Network*, September 1, 2005. See also Shambaugh, "China Engages Asia," 65.

127. Data from Asian Development Bank, *Asian Development Outlook*.

128. Acharya, "Ideas, Identity, and Institution-Building," 342.

129. See Walt, *Origins of Alliances*, 148–53.

Chapter 4

1.   Weatherbee, *International Relations*, 2.

2.   See Ji, "Current Security Issues," 977–78; Connor, "Prospects for Stability," 32–35; and Battersby, "Border Politics," 474.

3.   See Snitwongse, "Soviet-Vietnamese Alliance," 57; Acharya, "New Regional Order," 17–27; Lau, "Challenge to ASEAN," 106; Wanandi, "Dimensions of Southeast Asian Security," 334–35; and Jackson, "Post-Colonial Rebellion," 3.

4.   Simon, "Parallel Tracks," 30–31.

5.   "Indonesia to Maintain Neutrality among Global Powers—Defense Minister," *Jakarta Post*, March 15, 2010.

6.   Suryadinata, *Indonesia's Foreign Policy*, 11–12; Leifer, "Indonesia and the Dilemmas of Engagement," 101; and Dupont, "Indonesia Defence Strategy," 277–78.

7.   Indonesian Department of Defence and Security, *Defending the Country*, vi–ix.

8.   Anwar, "Indonesia: Domestic Priorities," 477–78, 489–96.

9.   Cribb, "Unresolved Problems," 550–63.

10.   Sukma, "Recent Developments," 36–37, 41–42; Van der Kroef, "'Normalizing' Relations," 189–90; and Wanandi, "Politico-Security Dimensions," 772–73.

11.   Wanandi, "Conflict and Cooperation," 504.

12.   See "Mochtar Discusses PRC Ties, Cambodia Talks," *FBIS Asia-Pacific*, May 28, 1985, N1; Owen, "Economic and Social Change," 168; Wanandi, "Dimensions of Southeast Asian Security," 337; and Ji, "Current Security Issues," 986–89.

13.   Purdey, "Problemizing the Place of Victims," 605–22.

14.   Chin, "Reflections," 6; Leifer, "Indonesia and the Dilemmas of Engagement," 90; and Dupont, "Indonesia Defence Strategy," 285–90.

15.   Indonesian Department of Defence and Security, *The Policy*, 7–12.

16.   Simon, "ASEAN's Strategic Situation," 83.

17.   See "We Believe Hanoi: Murdani," *New Straits Times*, April 18, 1985, 1.

18.   *Asiaweek*, May 4, 1986, 39.

19.   See, e.g., Wanandi, "Conflict and Cooperation," 514–15; Wanandi, "Politico-Security Dimensions," 774–75; Suryadinata, *Indonesia's Foreign Policy*, 11–12; and Leifer, "Indonesia and the Dilemmas of Engagement," 89–90, 105–06.

20.   Emmers, "Regional Hegemonies," 645–49.

21.   Leifer, "Indonesia and the Dilemmas of Engagement," 87, 99.

22.   Interview of President Suharto, excerpted in *Agence France Presse*, August 14, 1996; and Lowry, "Indonesian Defence Policy," 12–13. For a contrary view, see Ravenhill, "Is China an Economic Threat," 653–74.

23.   Simon, "ASEAN's Strategic Situation," 79–80; and Suryadinata, *Indonesia's Foreign Policy*, 140–41.

24.   Emmerson, "Indonesia, Malaysia, Singapore," 39; and Vatikiotis, "Indonesia's Foreign Policy," 353–57.

25.   Indonesian Department of Defence and Security, *The Policy*, 1–12.

26.   Wiranto's response to question by the author, Ampro Business Club Address, "Indonesia in Transition," Singapore, February 25, 2004. See also Sukma, "Indonesia and Regional Security," 75.

27.   Malik, "Djakarta's Conference," 74.

28.   Interview with Barry Desker, Singapore, March 29, 2004. See also Wanandi, "Politico-Security Dimensions," 788.

29.   Cited in Sukma, "Indonesia and Regional Security," 75.

30.   Anwar, "Indonesia: Domestic Priorities," 496–97. See also Leifer, "Indonesia and the Dilemmas of Engagement," 97–98.

31.   Johnson and Um, "The United States and Asia," 10, excerpting from remarks by Reagan and Mokhtar in Bali on April 25, 1986.

32.   Smith, "Reluctant Partner," 4.

33.   "Foreign Power Made Me Quit, Says Suharto," *Straits Times*, Jan. 28, 1999.

34.   See, e.g., Marian Wilkinson, "Megawati Hits Out at U.S. for War on Terrorism," *Sydney Morning Herald*, September 25, 2003; Ron Hutcheson, "Bush Hears Muslims' Criticism in Indonesia," *Philadelphia Inquirer*, October 23, 2003; and Ron Hutcheson and Terence Hunt, "Tense Visit as Bush Cursed by Protesters," *Herald Sun* (Australia), November 21, 2006.

35.   Alatas, *Voice for a Just Peace*, 253.

36.   Wanandi, "Politico-Security Dimensions," 791.

37.   Emmerson, "Critical Terms," 21–22.

38. See Vatikiotis, "Indonesia's Foreign Policy," 356–57; MacIntyre, "Interpreting Indonesian Foreign Policy," 528–29; and Weinstein, *Indonesian Foreign Policy*, 189.

39. John E. Dougherty, "New Eurasian Alliance Seen Coming: Move Intended to Check U.S. Global Hegemony," *World Net Daily*, October 15, 1999. See also *South China Morning Post*, October 12, 1999.

40. Weinstein, *Indonesian Foreign Policy*, 161; and Huxley, "Insecurity in the ASEAN Region," 24–25.

41. Interview with Barry Desker, Singapore, March 29, 2004.

42. *Jakarta Post*, April 29, 1984.

43. *Indonesian Times*, December 17, 1979, cited in MacIntyre, "Interpreting Indonesian Foreign Policy," 517.

44. Interview with Barry Desker, Singapore, March 29, 2004.

45. See Frank Ching, "Malaysia Charts China Course: Kuala Lumpur Warms to Beijing as China's Policies Shift," *Far Eastern Economic Review*, February 23, 1995, excerpting from Mahathir's remarks at a Malaysia-China forum. See also Leong, "Malaysia and the People's Republic," 1112–13

46. *New Straits Times*, September 30, 1981.

47. *New Straits Times*, October 21, 1985.

48. *Straits Times*, August 23, 1981. See also Nathan, "Malaysia and the Soviet Union," 1066–67, 1070–71.

49. See Ghazali Shafie, "On Development," 17.

50. "Mahathir: Vietnam Won't Attack Us," *Bangkok Post*, August 15, 1981, 1. See also Wanandi, "Politico-Security Dimensions," 773–74; and Nordin Sopiee, "The ASEAN States Are Unruffled by the Soviet Giant," *International Herald Tribune,* May 3–4, 1986, 6.

51. See Acharya, "Malaysia's Response," 132–33; and "Malaysia: Preparing for Change," *Jane's Defence Weekly*, July 29, 1989, 159.

52. Acharya, *Quest for Identity*, 131; and Gallagher, "China's Illusory Threat," 170.

53. Nathan, "Malaysia and the Soviet Union," 1071–72.

54. Sodhy, "U.S.-Malaysian Relations," 379.

55. See Albar, Keynote Remarks.

56. Emmerson, "Critical Terms," 21.

57. Razak, Remarks.

58. Ghazali Shafie, "ASEAN's Response," 23.

59. See Michael Richardson, "ASEAN Split on Anti-Terror Tactics: Backing Regional Unity, Malaysia Questions U.S. Role in Philippines," *International Herald Tribune*, February. 4, 2002.

60. Mahathir, "Global Community Forum," cited in Mak, "Malaysian Defense and Security," 128.

61. Mahathir, "First ISIS National Conference," cited in Mak, "Malaysian Defense and Security," 129.

62. Acharya, *Quest for Identity*, 140; Alagappa, "Asian Practice of Security," 634; and Narine, "ASEAN and the Management," 210.

63. Mahathir and Ishihara, *Voice of Asia*, 19–21.

64. Roger Mitton, "The Man behind the Vision," *Asiaweek*, May 9, 1997. See also Acharya, "New Regional Order," 143.

65. Albar, Keynote Address at the U.S.-Malaysia Colloquium.

66. Rithauddeen, "Kampuchean Problem," 208.

67. "Mahathir: Vietnam Won't Attack Us," *Bangkok Post*, August 15, 1981, 1.

68. Wanandi, "Politico-Security Dimensions," 788; and Leifer, *ASEAN and the Security of South-East Asia*, 102–03, noting that other ASEAN officials harbored similar concerns.

69. Nathan, "Malaysia and the Soviet Union," 1066.

70. Acharya, *Quest for Identity*, 144–45, arguing that Malaysia is "steering a middle course somewhere between containment and engagement" of China.

71. Mak, "Malaysian Defence and Security," 130–44.

72. Mahathir Mohamad, "Much Confidence in Malaysia, Its Economic Management," *New Straits Times*, June 4, 1998, 10.

73. Sodhy, "U.S.-Malaysian Relations," 370.

74. Quoted in "Anti-Terrorism Centre opens in Kuala Lumpur," *Straits Times* (Singapore), July 2, 2003.

75. Albar, Keynote Remarks.

76. Interview with Khairy Jamaluddin, September 5, 2003. For a similar view, see Sodhy, "U.S.-Malaysian Relations," 376.

77. Kershaw, "Partners in Realism," 51.

78. Interview with Jatswan Sidhu, Kuala Lumpur, September 3, 2003; Emmers, *Cooperative Security*, 69–73; Singh, "Brunei in 1985," 169–70.

79. Ahmad, "Oil and Security," 183–85.

80. Kershaw, "Partners in Realism," 46–47.

81. Horton, "Brunei in 2004," 184.

82. Leifer, *Singapore's Foreign Policy*, 4, 15. See also Tan, "Singapore's Defense"; and Tow, "Southeast Asia," 441.

83. Cited in Leifer, "Indonesia and the Dilemmas of Engagement," 9.

84. "To Forestall Soviet Intimidation, U.S. Fleet Needed in Indian Ocean," *Straits Times*, February 2, 1982, 1, 7–11. See also Leifer, *Singapore's Foreign Policy*, 11–12; and Kwa, "Relating to the World," 113–22.

85. *Asiaweek*, March 28, 1980, 25.

86. Khong, "Singapore," 111–13; and Goh, "Singapore and the United States," 1–2.

87. Lee, Speech to Nixon Center.

88. Quoted in Bernstein and Munro, "Coming Conflict," 22–23.

89. See Doug Struck and Rajiv Chandrasekaran, "Nations Across asia Keep Watch on China," *Washington Post*, October 19, 2001.

90. See Fareed Zakaria, "Burgeoning China Can't Deny Its Past," *Detroit Free Press*, May 24, 2005.

91. See Baker, "China-Philippines Relations," 204.

92. Goh Chok Tong, "Will a Singapore Tribe Emerge?" *Straits Times*, May 6, 1999. Goh warned citizens not to "think that racial riots [will] never break out again in Singapore."

93. Goh, "Meeting the China Challenge," 14–15; and "Singapore and the United States," 1.

94. Ganesan, *Realism and Interdependence*, 118–19; and Acharya, "A New Regional Order," 66; and Goh, "Singapore and the United States," 4–5.

95. Lee, "We Want to Be Ourselves."

96. Lee, Speech to the U.S.-ASEAN Business Council.

97. Interview with Derek Da Cunha, Singapore, September 15, 2003.

98. Goh, Keynote Address.

99. Lee, Speech to the U.S.-ASEAN Business Council.

100. Goh, Remarks at the Signing.

101. Quoted in Chan and Haq, *S. Rajaratnam*, 493.

102. Khong, "Singapore," 119–20. See *Straits Times*, weekend edition, June 24, 1995; Lee, "ASEAN Must Balance," 416; and Tow, "Southeast Asia," 442–43.

103. Frank Ching, "Lee Kuan Yew on Hong Kong," *Far Eastern Economic Review*, November 11, 1999, excerpting from an interview with Lee.

104. Leifer, *Singapore's Foreign Policy*, 104–05.

105. Interview with Bilahari Kausikan, Singapore, September 22, 2003.

106. Khong, "Singapore," 112.

107. See Natalie Soh, "S'pore a Friend of the U.S., Not a Client State, Says PM," *Straits Times*, November 28, 2002. For a similar view of the basis for strong Singapore-U.S. cooperation, see Leifer, *Singapore's Foreign Policy*, 16.

108. Sue-Ann Chia, "Ties with U.S., China Not Zero-Sum Game: PM Lee," *Straits Times*, November 14, 2009.

109. Tan and Cohen, News Briefing.

110. See Jayakumar, Remarks in Parliament.

111. Interview with Naranyan Ganesan, Singapore, September 22, 2003.

112. *Straits Times*, July 26, 2001. See also Khong, "Singapore," 124.

113. Khong, "Singapore," 116–23.

114. Goh's remarks at a memorial service for victims of the September 11 attack, excerpted in "Singapore Stands with U.S. against Terrorism," *Straits Times*, September 24, 2001.

115. Goh Chok Tong, "Coping with the Terror Threat in S'pore," *Straits Times*, October 15, 2002.

116. Singaporean Ministry of Defence, *Fight against Terror*, 7–25.

117. Huxley, "Singapore in 2001," 164; and Natalie Soh, "S'pore a Friend of U.S., Not a Client State, Says PM," *Straits Times*, November 28, 2002.

118. Kausikan, "Asia's Different Standard," 36. See also Neher, *Southeast Asia*, 174.

119. Kivimäki, *U.S.-Indonesian Hegemonic Bargaining*, 2.

120. Goh, "Singapore and the United States," 4; and Goh, "Meeting the China Challenge," 25–26.

121. Interview with Bilahari Kausikan, Singapore, September 22, 2003.

122. Khong and Abdullah, "Security Co-operation in ASEAN," 135; and Leifer, *ASEAN and the Security*, 72.

123. *Straits Times*, November 26, 1975.

124. "For U.S., Still a 'Wide Reservoir of Good Will': President of Philippines Speaks His Mind," *U.S. News & World Report*, September 20, 1976.

125. Marcos, *Five Years*, 135–39; and "Manila Reviewing Status of U.S. Bases," *New York Times*, April 13, 1975, 19.

126. See, e.g., Brands, *Bound to Empire*, 284–85.

127. Henze, "U.S.-Philippine Economic Relations," 319–20, 336–37, citing an interview with former Foreign Minister Raul Manglapus. See also Simon, "Great Powers and Southeast Asia," 928; and Simon, "ASEAN's Strategic Situation," 90.

128. Marcos, *Five Years*, 142–43. See also Solidum, "Philippine Perceptions," 537–38.

129. Corning, "Philippine Bases," 19; Simon, "ASEAN's Strategic Situation," 90; and Storey, "Creeping Assertiveness," 102.

130. "Manila Reviewing Status of U.S. Bases," *New York Times*, April 13, 1975, 19; and Simon, "ASEAN's Strategic Situation," 77.

131. Ford, "Memorandum of Conversation," 2.

132. Van der Kroef, "Hanoi and ASEAN," 172.

133. Zagoria, "Soviet Policy and Prospects," 77; "Strategic Environment," 9.

134. Simon, "Great Powers and Southeast Asia," 928; and "Facing Up to Security," *Far Eastern Economic Review*, August 6, 1992.

135. Villegas, "Philippines in 1986," 201–02.

136. Corning, "Philippine Bases," 16–18.

137. Acharya, "New Regional Order," 17–18; and De Castro, "Triumph," 157.

138. *Philippine Daily Inquirer*, September 19, 1990.

139. Tow, "Southeast Asia," 445; Yahuda, *International Relations*, 144; and Leifer, "ASEAN Regional Forum," 19.

140. Neher, *Southeast Asia*, 106; Buszynski, "Realism, Institutionalism, and Philippine Security," 486–87; Storey, "Creeping Assertiveness," 102–03; and Simon, "ASEAN's Strategic Situation," 89–90.

141. Neher, *Southeast Asia*, 105.

142. De Castro, "Ghost," 976. See also Storey, "Creeping Assertiveness," 109–10.

143. Buszynski, "Realism, Institutionalism, and Philippine Security" 489.

144. Data from Asian Development Bank, *Asian Development Outlook*.

145. *Agence France Presse*, October 17, 1995.

146. Ramos's speech in Hawaii, October 17, 1995, excerpted in Nirmal Ghosh, "Integrating China into Region the Key to Stability, Says Ramos," *Straits Times*, October 18, 1995.

147. Philippine Department of National Defense, *In Defense of the Philippines*, chap. 1.

148. Philippine Department of National Defense, *In Defense of the Philippines*, chap. 1.

149. Quoted in Limaye, "Minding the Gaps," 84–85. See also De Castro, "Ghost," 977–81, describing the specific types of assistance provided.

150. See "Philippines Urges China, U.S. to Settle Row," *FBIS Asia-Pacific*, May 22, 2001.

151. Tow, "Southeast Asia," 447; and Capie, "Hegemon and a Hard Place," 235.

152. Hrvoje Hranjske, "U.S. Denies Troops Involved in Combat in Philippines," *Associated Press*, August 27, 2009.

153. "Philippine Supreme Court Rules U.S. Visiting Forces Agreement Legal," *Philippine Inquirer*, March 3, 2010.

154. De Castro, "Ghost," 982; and Storey, "Creeping Assertiveness," 111–12.

155. Tow, "Southeast Asia," 447–48.

156. See summary of American Enterprise Institute, "China in Asia."

157. Goldstein, "Balance of Power Politics," 193.

158. See Scalapino, "Political Influence of the USSR," 90; Evans, *A Short History*, 189–90; Simon, "Great Powers and Southeast Asia," 931–37; and Zagoria, "Soviet Policy and Prospects," 73.

159. Simon, "Parallel Tracks of Asian Multilaterialism," 21.

160. Ross, "Beijing as a Conservative Power," 35–40.

Chapter 5

1. See Liang, *Burma's Foreign Relations*, 67; Neher, *Southeast Asia*, 205; Steinberg, "Crisis in Burma," 46; and Malik, "Sino-Indian Rivalry," 139.

2. Convocation Address to Rangoon University, cited in Liang, *Burma's Foreign Relations*, 63.

3. See Haacke, "Myanmar's Foreign Policy," 19.

4. See Trager and Scully, "Third Congress;" "Burma in 1977."

5. Malik, "Burma's Role in Regional Security—Pawn or Pivot?" 130; and Haacke, "Myanmar's Foreign Policy," 25–26.

6. Steinberg, "Crisis in Burma," 47.

7. See Lee, "China's Expanding Maritime Ambitions," 553–54; Malik, "Burma's Role in Regional Security—Pawn or Pivot?" 111; Joshua Kurlantzick, "China's Influence Waxes as Washington's Wanes," *Washington Times*, December 4, 2000; James, "Myanmar's International Relations Strategy," 539–42; and Malik, "Sino-Indian Rivalry," 139–40.

8. Haacke, "Myanmar's Foreign Policy," 61–64; and Steinberg, "Crisis in Burma," 13–15.

9. Malik, "Burma's Role in Regional Security—Pawn or Pivot?," 110–11; Battersby, "Border Politics," 487; and Haacke, "Myanmar's Foreign Policy," 17–18.

10.   Steinberg, *Burma*, 292–93.

11.   See "Myanmar, Regional Security to Top ASEAN Meeting," *Straits Times* (Singapore), June 16, 2003.

12.   Nyunt, Keynote Address, cited in Steinberg, *Burma: The State of Myanmar*, 280.

13.   Message from the chairman of the State Peace and Development Council Senior General Than Shwe on the 79th Anniversary of National Day, Yangon, December 2, 1999, http://www.burmalibrary.org/reg.burma/archives/199912/msg00075.html. See also "Myanmar Regime Accuses NLD of Threatening National Security," *Agence France Presse*, September 4, 2000; Haacke, "Myanmar's Foreign Policy," 21–22; and "Myanmar Regime Accuses NLD of Threatening National Security," *Agence France Presse*, September 4, 2000.

14.   Than, "Myanmar: Preoccupation with Regime," 415.

15.   See "Myanmar Urges U.S. to Abandon Efforts to Destabilize It," *Xinhua News Agency*, January 28, 2004; and "Myanmar Accuses United States of Working to Destabilize Asia," *Agence France Presse*, January 28, 2004.

16.   Steinberg, *Burma*, 293, citing personal interviews with SPDC officials. On the move to Naypidaw, see "Diplomats Greet Move with Shock," *The Nation* (Thailand), November 8, 2005, 5A.

17.   Interview with Kyaw Yin Hlaing, Singapore, September 22, 2003.

18.   See Steinberg, "Crisis in Burma," 48–54; Steinberg, *Burma*, 225–30; and Michael Vatikiotis, "Burma: Border Bushfires," *Far Eastern Economic Review*, February 16, 1995.

19.   Steinberg, *Burma*, 238; Haacke, "Myanmar's Foreign Policy," 27–28; Michael Vatikiotis, "Burma: Border Bushfires," *Far Eastern Economic Review*, February 16, 1995; and James, "Myanmar's International Relations Strategy," 535–36.

20.   Than, "Myanmar and China," 189–90; Selth, "Burma," 224–27; and Haacke, "Myanmar's Foreign Policy," 9–10, 28.

21.   Interview with Sunait Chitintaranond, Bangkok, November 8, 2005, arguing that balancing its ties with the great powers has been a core element of modern Burmese security policy. See also Malik, "Burma's Role in Regional Security—Pawn or Pivot?" 113.

22.   "Myanmar and China: But Will the Flag Follow Trade?" *The Economist*, October 8, 1994, 35–36.

23.   Joshua Kurlantzick, "China's Chance," *Prospect Magazine* no. 108, March 17, 2005.

24.   Amer, "Sino-Vietnamese Normalization," 362; and Simon, "Davids and Goliaths," 311.

25.   See Emmers, "Regional Hegemonies," 645–49; Elliott, "Third Indochina Conflict," 4–5; and Kenny, *Shadow of the Dragon*, 21–50.

26.   Colbert, "Changing Relationships," 79.

27.   Snitwongse, "Soviet-Vietnamese Alliance," 48; and Singh, "Singapore's Perspectives," 64–68.

28.   *Tap Chi Cong San*, August 1982, cited in Pike, "Vietnam and China," 335–36. See also Horn, "Vietnam and Sino-Soviet Relations," 738.

29.   *Le Monde*, January 1, 1983, cited in Van der Kroef, "Kampuchean Problem," 269–70.

30.   Porter, "Vietnamese Policy," 69–71; and Horn, "Vietnam and Sino-Soviet Relations," 738, citing an article by Hoang Tung in *Partinaya Zhizn* (Moscow), no. 24, December 1984.

31.   On the nature of Soviet military and economic aid in the late 1970s and early 1980s, see Colbert, "Changing Relationships," 79; Thien, "Vietnam's New Economic Policy," 692–95; Donnell, "Vietnam 1979," 25–26; Simon, "Peking and Indochina," 403; Niehaus, "Vietnam in 1978," 87; and Pike, "USSR and Vietnam," 1164–66.

32.   Alagappa, "Soviet Policy," 329.

33.   "Moscow and Hanoi in a Bind," *Straits Times*, November 3, 1982, 17.

34.   Alagappa, "Soviet Policy," 331–32.

35. Scalapino, "Political Influence," 92.

36. Chanda, *Brother Enemy*, 322; and Elliott, "Vietnam: Tradition under Challenge," 135.

37. Zagoria and Simon, "Soviet Policy," 164. See also "Moscow and Hanoi in a Bind," *Straits Times*, November 3, 1982, 17; and Simon, "Superpowers in Southeast Asia," 73.

38. Zagoria and Simon, "Soviet Policy," 163–64.

39. Interview reprinted in H.D.S. Greenway, "View of the World from Vietnam," *Boston Globe*, November 15, 1982.

40. Zagoria and Simon, "Soviet Policy," 159.

41. Anderson, Memorandum to Ambassador Holdridge.

42. Duiker, "Vietnam in 1985," 107.

43. Simon, "Superpowers in Southeast Asia," 72.

44. Esterline, "Vietnam in 1987," 91.

45. Heder, "Kampuchean-Vietnamese Conflict," 57; and Jackson, "Cambodia 1978," 80.

46. Gordon, "Asian Angst," 57; Chang, "Vietnam and China," 138; and Amer, "Sino-Vietnamese Normalization," 362.

47. On Pham Van Dong, see "Seeking the West's Goodwill," *Far Eastern Economic Review*, May 18, 1979, 13. On Nguyen Co Thach, see H. D. S. Greenway, "View of the World from Vietnam," *Boston Globe*, November 15, 1982.

48. "Interview with SRV Foreign Minister Nguyen Co Thach," *FBIS Asia-Pacific*, December 22, 1983, K2.

49. "China-Vietnam: Fighting Likely to Escalate."

50. For a similar view, see Cima, "Vietnam in 1989," 88–89.

51. Bui Dinh Nguyen, "Military Region 9 Coordinates National Defense with the Economy," *Nhan Dan*, April 10, 1989, cited in Thayer, "Vietnam People's Army," 15.

52. Wheeler, *Thai-Vietnamese Relations*, 17; Leifer, "Indochina and ASEAN," 273; and Thayer, "Laos in 1998," 2.

53. Quoted in Porter, "Transformation," 7.

54. Meeting with Vietnamese officials, Institute of International Relations, Vietnamese Foreign Ministry, Hanoi, January 24, 2008. See also Giap, "Relationship with Great Powers."

55. Elliott, "Vietnam: Tradition under Challenge," 125–26.

56. Doan Khue, "Understanding the Resolution of the Third Plenum of the VCP Central Committee: Some Basic Issues Regarding the Party's Military Line in the New Stage," *Tap Chi Quoc Phong Toan Dan*, August 1992, 3–15, cited in Thayer, "Beyond Indochina," 21–22. See also Kenny, *Shadow of the Dragon*, 110.

57. See "Vietnam: Foreign Interference Poses Great Threat to Security," *Xinhua News Agency*, September 24, 1998.

58. See "Vietnam Party Warns U.S. Trade Pact Could be Trojan Horse," *Reuters*, November 29, 2001.

59. *Vietnam: Consolidating Peace, Securing the Homeland*, Hanoi: Ministry of National Defense, 1998, 13–14, cited in Wheeler, "Thai-Vietnamese Relations," 78.

60. Nayan Chanda, "Pulled Two Ways: It May Be Reaching Out to the West, but Vietnam Must Still Keep an Eye on China," *Far Eastern Economic Review*, August 29, 1999.

61. See, e.g., Nayan Chanda, "Friend or Foe: Hanoi Has Embarked on a Controversial Policy of Closer Ties with Its Oldest Enemy—China," *Far Eastern Economic Review*, June 22, 2000.

62. Goh, "Meeting the China Challenge," 19–23; Amer, "Assessing Sino-Vietnamese Relations," 321–23; and Pike, "Vietnam and China," 326–28.

63. See "Three Decades after Vietnam Warm, Visit by American Ship Signals New Military Ties," *Associated Press Wire*, November 19, 2003; Goh, "Meeting the China Challenge," 23;

and Jane Perlez, "U.S. Competes with China for Vietnam's Allegiance," *New York Times*, June 19, 2006. On the historical legacy, see also Storey, "Vietnam and the United States," 1–2; and Kenny, *Shadow of the Dragon*, 10–11.

64. "Journal Stresses Importance of Defense Work," *FBIS East Asia Service*, May 6, 1994 (italics in the original).

65. Interview with Dang Dinh Quy, Deputy Director, Institute of International Relations, Vietnamese Foreign Ministry, Hanoi, January 24, 2008.

66. Stuart-Fox, "National Defence," 220–21.

67. "Lao Party-Government Delegation in Cambodia," *FBIS Asia-Pacific*, December 18, 1975, A9.

68. *FBIS Asia-Pacific*, December 19, 1975.

69. Brown and Zasloff, "Laos 1978," 100. See also Nayan Chanda, "Acid Test Exposes Alliances," *Far Eastern Economic Review*, July 28, 1978, 26–28.

70. Simon, "Peking and Indochina," 405; and Stuart-Fox, *Laos: Politics, Economics, and Society*, 184.

71. *FBIS*, October 18, 1978, cited in Stuart-Fox, *Laos*, 186.

72. "President Souphanouvong Addresses Opening of Heroes Congress, *FBIS Asia-Pacific*, 9 April 1979, I2; Gunn, "Foreign Relations," 996; and Brown and Zasloff, "Laos 1979," 106.

73. "Kaysone Phomvihan Article for Tap Chi Cong San," *FBIS Asia-Pacific*, March 27, 1985, I1.

74. *Vietnam News Agency*, October 18, 1975, cited in Simon, "Peking and Indochina," 404–05. See also "Commentary Decries Missions to Find U.S. POWs," *FBIS Asia-Pacific*, April 8, 1983, I1.

75. Gunn, "Foreign Relations," 1005; and Ngaosyvathn, *Kith and Kin*, preface; Evans, *Politics of Ritual*, 179; and Abuza, "Laos," 162.

76. *Siam Rath* (Bangkok), February 23, 1988, cited in Ngaosyvathn, *Kith and Kin*, 2.

77. Ngaosyvathn, *Kith and Kin*, 1; and Viraphol, *Directions in Thai Foreign Policy*, 42–44.

78. *FBIS Asia-Pacific*, December 6, 1976, excerpting from a Kaysone Phomvihane article in the Soviet journal *Pravda*; and Stuart-Fox, *History of Laos*, 177–78, 199.

79. Gunn, "Foreign Relations," 1002, citing a Lao Embassy handout of Khamphay Boupha, "Letter dated 26 April 1979 from the Acting Minister for Foreign Affairs of the Lao People's Democratic Republic addressed to the Secretary-General (UN)," April 26, 1979.

80. Remarks by Lao Prime Minister Kaysone Phomvihane, Vientiane, December 2, 1985, *Asian Recorder*, January 22–25, 1986, cited in Joiner, "Laos in 1986," 104.

81. Stuart-Fox, *History of Laos*, 200; and Neher, *Southeast Asia*, 275–76.

82. Johnson, "Laos in 1991," 86; Thayer, "Beyond Indochina," 21–25; and Gunn, "Laos in 1990," 92.

83. Johnson, "Laos in 1992," 75 (citing an October 5 Politburo resolution).

84. Abuza, "Laos," 170–71.

85. Freeman, "Laos," 132.

86. Elliott, "Third Indochina Conflict," 5–6; and Pouvatchy, "Cambodian-Vietnamese Relations," 440.

87. Heder, "Kampuchean-Vietnamese Conflict," 35–40.

88. "After Victory: Pointers toward a Neutral Future," *Far Eastern Economic Review*, May 9, 1975, 20.

89. Kissinger, *Years of Renewal*, 559–64, citing *AP Report*, May 13, 1975.

90. "Sihanouk's Address to the UN General Assembly," *FBIS Asia-Pacific*, October 7, 1975.

91. *BBC Summary of World Broadcasts*, September 21, 1977, cited in Jackson, "Cambodia 1977," 83.

92. Porter, "Vietnamese Policy," 95–96. See also "Minutes on the Standing Committee's Visit to the Southwest Zone," August 20–24, 1975, Documentation Center of Cambodia Catalogue Number L01022 (01bbk).

93. Jackson, "Cambodia 1977," 82; and Morris, *Why Vietnam Invaded Cambodia.*

94. Jackson, "Cambodia 1978," 80; and Chanda, "China and Cambodia," 4.

95. Van der Kroef, "Cambodian-Vietnamese War," 93.

96. "Cambodia's Pol Pot Comments on SRV Coup Plots," *FBIS-PRC,* 29 September 1978, A22. See also Porter, "Vietnamese Policy," 93–94.

97. Niehaus, "Vietnam in 1978," 90.

98. *Le Monde,* July 26, 1983, cited in Pouvatchy, "Cambodian-Vietnamese Relations," 449.

99. Pouvatchy, "Cambodian-Vietnamese Relations," 449–50.

100. Shawcross, "Cambodia's New Deal," 47–50.

101. Royal Government of Cambodia, *Defending the Kingdom (2000),* 11.

102. Royal Government of Cambodia, *Strategic Review,* 7–9; and Royal Government of Cambodia, *Defending the Kingdom (2006),* 15–19.

103. Hun Sen's Remarks at a News Conference, May 3, 1996, cited in Öjendal and Antlöv, "Asian Values," 533.

104. 1993 Cambodian Constitution, art. 53.

105. Chanda, "China and Cambodia," 8.

106. Un and Ledgerwood, "Cambodia in 2001," 103.

107. See Jane Perlez, "China Competes with West in Aid to Its Neighbors," *New York Times,* September 18, 2006, A2. By 2002, China emerged as Cambodia's second largest aid donor, after Japan. See Chanda, "China and Cambodia," 7.

108. See Julio Jeldres, "China-Cambodia: More Than Just Friends?" *Asia Times Online,* September 16, 2003.

109. Sim Chi Yin, "Cambodia Welcomes New Best Friend: China," *Straits Times* (Singapore), June 21, 2009.

110. Perlez, "China Competes with West," A2.

111. See "Southern Hospitality: The U.S. and China Are Once Again Vying for Influence in Cambodia," *Far Eastern Economic Review,* May 24, 2001.

112. Data from Asian Development Bank, *Asian Development Outlook.*

113. Wattanayagorn, "Thailand," 436; and Haacke, *ASEAN's Diplomatic and Security Culture,* 83–84.

114. See Wattanayagorn, "Thailand," 438–39; Liang, *Burma's Foreign Relations,* 97–101; and Buszynski, "Thailand and Myanmar," 292–99.

115. Polomka, "ASEAN Perspectives on China," 89; and Battersby, "Border Politics," 474.

116. Paribatra, "Challenge of Co-existence," 8.

117. Yahuda, *International Relations,* 34; and Buszynski, "Thailand: The Erosion," 1037.

118. Paribatra, "Challenge of Co-existence," 6.

119. Snitwongse, "Thai Government Responses," 259–60.

120. Wanandi, "Politico-Security Dimensions," 782–83.

121. Acharya, *Quest for Identity,* 70; and Yahuda, *International Relations,* 90.

122. "Thai Aide Calls U.S. Immoral," *Washington Post,* May 3, 1975, A1.

123. Paribatra, "Thailand," 105.

124. "Memorandum of Conversation: President Ford and Prime Minister Lee Kuan Yew of Singapore, May 8, 1975," NSC Meeting Memoranda, Spring 1975, Gerald R. Ford Presidential Library, 5–6.

125. See "Threat to Relations; Thailand Reports Withdrawal of U.S. Marines after Protest," *New York Times,* May 15, 1975, A1.

126. Whiting, "ASEAN Eyes China," 315; and Teo, "New Omnidirectional Overtures," 747.

127. Neher, "Post-Cold War Security Issues," 154.

128. Paribatra, "Challenge of Co-existence," 36–37.

129. See "Thanat Warns: Beware the Tiger," *Bangkok Post,* February 9, 1982, 9.

130. Wanandi, "Dimensions of Southeast Asian Security," 340–41.

131. Duncanson, "Sino-Soviet Rivalry," 375–77.

132. Simon, "Great Powers," 923.

133. John McBeth, "Thailand's Push to Re-Arm," *Far Eastern Economic Review,* 19 October 1979, 28–29. See also Niksch, "Thailand in 1980," 228.

134. Theeravit and Brown, "Introduction," vi.

135. Simon, "Great Powers," 923–24.

136. Paribatra, "Challenge of Co-existence," 6–7.

137. Viraphol, "Thai-American Relations," 142–48; and Teo, "New Omnidirectional Overtures," 748.

138. Teo, "New Omnidirectional Overtures," 756–57; and Simon, "ASEAN's Strategic Situation," 77.

139. Tilman, "Enemy Beyond," 32, citing the author's personal interview.

140. Emmers, *Cooperative Security,* 99–100; Simon, "Davids and Goliaths," 310; and Teo, "New Omnidirectional Overtures," 756.

141. Viraphol, "Thailand's Perspectives," 23; and Teo, "New Omnidirectional Overtures," 755.

142. Simon, "Two Southeast Asias," 523.

143. Interview with Suchit Bunbongkarn, Bangkok, November 8, 2005.

144. Paribatra, "Challenge of Co-existence," 24–25.

145. Cited in Paribatra, "Challenge of Co-existence," 24. See also "Unlikely Alliance Offers Security," *Bangkok Post,* February 2, 1981, 4; and Tongdhammachart et al., *Thai Elite's National Security Perspectives.*

146. Teo, "New Omnidirectional Overtures," 755–56; Samudavanija and Paribatra, "Development for Security," 202–03; and Paribatra, "Challenge of Co-existence," 43–44.

147. Buszynski, "Thailand: The Erosion," 1039.

148. Ibid., 1052.

149. See Dupont, "Non-Traditional Threats," 93–105; and Neher, *Southeast Asia,* 70.

150. Simon, "Asian Armed Forces," 14–15.

151. Stubbs, "Subregional Security Cooperation," 398, 401; and Thayer, "Beyond Indochina," 38–41.

152. "Thais Need to Remain Ever Vigilant," *Bangkok Post,* January 7, 2000. See also Bertil Lintner, "Natural Allies: Thailand's Neighbours Forge Closer Bonds," *Far Eastern Economic Review,* April 18, 1996, 23.

153. Bertil Lintner and Rodney Tasker, "Border Bravado," *Far Eastern Economic Review,* March 8, 2001.

154. Surath Jinakul, "Dangerous Escalations," *Bangkok Post,* May 20, 2001; "Opposing Positions on Burma Conflict," *Bangkok Post,* February 27, 2001; and Saritdet Marukatat and Wassana Nannuam, "Burma Is Given Topmost Priority," *Bangkok Post,* August 30, 2000.

155. Chambers, "U.S.-Thai Relations," 462.

156. Simon and Ellings, "Postscript," 221–26.

157. Chanlett-Avery, "Thailand," 9; and interview with Panitan Wattanayagorn, former senior advisor to the Thai government and current secretary-general for the deputy prime minister and acting government spokesman, Bangkok, November 4, 2005.

158. Interview with Sek Wannamethee, director of policy planning, Thai Ministry of Foreign Affairs, Bangkok, January 14, 2008; and interview with Pranee Thiparat, director of the Thai Institute of Security and International Studies, Bangkok, November 4, 2005.

159. Roy, "Southeast Asia and China," 313.

160. Thai Ministry of Defense, *Defense of Thailand 1994*.

161. Wheeler, "Thai-Vietnamese Relations," 69, citing an interview with an official at the Thai embassy in Hanoi.

162. James, "Myanmar's International Relations Strategy," 533.

163. Interview with Sek Wannamethee, director of policy planning, Thai Ministry of Foreign Affairs, Bangkok, January 14, 2008.

164. Tow, "Southeast Asia," 452–53.

165. *The Nation* (Thailand), September 15, 2001.

166. Interview with Panitan Wattanayagorn, former senior advisor to the Thai government and current secretary-general for the deputy prime minister and acting government spokesman, Bangkok, November 4, 2005.

167. Dosch, *Changing Dynamics*, 187–88.

Chapter 6

1. See Michael Richardson, "Nonaligned Nations Seeking to Big-Power Control of the UN," *International Herald Tribune*, September 2, 1992, 2.

2. Acharya, "New Regional Order," 29–30.

3. See, e.g., "Southeast Asian Antiterror Centre Opens in Malaysia," *Japan Economic Newswire*, July 1, 2003.

4. Acharya, "Malaysia's Response," 143–47; and Acharya, "Will Asia's Past," 153 and note 7.

5. Lau, "ASEAN and the Cambodian Problem," 558; Zagoria, "Strategic Environment," 9–10; and Simon, "Davids and Goliaths," 307.

6. Leifer, "Chinese Economic Reform," 56–57.

7. Mark Valencia, "Why the U.S. Is Back in Asia for Keeps," *Straits Times*, January 28, 2010.

8. Simon, "ASEAN's Strategic Situation," 80–81.

9. Snitwongse, "Strategic Outlook," 137.

10. Limaye, "Minding the Gaps," 74–79. See also David E. Sanger, "Asian Countries, in Shift, Weigh Defense Forum," *New York Times*, May 23, 1993, A16.

11. Wanandi, "ASEAN's China Strategy;" Acharya, "Association of Southeast Asian Nations," 172; and Leifer, "ASEAN Regional Forum," 53.

12. Cited in Snitwongse, "Strategic Outlook," 126–27.

13. "Bashir Wants Anti-Terror Force 'Eradicated,'" *ABC News Report*, June 27, 2007.

14. Acharya, "New Regional Order," 10–11.

15. See generally Kurlantzik, *Charm Offensive*.

16. See Chambers, "U.S.-Thai Relations," 466.

17. Caballero-Anthony, "Challenging Change," 193–204; Caballero-Anthony et al., *Non-Traditional Security*, chaps. 1, 3–5, 10–11.

18. See Herschede, "Trade between China and ASEAN," 179–93.

19. Leifer, "ASEAN Regional Forum," 18.

20. See Jane Perlez, "China Competes with West in Aid to Its Neighbors," *New York Times*, September 18, 2006.

21. Ba, "China and ASEAN," 638–44; and "Indonesia, China Sign $20 Billion Worth of Trade, Investment Deals," *Xinhua Financial Network*, September 1, 2005. Data from Asian Development Bank, *Asian Development Outlook 2008*.

22. Chung, "Southeast Asia-China Relations," 35.

23. Chin, "Reflections," 9.

24. Acharya, *Constructing a Security Community*, 143.

25. Narine, "ASEAN and the Management," 195.

26. Simon, "ASEAN's Strategic Situation," 88–89; and Sukma, "Indonesia's Bebas-Aktif Foreign Policy," 231. See also Khong, "ASEAN's Post-Ministerial Conference," 51.

27. Acharya, "Will Asia's Past," 150.

28. See, e.g., Foot, "China in the ASEAN," 427–31, 435–39; Ba, "Who's Socializing Whom?"; and Goh, "Great Powers."

29. See Deutsch, "Security Communities." On ASEAN's effort to develop into a robust security community, see Emmers, *Cooperative Security*, 27–30, 122–23; Kuhonta, "Walking a Tightrope," 341–43; and Narine, "ASEAN and the Management," 201–13.

30. See Goh, "Meeting the China Challenge," 2–5; and Foot, "Chinese Strategies," 88.

31. Khong, "Southeast Asia's Post-Cold War Strategy;" "Coping with Uncertainty."

32. Leifer, "Indochina and ASEAN," 275–76.

33. See Stuart-Fox, "Southeast Asia and China," 118–31.

34. "The New Concepts of Security," address before the Temasek Society, July 28, 1993, reprinted in Alatas, *Voice for a Just Peace*, 96–108.

35. Reiter, "Learning, Realism, and Alliances."

36. Friedberg, "Ripe for Rivalry"; "Will Europe's Past"; and "Struggle for Mastery," 17–26.

37. Brzezinski and Mearsheimer, "Clash of the Titans." See also Mearsheimer, "The Future," 46–61; and Hoge, "Global Power Shift," 5.

38. Ross, "Balance of Power Politics," 357–65. See also Khoo and Smith, "China Engages Asia?" 200–03.

39. Brzezinski and Mearsheimer, "Clash of the Titans."

40. Ross, "Geography of the Peace," 101–08.

41. Ross, "Balance of Power Politics," 358.

42. Quoted in Christian Caryl, "Asia's Dangerous Divide," *Newsweek*, September 10, 2007.

43. Shambaugh, "China Engages Asia," 67–99.

44. Kang, "Getting Asia Wrong," 58–85.

45. Stuart-Fox, "Southeast Asia and China," 131–36.

46. Chung, "Southeast Asia-China Relations," 50–51.

47. Christofferson, "Role of East Asia," 380.

48. Tow, "Southeast Asia," 436.

49. Cited in Huxley, "Insecurity in the ASEAN," 25.

50. See, for example, Ignatius Low, "DPM Lee – U.S. Must continue Key S-E Asia Role," *Straits Times*, November 13, 2002.

51. Quoted in Limaye, "Minding the Gaps," 84.

52. Mueller, "Patterns of Alliance," 41–43.

53. Foot, "Pacific Asia," 234.

54. See Scott, "Patron-Client Politics," 411–25; and Handel, *Weak States*, 30–46, 129–48.

55. Chen, *Strategic Triangle*, 3.

56. As Leifer writes, ASEAN-6 states have sought to find the political center of gravity among regional actors. "ASEAN Regional Forum," 47.

57. See Sarah Abrams, "Philippines' Ramos Stresses Cooperation for Asian Countries," *Kennedy School of Government Press Release*, April 27, 2001.

58. Goh, "Great Powers," 121; and Acharya, "Will Asia's Past" 153.

59.   Ciorciari, "Balance of Great-Power Influence," 165–91 (providing a review of recent literature on the subject and an assessment of the empirical picture).

60.   Leifer, "ASEAN Regional Forum," 57–58. See also Haacke, "Michael Leifer," 46–47, 52–54.

61.   See Khong, "Making Bricks without Straw," 296–98.

Conclusion

1.   Menon, *End of Alliances*, chap. 1; "End of Alliances," 1–16.

2.   Miller, "International System," 261.

3.   See David R. Sands, "Iran Hits Bush Trip as Unwelcome," *Washington Times,* January 7, 2008, A16; and Borzou Daragahi, "Arabs Unmoved by Bush Visit," *Los Angeles Times*, January 19, 2008, A3.

4.   Cohen, "Conclusion," 203–04.

5.   Lake, "Escape from the State," 50–56.

6.   See Bull, *Anarchical Society*, 214–16.

7.   Art, *Grand Strategy for America*, 145.

8.   Parag Khanna, "Waving Goodbye to Hegemony," *New York Times Magazine*, January 27, 2008, 34–40.

Glossary

Balikatan: "shoulder-to-shoulder," the name for annual U.S.-Philippine military exercises

Ban phi muang nong: a relationship between older and younger siblings, sometimes used by Thais to describe relations with Laos

Barrios: local administrative units in the Philippines

Bebas-aktif: "independent and active," referring to the dual goals of Indonesian foreign policy in the postcolonial period

Bumiputera: indigenous people of the Malay archipelago

Doc lap: "independence" in Vietnamese.

Doi Moi: "opening," Vietnamese policy akin to glasnost in the Soviet Union and introduced in 1986

Dwifungsi: "dual function," referring to the long-standing mixture of political and military roles of the Indonesian armed forces

Glasnost: "opening" in Soviet policy under Gorbachev after 1985

Golkar: abbreviation of *golongan karya* ("functional group"), the military-led party set up by Suharto

Ketahanan: "resilience" in Indonesian

Konfrontasii: "confrontation" in Indonesian foreign policy with its regional neighbors between 1965 and 1967

Musjawarah-mufakat: "consultation and consensus," referring to a style of consensus-building diplomacy in ASEAN

Paukphaw: "brotherly," referring to Sino-Myanmar ties

Perestroika: "reconstruction" of the Soviet system under Gorbachev

Suvannaphum: "golden land," suggesting the goal of a prosperous economic community in mainland Southeast Asia

Tatmadaw: armed forces of the state of Myanmar

Viet Minh: "League for the Independence of Vietnam," the principal communist insurgents during the Vietnam War

Wawasan-nusantara: "archipelagic outlook," referring to Indonesia's priority on stability across its vast island chain

Bibliography

Abuza, Zachary. "Laos: Maintaining Power in a Highly Charged Region." In *Small States in World Politics: Explaining Foreign Policy Behavior*, edited by Jeanne A. K. Hey. Boulder, CO: Lynne Rienner, 2003.

Acharya, Amitav. "The Association of Southeast Asian Nations: 'Security Community' or 'Defence Community?'" *Pacific Affairs* 64, no. 2 (1991): 159–78.

———. "A New Regional Order in South-East Asia: ASEAN in the Post-Cold War Era." *Adelphi Paper* 279. London: Institute for International and Strategic Studies, 1993.

———. "Ideas, Identity, and Institution-Building: From the 'ASEAN Way' to the 'Asia-Pacific Way?'" *Pacific Review* 10, no. 3 (1997): 319–46.

———. "Malaysia's Response to China's Rise." In *Engaging China*, edited by Alastair Iain Johnston and Robert S. Ross. London: Routledge, 1999.

———. "A Concert of Asia?" *Survival* 41, no. 3 (1999): 84–101.

———. *The Quest for Identity: International Relations of Southeast Asia.* Singapore: Oxford University Press, 2000.

———. *Constructing a Security Community in Southeast Asia: ASEAN and the Problem of Regional Order.* London/New York: Routledge, 2001.

———. "Will Asia's Past Be Its Future?" *International Security* 28, no. 3 (2003): 149–64.

Ahmad, Hamzah. "Oil and Security in Brunei." *Contemporary Southeast Asia* 2, no. 2 (1980): 182–91.

Alagappa, Muthiah. "Soviet Policy in Southeast Asia: Towards Constructive Engagement." *Pacific Affairs* 63, no. 3 (1990): 321–50.

———. "Regional Arrangements and International Security in Southeast Asia: Going beyond Zopfan." *Contemporary Southeast Asia* 12, no. 4 (1991): 269–305.

———. "Asian Practice of Security: Key Features and Explanations." In *Asian Security Practice*, edited by Muthiah Alagappa. Stanford, CA: Stanford University Press, 1998.

Alatas, Ali. *A Voice for a Just Peace: A Collection of Speeches.* Singapore: Institute of Southeast Asian Studies, 2001.

Albar, Dato Seri Syed Hamid. Keynote Remarks at U.S.-Malaysia Colloquium on "Malaysia–U.S. Relations: Promoting Understanding and Co-operation," Washington, DC, September 26, 2005.

Allison, Roy. "The Military and Political Security Landscape in Russia and the South." In *Russia, the Caucasus, and Central Asia: The 21st Century Security Environment*, edited by Rajan Menon, Yuri E. Federov, and Ghia Nodia. Armonk, NY: M. E. Sharpe, 1999.

Altfeld, Michael F. "The Decision to Ally: A Theory and Test." *Western Political Quarterly* 37, no. 4 (1984): 523–44.

Amer, Ramses. "Sino-Vietnamese Normalization in Light of the Crisis of the Late 1970s." *Pacific Affairs* 67, no. 3 (1994): 357–83.

———. "Assessing Sino-Vietnamese Relations through the Management of Contentious Issues." *Contemporary Southeast Asia* 26, no. 2 (2004): 320–45.

287

American Enterprise Institute. "China in Asia: Chinese Influence, Asian Strategies, U.S. Policy Responses." *China in Asia Seminar Series.* Washington, DC: American Enterprise Institute and National Defense University, February 23, 2006.

Anderson, L. Desaix. Memorandum to Ambassador Holdridge, August 9, 1982. Richard Childress files, box 92402, folder "Vietnam 1983–1984," 2 of 3. Simi Valley, CA: Ronald Reagan Presidential Library, 1982.

Ang, Cheng Guan. "Vietnam: Another Milestone and the Country Plods On." *Southeast Asian Affairs 2002.* Singapore: Institute for Southeast Asian Studies, 2002.

Anwar, Dewi Fortuna. "Indonesia: Domestic Priorities Define National Security." In *Asian Security Practice: Material and Ideational Influences,* edited by Muthiah Alagappa. Stanford, CA: Stanford University Press, 1998.

———. "Indonesia: Ketahanan Nasional, Wawasan Nusantara, Hankamrata." In *Strategic Cultures in the Asia-Pacific Region,* edited by Ken Booth and Russell Trood. Basingstoke: Macmillan, 1999.

———. "A Southeast Asian Perspective." *Australian Journal of International Affairs* 55, no. 2 (2001): 213–23.

Arreguín-Toft, Ivan. "How the Weak Win Wars: A Theory of Asymmetric Conflict." *International Security* 26, no. 1 (2001): 93–128.

Art, Robert J. *A Grand Strategy for America.* Ithaca, NY: Cornell University Press, 2003.

———. "Europe Hedges Its Security Bets." In *Balance of Power Revisited: Theory and Practice in the 21st Century,* edited by T.V. Paul, James J. Wirtz, and Michel Fortmann. Stanford, CA: Stanford University Press, 2004.

ASEAN Secretariat. "Plan of Action to Implement the Joint Declaration on ASEAN-China Strategic Partnership for Peace and Prosperity," October 7, 2003. http://www.aseansec .org/16805.htm (accessed February 16, 2010).

Asian Development Bank. *Asian Development Outlook 2008: Key Indicators.* Manila: Asian Development Bank, 2008.

Atkins, G. Pope. *Latin America in the International Political System,* 3rd ed. Boulder, CO: Westview, 1995.

Axelrod, Robert, and Robert E. Keohane. "Achieving Cooperation under Anarchy: Strategies and Institutions." *World Politics* 38, no. 1 (1985): 226–54.

Ayoob, Mohammad. "The Security Problematic of the Third World." *World Politics* 43, no. 2 (1991): 257–83.

Aziz, Tariq. "The Post-Cold War Era: 'Facts and Prospects.'" In *After the Cold War,* edited by Keith Philip Lepor. Austin: University of Texas Press, 1997.

Ba, Alice D. "China and ASEAN: Renavigating Relations for a 21st-Century Asia." *Asian Survey* 43, no. 4 (2003): 622–47.

———. "Who's Socializing Whom? Complex Engagement in Sino-ASEAN Relations." *Pacific Review* 19, no. 2 (2006): 157–79.

Badgley, John. "Myanmar in 1993: A Watershed Year." *Asian Survey* 34, no. 2 (1994): 153–59.

Baker, Carl. "China-Philippines Relations: Cautious Cooperation." *Asia-Pacific Center Special Assessment.* Honolulu: Asia-Pacific Center for Security Studies, 2004.

Banlaoi, Rommel C. "The Role of Philippine-American Relations in the Global Campaign against Terrorism: Implications for Regional Security." *Contemporary Southeast Asia* 24, no. 2 (2002): 278–96.

Barnds, William J. "Political and Security Relations." In *Crisis in the Philippines,* edited by John Bresnan. Princeton, NJ: Princeton University Press, 1986.

Barnett, Michael N. "Alliances and Identity in the Middle East." In *The Culture of National*

Security: Norms and Identity in World Politics, edited by Peter Katzenstein. New York: Columbia University Press, 1996.

Barnett, Michael N., and Jack S. Levy. "Domestic Sources of Alliances and Alignments: The Case of Egypt, 1962–73." *International Organization* 45, no. 3 (1991): 369–95.

Battersby, Paul. "Border Politics and the Broader Politics of Thailand's International Relations in the 1990s: From Communism to Capitalism." *Pacific Affairs* 71, no. 4 (1998/99): 473–88.

Bedlington, Stanley S. "Laos in 1980: The Portents are Ominous." *Asian Survey* 21, no. 1 (1981): 102–11.

———. "Laos in 1981: Small Pawn on a Larger Board." *Asian Survey* 22, no. 1 (1982): 88–98.

Bennett, D. Scott. "Testing Alternative Models of Alliance Duration, 1816–1984." *American Journal of Political Science* 41, no. 3 (1997): 846–78.

Bercovitch, Jacob. "Superpowers and Client States: Analyzing Relations and Patterns of Influence." In *Superpowers and Client States in the Middle East: The Imbalance of Influence*, edited by Moshe Efrat and Jacob Bercovitch. London: Routledge, 1991.

Bernstein, Richard, and Ross H. Munro. "The Coming Conflict with America." *Foreign Affairs* 76, no. 2 (1997): 18–32.

Bessho, Koro. "Identities and Security in East Asia." *Adelphi Paper* 325. London: International Institute for Strategic Studies, 1999.

Bhutto, Benazir. "Pakistan's Foreign Policy: Challenges and Responses in the Post-Cold War Era." In *After the Cold War*, edited by Keith Philip Lepor. Austin: University of Texas Press, 1997.

Blaiser, Cole. "Security: The Extracontinental Dimension." In *Latin America in the 1980s: Contending Perspectives on a Decade of Crisis*, edited by Kevin J. Middlebrook and Carlos Rico. Pittsburgh: University of Pittsburgh Press, 1986.

Bourdet, Yves. "Laos in 1995: Reform Policy, Out of Breath?" *Asian Survey* 36, no. 1 (1996): 89–94.

———. "Laos in 1996: Please Don't Rush!" *Asian Survey* 37, no. 1 (1997): 72–78.

———. "Laos in 2000: The Economics of Political Immobilism." *Asian Survey* 41, no. 1 (2001): 164–70.

———. "Laos in 2001: Political Introversion and Economic Respite." *Asian Survey* 42, no. 1 (2002): 107–14.

Brand, Laurie A. "Economics and Shifting Alliances: Jordan's Relations with Syria and Iraq, 1975–1981." *International Journal of Middle East Studies* 26, no. 3 (1994): 393–413.

Brands, H. W. *Bound to Empire: The United States and the Philippines*. New York: Oxford University Press, 1992.

Brooks, Stephen G., and William C. Wohlforth. "Hard Times for Soft Balancing." *International Security* 30, no. 1 (2005): 72–108.

Brown, MacAlister, and Joseph J. Zasloff. "Laos 1975: People's Democratic Revolution—Lao Style." *Asian Survey* 16, no. 2 (1976): 193–99.

———. "Laos 1976: Faltering First Steps toward Socialism." *Asian Survey* 17, no. 2 (1977): 107–15.

———. "Laos 1977: The Realities of Independence." *Asian Survey* 18, no. 2 (1978): 164–74.

———. "Laos 1978: The Ebb and Flow of Adversity." *Asian Survey* 19, no. 2 (1979): 95–103.

———. "Laos 1979: Caught in Vietnam's Wake." *Asian Survey* 20, no. 2 (1980): 103–11.

Brzezinski, Zbigniew, and John J. Mearsheimer. "Clash of the Titans." *Foreign Policy* no. 146 (January-February 2005).

Buchan, Alastair. "Problems of an Alliance Policy: An Essay in Hindsight." In *The Theory and Practice of War*, edited by Michael Howard. Bloomington: Indiana University Press, 1965.

Bull, Hedley. *The Anarchical Society*. London: Macmillan, 1977.

Burchett, Wilfred. *The China-Cambodia-Vietnam Triangle*. London: Zed Press, 1981.

Burns, William J. *Economic Aid and American Policy toward Egypt, 1955–1981*. Albany: State University of New York Press.

Bush, George W. Address to Joint Session of Congress and the American People, United States Capitol, Washington, DC, September 20, 2001, http://georgewbush-whitehouse.archives .gov/news/releases/2001/09/20010920-8.html.

Busse, Nikolas. "Constructivism and Southeast Asian Security." *Pacific Review* 12, no. 1 (1999): 39–60.

Buszynski, Leszek. "Thailand: The Erosion of a Balanced Foreign Policy." *Asian Survey* 22, no. 11 (1982): 1037–55.

———. "New Aspirations and Old Constraints in Thailand's Foreign Policy." *Asian Survey* 29, no. 11 (1989): 1057–72.

———. "ASEAN's New Challenges." *Pacific Affairs* 70, no. 4 (1997/98): 555–77.

———. "Thailand and Myanmar: the Perils of 'Constructive Engagement.'" *Pacific Review* 11, no. 2 (1998): 290–305.

———. "Realism, Institutionalism, and Philippine Security." *Asian Survey* 42, no. 3 (2002): 483–501.

Buzan, Barry. "Civilizational *Realpolitik* as the New World Order?" *Survival* 39, no. 1 (1997): 180–83.

Caballero-Anthony, Mely. "Challenging Change: Nontraditional Security, Democracy, and Regionalism." In *Hard Choices: Security, Democracy, and Regionalism in Southeast Asia*, edited by Donald K. Emmerson. Stanford, CA: Stanford University Press, 2008.

Caballero-Anthony, Mely, Ralf Emmers, and Amitav Acharya, eds. *Non-Traditional Security in Asia: Dilemmas in Securitization*. London: Ashgate, 2006.

Capie, David. "Between a Hegemon and a Hard Place: The 'War on Terror' and Southeast Asian-U.S. Relations." *Pacific Review* 17, no. 2 (2004): 223–48.

Carr, Edmund Hallett. *The Twenty Years' Crisis, 1919–1939*, reissued ed. Basingstoke: Palgrave, 2001.

Cassidy, Robert M. "Why Great Powers Fight Small Wars Badly." *Military Review* no. 82 (Sept.-Oct. 2000): 41–53.

Cha, Victor D. "The Ideational Dimension of America's Alliances in Asia." In *Reassessing Security Cooperation in the Asia-Pacific*, edited by Evelyn Goh and Amitav Acharya. Cambridge, MA: MIT Press, 2007.

Chambers, Paul. "U.S.-Thai Relations after 9/11: A New Era in Cooperation?" *Contemporary Southeast Asia* 26, no. 3 (2004): 460–79.

Chan, Heng Chee, and Obaid Ul Haq, eds. *S. Rajaratnam: The Prophetic and the Political*. Singapore: Graham Brash, 1987.

Chanda, Nayan. *Brother Enemy: The War after the War*. San Diego, CA: Harcourt Brace Jovanovich, 1986.

———. "China and Cambodia: In the Mirror of History." *Asia-Pacific Review* 9, no. 2 (2002): 1–11.

Chandler, David P. *A History of Cambodia*, 2nd ed. Boulder, CO: Westview, 1996.

Chang, C. Y. "The Sino-Vietnam Rift: Political Impact on China's Relations with Southeast Asia." *Contemporary Southeast Asia* 4, no. 4 (1983): 538–64.

Chang, Pao-Min. "Vietnam and China: New Opportunities and New Challenges." *Contemporary Southeast Asia* 19, no. 2 (1997): 136–51.

Chanlett-Avery, Emma. "Thailand: Background and U.S. Relations." *CRS Report for Congress*, Washington, DC: The Library of Congress, 2005.

Chen, Min. *The Strategic Triangle and Regional Conflicts: Lessons from the Indochina Wars.* Boulder, CO: Lynne Rienner, 1992.

Cheng, Joseph Y. S. "Sino–ASEAN Relations in the Early Twenty-First Century." *Contemporary Southeast Asia* 23, no. 3 (2001): 420–52.

Chin, Kin Wah. "Reflections on the Shaping of Strategic Cultures in Southeast Asia." In *Southeast Asian Perspectives on Security*, edited by Derek Da Cunha. Singapore: Institute for Southeast Asian Studies, 2000.

"China-Vietnam: Fighting Likely to Escalate." Intelligence Estimate, May 4, 1984. Richard Childress files, box 92402, folder "Vietnam 1983–84," 2 of 3. Simi Valley, CA: Ronald Reagan Presidential Library, 1984.

The Chinese Rulers' Crimes against Kampuchea. Phnom Penh: People's Republic of Kampuchea, Ministry of Foreign Affairs, 1984.

Chinh, Nguyen Huu. "Big Powers vis-à-vis Southeast Asia." *Indonesian Quarterly* 7, no. 2 (1984): 171–81.

Christensen, Thomas J., and Jack Snyder. "Chain Gangs and Passed Bucks: Predicting Alliance Patterns in Multipolarity." *International Organization* 44, no. 2 (1990): 137–68.

Christofferson, Gaye. "The Role of East Asia in Sino-U.S. Relations." *Asian Survey* 42, no. 3 (2002): 369–96.

Chubin, Shahram, and Sepehr Zabih. *The Foreign Relations of Iran: A Developing State in the Zone of Great-Power Conflict.* Berkeley: University of California Press, 1974.

Chung, Chien-Peng. "Southeast Asia-China Relations: Dialectics of 'Hedging' and 'Counter-Hedging.'" In *Southeast Asian Affairs 2004.* Singapore: Institute of Southeast Asian Studies, 2004.

Cima, Ronald J. "Vietnam in 1989: Initiating the Post-Cambodia Period." *Asian Survey* 30, no. 1 (1990): 88–95.

Ciorciari, John D. "The Balance of Great-Power Influence in Contemporary Southeast Asia." *International Relations of the Asia-Pacific* 9, no. 1 (2009): 157–96.

Clapham, Christopher. *Third World Politics.* Madison: University of Wisconsin Press, 1985.

Cohen, Ariel. "Conclusion." In *Eurasia in Balance: The U.S. and the Regional Power Shift.* Aldershot, UK: Ashgate, 2005.

Colbert, Evelyn. "Changing Relationships in Southeast Asia: ASEAN, Indochina, and the Great Powers." *Contemporary Southeast Asia* 4, no. 1 (1982): 76–85.

Connor, Walker. "Prospects for Stability in Southeast Asia: The Ethnic Barrier." In *Durable Stability in Southeast Asia*, edited by Kusuma Snitwongse and Sukhumbhand Paribatra. Singapore: Institute of Southeast Asian Studies, 1987.

Cooper, Scott. "State-Centric Balance-of-Threat Theory: Explaining the Misunderstood Gulf Cooperation Council," *Security Studies* 13, no. 2 (2003/04): 306–49.

Copper, John F. "China and Southeast Asia." *Southeast Asia Divided: The ASEAN-Indochina Crisis*, edited by Donald E. Weatherbee. Boulder, CO: Westview, 1985.

Corning, Gregory P. "The Philippine Bases and U.S. Pacific Strategy." *Pacific Affairs* 63, no. 1 (1990): 6–23.

Cribb, Robert. "Unresolved Problems in the Indonesian Killings of 1965–1966." *Asian Survey* 42, no. 4 (2002): 550–63.

David, Steven R. "Explaining Third World Alignment." *World Politics* 43, no. 2 (1991): 233–56.

———. *Choosing Sides: Alignment and Realignment in the Third World.* Baltimore, MD: Johns Hopkins University Press, 1991.

De Castro, Renato Cruz. "The Revitalized Philippine-U.S. Security Relations: A Ghost from the Cold War or an Alliance for the 21st Century?" *Asian Survey* 43, no. 6 (2003): 971–88.

————. "The Revitalized Philippine-U.S. Security Relations: The Triumph of Bilateralism over Multilateralism in Philippine Foreign Policy?" In *Asia-Pacific Security Cooperation: National Interests and Regional Order*, edited by See Seng Tan and Amitav Acharya. Armonk, NY: M. E. Sharpe, 2004.

Dent, Richard W. "Ecuador: The Fragility of Dependant Democracy." In *Latin American Politics and Development*, 6th ed., edited by Howard J. Wiarda and Harvey F. Kline. Boulder, CO: Westview, 2007.

————. *Australia's Alliance with America*. Parkville, VIC: University of Melbourne, 2003.

Deutch, Karl. "Security Communities." In *International Politics and Foreign Policy: A Reader in Research and Theory*, edited by James Rosenau. New York: Free Press, 1961.

De Wijk, Rob. "The Limits of Military Power." *Washington Quarterly* 25, no. 1 (2002): 3–28.

————. "Australia's Alliance with America." *Melbourne Asia Policy Papers* 1, no. 1 (2003): 1–12.

Dibb, Paul. "Towards a New Balance of Power in Asia." *Adelphi Paper* 295. London: International Institute for Strategic Studies, 1995.

Dommen, Arthur J. "Laos in 1994: Among Generals, Among Friends." *Asian Survey* 35, no. 1 (1995): 84–91.

Donnell, John C. "Vietnam 1979: Year of Calamity." *Asian Survey* 20, no. 1 (1980): 19–32.

Dosch, Jörn. *The Changing Dynamics of Southeast Asian Politics*. Boulder, CO: Lynne Rienner, 2007.

Duiker, William J. "Vietnam in 1985: Searching for Solutions." *Asian Survey* 26, no. 1 (1986): 102–11.

Duncanson, Dennis. "Sino-Soviet Rivalry in Southeast Asia." *Contemporary Southeast Asia* 1, no. 4 (1980): 367–81.

Dupont, Alan. "Is There an 'Asian Way?'" *Survival* 38, no. 2 (1996): 13–34.

————. "Indonesia Defence Strategy and Security: Time for a Rethink?" *Contemporary Southeast Asia* 18, no. 3 (1996): 275–97.

————. "Non-Traditional Threats to Thailand." In *Thailand, Australia and the Region: Strategic Developments in Southeast Asia*, edited by Cavan Hogue. Canberra: National Thai Studies Centre, 2001.

Eban, Abba. "Statement to the UN Security Council." New York, June 6, 1967. Israeli Ministry of Foreign Affairs. http://www.mfa.gov.il/MFA/Foreign Relations/Israels Foreign Relations since 1947/1947-1974/19 Statement to the Security Council by Foreign Mi.

Eckstein, Harry. "Case Study and Theory in Political Science." In *Handbook of Political Science*, vol. VII, edited by Fred Greenstein and Nelson Polsby. Reading, MA: Addison-Wesley, 1975.

Ellings, Richard J., and Sheldon W. Simon, eds. *Southeast Asian Security in the New Millennium*. Armonk, NY: M.E. Sharpe, 1996.

Elliott, David W. P. "The Third Indochina Conflict: Introduction." In *The Third Indochina Conflict*, edited by David W.P. Elliott. Boulder, CO: Westview, 1981.

————. "Vietnam: Tradition under Challenge." In *Strategic Cultures in the Asia-Pacific Region*, edited by Ken Booth and Russell Trood. Basingstoke: Macmillan, 1996.

Emmers, Ralf. "The Influence of the Balance of Power Factor within the ASEAN Regional Forum." *Contemporary Southeast Asia* 23, no. 2 (2001): 275–91.

————. *Cooperative Security and the Balance of Power Factor in ASEAN and the ARF*. London: Routledge, 2003.

————. "Regional Hegemonies and the Exercise of Power in Southeast Asia: A Study of Indonesia and Vietnam." *Asian Survey* 45, no. 4 (2005): 645–65.

Emmerson, Donald K. "Indonesia, Malaysia, Singapore: A Regional Security Core?" In *Southeast Asian Security in the New Millennium*, edited by Richard J. Ellings and Sheldon W. Simon. Armonk, NY: M. E. Sharpe, 1996.

———. "Whose Eleventh? Indonesia and the United States since 11 September." *Brown Journal of World Affairs* 9, no. 1 (2002): 115–26.

———. "What Do the Blind-Sided See? Reapproaching Regionalism in Southeast Asia." *Pacific Review* 18, no. 1 (2005): 1–21.

———. "Critical Terms: Security, Democracy, and Regionalism in Southeast Asia." In, *Hard Choices: Security, Democracy, and Regionalism in Southeast Asia*, edited by Donald K. Emmerson. Stanford, CA: Shorenstein APARC, 2008.

Esterline, John H. "Vietnam in 1987: Steps Toward Rejuvenation." *Asian Survey* 28, no. 1 (1988): 86–94.

Evans, Grant. *The Politics of Ritual and Rememberance: Laos since 1975*. Bangkok: Silkworm Books, 1998.

———. *A Short History of Laos: The Land in Between*. London: Allen & Unwin, 2002.

Fisher, Richard D. "Rebuilding the U.S.-Philippine Alliance." *Heritage Foundation Backgrounder No. 1255*. Washington, DC: Heritage Foundation, 1999.

Foot, Rosemary. "Pacific Asia: The Development of Regional Dialogue." In *Regionalism in World Politics: Regional Organization and International Order*, edited by Louise Fawcett and Andrew Hurrell. Oxford: Oxford University Press, 1995.

———. "China in the ASEAN Regional Forum: Organizational Processes and Domestic Modes of Thought." *Asian Survey* 38, no. 5 (1998): 425–40.

———. "Chinese Strategies in a U.S.-Hegemonic Global Order: Accommodating and Hedging." *International Affairs* 82, no. 1 (2006): 77–94.

Ford, Gerald. "Memorandum of Conversation: President Ford and Prime Minister Lee Kuan Yew of Singapore, May 8, 1975," NSC Meeting Memoranda Files, Spring 1975. Austin, TX: Gerald R. Ford Presidential Library, 1975.

Fox, Annette Baker. *The Power of Small States: Diplomacy in World War Two*. Chicago: University of Chicago Press, 1959.

Freeman, Nick J. "Laos: Exiguous Evidence of Economic Reform and Development." In *Southeast Asian Security 2004*. Singapore: Institute of Southeast Asian Studies, 2004.

Friedberg, Aaron L. "Ripe for Rivalry: Prospects for Peace in a Multipolar Asia." *International Security* 18, no. 3 (1993/94): 5–33.

———. "Will Europe's Past Be Asia's Future?" *Survival* 42, no. 3 (2000): 147–60.

———. "The Struggle for Mastery in Asia." *Commentary* 110, no. 4 (2000): 17–26.

Fujimori, Alberto. "Peru and Latin America in the Post-Cold War World." In *After the Cold War*, edited by Keith Philip Lepor. Austin: University of Texas Press, 1997.

Gaddis, John Lewis. "History, Science and the Study of International Relations." In *Explaining International Relations since 1945*, edited by Ngaire Woods. Oxford: Oxford University Press, 1996.

———. *We Now Know: Rethinking Cold War History*. Oxford: Oxford University Press, 1997.

Gallagher, Michael G. "China's Illusory Threat to the South China Sea." *International Security* 19, no. 1 (1994): 169–94.

Ganesan, Naranyan. "ASEAN's Relations with Major External Powers." *Contemporary Southeast Asia* 22, no. 2 (2000): 258–78.

———. *Realism and Interdependence in Singapore's Foreign Policy*. London: Routledge, 2005.

Ghazali Shafie, Tan Sri Mohamad. "ASEAN's Response to Security Issues in Southeast Asia." In *Regionalism in Southeast Asia*. Jakarta: Centre for Strategic and International Studies, 1975.

———. "On Development and Security." *Asian Defence Journal* (Malaysia) (September 1981).

Giap, Nguyen Hoang. "Relationship with Great Powers in Our Party and State's Foreign Policy under Doi Moi." *International Studies* no. 2 (2005): 30–38.

Gilderhus, Mark T. *The Second Century: U.S.-Latin American Relations since 1889.* Wilmington, DE: SR Books, 2000.

Goh, Chok Tong. Remarks at the Signing of the Singapore-U.S. Free Trade Agreement. Washington, DC, May 6, 2003. http://malaysia.usembassy.gov/wf/wf0506_bush.html.

———. Keynote Address to the Asia Society, Washington, DC, May 7, 2003. http://app.mfa.gov.sg/pr/read_content.asp?view,1899,.

Goh, Evelyn. "Meeting the China Challenge: The U.S. in Southeast Asian Regional Security Strategies." *Policy Studies* 16. Washington, DC: East-West Center Washington, 2005.

———. "Singapore and the United States: Cooperation in Transnational Security Threats." Paper for the 26th Annual Pacific Symposium. Honolulu (June 8–10, 2005).

———. "Great Powers and Hierarchical Order in Southeast Asia: Analyzing Regional Security Strategies." *International Security* 32, no. 3 (2008): 113–57.

Goldstein, Avery. "Great Expectations: Interpreting China's Arrival." *International Security* 22, no. 3 (1997/98): 36–73.

———. "Balance of Power Politics: Consequences for Asian Security Order." In *Asian Security Order: Material and Ideational Influences,* edited by Muthiah Alagappa. Stanford, CA: Stanford University Press, 1998.

Goncharenko, Alexander. "Ukraine: National Interests between the CIS and the West." In *Security Dilemmas in Russia and Eurasia,* edited by Roy Allison and Christopher Bluth. London: Royal Institute of International Affairs, 1998.

Goodman, Allan E. "Vietnam in 1994: With Peace at Hand." *Asian Survey* 35, no. 1 (1995): 92–99.

Goodman, David S. G. "Are Asia's 'Ethnic Chinese' a Regional-Security Threat?" *Survival* 39, no. 4 (1997): 140–55.

Gordon, Bernard K. "Asian Angst and American Foreign Policy." *Foreign Policy* no. 47 (1982): 46–65.

Gordon, Bernard K., with Lloyd R. Vasey. "Security in East Asia-Pacific." In *Threats to Security in East Asia-Pacific,* edited by Charles E. Morrison. Toronto: Lexington Books, 1985.

Gowa, Joanne, and Edward D. Mansfield. "Power Politics and International Trade." *American Political Science Review* 87, no. 2 (1993): 408–20.

Grieco, Joseph M. "Anarchy and the Limits of Cooperation: A Realist Critique of the Newest Liberal Institutionalism." *International Organization* 42, no. 3 (1988): 485–507.

———. "Realist International Theory and the Study of World Politics." In *New Thinking in International Relations Theory,* edited by Michael Doyle and John G. Ikenberry. Boulder, CO: Westview Press, 1997.

Gunn, Geoffrey C. "Foreign Relations of the Lao People's Democratic Republic: The Ideological Imperative." *Asian Survey* 20, no. 10 (1980): 990–1007.

———. "Laos in 1989: Quiet Revolution in the Marketplace." *Asian Survey* 30, no. 1 (1990): 81–87.

———. "Laos in 1990: Winds of Change." *Asian Survey* 31, no. 1 (1991): 87–93.

Haacke, Jürgen. *ASEAN's Diplomatic and Security Culture: Origins, Development and Prospects.* London: Routledge, 2002.

———. "Myanmar's Foreign Policy: Domestic Influences and International Implications." *Adelphi Paper* 381. London: International Institute for Strategic Studies, 2006.

———. "Michael Leifer, the Balance of Power, and International Relations Theory." In *Order and Security in Southeast Asia: Essays in Memory of Michael Leifer,* edited by Joseph Chinyong Liow and Ralf Emmers. London: Routledge, 2006.

Haas, Mark L. "Ideology and Alliances: British and French Balancing Decisions in the 1930s." *Security Studies* 12, no. 4 (2003): 34–79.

Habib, Hasnan. "Remarks by General Hasnan Habib, 22 May 1996." *KOMPAS*, May 23–24, 1996.

Handel, Michael. *Weak States in the International System*. London: Frank Cass, 1981.

Harknett, Richard J., and Jeffrey A. VanDenBerg. "Alignment Theory and Interrelated Threats: Jordan and the Persian Gulf Crisis." *Security Studies* 6, no. 3 (1997): 112–53.

Heder, Stephen P. "The Kampuchean-Vietnamese Conflict." In *The Third Indochina Conflict*, edited by David W. P. Elliott. Boulder, CO: Westview, 1981.

Heginbotham, Eric, and Richard J. Samuels. "Japan's Dual Hedge." *Foreign Affairs* 81, no. 5 (2002): 110–21.

Henze, Laura Jeanne. "U.S.-Philippine Economic Relations and Trade Negotiations." *Asian Survey* 16, no. 4 (1976): 319–37.

Hermann, Margaret G., and Charles W. Kegley, Jr. "Rethinking Democracy and International Peace: Perspectives from Political Psychology." *International Studies Quarterly* 39, no. 4 (1995): 511–33.

Herschede, Fred. "Trade between China and ASEAN: The Impact of the Pacific Rim Area." *Pacific Affairs* 64, no. 2 (1991): 179–93.

Hirschmann, Albert O. *National Power and the Structure of Foreign Trade*. Berkeley: University of California Press, 1980.

Hoge, James F. Jr. "A Global Power Shift in the Making." *Foreign Affairs* 83, no. 4 (2004): 2–7.

Holsti, Ole R. "The Belief System and National Images: A Case Study." *Journal of Conflict Resolution* 6, no. 3 (1962): 244–52.

Holsti, Ole R., Terrence Hopmann, and John D. Sullivan. *Unity and Disintegration in International Alliances*. New York: Wiley, 1973.

Horn, Robert C. *Soviet-Indian Relations: Issues and Influence*. New York: Praeger, 1982.

———. "Southeast Asian Perceptions of U.S. Foreign Policy." *Asian Survey* 25, no. 6 (1985): 678–91.

———. "Vietnam and Sino-Soviet Relations: What Price Rapprochement?" *Asian Survey* 27, no. 7 (1987): 729–47.

Horton, A. V. M. "Brunei in 2004: Window-Dressing an Islamizing Sultanate." *Asian Survey* 45, no. 1 (2005): 180–85.

Hun, Sen. "Kampuchean Foreign Policy: A Policy of Peace, Friendship, and Cooperation." *International Affairs* (Moscow) no. 7 (1984): 28–34.

Hung, Nguyen Manh. "Vietnam in 1999: The Party's Choice." *Asian Survey* 40, no. 1 (2000): 98–111.

Huntington, Samuel P. *The Clash of Civilizations and the Remaking of World Order*. London: Touchstone, 1998.

———. "The Lonely Superpower." *Foreign Affairs* 78, no. 2 (1999): 35–49.

Huxley, Tim. "Insecurity in the ASEAN Region." *Whitehall Paper* 23. London: Royal United Services Institute for Defence Studies, 1993.

———. "Singapore in 2001: Political Continuity Despite Deepening Recession." *Asian Survey* 42, no. 1 (2002): 156–64.

———. "Singapore's Strategic Outlook and Defence Policy." In *Order and Security in Southeast Asia: Essays in Memory of Michael Leifer*, edited by Joseph Liow and Ralf Emmers. London: Routledge, 2006.

Ikenberry, G. John. "Institutions, Strategic Restraint, and the Persistence of American Postwar Order." *International Security* 23, no. 3 (1998/99): 43–78.

Indonesian Department of Defence and Security. *The Policy of the State Defence and Security of the Republic of Indonesia*. Jakarta: Republic of Indonesia, 1997.

Indorf, Hans H. "Malaysia in 1977: A Prelude to Premature Parliamentary Elections." *Asian Survey* 18, no. 2 (1978): 186–93.

―――. "ASEAN in Extra-Regional Perspective." *Contemporary Southeast Asia* 9, no. 2 (1987): 86–105.

Jackson, Karl D. "Cambodia 1977: Gone to Pot." *Asian Survey* 18, no. 1 (1978): 76–90.

―――. "Cambodia 1978: War, Pillage and Purge in Democratic Kampuchea." *Asian Survey* 19, no. 1 (1979): 72–84.

―――. "Post-Colonial Rebellion and Counterinsurgency in Southeast Asia." In *Governments and Rebellions in Southeast Asia*, edited by Chandran Jeshurun. Singapore: Institute of Southeast Asian Studies, 1985.

James, Helen. "Myanmar's International Relations Strategy: The Search for Security." *Contemporary Southeast Asia* 26, no. 3 (2004): 530–53.

Jayakumar, S. Remarks on Strategic Review in the World. Singapore, March 14, 2003. http://app.mfa.gov.sg/2006/idx_fp.asp?web_id=14.

Ji, Guoxing. "Current Security Issues in Southeast Asia." *Asian Survey* 26, no. 9 (1986): 973–90.

Johnson, Chalmers, and Katharya Um. "The United States and Asia in 1986: Demands for Democracy." *Asian Survey* 27, no. 1 (1987): 10–22.

Johnson, Stephen T. "Laos in 1991: Year of the Constitution." *Asian Survey* 32, no. 1 (1992): 82–87.

―――. "Laos in 1992: Succession and Consolidation." *Asian Survey* 33, no. 1 (1993): 75–82.

Johnston, Alastair Iain, and Robert S. Ross, eds. *Engaging China: The Management of An Emerging Power*. London: Routledge, 1999.

Joiner, Charles A. "Laos in 1986: Administrative and International Partially Adaptive Communism." *Asian Survey* 27, no. 1 (1987): 104–14.

Kang, David C. *Culture, Hierarchy and Stability in Asian International Relations*. Hanover, NH: Dartmouth College Press, 2000.

―――. "Getting Asia Wrong: The Need for New Analytical Frameworks." *International Security* 27, no. 4 (2003): 57–85.

―――. *China Rising: Peace, Power and Order in East Asia*. New York: Columbia University Press, 2007.

Kann, Robert A. "Alliances versus Ententes." *World Politics* 28, no. 4 (1976): 611–21.

Kasenov, Oumirserik. "Central Asia: National, Regional, and Global Aspects of Security." In *Security Dilemmas in Russia and Eurasia*, edited by Roy Allison and Christopher Bluth. London: Royal Institute of International Affairs, 1998.

Kaufman, Robert G. "'To Balance or Bandwagon?' Alignment Decisions in 1930s Europe." *Security Studies* 1, no. 3 (1992): 417–47.

Kausikan, Bilahari. "Asia's Different Standard." *Foreign Policy* 92 (1993): 24–41.

Kechichian, Joseph A. "Trends in Saudi National Security." *Middle East Journal* 53, no. 2 (1999): 232–53.

Kegley, Charles W., and Gregory A. Raymond. *When Trust Breaks Down: Alliance Norms and World Politics*. Columbia: University of South Carolina Press, 1990.

Kennan, George F. *The Fateful Alliance: France, Russia, and the Coming of the First World War*. New York: Pantheon Books, 1984.

Kenny, Henry J. *Shadow of the Dragon: Vietnam's Continuing Struggle with China and the Implications for U.S. Foreign Policy*. Washington, DC: Brassey's, 2002.

Keohane, Robert E. "The Big Influence of Small Allies." *Foreign Policy* no. 2 (1971): 161–82.

―――, ed. *Neorealism and Its Critics*. New York: Columbia University Press, 1986.

Kershaw, Roger. "Partners in Realism: Britain and Brunei amid Recent Turbulence." *Asian Affairs* 34, no. 1 (2003): 43–53.

Khong, Kim Hoong, and Abdul Razak Abdullah. "Security Co-operation in ASEAN." *Contemporary Southeast Asia* 9, no. 2 (1987): 129–39.

Khong, Yuen Foong. "ASEAN's Post-Ministerial Conference and Regional Forum: A Convergence of Post-Cold War Security Strategies." In *U.S.-Japan Relations and International Institutions after the Cold War*, edited by Peter Gourevitch, Takashi Inoguchi, and Courtney Purrington. San Diego: University of California Press, 1995.

———. "Making Bricks without Straw in the Asia-Pacific?" *Pacific Review* 10, no. 2 (1997): 289–300.

———. "Singapore: A Time for Political and Economic Engagement." In *Engaging China*, edited by Alastair Iain Johnston and Robert S. Ross. New York: Routledge, 1999.

———. "Coping with Strategic Uncertainty: The Role of Institutions and Soft Balancing in Southeast Asia's Post-Cold War Strategy." In *Rethinking Security in East Asia: Identity, Power, and Efficiency*, edited by J. J. Suh, Peter Katzenstein, and Allen Carlson. Stanford, CA: Stanford University Press, 2004.

———. "Southeast Asia's Post–Cold War Strategy." Paper presented at the Weatherhead Center for International Affairs, Harvard University, March 15, 2004.

Khoo, Nicholas, and Michael L. R. Smith. "China Engages Asia? Caveat Lector." *International Security* 30, no. 1 (2005): 196–211.

Kiernan, Ben. *The Pol Pot Regime: Race, Power, and Genocide under the Khmer Rouge, 1975–1979*. New Haven, CT: Yale University Press, 1996.

King, Gary, Robert E. Keohane, and Sidney Verba. *Designing Social Inquiry: Scientific Inference in Qualitative Research*. Princeton, NJ: Princeton University Press, 1994.

Kintner, William R. *Soviet Global Strategy*. Fairfax, VA: Hero Books, 1987.

Kirk, Donald. *Looted: The Philippines after the Bases*. London: Palgrave Macmillan, 2000.

Kissinger, Henry. *Years of Renewal*. New York: Simon & Schuster, 1999.

Kivimäki, Timo. *U.S.-Indonesian Hegemonic Bargaining: Strength of Weakness*. Aldershot: Ashgate, 2003.

Koh, Tommy. *The Quest for World Order*. Singapore: Times Academic Press, 1998.

Kuhonta, Erik Martinez. "Walking a Tightrope: Democracy versus Sovereignty in ASEAN's Illiberal Peace." *Pacific Review* 19, no. 3 (2006): 337–58.

Kurlantzick, Joshua. *Charm Offensive: How China's Soft Power Is Transforming the World*. New Haven, CT: Yale University Press, 2007.

Kwa, Chong Guan. "Relating to the World: Images, Metaphors, and Analogies." In *Singapore in the New Millennium: Challenges Facing the City-State*, edited by Derek DaCunha. Singapore: Institute for Southeast Asian Studies, 2002.

Labs, Eric J. "Do Weak States Bandwagon?" *Security Studies* 1, no. 3 (1992): 383–416.

Lai, Brian, and Dan Reiter. "Democracy, Political Similarity, and International Alliances, 1816–1992." *Journal of Conflict Resolution* 44, no. 2 (2000): 203–27.

Laïdi, Zaki. *The Superpowers and Africa: The Constraints of a Rivalry*, translated edition. Chicago: University of Chicago Press, 1990.

Lake, David A. "Escape from the State of Nature: Authority and Hierarchy in World Politics." *International Security* 32, no. 1 (2007): 47–79.

Lam, Lai Sing. "A Short Note on ASEAN-Great Power Interaction." *Contemporary Southeast Asia* 15, no. 4 (1993): 451–63.

Lampton, David M. "Paradigm Lost: The Demise of 'Weak China,'" *National Interest* no. 81 (Fall 2005): 73–80.

Larrabee, F. Stephen. "Turkey Rediscovers the Middle East." *Foreign Affairs* 86, no. 4 (2007): 103–14.

Larson, Deborah Welch. "Bandwagon Images in American Foreign Policy: Myth or Reality?" In *Dominoes and Bandwagons: Strategic Beliefs and Great-Power Competition in the Eurasian Rimland*, edited by Robert Jervis and Jack Snyder. Oxford: Oxford University Press, 1991.

Lau, Teik Soon. "ASEAN and the Cambodian Problem." *Asian Survey* 22, no. 6 (1982): 548–60.

———. "The Challenge to ASEAN Political Co-operation." *Contemporary Southeast Asia* 9, no. 2 (1987): 106–12.

Layne, Christopher. "The Unipolar Illusion: Why New Great Powers Will Rise." *International Security* 17, no. 4 (1993): 5–51.

Lee, Hsien Loong. Speech to the U.S. ASEAN Business Council, Washington, DC, July 12, 2005.

Lee, Jae-Hyung. "China's Expanding Maritime Ambitions in the Western Pacific and the Indian Ocean." *Contemporary Southeast Asia* 24, no. 3 (2002): 549–68.

Lee, Kuan Yew. "We Want to Be Ourselves." Speech delivered at the National University of Singapore, October 9, 1966.

———. Speech to the Nixon Center, Washington, DC, November 11, 1996. http://www.nixoncenter.org/publications/YEW96.html.

———. "ASEAN Must Balance China in Asia." *New Perspectives Quarterly* 18, no. 3 (2001): 20–23.

Lefebvre, Jeffrey A. "Moscow's Cold War and Post-Cold War Policies in Africa." In *Africa in the New International Order: Rethinking State Sovereignty and Regional Security*, edited by Edmond J. Keller and Donald Rothchild. Boulder, CO: Lynne Rienner, 1996.

Leifer, Michael. "Kampuchea 1979: From Dry Season to Dry Season." *Asian Survey* 20, no. 1 (1980): 33–41.

———. *Indonesia's Foreign Policy*. London: George Allen & Unwin, 1983.

———. *ASEAN and the Security of South-East Asia*. London: Routledge, 1989.

———. "Indochina and ASEAN: Seeking a New Balance." *Contemporary Southeast Asia* 15, no. 3 (1993): 269–79.

———. "Chinese Economic Reform and Security Policy: The South China Sea Connection." *Survival* 37, no. 2 (1995).

———. "The ASEAN Regional Forum." *Adelphi Paper* 302. London: International Institute for Strategic Studies, 1996.

———. "Indonesia and the Dilemmas of Engagement." In *Engaging China*, edited by Alastair Iain Johnston and Robert S. Ross. New York: Routledge, 1999.

———. *Singapore's Foreign Policy: Coping with Vulnerability*. London: Routledge, 2000.

Leong, Stephen. "Malaysia and the People's Republic of China in the 1980s: Political Vigilance and Economic Pragmatism." *Asian Survey* 27, no. 10 (1987): 1109–26.

Levi, Werner. "Ideology, Interests, and Foreign Policy." *International Studies Quarterly* 14, no. 1 (1970): 1–31.

Liang, Chi-shad. *Burma's Foreign Relations: Neutralism in Theory and Practice*. New York: Praeger, 1990.

Limaye, Satu P. "Minding the Gaps: The Bush Administration and U.S.-Southeast Asia Relations." *Contemporary Southeast Asia* 26, no. 1 (2004): 73–93.

Lipson, Charles. "International Cooperation in Economic and Security Affairs." *World Politics* 37, no. 1 (1984): 1–23.

Liska, George. *Nations in Alliance: The Limits of Interdependence*. Baltimore, MD: Johns Hopkins University Press, 1962.

———. *Alliances and the Third World*. Baltimore, MD: Johns Hopkins University Press, 1968.

Lizée, Pierre P. "Cambodia in 1996: Of Tigers, Crocodiles, and Doves." *Asian Survey* 37, no. 1 (1997): 65–71.

Lowry, Bob. "Indonesian Defence Policy and the Indonesian Armed Forces." *Canberra Papers on Strategy and Defence* 99. Canberra: Strategic and Defence Studies Centre, 1993.

Lyall, Jason, and Isaiah Wilson III. "Rage against the Machines: Explaining Outcomes in Counterinsurgency Wars." *International Organization* 63, no. 1 (2009): 67–106.

MacFarlane, Neil. *Superpower Rivalry and Third World Radicalism: The Idea of National Liberation.* Baltimore, MD: Johns Hopkins University Press, 1985.

MacIntyre, Andrew J. "Interpreting Indonesian Foreign Policy: The Case of Kampuchea, 1979–1986." *Asian Survey* 27, no. 5 (1987): 515–34.

Mahathir, Mohamad. Keynote address to the Global Community Forum, Kuala Lumpur, December 3, 1984. http://www.pmo.gov.my/ucapan/?m=p&p=mahathir&id=1142.

———. Keynote address to the First ISIS National Conference on Security, Kuala Lumpur, August 1986, reprinted in *ISIS Focus* no. 17 (August 1986): 16.

———. Speech at Opening Session of the 23rd Summit Meeting of the Non-Aligned Movement. Kuala Lumpur, February 24, 2003. http://www.nam.gov.za/media/030225na.htm.

Mahathir, Mohamad, and Shintaro Ishihara. *The Voice of Asia: Two Leaders Discuss the Coming Century.* Tokyo: Kodansha International, 1995.

Mak, Joon Nam. "The Chinese Navy and the South China Sea: A Malaysian Assessment." *Pacific Review* 4, no. 2 (1991): 150–61.

———. "Malaysian Defense and Security Cooperation: Coming Out of the Closet." In *Asia-Pacific Security Cooperation: National Interests and Regional Order*, edited by See Seng Tan and Amitav Acharya. Armonk, NY: M. E. Sharpe, 2004.

Malik, Adam. "Djakarta's Conference and Asia's Political Future." *Pacific Community* 2, no. 1 (1970): 66–91.

Malik, J. Mohan. "Sino-Indian Rivalry in Myanmar: Implications for Regional Security." *Contemporary Southeast Asia* 16, no. 2 (1994): 137–56.

———. "Burma's Role in Regional Security—Pawn or Pivot?" In *Burma: Prospects for a Democratic Future*, edited by Robert I. Rotberg. Washington, DC: Brookings Institution Press, 1998.

Maranan, Edgardo. "China and the Philippines." In *ASEAN and China: An Evolving Relationship*, edited by Joyce Kallgren, Mohamed Noordin Sopiee, and S. Soedjati Djiwandono. Berkeley: Institute of East Asian Studies, University of California, 1988.

Marcos, Ferdinand. *Five Years of the New Society.* Manila, PI: Marcos Foundation, 1978.

Markey, Daniel. "A False Choice in Pakistan." *Foreign Affairs* 86, no. 4 (2007): 85–102.

Martin, Edwin W. "Burma in 1975: New Dimensions to Non-Alignment." *Asian Survey* 16, no. 2 (1976): 173–77.

Mastanduno, Michael. "Economics and Security in Statecraft and Scholarship." *International Organization* 52, no. 4 (1998): 825–54.

Mat Arshad, Che Mohamad Noor. Paper presented to the Conference "Land Forces in the Twenty-First Century: The Challenge for the Malaysian and Regional Armies," Kuala Lumpur, November 20–21, 1995.

Maung, Aung Myoe. "Neither Friend nor Foe: Myanmar's Relations with Thailand since 1988." *IDSS Monograph No. 1.* Singapore: Institute of Defence and Strategic Studies, 2002.

Mearsheimer, John J. "The False Promise of International Institutions." *International Security* 19, no. 3 (1994/95): 5–49.

———. "The Future of the American Pacifier." *Foreign Affairs* 80, no. 5 (2001): 46–61.

———. *The Tragedy of Great Power Politics.* New York: W. W. Norton, 2001.

Medeiros, Evan S. "Strategic Hedging and the Future of Asia-Pacific Stability." *Washington Quarterly* 29, no. 1 (2005): 145–67.

Mediansky, F. A. "The New People's Army: A Nation-wide Insurgency in the Philippines." *Contemporary Southeast Asia* 8, no. 1 (1986): 1–17.

Menon, K. U. "Brunei Darussalam in 1986." In *Southeast Asian Affairs 1986*. Singapore: Institute of Southeast Asian Studies, 1986.

———. "Brunei Darussalam in 1987: Modernizing Autocracy." *Asian Survey* 28, no. 2 (1988): 252–58.

Menon, Rajan. "The End of Alliances." *World Policy Journal* 20, no. 2 (2003): 1–20.

———. *The End of Alliances*. Oxford: Oxford University Press, 2007.

Miller, Benjamin. "The International System and Regional Balance in the Middle East." In *Balance of Power: Theory and Practice in the 21st Century*, edited by T. V. Paul, James J. Wirtz, and Michel Fortmann. Stanford, CA: Stanford University Press, 2004.

Mohan, C. Raja. *Crossing the Rubicon: The Shaping of India's New Foreign Policy*. New Delhi: Viking, 2003.

Morgenthau, Hans. *Politics among Nations: The Struggle for Power and Peace*, 6th ed. New York: Alfred A. Knopf, 1985.

Morris, Stephen J. *Why Vietnam Invaded Cambodia: Political Culture and the Causes of War*. Stanford, CA: Stanford University Press, 1999.

Morrow, James D. "Alliances and Asymmetry: An Alternative to the Capability Aggregation Model of Alliances." *American Journal of Political Science* 35, no. 4 (1991): 904–33.

———. "Arms versus Allies: Trade-Offs in the Search for Security." *International Organization* 47, no. 2 (1993): 207–33.

Mueller, John. *The Remnants of War*. Ithaca, NY: Cornell University Press, 2004.

Mueller, Karl. "Patterns of Alliance: Alignment Balancing and Stability in Eastern Europe." *Security Studies* 5, no. 1 (1995): 38–76.

Mulliner, K. "Brunei in 1984: Business as Usual after the Gala." *Asian Survey* 25, no. 2 (1985): 214–19.

Muni, S. D. "China's Strategic Engagement with the New ASEAN." *IDSS Monograph No. 2*. Singapore: Institute of Defence and Strategic Studies, 2002.

Narine, Shaun. "ASEAN and the Management of Regional Security." *Pacific Affairs* 71, no. 2 (1998): 195–214.

Nathan, K. S. "Malaysia and the Soviet Union: A Relationship with a Distance." *Asian Survey* 27, no. 10 (1987): 1059–73.

Neher, Clark D. "Post-Cold War Security Issues in Thailand and the Philippines." In *Southeast Asian Security in the New Millennium*, edited by Richard J. Ellings and Sheldon W. Simon. Armonk, NY: M. E. Sharpe, 1996.

———. *Southeast Asia in the New International Era*, 4th ed. Boulder, CO: Westview, 2002.

Ngaosyvathn, Mayoury, and Pheuiphanh Ngaosyvathn. *Kith and Kin: The Relationship between Laos and Thailand*. Manila: Journal of Contemporary Asia Publishers, 1993.

Niehaus, Marjorie. "Vietnam in 1978: The Elusive Peace." *Asian Survey* 19, no. 1 (1979): 85–94.

Niksch, Larry A. "Thailand in 1980: Confrontation with Vietnam and the Fall of Kriangsak." *Asian Survey* 21, no. 2 (1981): 223–31.

Novicio, Noel M. "The South China Sea Dispute in Philippine Foreign Policy: Problems, Challenges, and Prospects." *IDSS Monograph No. 5*. Singapore: Institute of Defence and Strategic Studies, 2003.

Nyunt, Khin Maung. Keynote Address to the Symposium on Interaction for Progress: Myanmar in ASEAN. Myanmar Ministry of Defence, Yangon, October 23–24, 1998.

Oelsner, Andrea. *International Relations in Latin America: Peace and Security in the Southern Cone*. New York: Routledge, 2005.

Office of the Press Secretary, "September 11, 2001: Attack on America." Joint Statement between the United States of America and the Republic of the Philippines. Washington,

DC: Government Printing Office, November 20, 2001. http://avalon.law.yale.edu/
sept11/joint_007.asp.

Öjendal, Joakim, and Hans Antlöv. "Asian Values and Its Political Consequences: Is Cambodia
the First Domino?" *Pacific Review* 11, no. 4 (1998): 525–40.

O'Reilly, Marc J. "Omanibalancing: Oman Confronts an Uncertain Future." *Middle East Journal*
52, no. 1 (1998): 70–84.

Osgood, Robert E. *Alliances and American Foreign Policy*. Baltimore, MD: Johns Hopkins University Press, 1968.

Owen, John M. IV. "Transnational Liberalism and American Primacy; or, Benignity Is in the
Eye of the Beholder." In *America Unrivaled: The Future of the Balance of Power*, edited by G.
John Ikenberry. Ithaca, NY: Cornell University Press, 2002.

Owen, Norman G. "Economic and Social Change." In *The Cambridge History of Southeast Asia:
From World War II to the Present*, vol. II, part II, edited by Nicholas Tarling. Cambridge:
Cambridge University Press, 1999.

Palmer, David Scott. "Peru: Authoritarian Traditions, Troubled Democracy." In *Latin American
Politics and Development*, 6th ed., edited by Howard J. Wiarda and Harvey F. Kline. Boulder, CO: Westview, 2007.

Papayoanou, Paul A. "Interdependence, Institutions, and the Balance of Power: Britain, Germany, and World War I." *International Security* 20, no. 4 (1996): 42–76.

Pape, Robert A. "Soft Balancing against the United States." *International Security* 30, no. 1 (2005):
7–45.

Paribatra, Sukhumbhand. "The Challenge of Co-existence: ASEAN's Relations with Vietnam
in the 1990s." *Contemporary Southeast Asia* 9, no. 2 (1987): 140–56.

———. "Thailand: Defense Spending and Threat Perceptions." In *Defense Spending in Southeast
Asia*, edited by Chin Kin Wah. Singapore: Institute for Southeast Asian Studies, 1987.

Paul, T. V. "Introduction: The Enduring Axioms of Balance of Power Theory and Their Contemporary Relevance." In *Balance of Power: Theory and Practice in the 21st Century*, edited
by T. V. Paul, James J. Wirtz, and Michel Fortmann. Stanford, CA: Stanford University
Press, 2004.

———. "Soft Balancing in the Age of U.S. Primacy." *International Security* 30, no. 1 (2005):
46–71.

Paznyak, Vyachaslau. "Belarus: In Search of a Security Identity." In *Security Dilemmas in Russia
and Eurasia*, edited by Roy Allison and Christopher Bluth. London: Royal Institute of
International Affairs, 1998.

Peou, Sorpong. *Cambodia after the Cold War: The Search for Security Continues*. Working Paper No.
96. Clayton, VIC: Monash University Center for Southeast Asian Studies, 1995.

Philippine Department of National Defense. *In Defense of the Philippines: 1998 Defense Policy
Paper*. Manila: Philippine Department of National Defense, 1998.

Pike, Douglas. "The USSR and Vietnam: Into the Swamp." *Asian Survey* 19, no. 12 (1979):
1159–170.

———. "Vietnam and China." In *ASEAN and China: An Evolving Relationship*, edited by Joyce
K. Kallgren, Nordin Sopiee, and Soedjati Djiwandono. Berkeley, CA: Institute of East
Asian Studies, 1988.

———. "Vietnam in 1990: The Last Picture Show." *Asian Survey* 31, no. 1 (1991): 79–86.

———. "Vietnam in 1991: The Turning Point." *Asian Survey* 32, no. 1 (1992): 74–81.

Polomka, Peter. "ASEAN Perspectives on China: Implications for Western Interests." *Australian
Journal of Chinese Affairs* no. 8 (1982): 85–99.

Poole, Peter A. "Cambodia 1975: The *GRUNK* Regime." *Asian Survey* 16, no. 1 (1976): 23–20.

Porter, Gareth. "Vietnamese Policy and the Indochina Crisis." In *The Third Indochina Conflict*, edited by David W. P. Elliott. Boulder, CO: Westview, 1981.

———. "The Transformation of Vietnam's World View: From Two Camps to Interdependence." *Contemporary Southeast Asia* 12, no. 1 (1990): 1–19.

Posen, Barry R. "The Struggle against Terrorism: Grand Strategy, Strategy, and Tactics." *International Security* 26, no. 3 (2001/02): 39–55.

———. "European Union Security and Defense Policy: Response to Unipolarity?" *Security Studies* 15, no. 2 (2006): 149–86.

Pouvatchy, Joseph R. "Cambodian-Vietnamese Relations." *Asian Survey* 26, no. 4 (1986): 440–51.

Press-Barnathan, Galia. "Managing the Hegemon: NATO under Unipolarity." *Security Studies* 15, no. 2 (2006): 271–309.

Purdey, Jemma. "Problematizing the Place of Victims in Reformasi Indonesia: A Contested Truth about the May 1998 Violence." *Asian Survey* 42, no. 4 (2002): 605–22.

Quinn, Kenneth M. "Cambodia in 1976: Internal Consolidation and External Expansion." *Asian Survey* 17, no. 1 (1977): 43–54.

Ramazani, Rouhallah K. *Iran's Foreign Policy: A Study of Foreign Policy in Modernizing Nations*. Charlottesville: University of Virginia Press, 1975.

———. Remarks at a special seminar as Malaysian Defence Minister, St. Antony's College, Oxford, January 31, 2003.

Rashid, Ahmed. *Jihad: The Rise of Militant Islam in Central Asia*. New Haven, CT: Yale University Press, 2002.

Ravenhill, John. "Is China an Economic Threat to Southeast Asia?" *Asian Survey* 46, no. 5 (2006): 653–74.

Razak, Najib bin Tun Abdul. "U.S.-Malaysia Defense Cooperation: A Solid Success Story," Speech to the Heritage Foundation (Lecture 742), Washington, DC, May 3, 2002. http://www.heritage.org/Research/AsiaandthePacific/HL742.cfm.

Reagan, Ronald. Address before a Joint Session of Congress on Central America, April 27, 1983, Washington, DC. http://www.reagan.utexas.edu/archives.

Reiter, Dan. "Learning, Realism, and Alliances: The Weight of the Shadow of the Past." *World Politics* 46, no. 4 (1994): 490–526.

Rithauddeen, Tengku Ahmad. "The Kampuchean Problem and the Non-Aligned Movement." *Contemporary Southeast Asia* 1, no. 3 (1979): 205–10.

Rogers, Steven. "Beyond the Abu Sayyaf: The Lessons of Failure in the Philippines." *Foreign Affairs* 83, no. 1 (2004): 15–21.

Ross, Robert S. *The Indochina Tangle: China's Vietnam Policy 1975–1979*. New York: Columbia University Press, 1988.

———. "Beijing as a Conservative Power." *Foreign Affairs* 76, no. 2 (1997): 33–44.

———. "The Geography of the Peace: East Asia in the Twenty-First Century." *International Security* 23, no. 4 (1999): 81–118.

———. "Balance of Power Politics and the Rise of China: Accommodation and Balancing in East Asia." *Security Studies* 15, no. 3 (2006): 355–95.

Rothstein, Robert L. *Alliances and Small Powers*. New York: Columbia University Press, 1968.

Roy, Denny. "Southeast Asia and China: Balancing or Bandwagoning?" *Contemporary Southeast Asia* 27, no. 2 (2005): 305–22.

Royal Government of Cambodia. *Defending the Kingdom of Cambodia: Security and Development*. Phnom Penh, 2000.

———. *Strategic Review 2002*. Phnom Penh, 2002.

———. *Defending the Kingdom of Cambodia: Security, Development, and International Cooperation*. Phnom Penh, 2006.

Russett, Bruce. "An Empirical Typology of International Military Alliances." *Midwest Journal of Political Science* 15, no. 2 (1971): 262–89.

Ryan, Curtis R. "Jordan: The Politics of Alliance and Foreign Policy." In *Small States in World Politics: Explaining Foreign Policy Behavior*, edited by Jeanne A. K. Hey. Boulder, CO: Lynne Rienner, 2003.

Sabrosky, Alan N. "Interstate Alliances: Their Reliability and the Expansion of War." In *The Correlates of War: II. Testing Some Realpolitik Models*, edited by J. David Singer. New York: Free Press, 1980.

Samudavanija, Chai-Anan, and Sukhumbhand Paribatra, "Development for Security, Security for Development: Prospects for Durable Stability in Southeast Asia." In *Durable Stability in Southeast Asia*, edited by Kusuma Snitwongse and Sukhumbhand Paribatra. Singapore: Institute of Southeast Asian Studies, 1987.

Savetsila, Siddhi. "Thailand's View on the Present Situation in Southeast Asia." Speech to the Council of Foreign Relations, New York, May 20, 1985.

Scalapino, Robert A. "The Political Influence of the USSR in Asia." In *Soviet Policy in East Asia*, edited by Donald S. Zagoria. New Haven, CT: Yale University Press, 1982.

Schier, Peter. "The Indochina Conflict from the Perspective of Singapore." *Contemporary Southeast Asia* 4, no. 2 (1982): 226–35.

Schoultz, Lars. *National Security and United States Policy toward Latin America*. Princeton, NJ: Princeton University Press, 1987.

Schraeder, Peter J. "Removing the Shackles? U.S. Foreign Policy toward Africa after the End of the Cold War." In *Africa in the New International Order: Rethinking State Sovereignty and Regional Security*, edited by Edmond J. Keller and Donald Rothchild. Boulder, CO: Lynne Rienner, 1996.

Schroeder, Paul W. "Alliances, 1815–1945: Weapons of Power and Tools of Management." In *Historical Dimensions of National Security Problems*, edited by Klaus Knorr. Lawrence: University Press of Kansas, 1976.

———. "Historical Reality vs. Neo-Realist Theory." *International Security* 19, no. 1 (1994): 108–48.

Schweller, Randall L. "Bandwagoning for Profit: Bringing the Revisionist State Back In." *International Security* 19, no. 1 (1994): 72–107.

———. *Deadly Imbalances: Tripolarity and Hitler's Strategy of World Conquest*. New York: Columbia University Press, 1998.

———. "Unanswered Threats: A Neoclassical Realist Theory of Underbalancing." *International Security* 29, no. 2 (2004): 159–201.

———. *Unanswered Threats: Political Constraints on the Balance of Power*. Princeton, NJ: Princeton University Press, 2006.

Scobell, Andrew. *China's Use of Military Force*. Cambridge: Cambridge University Press, 2003.

Scott, James C. "Patron-Client Politics and Political Change in Southeast Asia." *American Political Science Review* 64, no. 2 (1972): 91–113.

Scully, William L., and Frank N. Trager. "Burma 1979: Reversing the Trend." *Asian Survey* 20, no. 2 (1980): 168–75.

Seekins, Donald M. "Burma in 1999: A Slim Hope." *Asian Survey* 40, no. 1 (2000): 16–24.

Segal, Gerald. *The Great Power Triangle*. London: Macmillan, 1982.

Seligson, Mitchell A. "Costa Rica." In *Latin American Politics and Development*, 6th ed., edited by Howard J. Wiarda and Harvey F. Kline. Boulder, CO: Westview, 2007.

Selth, Andrew. "Burma and the Strategic Competition between China and India." *Journal of Strategic Studies* 19, no. 2 (1996): 213–30.

Shambaugh, David. "China Engages Asia: Reshaping the Regional Order." *International Security* 29, no. 3 (2004/05): 64–99.

Shambaugh, David, and Karl F. Inderfurth. "China and the U.S.: To Hedge or Engage." *Yale-Global* (April 11, 2007).

Shawcross, William. "Cambodia's New Deal." *Contemporary Issues Paper No. 1.* Washington, DC: Carnegie Endowment for International Peace, 1994.

Shee, Poon-Kim. "Singapore in 1977: Stability and Growth." *Asian Survey* 18, no. 2 (1978): 194–201.

Sidel, Mark. "Vietnam in 1998: Reform Confronts the Regional Crisis." *Asian Survey* 39, no. 1 (1999): 89–98.

Sigmund, Paul E. "Chile." In *Latin American Politics and Development*, 6th ed., edited by Howard J. Wiarda and Harvey F. Kline. Boulder, CO: Westview, 2007.

Simon, Sheldon W. "Peking and Indochina: The Perplexity of Victory." *Asian Survey* 16, no. 5 (1976): 401–10.

———. "China, Vietnam, and ASEAN: The Politics of Polarization." *Asian Survey* 19, no. 12 (1979): 1171–88.

———. "Davids and Goliaths: Small Power-Great Power Security Relations in Southeast Asia." *Asian Survey* 23, no. 3 (1983): 302–15.

———. "The Two Southeast Asias and China: Security Perspectives." *Asian Survey* 24, no. 5 (1984): 519–33.

———. "The Great Powers and Southeast Asia: Cautious Minuet or Dangerous Tango?" *Asian Survey* 25, vol. 9 (1985): 918–42.

———. "The Superpowers in Southeast Asia: A Security Assessment." In *Southeast Asia Divided: The ASEAN-Indochina Crisis*, edited by Donald E. Weatherbee. Boulder, CO: Westview, 1985.

———. "ASEAN's Strategic Situation in the 1980s." *Pacific Affairs* 60, no. 1 (1987): 73–93.

———. "Realism and Neoliberalism: International Relations Theory and Southeast Asian Security." *Pacific Review* 8, no. 1 (1995): 5–24.

———. "The Parallel Tracks of Asian Multilateralism." In *Southeast Asian Security in the New Millennium*, edited by Richard J. Ellings and Sheldon W. Simon. Armonk, NY: NBR Press, 1996.

———. "Asian Armed Forces: Internal and External Tasks and Capabilities." *NBR Analysis* 11, no. 1 (May 2000).

———. "President Bush Presses Antiterror Agenda in Southeast Asia." *Comparative Connections* 5, no. 4 (2004): 67–78.

Simon, Sheldon W., and Richard J. Ellings. "A Postscript on U.S. Policy." In *Southeast Asian Security in the New Millennium*, edited by Richard J. Ellings and Sheldon W. Simon. Armonk, NY: NBR Press, 1996.

Singaporean Ministry of Defence. *The Fight against Terror: Singapore's National Security Strategy.* Singapore: National Security Coordination Centre, 2004.

Singer, J. David, and Melvin Small. *Resort to Arms: International and Civil Wars, 1816–1980.* Beverly Hills, CA: Sage Publications, 1982.

Singh, Bilveer. "Singapore's Perspectives on the Soviet-Vietnamese Alliance and the Security of Southeast Asia." In *The Soviet-Vietnamese Alliance and the Security of Southeast Asia.* Bangkok: International Security Council, 1986.

———. "The Soviet Union in Southeast Asia: National Perspectives from the Region." *Contemporary Southeast Asia* 8, no. 4 (1987): 276–97.

————. *The Vulnerability of Small States Revisited: A Study of Singapore's Post-Cold War Foreign Policy.* Yogyakarta, Indonesia: Gadjah Mada University Press, 1999.

Singh, D. S. Ranjit. "Brunei in 1985: Domestic Factors, Political and Economic Externalities." *Asian Survey* 26, no. 2 (1986): 168–73.

Siverson, Randolph M., and Juliann Emmons. "Birds of a Feather: Democratic Political Systems and Alliance Choices in the Twentieth Century." *Journal of Conflict Resolution* 35, no. 2 (1991): 285–306.

Siverson, Randolph M., and Harvey Starr. "Regime Change and the Restructuring of Alliances." *American Journal of Political Science* 38, no. 1 (1994): 145–61.

Smith, Anthony L. "Reluctant Partner: Indonesia's Response to U.S. Security Policies." *Special Assessment.* Honolulu: Asia-Pacific Center for Security Studies, 2003.

Snitwongse, Kusuma. "Thai Government Responses to Armed Communist and Separatist Movements." In *Governments and Rebellions in Southeast Asia*, edited by Chandran Jeshurun. Singapore: Institute of Southeast Asian Studies, 1985.

————. "Soviet-Vietnamese Alliance and the Security of Southeast Asia: A Southeast Asian Perspective." In *The Soviet-Vietnamese Alliance and the Security of Southeast Asia.* Bangkok: International Security Council, 1986.

————. "ASEAN Security Cooperation: Searching for a Regional Order." *Pacific Review* 8, no. 3 (1995): 518–30.

————. "Strategic Outlook for the Asia Pacific Region: A Thai Perspective on the U.S. Stabilizing Role." In *Thailand, Australia and the Region: Strategic Developments in Southeast Asia*, edited by Cavan Hogue. Canberra: National Thai Studies Centre, 2001.

Snyder, Glenn H. "The Security Dilemma in Alliance Politics." *World Politics* 36, no. 4 (1984): 461–95.

————. "Alliances, Balance, and Stability." *International Organization* 45, no. 1 (1991): 121–42.

————. *Alliance Politics.* Ithaca, NY: Cornell University Press, 1997.

————. "Mearsheimer's World: Offensive Realism and the Struggle for Security: A Review Essay." *International Security* 27, no. 1 (2002): 149–73.

Snyder, Jack. "The Concept of Strategic Culture: Caveat Emptor." In *Strategic Power: USA/USSR*, edited by Carl G. Jacobsen. New York: St. Martin's Press, 1990.

Sodhy, Pamela. *The U.S.-Malaysian Nexus: Themes in Superpower-Small State Relations.* Kuala Lumpur: Institute for Strategic and International Studies, 1991.

————. "U.S.-Malaysian Relations during the Bush Administration: The Political, Economic, and Security Aspects." *Contemporary Southeast Asia* 25, no. 3 (2003): 363–86.

Solidum, Estrella D. "Philippine Perceptions of Crucial Issues Affecting Southeast Asia." *Asian Survey* 22, no. 6 (1982): 536–47.

SRV Foreign Ministry. "Facts about the Vietnam-Kampuchea Border Question." *Kampuchea Dossier* 1 (1978): 126.

————. "Statement of the Government of the Socialist Republic of Vietnam on the Vietnam-Kampuchea Border Issues." *Kampuchea Dossier* 1 (1978): 81.

Steinberg, David I. "Crisis in Burma: Stasis and Change in a Political Economy in Turmoil." *ISIS Paper* 5. Bangkok: Institute of Security and International Studies, 1989.

————. *Burma: The State of Myanmar.* Washington, DC: Georgetown University Press, 2001.

Storey, Ian. "Creeping Assertiveness: China, the Philippines, and the South China Sea Disputes." *Contemporary Southeast Asia* 21, no. 1 (1999): 95–118.

————. "Indonesia's China Policy in the New Order and Beyond: Problems and Prospects." *Contemporary Southeast Asia* 22, no. 1 (2000): 145–74.

————. "China and Vietnam's Tug of War over Laos." *China Brief* 5, no. 13 (June 7, 2005).

————. "Vietnam and the United States, 2004–2005: Still Sensitive, but Moving Forward." Special Assessment for the Asia-Pacific Center for Security Studies, 2005.

————. "China and Thailand: Enhancing Military-Security Ties in the 21st Century." *China Brief* 8, no. 14 (July 3, 2008).

Storey, Ian, and Carlyle Thayer. "Cam Ranh Bay: Past Imperfect, Future Uncertain." *Contemporary Southeast Asia* 23, no. 3 (2001): 452–73.

Stryker, Sheldon, and George Psathas. "Research on Coalitions in the Triad: Findings, Problems and Strategy." *Sociometry* 23, no. 3 (1960): 217–30.

Stuart-Fox, Martin. "National Defence and Internal Security in Laos." In *Contemporary Laos: Studies in the Politics and Society of the Lao People's Democratic Republic*, edited by Martin Stuart-Fox. St. Lucia, AU: University of Queensland Press, 1982.

————. *Laos: Politics, Economics, and Society.* London: Frances Pinter, 1984.

————. "Laos in 1988: In Pursuit of New Directions." *Asian Survey* 29, no. 1 (1989): 81–88.

————. "Foreign Policy of the Lao People's Democratic Republic." In *Laos: Beyond the Revolution*, edited by Joseph J. Zasloff and Leonard Unger. New York: St. Martin's Press, 1991.

————. *A History of Laos.* Cambridge: Cambridge University Press, 1997.

————. "Southeast Asia and China: The Role of History and Culture in Shaping Future Relations." *Contemporary Southeast Asia* 26, no. 1 (2004): 116–39.

Stubbs, Richard. "Subregional Security Cooperation in ASEAN: Military and Economic Imperatives and Political Obstacles." *Asian Survey* 32, no. 5 (1992): 397–410.

Sukma, Rizal. "Recent Developments in Sino-Indonesian Relations: An Indonesian View." *Contemporary Southeast Asia* 16, no. 1 (1994): 35–45.

————. "Indonesia's Bebas-Aktif Foreign Policy and the 'Security Agreement' with Australia." *Australian Journal of International Affairs* 51, no. 2 (1997): 231–41.

————. "Indonesia and Regional Security: The Quest for Cooperative Security." In *Asia-Pacific Security Cooperation: National Interests and Regional Order*, edited by See Seng Tan and Amitav Acharya. Armonk, NY: M. E. Sharpe, 2004.

Sulaiman, Hamzah. "Negara Brunei Darussalam: Socio-Economic Concerns Amid Stability and Plenty." In *Southeast Asian Affairs 2003.* Singapore: Institute of Southeast Asian Studies, 2003.

Suryadinata, Leo. *Indonesia's Foreign Policy under Suharto: Aspiring to International Leadership.* Singapore: Times Academic Press, 1996.

Tan, Andrew T. H. "Singapore's Defense: Capabilities, Trends, and Implications." *Contemporary Southeast Asia* 21, no. 3 (1999): 451–74.

Tan, Tony Keng Yam, and William Cohen. News Briefing at the U.S. Department of Defense. Arlington, VA, November 10, 1998.

Teo, Eric Chu Cheow. "New Omnidirectional Overtures in Thai Foreign Policy." *Asian Survey* 26, no. 7 (1986): 745–58.

Thai Ministry of Defense. *The Defense of Thailand 1994.* Bangkok: Strategic Research Institute, 1994.

Than, Tin Maung Maung. "Myanmar: Preoccupation with Regime Survival, National Unity, and Stability." In *Asian Security Practices: Material and Ideational Influences*, edited by Muthiah Alagappa. Stanford, CA: Stanford University Press, 1998.

————. "Myanmar (Burma) in 2000: More of the Same?" *Asian Survey* 41, no. 1 (2001): 148–55.

————. "Myanmar and China: A Special Relationship?" In *Southeast Asian Affairs 2003.* Singapore: Institute of Southeast Asian Studies, 2003.

Thayer, Carlyle A. "Laos and Vietnam: The Anatomy of a 'Special Relationship.'" In *Contemporary Laos: Studies in the Politics and Society of the Lao People's Democratic Republic*, edited by Martin Stuart-Fox. St. Lucia, Australia: University of Queensland Press, 1982.

————. "Laos in 1983: Pragmatism in the Transition to Socialism." *Asian Survey* 24, no. 1 (1984): 49–59.

————. "The Vietnam People's Army under *Doi Moi.*" *Pacific Strategic Paper* no. 7. Singapore: Institute of Southeast Asian Studies, 1994.

————. "Beyond Indochina." *Adelphi Paper* 297. London: International Institute for Strategic Studies, 1995.

————. "Laos in 1998: Continuity under New Leadership." *Asian Survey* 39, no. 1 (1999): 38–42.

————. "Vietnamese Foreign Policy: Multilateralism and the Threat of Peaceful Evolution." In *Vietnamese Foreign Policy in Transition*, edited by Carlyle A. Thayer and Ramses Amer. Singapore: Institute of Southeast Asian Studies, 1999.

————. "Laos in 1999: Economic Woes Drive Foreign Policy." *Asian Survey* 40, no. 1 (2000): 43–48.

————. "Vietnam in 2000: Toward the Ninth Party Congress." *Asian Survey* 41, no. 1 (2001): 181–88.

————. "China's International Security Cooperation Diplomacy and Southeast Asia." Paper presented at the International Studies Association Annual Meeting, San Diego, CA, March 2006.

Theeravit, Khien, and MacAlister Brown, eds. "Introduction." In *Indochina and Problems of Security and Stability in Southeast Asia.* Bangkok: Chulalongkorn University Press, 1981.

Thien, Ton That. "Vietnam's New Economic Policy." *Pacific Affairs* 56, no. 4 (1983/84): 691–712.

Thomas, Ragu C. G. "The South Asian Security Balance in a Western Dominant World." In *Balance of Power: Theory and Practice in the 21st Century*, edited by T. V. Paul, James J. Wirtz, and Michel Fortmann. Stanford, CA: Stanford University Press, 2004.

Tilman, Robert O. "The Enemy Beyond: External Threat Perceptions in the ASEAN Region." *Research Notes and Discussion Paper No. 42.* Singapore: Institute of Southeast Asian Studies, 1984.

Tongdhammachart, Kramol, Kusuma Snitwongse, Sarasin Viraphol, Arong Suthasasna, Wiwat Mungkandi, and Sukhumbhand Paribatra. *The Thai Elite's National Security Perspectives: Implications for Southeast Asia.* Bangkok: Chulalongkorn University Press, 1983.

Tow, Shannon. "Southeast Asia in the Sino-U.S. Strategic Balance." *Contemporary Southeast Asia* 26, no. 3 (2004): 434–59.

Trager, Frank N., and William L. Scully. "The Third Congress of the Burma Socialist Programme Party: 'The Need to Create Continuity and Dynamism of Leadership.'" *Asian Survey* 17, no. 9 (1977): 830–38.

————. "Burma in 1977: Cautious Changes and a Careful Watch." *Asian Survey* 18, no. 2 (1978): 142–52.

Turley, William S. "Thai-Vietnamese Rivalry in the Indochina Conflict." In *East Asian Conflict Zones: Prospects for Regional Stability and Deescalation*, edited by Lawrence E. Ginter and Young Whan Kihl. New York: St. Martin's Press, 1987.

Turnbull, C. M. "Regionalism and Nationalism." In *The Cambridge History of Southeast Asia: From World War II to the Present*, vol. II, part II, edited by Nicholas Tarling. Cambridge: Cambridge University Press, 1999.

Tymoshenko, Yuliya. "Containing Russia." *Foreign Affairs* 86, no. 3 (2007): 69–82.

Un, Kheang, and Judy Ledgerwood. "Cambodia in 2001: Toward Democratic Consolidation?" *Asian Survey* 42, no. 1 (2002): 100–06.

————. "Cambodia in 2002: Decentralization and its Effects on Party Politics." *Asian Survey* 43, no. 1 (2003): 113–19.

Valencia, Mark J. "China and the South China Sea Disputes." *Adelphi Paper 298*. London: International Institute for Strategic Studies, 1995.

Van der Kroef, Justus M. "Hanoi and ASEAN: Is Co-Existence Possible?" *Contemporary Southeast Asia* 1, no. 2 (1979): 164–78.

———. "The Cambodian-Vietnamese War: Some Origins and Implications." *Asia Quarterly* no. 2 (1979): 169–82.

———. "'Normalizing' Relations with the People's Republic of China: Indonesia's Rituals of Ambiguity." *Contemporary Southeast Asia* 3, no. 3 (1981): 187–218.

Vatikiotis, Michael R. J. "Indonesia's Foreign Policy in the 1990s." *Contemporary Southeast Asia* 14, no. 4 (1993): 352–67.

Villegas, Bernardo M. "The Philippines in 1986: Democratic Reconstruction in the Post-Marcos Era." *Asian Survey* 27, no. 2 (1987): 194–205.

Viraphol, Sarasin. *Directions in Thai Foreign Policy*. Singapore: Institute of Southeast Asian Studies, 1976.

———. "Thai-American Relations in the Post-1975 Period." In *A Century and A Half of Thai-American Relations*, edited by Wiwat Mungkandi and William Warren. Bangkok: Chulalongkorn University Press, 1982.

———. "Thailand's Perspectives on Its Rivalry with Vietnam." In *Confrontation and Coexistence: the Future of ASEAN-Vietnam Relations*, edited by William S. Turley. Bangkok: Institute of Security and International Studies, Chulalongkorn University, 1985.

Vital, David. *The Survival of Small States: Studies in Small Power/Great Power Conflict*. Oxford: Oxford University Press, 1971.

Walt, Stephen M. *The Origins of Alliances*. Ithaca, NY: Cornell University Press, 1987.

——— "Testing Theories of Alliance Formation: The Case of Southwest Asia." *International Organization* 42, no. 2 (1988): 275–316.

———. "Alliance Formation in Southwest Asia: Balancing and Bandwagoning in Cold War Competition." In *Dominoes and Bandwagons: Strategic Beliefs and Great-Power Competition in the Eurasian Rimland*, edited by Robert Jervis and Jack Snyder. Oxford: Oxford University Press, 1991.

———. "Why Alliances Endure or Collapse." *Survival* 39, no. 1 (1997): 156–79.

———. "Building Up New Bogeymen." *Foreign Policy* 106 (1997): 176–89.

———. "Keeping the World 'Off-Balance': Self-Restraint and U.S. Foreign Policy." In *America Unrivaled: The Future of the Balance of Power*, edited by G. John Ikenberry. Ithaca, NY: Cornell University Press, 2002.

———. "Alliances in a Unipolar World." *World Politics* 61, no. 1 (2009): 86–120.

Waltz, Kenneth N. *Theory of International Politics*. Reading, MA: Addison-Wesley, 1979.

———. "International Politics Is Not Foreign Policy." *Security Studies* 6, no. 1 (1996): 54–57.

———. "Evaluating Theories." *American Political Science Review* 91, no. 4 (1997): 913–17.

———. "Structural Realism after the Cold War." *International Security* 25, no. 1 (2000): 5–41.

Wanandi, Jusuf. "Politico-Security Dimensions of Southeast Asia." *Asian Survey* 17, no. 8 (1977): 771–92.

———. *Security Dimensions of the Asia-Pacific Region in the 1980s*. Jakarta: Centre for Strategic and International Studies, 1979.

———. "Dimensions of Southeast Asian Security." *Contemporary Southeast Asia* 1, no. 4 (1980): 334–47.

———. "Conflict and Cooperation in the Asia-Pacific Region: An Indonesian Perspective." *Asian Survey* 22, no. 6 (1982): 503–15.

———. "ASEAN's China Strategy: Towards Deeper Engagement." *Survival* 38, no. 3 (1996): 117–28.

Wanandi, Jusuf, and Hadi Soesastro. "Indonesia's Security and Threat Perceptions." In *Threats to Security in East Asia-Pacific*, edited by Charles E. Morrison. Toronto: Lexington Books, 1983.

Wattanayagorn, Panitan. "Thailand: The Elite's Shifting Conceptions of Security." In *Asian Security Practice*, edited by Muthiah Alagappa. Stanford, CA: Stanford University Press, 1998.

Weatherbee, Donald E. "U.S. Policy and the Two Southeast Asias." *Asian Survey* 18, no. 4 (1978): 408–21.

———. "Indonesia in 1984: Pancasila, Politics, and Power." *Asian Survey* 25, no. 2 (1985): 187–97.

———. *International Relations in Southeast Asia: The Struggle for Autonomy*, 2nd ed. Lanham, MD: Rowman & Littlefield, 2009.

Weinstein, Franklin B. *Indonesian Foreign Policy and the Dilemma of Dependence: From Sukarno to Suharto*. Ithaca, NY: Cornell University Press, 1976.

Weitsman, Patricia A. "Alliance Cohesion and Coalition Warfare: The Central Powers and Triple Entente." *Security Studies* 12, no. 3 (2003): 79–113.

Welch, David A. "The 'Clash of Civilizations' Thesis as an Argument and as a Phenomenon." *Security Studies* 6, no. 4 (1997): 197–216.

Wendt, Alexander. "Collective Identity Formation and the International State." *American Political Science Review* 88, no. 2 (1988): 384–96.

Wheeler, Matthew Z. "Thai-Vietnamese Relations in the Post-Cold War Period, 1988–2000." *ISIS Paper 4*. Bangkok: Institute of Security and International Studies, 2001.

Whiting, Allen S. "ASEAN Eyes China: The Security Dimension." *Asian Survey* 37, no. 4 (1997): 299–322.

Williams, Michael C. *Vietnam at the Crossroads*. London: Royal Institute of International Affairs, 1992.

Wohlforth, William C. "The Stability of a Unipolar World." *International Security* 24, no. 1 (1999): 5–41.

———. "U.S. Strategy in a Unipolar World." In *America Unrivaled: The Future of the Balance of Power*, edited by G. John Ikenberry. Ithaca, NY: Cornell University Press, 2002.

———. "Revisiting Balance of Power Theory in Central Eurasia." In *Balance of Power: Theory and Practice in the 21st Century*, edited by T.V. Paul, James J. Wirtz, and Michel Fortmann. Stanford, CA: Stanford University Press, 2004.

World Bank. *World Development Indicators 2007*. Washington, DC: The World Bank Group, 2007.

Wright, Quincy. *A Study of War*, 2nd ed., abridged by Louise Leonard Wright, Chicago: University of Chicago Press, 1965.

Yahuda, Michael. *The International Relations of the Asia-Pacific, 1945–1995*. London: Routledge, 1996.

Zabih, Sepehr. "Iran's International Posture: De Facto Non-Alignment within a Pro-Western Alliance." *Middle East Journal* 24, no. 3 (1970): 302–18.

Zagoria, Donald S. "Soviet Policy and Prospects in East Asia." *International Security* 5, no. 2 (1980): 66–78.

———. "The Strategic Environment in East Asia." In *Soviet Policy in East Asia*, edited by Donald S. Zagoria. New Haven, CT: Yale University Press, 1982.

Zagoria, Donald S., and Sheldon W. Simon. "Soviet Policy in Southeast Asia." In *Soviet Policy in East Asia*, edited by Donald S. Zagoria. New Haven, CT: Yale University Press, 1982.

Zakaria, Fareed. "Culture Is Destiny: A Conversation with Lee Kuan Yew." *Foreign Affairs* 73, no. 2 (1994): 109–26.

Zimmerman, Robert F. "Thailand 1975: Transition to Constitutional Democracy Continues." *Asian Survey* 16, no. 2 (1976): 159–72.

Index

Note: Page numbers in italics represent illustrations.